Inhabiting Technologies/Modernities

Inhabiting Technologies/Modernities

Media and Cultural Practices in South Asia

Edited by

P. Thirumal
K. A. Nuaiman

With a Foreword by

Arjun Appadurai

Orient BlackSwan

INHABITING TECHNOLOGIES/MODERNITIES: MEDIA AND CULTURAL PRACTICES IN SOUTH ASIA

ORIENT BLACKSWAN PRIVATE LIMITED

Registered Office
3-6-752 Himayatnagar, Hyderabad 500 029, Telangana, India
e-mail: centraloffice@orientblackswan.com

Other Offices
Bengaluru, Chennai, Guwahati, Hyderabad, Kolkata,
Mumbai, New Delhi, Noida, Patna

First published 2025

ISBN 978-93-5442-892-0

041949

Typeset in
Goudy Oldstyle Std 11/13
by Le Studio Graphique, Gurgaon 122 007

Printed in India at
Kensington Printing & Packaging, Noida 201 301

Published by
Orient Blackswan Private Limited
3-6-752 Himayatnagar, Hyderabad 500 029, Telangana, India
e-mail: info@orientblackswan.com

Contents

Abbreviations *vii*
List of Images and Figures *ix*
Foreword *xi*
Arjun Appadurai
Acknowledgements *xiii*
Publisher's Acknowledgements *xv*

1. Introduction 1
P. Thirumal and K. A. Nuaiman

2. Telegraphy and Journalism in Colonial India, c. 1830s to 1900s 27
Amelia Bonea

3. Indian Films and Nigerian Lovers 46
Media and the Creation of Parallel Modernities
Brian Larkin

4. A Community in Print 95
Islam and Print Culture in Malabar, South India
K. A. Nuaiman

5. Listening to the Sonorous 132
Digital Archiving as a Political Practice
P. Thirumal and Sai Amulya Komarraju

6. From Invisibility to Hypervisibility and Back? 156
The Lost Same-sex Object in Media History in India
Ashley Tellis

7. CAST OUT WORLDS IN PRINT 175
Iyothee Thass (1845–1914) and the Tamil Public Sphere
Dickens Leonard

8. 'REALITY MUST IMPROVE' 210
The Perversity of Expertise and the Belatedness of Indian Development Television
William Mazzarella

9. CITY AS A CONTINUUM 251
Cinematic Geography of Kochi in Malayalam Cinema
Carmel Christy K. J.

10. LAMPOONING THE RAJ 273
The Cartoon in Pre-independence Tamil Journalism
A. R. Venkatachalapathy

11. THE MACHINE IN THE COLONY 289
Technology, Politics, and the Typography of Devanagari in the Early Years of Mechanisation
Vaibhav Singh

12. POLITICS OF SCRIPT SELECTION AND MEETEI IDENTITY, 1978–1979 320
Thongam Bipin

13. THE LATE COLONIAL TELUGU TEXTBOOK 337
A Material Embodiment of Dissent, Debate, and Knowledge
Sasi Kiran R. Mallam

Notes on the Contributors 364
Index 367

Abbreviations

ACJ	Asian College of Journalism
AIR	All India Radio
AMPECA	American Motion Picture Exporters and Cinema Association
AMU	Aligarh Muslim University
BBC	British Broadcasting Corporation
CAA	Citizenship Amendment Act
CMP	Coronation Memorial Press
CTV	City Television Kano
DD	Doordarshan
ISRO	Indian Space Research Organisation
L&M	Linotype & Machinery
LGBTQI	Lesbian, Gay, Bisexual, Transgender, Queer, Intersex
MEELAL	Meetei Eyek Erol Loinasillon Apunba Lup
MSM	Men Who Have Sex With Men
NASA	National Aeronautics and Space Administration
NFDC	Nigerian Film Distribution Company
NMAH	National Museum of American History, Washington, D.C.
SAC	Space Applications Centre
SAP	Structural Adjustment Programme
SITE	Satellite Television Instructional Experiment
SPCK	Society for Promoting Christian Knowledge
SSLC	Secondary School Leaving Certificate
VC	Vice-Chancellor

Images and Figures

Images

3.1a, b	*Soyayya* books on sale at Gidan Dabino, bookseller and publisher.	66
3.2	An illustrated cover of a *soyayya* book.	70
3.3	An illustrated cover of a *soyayya* book.	71
3.4	An illustrated cover of a *soyayya* book.	72
5.1	'Manemma', Water painting.	133
10.1	The English suck Rs 45 crore from India every year.	275
10.2	Lord Morley milks the cow (India) dry, while the calves (Indians) starve.	276
10.3	The owls (the Moderates) seek refuge from sunlight (Swadeshism) by hiding in a tree hole (the Madras Congress Convention).	277
10.4	The thief (Lord Morley) who has come to loot the mansion (India) throws a few bones (honours) to the dogs (the Moderates), while the lion (Tilak) is in prison.	278
10.5	The British official claims to provide security to the people; but what they want is food, which is being shipped off.	279

FIGURES

11.1 A page from the patent application showing Govil's scheme for the formation of Devanagari characters by the combination of separate components. 295

11.2 A schematic comparison of alphabetic and syllabic script composition in type sorts. 306

11.3 Front page of Hindi newspaper *Vishwamitra*, 21 April 1950. 309

Foreword

I am honoured to provide this brief Foreword for an extremely rich and timely collection of essays on the general topic of media, technology, and modernity in India in the last five centuries. I learned a great deal from the essays (and the Introduction by the Editors) and I want to highlight a few major interventions in the book which will help scholars, theorists, and practitioners in the space of media in India to revitalise this field.

The first striking effect of the volume (taken as a whole) is to show that *the decolonial without the precolonial is an incomplete object*. Thus, many of the authors in this volume reach back to the early modern history of many parts of the subcontinent to unpack the history of scripts, genres, and rhetorics, as well as typesetting, mass distribution, broadcasting, and televisuality, and illuminate these long histories. The plurality and density of these prehistories has the effect of diluting the exaggerated emphasis on colonialism and nationalism, which are too often seen as the only forces of change in an otherwise sleepy *longue durée*.

This shift in perspective is achieved without flattening or homogenising the different temporalities or variations across sub-regions. Even more significant is the resistance to linear history, with its clear ideas of development, sequence, and teleology. The Editors and the authors are keenly aware that media histories in India are discontinuous, disjunct, and contingent. Taken as a whole, the reader is introduced to the ways in which different media ecologies evolve in India, through complex processes of translation, distribution, and influence. The scholars in this volume are careful to avoid technological determinism, while recognising that graphic, reproductive, and design technologies themselves emerge from contingent cultural and historical contexts.

This approach to history and temporality enables the essays in this volume to pay special attention to the amnesia, marginalisation, and silence which have burdened minor voices, classes, forms, and ideologies, and obscured their significance in the history of India. This leads the authors to pay attention to examples such as the typographical and lithographic history of Islam in Kerala, the oddities of the efforts to link development goals to television audiences in this much forgotten State-sponsored mass communication, the growth of media platforms geared to the special horizons of Dalit digitality, and the largely untold story of the repatriation of Malayalam cinema to Kerala after a long history in Chennai.

As several essays in this book richly show, in the spirit of Gilles Deleuze and Felix Guattari's classic essay on 'minor' literatures, the category of the minor is the key prerequisite of any effort to claim 'majority', and must be produced before being naturalised as props on the proscenium of the major. The critical histories of media forms and practices in this volume lend a new urgency to the idea that India is a land of an infinity of minorities, which provide the context, the subjectivities, and the counter-hegemonies that make any Indian majority a precarious project.

This powerful role of the 'minor' applies to social groups, disciplines, and archives. This volume reveals the power of bringing together a diversity of minor or occluded archives to unseat the landscape of majority in India.

Arjun Appadurai
Berlin, December 2024

Acknowledgements

This volume is dedicated to those who teach theory and history of media in the Departments of Communication and Journalism in Indian universities. Recognising the need for a reader to ground their teaching in research-oriented materials based in South Asia, this volume attempts to incite the historical in the theoretical and the theoretical in the historical. In that endeavour, the contributing authors dig spatially and temporally to understand the multiple conceptions and origins of South Asian media technologies/modernities, and move away from the restrictive gaze of received binaries such as colonialism *versus* nationalism. Thus, the chapters in the volume advocate for reconfiguring media theories by locating them both vertically and contingently within media histories.

The idea for this volume grew from a series of academic events that we conducted at SN School of Arts and Communication, University of Hyderabad, namely the Symposium on Curatorial Practices of Alternative Publishing Enterprises (2018), with the help of the Swiss Arts Council, and 'Histories of Media: Political, Cultural and Deep Pasts of Media' (2019). We remember warmly the support of Akshay Pathak and G. Aloysius in conducting these events.

The Department of Communication, University of Hyderabad, has produced several important dissertations in the area of social, cultural, and theoretical history of media, where they have problematised the terms technologies, modernities, and inhabitation. Some of these articulations appear in this volume. Among other things, this book is a product of pedagogical research into and the political practice of doing and thinking media history in South Asia.

We acknowledge our deep gratitude to Professor Arjun Appadurai for writing an insightful Foreword for this volume. We have gained immensely from his erudite advice and generous demeanour. We take this opportunity to wish him a long creative-intellectual presence.

We profusely thank Brian Larkin, William Mazzarella, Venkatachalapathy, Amelia Bonea, and Vaibhav Singh for consenting to republish their research in this volume. Thanks to John Wiley and Sons, Cambridge University Press, Brill, Indian Institute of Advanced Studies, and Sage for granting permission to reprint their chapters.

We also thank our younger scholars for writing fresh chapters for this collection: Ashley Tellis, Dickens Leonard, Carmel Christie, Thongam Bipin, and Amulya Komarraju. Our research scholars Chinar, Amrita, Hima, and Bindu read several chapters while initially putting them together; Arjun, Deviender, Rohit, Sparsh, Adrita, Jumuna, Roger, and Noufal have been additions to this list. Special mention should be made of Shahal, who stayed with the twists and turns that the book followed.

We thank Professor Jyotirmoyi Sharma immensely for his counselling and encouragement of this work, and our friend, Professor Sanjay Palshikar, for being a silent support and well-wisher. Namitha Sahajan has designed such a marvellous cover, and we express our gratitude to her. Our thanks to Nilanjana Majumdar at Orient BlackSwan for making this book happen. Finally, Proteeti Banerjee (at Orient BlackSwan) made our work simpler and efficient, and we sincerely appreciate her robust involvement in editing this volume.

We gratefully acknowledge the generous funding that we received from the Institution of Eminence (IOE), University of Hyderabad.

P. Thirumal

K. A. Nuaiman

Publisher's Acknowledgements

Chapter 2, 'Telegraphy and Journalism in Colonial India, c.1830s to 1900s' by Amelia Bonea, was first published as 'Telegraphy and Journalism in Colonial India, c. 1830s to 1900s', *History Compass* 12 (5), 7 May 2014. Reproduced here with the kind permission of John Wiley and Sons.

Chapter 3, 'Indian Films and Nigerian Lovers: Media and the Creation of Parallel Modernities' by Brian Larkin, was first published as 'Indian Films and Nigerian Lovers: Media and the Creation of Parallel Modernities', in *Africa: Journal of the International African Institute* 67 (3), 406–440. Reproduced here with the kind permission of Cambridge University Press.

Chapter 5, 'Listening to the Sonorous: Digital Archiving as a Political Practice', by Thirumal P. and Sai Amulya Komarraju, was first published 'Listening to the Sonorous: Digital Archiving as a Political Practice', in *Summer Hill* XXII (1), Summer 2016, published by the Indian Institute of Advanced Study. Reproduced here with the kind permission of the Indian Institute of Advanced Study, Shimla.

Chapter 8, '"Reality Must Improve" The Perversity of Expertise and the Belatedness of Indian Development Television', was first published as '"Reality Must Improve" The Perversity of Expertise and the Belatedness of Indian Development Television', *Global Media and Communication* 8 (December), 2012, 215–41. Copyright © 2012 by SAGE Publications Ltd. Reprinted with the permission of SAGE Publications Ltd.

Chapter 10, 'Lampooning the Raj: The Cartoon in Pre-independence Tamil Journalism', was first published as 'Lampooning the Raj: Subramania Bharati and the Cartoon in

Tamil Journalism, 1906-1910', *CCTR Journal* V (1–2), 1996. Reprinted with permission.

Chapter 11, 'The Machine in the Colony: Technology, Politics, and the Typography of Devanagari in the Early Years of Mechanization', was first published as 'The Machine in the Colony: Technology, Politics, and the Typography of Devanagari in the Early Years of Mechanization' in *Philological Encounters* 3 (4), 2018, 469–495. Reprinted with permission from Brill.

1

Introduction

P. Thirumal and K. A. Nuaiman

This book grew out of a conference titled 'Media Histories: Political, Cultural and Deep Pasts of Media', organised by the Sarojini Naidu School of Arts and Communication, University of Hyderabad, in February 2018. The conference was primarily concerned with addressing the lack of academic visibility for teaching and researching the 'theory and history' of media in media and journalism schools in India. With India attaining independence, journalism as an anti-establishment trade of the cultural elites had to find a new direction and purpose. In the early decades of independence, newer groups and communities sought political attention and the redistribution of resources primarily through the electoral mechanism. Partha Chatterjee's (2004) analytical-descriptive concept of 'political society', which addressed the emergence of constituencies that were denied a claim to civil society, hardly finds mention in any theory of the discipline.

In a slightly different context, one of India's noted communication scholars, K. E. Eapen, proposed the setting up of an advanced multidisciplinary research centre for the study of communication, with the aim of dovetailing the political churning into a manageable development ideology (Eapen 1995). This move demanded that the pedagogy and research of communication emphasise the generative character of social and cultural institutions and facilitate the application of communication for planned social development. Aspirations for a modern associational life had to engage with the ubiquity and ever-rejuvenating, self-replenishing, generative cultural authority of caste, gender, and communal relations. There was a tendency for upper-caste professionals across diverse modern occupations to deny the power of caste in order to tacitly direct one's orientation towards ideas, objects, and people. For Eapen, the training of journalists was too important a task to be left to journalists themselves. Notwithstanding Eapen's provocation, research as a domain of academic practice was not recognised as an integral part of disciplinary concerns until recently. However, with the 2018 move by the University Grants Commission (UGC) to make a doctoral degree a minimum requirement for a teaching position in university departments, including the practice-related disciplines, a tradition of research is now emerging in these disciplines.[1] Also, the incentives given to teachers who hold doctoral degrees, in terms of promotion and upward mobility, further facilitate the consideration of research as integral to the academic programme in many universities.

This formalisation is not merely restricted to journalism, but applies to liberal and performing arts disciplines such as fine arts, theatre arts, and dance as well. Art History has traditionally had traction among the expressive arts and involved expressing, transgressing, and translating the desires of the nation, nationalism, or colonialism. Unlike the more critical approach associated with Art History, disciplines like Dance and Theatre taught and wrote eulogies and largely produced unexamined histories and documentation of personalities, performative traditions, and art institutions of ancient, colonial, and post-independence India. These disciplines did not produce a critical vocabulary or a theoretical framework for ushering in an egalitarian society. Their purpose was to acknowledge and announce the arrival of an emergent State society, and they provided an aesthetic for the formation and conduct of the nascent Indian State (Natarajan 2018; Soneji 2012, 2013).

At a time when cultural and literary historians from South Asia were offering a variety of critical perspectives to account for the history of modern Indian languages, literary cultures, performative traditions, and print and book histories (see

Blackburn and Dalmia 2013; Ghosh 2006; Gupta and Chakravorty 2004, 2008; Harder 2010; Joshi 1998; Orsini 2009; Pollock 2003; Starke 2008; Venkatachalapathy 2012), the discipline of Communication, along with Dance and Theatre, failed to partake in the methodological and theoretical churning taking place in neighbouring fields. For example, historical studies on media/technologies in India have mainly confined themselves to chronicling major events in the course of their introduction and inhabitation (see Ghose 1952; Kesavan 1984; Krishnamurthi 1966; Muniruddin 2005; Natarajan 1954). Privileging an instrumental view of media/technologies and their functioning in territorially bound geographies, stories of such developments are often told through the trope of nationalism or neoliberal economy. These studies followed a linear interpretation of media growth, media literacy, and the emergence of secular, liberal democratic institutions, and sometimes of the crises they faced. The resultant historiographical and theoretical approach tends to restrict their objects of inquiry to what can be broadly called the impact narrative of media/technologies. This is not surprising, given that media history in India is considered an ancillary subject within the narrow confines of journalism and mass communication studies and a less fashionable area of research and teaching in journalism and media schools, consequently providing a narrow and closed history of the media.

Journalists writing on media history have generally presented media's instrumental value, thereby foregrounding the functional character of media technologies. Cultural historians value technologies because they think the latter constitute humans as much as humans constitute them. Cultural histories of media/technologies are concerned with establishing the connection between these new technologies and an earlier mode of production, consumption, and distribution of cultural artefacts. For instance, book historians in India increasingly view twentieth-century print culture as negotiating with artisanal cultures, alongside the fashioning of folklore, print performance, and pleasure (Blackburn 2003; Fraser 2008; Orsini 2009); or film studies scholars connect the arrival and popularity of cinema with an already existing visual culture and performative tradition prevalent in Indian society (Rajadhyaksha and Willemen 1994; Srivatsan 1993). While these studies have made significant contributions by emphasising the multiple origins of technologies that go beyond the formation of a nationalist political community, these attempts also seem to restrict our understanding of media/technology because of their sharper historical focus.

Although impact narratives and cultural histories of media/technology appear to have embarked on different projects, they not only meet at several points but also build up curious proximities and often draw each other into existence. This is more evident in the temporal logics they work with and what they exclude from their respective archives. It is important to examine the extent to which cultural historians of media/technology go to map the cultural currents of these media practices. Very often, such longer histories privilege a historiography that focuses on the nineteenth century, a time when (the nascent) Brahmin domination over modern cultural institutions, artefacts, and media practices was at its peak in India. By preoccupying itself with establishing a deep relationship between literary cultures and pre-modern Sanskrit/Indology, this approach systematically conceals archives that stem from and flourish in the interiors of non-Brahminic life-worlds.

One dominant approach to securing the life-world of media and literary practices prior to the nineteenth century is to look for a globally interconnected Perso-Arabic past. For instance, this approach attempts to look at the Indian past through the lens of Perso-Arabic literature produced in India. There is a growing body of literature that demonstrates how middlemen/journeymen and their travelling texts have established 'a sustainable Muslim print and literary culture in several distinct centres' (Green 2009, 203; see also Alam and Subrahmanyam 2007; Ho 2006; Ricci 2011) such as Tabriz, Cairo, and Lucknow within a transcultural framework in the eighteenth century. Scholars have established connections and traced the dynamic relationship between medieval calligraphy and modern print cultures across religious centres on both sides of the Arabian Sea (Messick 1993; Proudfoot 1997). However, does it exhaust all other vernacular literary and religious traditions that seemingly flowered or floundered during this somewhat amnesic period of history?

In this connection, it is important to point out that the strand of critical Indology that Sheldon Pollock and others have initiated and retrieved makes an advance over classical Indology by trying to orchestrate an intellectual history rather than resurrect a religious and mythological past. However, such an attempt to historically excavate a creative literary and discursive past did not proceed beyond the Vijayanagar period. For instance, for Pollock, the death of the Sanskrit language signified the death of a long commentarial tradition. Such a commentarial/dialectical tradition, which was used for philosophical and religious debates known as doxography, seems to have died out at exactly around the same time as the arrival of print, new modes of production, the exit of Buddhism from mainland India, and the entry of Christianity. For instance, what were the preferred choices of Hindu sacral texts highlighted by early modern religious commentators? Was there a dramatic change in preferred texts in nineteenth-century British India?

An amateur historian interested in cultural and intellectual history will maintain that the sixteenth to the early nineteenth century is a period of pronounced absence of any philosophical, aesthetic, and literary innovations in this dialectical tradition (Nicholson 2021; Pollock 2001). Heuristically, the Vaidika/Brahmanic/Hindu response to Western ideas, technologies, and practices lacked a distinct intellectual-ideological-embodied worldview. However, it was acutely conscious of the fact that these material/technological/discursive influences were embedded in a distinct religious (Christian) framework. It appears that the capacity for spiritually, politically, intellectually, and aesthetically unifying Hinduism or India was diminished during the period between the sixteenth and the eighteenth centuries (Bates 2005). It is perhaps for this precise historical reason that everything has to rest on nineteenth-century efforts at reimagining a unifying civilisational ethos. However, recent work that resurrects Saivism in south India roughly around this period of amnesis through archival researches is indicative of a creative fervour that challenges the existing view of this being a dark period.

While there is enough scholarly work that suggests a serious reordering of knowledge in the nineteenth century, there has not been much focus on what may have been the vernacular forms of knowledge from the sixteenth to the nineteenth century. Whitney Cox, the philologist, made this observation on pre-modern theoretical contributions:

> India provides the centre of gravity for our discussion, but—and this is important—we understand 'India' (or South Asia) to be a plural, polyglot, heterogenous [*sic*] social and semiotic space, one that is defined by the interaction of its constituent parts instead of as embodying any particular cultural essence. (Cox and Sharma 2024, 144)

Such a logic would question the circuitous way in which certain Hindu texts like the *Bhagavad Gita* and *Manu Smriti Dharma* became so central to the unifying impulse in nineteenth-century British India (Palshikar 2014). The colonial officials and missionaries retrieved these texts and nationalist thinkers such as Aurobindo, Bal Gangadhar Tilak, and Mahatma Gandhi had to produce a modern commentary about their cultural and ethical efficacy; Ambedkar went so far as to burn the *Manu Smriti*. In this three-way interaction of colonial Indology, nationalist appropriation, and subaltern resistance and condemnation, each fed into the other, discouraging any effort towards a longer view of history. Such an approach forecloses the possibility of a richer interpretation of the immediate vernacular past (1600–1800), that seems to have been more variegated in its choice of religious texts, nuanced hermeneutics, opulent production of manuscripts, and literary and performative cultures that were more likely to be working against the great Sanskritic/Vedic tradition. In the Kannada Saivite folklore, this period is referred to as one that saw the movement of religious and secular learning from the temple to the streets via itinerant Jangama mendicants, who did not appear to seek patronage from powerful kings. Such a religious disposition allowed the offering of moral and spiritual education to the masses. These early colonial public places of learning and worship were known as *Shalegudi* (school and temple) in Kannada. Perhaps, this was conjured up as Begumpura in Gail Omvedt's debt towards retrieving a pre-modern, pre-colonial lineage of anti-caste thinking. Otherwise, anti-caste thinking would be perceived as a derivative of colonial heritage.

These various forms of neglect acquire greater significance in a country like India, with its temporal/spatial depth and multiple traditions specific to regional/religious cultures. In such a context, a focus on the interaction of media/technologies with narrative traditions will possibly allow us to reconstruct media/technology themselves as new objects of inquiry, complete with their own internal life and logics, and enable us to write new genealogies of these while also offering new ways of thinking about media and history. For instance, Panchanan Karmakar, who created the first Bengali type for the printing press at Asiatic Society, was a goldsmith, blacksmith, and calligrapher. Unlike the Hindu cultural elite, the lack of excitement or any sense of novelty displayed by Panchanan when he was asked to fashion a new type for the printing press is suggestive of a technological history of continuity rather than a rupture with printing technology (Fraser 2008). Historians dealing with metallurgy associated with the Indic civilisation will be able to offer a better picture about the varieties of technology that have been instantiated since the period of proto-history. This, however, is too large a question for this volume to handle.

An emergent tradition presupposes a departure from the impact narrative approach and a cultural history approach. It may be construed as an opening into the ways in which disciplines construct an object of study and enable a rethinking of the discursive and non-discursive practices that surround the staging and academic judgement of that object. Following the thread of an emergent tradition is to ask questions, such as: What sort of a life is congealed in a colonial newspaper retrieved from a dusty state archive? The desire of the lower castes to be free, to think and act autonomously against the colonial master and the upper-caste nationalist elite, was rarely coded in the emergent journalistic discursive tradition. Such questions compel us to look at the constituent elements of media/technologies, their many incarnations, multifaceted characteristics, and unpredictable work in a given society. In other words, this approach tries to capture media/technologies as ontological/existential matter with their own life, substance, and afterlife, rather than as merely epistemological entities designed to represent and impact human life. This entails distributing the agency across technology and media to cinema, print, or the digital sphere, alongside social identities such as women, Dalits, and Muslims, or economic arrangements, without making a distinction among these heterogeneous components, emphasising instead the interaction among the constituent elements that mark this moment. Such a theoretical stance may emphasise either heterogeneity, relationality, and flux, or focus on power, politics, and agency.

In an altogether different context, Nikhil Anand's work on hydropolitics and citizenship in Mumbai studies the politics of access to water in the city largely from the point of view of the hydraulic infrastructure, built on the dynamic relationship among different stakeholders such as residents, plumbers, politicians, engineers, and the water pipes that bind them. For the purpose of our analysis, we need to recognise media/technology as part of a larger social assemblage, thereby foregrounding the need to study media/technology in society as part of a long and continuous process of infrastructure-building as well as in relational terms (Larkin 2008). It is this intersubjective relationality of media/technology with other infrastructures and human beings, or what can be called networks of the relationship between various infrastructures and its users, which provides them with the general conditions necessary for existence, an avenue to present and reveal themselves, along with the potential to transform.

The theoretical move mentioned above has the potential to understand the theory and history of media on a global scale. History and temporality can be differentiated; media anticipates, reflects, and constitutes history, and acts as a motor engine of history. The studies that magnify history rather than create it can arguably be seen as providing representation or content. Media history, as taught in university departments of Media Studies, has largely examined the representational nature of media. Very rarely has it focussed on how media reimagines time. This may require the discipline of Communication to make a definitive move from its current focus on an epistemic/cognitive understanding of media technology towards a more ontological/affective dimension, and thus invest more in understanding media technology as a way of presenting and revealing reality than simply as its representation (Huhtamo and Parikka 2011). The argument, then, is for an embodied understanding of the state of technology in a community rather than merely reproducing analytical frameworks offered by the restricted notions of Cartesian methodology, which tend to present technology as devoid of its subjects. How is the self actualised in media/technology? This question will obviously demand a different conception of media/technology as a matter with its own substance, life, and being. Borrowing from terms such as apparatus, infrastructure, dispositif, and equipmentality (from Heidegger [2008]), this emergent tradition connects the material with the cultural and disambiguates the distinction between life and knowledge.

This significant and inaugural moment in the life of the emergent tradition provided the occasion for organising another conference at the Sarojini Naidu School of Arts and Communication, titled 'Bodily Habitations: Cinema, Caste, Religious and Gender Practices', in March 2020. Together, these two conferences provided the intellectual ethos and the necessary impetus to put together this volume, with contributions from diverse scholars working with theoretical templates of varying sophistication, different historical periods, and media objects in India, South Asia, and elsewhere. While this volume comprises the writings of some of the scholars who presented their work at these conferences, many other senior scholars were also invited to write or republish their work for the volume. A special thanks to Brian Larkin, David Arnold, William Mazzarella, and Vaibhav Singh for giving us permission to republish their work. A. R. Venkatachalapathy and Amelia Boenne deserve special mention because they revised their chapters on cartoons and telegraph fully on our request. Ashley Tellis generously wrote a fresh chapter at short notice. Younger scholars like Dickens Leonard, K. A. Nuaiman, Thongam Bipin, Carmel Christy, and Sasikiran Reddy have all been part of the University of Hyderabad's politicised academic culture. The suicide of Dalit scholar Rohith Vemula led some of them to reflect on scholarly life and critically examine their participation in the production of knowledge, keeping in mind their own social and political backgrounds. Their work represents a promise and a hope for the emergent tradition of scholarship in media and cultural studies. The fact that the Rohith Vemula movement was met with solidarity and sympathy from top universities across the world (mostly Euro-American ones) owes much to digital activism, as also to the deeply ethical and political questions that Rohith's suicide note provoked.

Theme of the Book

'Inhabiting technologies' may be usefully replaced with an altered phrase, 'inhabiting modernity', or a more equitable phrase, 'inhabiting modernities' (Chakrabarty 2000). The singular 'modernity' connotes a historical derivation usually associated with the European Enlightenment, and indexes a particular way of thinking about and arriving at history. Such a deferred time constitutes one axis of writing the history of South Asia and writing the media history of India. Among the several sets of variables that constitute modernity, technologies of communication are considered the *desiderata* for becoming and claiming history. In this narrative, history succeeds the arrival of media. It is media that makes possible 'history' and, therefore, 'knowledge'. In a similar vein, media is expected to display its properties and functions everywhere, as they were designated in its place of origin, that is, Europe. The fact that the same media/technology can manifest different properties in a varied cultural and civilisational context is missing in this framework of diffusion of technology. The entity and being of technology were conflated in this construction of modernity, history, and the diffusion of media technology (Heidegger 2013; Latour 1996).

Impact narratives of media are derived from such an assumption of both history and media.[2] In such hegemonic narratives, historical and cultural specificities of the non-Western world are treated as less useful for theoretical purposes and formal knowledge production. This happens because of the pre-formed idea embedded in impact narratives that life and knowledge, value and facts, the sensible and the intelligible should be made distinct. Perhaps literary sources are useful in examining the intelligible along with the sensible. We now turn to a novel to highlight the fact that the castes of bodies are as important as castes of mind. A contemporary Kannada historical novel (Pai 2017) set in Portuguese Goa describes the reception of the first printing machine (in 1556). The Saraswat Brahmins, the cultural elites in the region, view this machine with enormous suspicion and call for a boycott. An extract from the novel is reproduced below to demonstrate the suspicion the machine engendered.

> 'Have you heard the news, Malappayya?' he asked. 'The *firangis* have brought a printing machine to Goa. It's as tall as a human being.... Paper is inserted on one side of the machine and a wheel is rotated.... All that is written appears on a paper. It's so easy. They say any number of copies can be printed in a single day. Isn't it surprising! People are flocking as in a shanty to see it.'
>
> Malappayya did not comprehend anything. 'What's it?' he asked, passing his work and climbing up from the field.
>
> ....
>
> Mangesh Kale ... made every effort to describe what he had seen: 'The machine is as tall as a human being. It has a wheel. A block with letters engraved on it is fixed to it. Ink is smeared to the block and placed in such a way that it touches paper. Paper is placed on a plank which is fixed below. A person turns the wheel. Another one keeps the paper and removes it. The ink on the letters engraved on the block appears on the paper. Not just one or two, but a hundred copies can be a printed in a day' ....

> In fact, Ramakrishna Gore made a trip to Goa one fine day accompanied by a few boys. On his return, he reported another new development: 'Malappayya, I believe the Brahmins of Goa have boycotted the machine. It's a wicked plan made by their means of livelihood. All these years, knowledge has been in the hands of Brahmins. Hundreds of Brahmins sit in rows in *Kavale Matha* [monastery] holding a stylus in their hands and inscribe over palm leaves making a grating sound. The task the Brahmins take years to complete is done by the machine in a day. Will they be left with any work? The ulterior motive is to make the Brahmins starve, and drive them to get converted! Hereafter, even people of the lower castes will get educated. Mark my words. They too will recite the Vedas and mythological texts. They'll also trifle with scriptures. Hence, those in Kavale Matha kept saying that our people shouldn't use the printing machine.' (Pai 2017, 88–89)

The layered meaning of technology that informed the call for a boycott of the machine in the novel shows that technology cannot be regarded in a purely technical sense. The sense of calamity which the new technology evoked cannot be explained by simply asserting that the Saraswat Brahmins were inherently opposed to technology. The social anxiety the machine provoked has its roots in the fear that the lower castes would now gain access to religious texts, which would in turn trivialise their sacrality. In a recent article, Thirumal, et al. (2024, 279) observe, 'Brahmanic comportment is the pre-theoretical existence of the elite cultural community where entities in the world are always already recognizable and seem to possess a framework of meaning to engage with hitherto unknown entities.' Since Brahmins as an elite cultural caste are one of the oldest historically continuous communities, their comportment has had a complex relationship with historical rationalities. As the novel is situated in the early colonial period, the power of the Brahmanic comportment to receive and order the heterogeneous and interacting components, namely the emerging moral, technical, economic, and social, was under threat.

To be a Brahmin means that one is nested in an ethical, social, and spiritual order. This nesting forms the condition that the above extract alludes to—the deeply ingrained activity of copying and composing religious texts on palm leaves, while sitting in rows in their monastery. The hand that does the copying is attuned to the pressures (both physical and metaphysical) attendant upon etching a poetic syllable or a Vedic text, even as it is directed by a force that it cannot comprehend, yet inevitably listens to. The nestedness allows them to anticipate how the impure bodies would assist in mechanically producing printed copies of any material, including sacred texts. The non-discriminating nature of the machine vis-à-vis the content and the bodies that attend to it are theorised together by Gopalakrishna Pai in *Swapna Saraswathe*. Such an affective and material history of media and technology is missing in the otherwise influential corpus of literary and cultural history, including the history of print or book history of India and South Asia. The above excerpt is suggestive of a phenomenological and ethical understanding of technology that goes beyond a blurring of the distinction between the natural and the social.

How does one engage with the following remark from one of the characters in the novel—'Malappayya, I believe the Brahmins of Goa have boycotted the machine'? A boycott connotes a suspension of thought, argument, or conversation and invokes judgement in its wake. To judge is to act. How does one see the Brahmanic mode of ordering via judgement as a way of putting things together? The psychic symbolises continuity and refers to both the discursive and the pre-discursive intelligibility referred to as the Brahmanic comportment. Personality would foreground the discursive and the historical character of Brahmin elites across particular epochs. Can one say that the consolidation of a range of disparate judgements founded on historical contingencies formed a constellation around which arose an opposing, collaborating, and contesting colonialism? It is not clear what discursive or epistemic registers were operational from the sixteenth to the eighteenth centuries. Does the Brahmanic worldview historically believe that the social—in a Latourian sense—may be extended to technology, or are there punctuated moments from the early modern period to the late nineteenth century where such a reading is theoretically possible? Or is it 'possible to differentiate a liminal unconscious into the threat of technology from a reasoned understanding of it' (R. Srivatsan, personal communication, 13 October 2021).

In the novel, the Saraswat Brahmins removed the deities from the temple, fearing the aggressive proselytisation of the Portuguese, and hid the idols in their homes (Pai 2017, 65). This act of shifting the idols from a sacral to a domestic locale deserves attention. Here, the Saraswat Brahmins brought in a topological sense of relative spatiality rather than a geographic sense of fixed territoriality. From the nineteenth century onwards, the nationalist social reformers invoked fixity rather than fluidity in matters relating to time and space. It was in this spatial manner that the sacral geography of India was grafted onto a political geography. The morphing of the sacred onto the political and vice versa is the axis around which mainstream media theory and history have to be situated. Brahmin comportment provides a range of responses to technology in general and media technology in particular. In this instance, the ability of the comportment to immediately offer a hegemonic Brahmin signification is held back. But, by the mid-nineteenth century, the Brahmin elites had managed to resignify the presence of print technology with newer meanings that did not disrupt the Brahmanic moral and aesthetic order.

Immanuel Kant's project of Enlightenment exhorts humans to have the courage to think, and as we have seen, the novel's historical response is to act in order to think (Bayly 2012; Kant n.d.). This response also marks the relative irrelevance of the Kantian distinction between public and private reason. The dominant approaches in media studies always prefer its scholars to measure their field by drawing on this distinction. The very existence of media practices is also rationalised in this tradition of political thought that advocates the relationship between the use of public reasoning and the formation of deliberative democracies. But a closer contextual scrutiny shows that this distinction is too vague, elusive, and inadequate to capture the multilayered works and nuances of media/technology in their everyday use and the possibilities they offer in one's life (Srivatsan 1993). The evaluative dispositions of both the media and its users fall outside the purview of consciousness, or what William Connolly refers to as 'visceral modes of appraisal' (Connolly 1999, 27), which transgress and transform any neat compartmentalisation of private spirituality from public reason. The pervasive role of the non-reflexive registers in shaping thought and action, as we can see in *Swapna Saraswathe*, demands an understanding of the body as an emotional and sensorial register in order to make sense of the media habitus and to restore intelligibility to 'forms of life that are otherwise impossible to recognize' (Spivak 2007).

Shifting dramatically from merchant capitalism of the sixteenth century to the age of liberalisation in the new millennium, Arjun Appadurai's (1998) work highlights some of the most visible and not-so-visible features of the new order of globalisation. The 'Global Now' (Fielder 2002, 165) has rendered the spatial, temporal, cosmic, and everyday mundane aspects of the local indeterminate, shaped by the flows of ethnicity, media, finance, technology, ideology, and culture. Then, does this formulation propose how an emergent subjectivity seems to address through imagination—rather than reason—the disjunctures associated with these 'runaway temporalities' and 'unruly spaces'? If one were to regard the 2019–2020 protests at Shaheen Bagh in New Delhi against the Citizenship Amendment Act (CAA), which preceded and continued towards the beginning of COVID-19, as 'the fearless idea' that questions 'life as it is', should we then see it as an 'uncommon association' against 'an uncommon assemblage'? (Leonard 2020). Shaheen Bagh must be viewed as one instance entangled with innumerable associations and assemblages from a variety of locations, and thus as an acknowledgement that these communities are yet to be imagined. Should studies connecting existents with existences, life and knowledge, history and spatiality through the application of novel approaches such as networks, infrastructure, and apparatus lead to merely eloquent and rich description, or should they raise ethical questions concerning disciplines and the very act of thinking? Working with the latter concerns will demand that we favour a radically different temporal and spatial framework, and think of media/technology from a planetary mode where they cannot be reduced to their materiality, history, or impact without and outside of which life will not be revealed. For instance, scholars working in digital humanities argue for what they call a 'networked being'. Singular images are less a product of single machines, but are consequences of multiple machines. This approach—the entanglement of media/technology and life—helps one to explore the transhistorical and transcultural experience of media technology. This is largely the spirit behind and the order in which the chapters in this volume have been assembled.

In an altogether different context, Arjun Appadurai addresses the important question of how a complex cultural form like cricket has been vernacularised through books, newspapers, radio, and television in contemporary India (Appadurai 2015). Cricket has now become 'an emblem of Indian nationhood at the same time that it became inscribed, as practice, into the Indian (male) body' (ibid., 21). Interestingly, Appadurai designates the acquired bodily repertoire of skills as 'agonistic skills', which means that they can also be read as exuding a new life form and as a body that disregards the weight of tradition and colonialism in one breath. The colony formally bequeaths knowledge and invisibly grooms the psychomotor dispositions needed to breathe life into the game. This transfer of passion, which then undergoes an unrecognisable transformation, gives rise to a collective fantasy attached to the idea of the nation. But what if the body is delinked from the nation? Will the collective fantasy still have significance for the body? This recalcitrant body, otherwise considered a product of techniques, technologies, geographies, and temporalities, mutates and transforms in ways that free it from its history and dominant spatial origins. (This transformation is focused on in Cultural Studies.) The body includes the animal and the human world. Sports trigger the most primal and supremely civil virtues. It is true that the colony has re-scripted the coloniser's body and the nationalists have tried to rewrite the cultural script inscribed on our bodies. But bodies contain histories of great temporal depth that may not necessarily be reducible to representation. It speaks to a deep time when the body remained uncoupled from the nation and matter spoke in an indeterminate fashion. The power of sport is more primal and goes beyond the limits of intelligibility situated in the artistry of the players or in the meaning attributed to it by spectators. In certain situations, in a Gadamerian sense, art addresses the community rather than community addressing art (Gadamer 2013). Sport makes possible a people, an orgiastic audience that is sociohistorically indeterminate. The uncoupling of the body from the figure, technology from anthropocentrism, and the history of caste from Brahminism is what makes this volume somewhat unique.

Organisation of the Volume

The chapters in this volume have been organised around theoretical affinities and their potential to explicate cultural values in disparate spaces and temporalities, in terms of a linear chronology or themes. The question of 'media history' and the attendant issues of actors, technology, political economy, imperialism, media genres, and audiences have been approached from nationalist, regional, transcultural, and global historical perspectives. The entrenched understanding of media history as national history is contested. Drawing on the globalisation theory of modernity, the chapters counter national perspectives and make an effort to retrieve and posit a subaltern and a lost LGBTQI imaginary to the making of media theory and history. From the question of whether television should be treated as an agent with the potential to fabricate a modernity, or as deployed to an already understood modernity, to questions related to the changing spatialities of film production and the concomitant challenges they pose to the representational order, the difficulties associated with the specificities of the historical understanding of media are all dealt with. The history of genres such as cartoons, textbooks, and newer cultural forms in mainland vernaculars, including technological questions such as the choice of script in the context of Northeast India, all receive attention.

Responding to the recent demand made by global historians that the intersection between telegraphy and journalism of the nineteenth century globally networked both telegraphy and journalism, Amelia Bonea (Chapter 2) focusses on the 'moments of cultural and technological transition' in Indian journalism. Her chapter undermines the predominant colonial and nationalist narratives of technological revolution. She argues that, in addition to geopolitical and commercial considerations, global flows of news were 'also shaped by the rationale of the network'. Historical studies of the press have been primarily motivated by nationalist, and in turn, anti-imperialist, concerns. Bonea's chapter belongs to a new genus of research which attempts to recast the history of the press and journalism as 'media history', an approach that has been strongly infused with the concerns of global historians who investigate connections and interactions beyond the traditional framework of the nation-State, and which has held particular appeal for many historians of the press in India.

Chapters 3, 4, and 5, by Brian Larkin, K. A. Nuaiman, and P. Thirumal and Amulya Komarraju, respectively, demonstrate how media practices are deployed to enhance the possibility of living life in accordance with cultural moorings that are at once open and closed. Appropriating Arjun Appadurai's work on parallel modernities, Brian Larkin proposes a completely new register on which to understand Bollywood cinema as globalised media by exploring the Nigerian Hausa attachment for Indian cinema. Such a move departs from viewing cinema as constituting the subject required for making a nation and related questions concerning citizenship and sovereignty. In engaging with the popularity of Bollywood films among the Muslim Hausa, Larkin proposes the concept of parallel modernities. Indian films, he argues (like many other scholars), are centred around family narratives, and provide a privileged site for witnessing the conflict between tradition and modernity. Interpreting the genre of *Soyayya* books to analyse the ethical and moral questions that overwhelm these works, Larkin draws parallels with Indian films. Rejecting the dominant thesis of Western cultural imperialism, Larkin, much like Arjun Appadurai, calls for a reworking of transnational cultural flows.

On the other hand, Nuaiman's *longue durée* understanding of lithography as a technology that is coeval with early medieval writerly cultures across globally connected Muslim religious centres in Malabar challenges the canonical understanding of the legacies of the typographic print revolution. His chapter focuses on Malabar Muslims' engagement with printing technologies, and questions the basic historical reasoning connected to print media and print cultures in the works of Elizabeth Einstein, among others, in the Western context. He also points out that even in historically specific works such as *Moveable Type* (2008), the ways in which printing technologies were utilised and adapted by religious communities in transcultural Muslim environments have not been adequately addressed. More specifically, he argues that there is a continuity between lithography and the pre-print writerly cultures of Malabar Muslims, which helps them retain forms of religious knowledge.

Thirumal and Komarraju explore the meaningful and productive relationship between online Dalit activism, digital archiving, and the making of anti-caste matter. Online portals such as *Dalit Camera*, *Round Table India*, and *Savari* are seen as producing textualities that are sonorous and sensible rather than graphic and intelligible. In analysing Subhadra's 'Kongu', the interpretation proposes that the poem does not only effectively counter an upper-caste meaning-making apparatus, but also exceeds the caste-restricted understanding of the thing called 'Kongu'. In doing so, anti-caste matter provides a horizon that is beyond caste *per se*.

Larkin, Nuaiman, and Thirumal and Komarraju note that the choices that Housas, Malabar Muslims, and Dalit communities make are crucial to engaging with media cultures. They argue against a naive media imperialism thesis, technological determinism, and an ethnocentric understanding of the agency of the typographic print revolution. Choosing Bollywood cinema instead of Hollywood, lithography over other printing technologies, and sonority over ocular-centric media practices is to retain agency as well as continuity with acknowledged forms of knowing.

In Chapters 6 and 7, respectively, Ashley Tellis and Dickens Leonard work with the idea that objects lost to history have to be reinstated with dignity—be it the desire of the gay professor from Aligarh Muslim University or Iyothee Thass's elaborately knitted anti-caste social imaginary. In a dialogue with Shad Naved's queer historiography, Tellis foregrounds the dismal manner in which queer identity and concerns multiply in the neoliberal media, yet fail to ground the psychic history of the queer subject. Leonard works with the iconic figure of Pandit Iyothee Thass and through a discussion of his prolific engagement with the Tamil language, and the press, attempts to revive civilisational debates related to religion, a retrieval of Buddhism, and polemics around Indian nationalism, questions the complete absence of Dalits in scholarly writings on media history. Leonard implies that all scholarly engagements have had an implicit bias against anti-caste social imaginaries, thereby offering tacit approval for hegemonic Hindu Brahmanism. Both Tellis and Leonard bring a reading strategy to the (affective) material they source in order to politically redeem a 'lost object' and an 'anti-caste imaginary', thus making an effort to rescue and resuscitate the 'petrified' objects they examine.

Contesting the popular perception that television in India transitioned from a statist model to a consumerist one, William Mazzarella (Chapter 8) offers a nuanced understanding of the historical moment that saw a transition from a statist to a liberalist TV system. In trying to posit the question, Mazzarella uses the label 'Development TV' to indicate independent India's desire to pursue 'a modernity that has both arrived and not yet been achieved'. Such an aspirational history actually moves from a TV that addresses a destined public to how State TV constitutes its own un-destined 'public'. Mazzarella closely reads the Joshi Report and the Kheda Project to study the locked possibilities of 'Development TV'.

Situating the spatiality of Kochi before and after the arrival of film studios and the setting up of the technological apparatus required for making films within the city, Carmel Christy (Chapter 9) discusses the spatiality of cinematic life through an analysis of the depiction of Kochi in Malayalam cinema. The partial relocation of the Malayalam film industry from Madras to Kochi through the establishment of studios created a discontinuity in the images related to the city of Kochi. Interestingly, this change coincided with changes in the visual and technical aspects of cinema, engendered by the liberalisation policies in the 1990s. Christy recounts the diverse ways in which social and cinematic life has evolved and suggests that the material and technical aspects of film production are intertwined with the social.

In Chapters 10 and 11, A. R. Venkatachalapathy and Vaibhav Singh provide insights into the affordances of technologies, including contested ideas regarding the choice of script, technology, and the historical and political reading of genres. Venkatachalapathy's chapter on cartoons evinces a historian's passion for tracing the genealogy of literary and cultural forms. Focusing primarily on the origin of cartoons in the Tamil region, the chapter offers a rich description of the anti-colonial spirit latent in these cartoons. Through his reading of popular Tamil periodicals, Venkatachalapathy demonstrates how the taste for the new art form was constructed among the Tamil-speaking population.

Vaibhav Singh details the complex context in which attempts were made to refine the Devanagari script in association with the American Mergenthler Linotype Company in the early decades of the twentieth century in a nationally contested space. Singh studies the debates and discussions around the introduction of the new type and script from the popular perspective, as well as academic, nationalist, and communal angles, and retrieves the ideological negotiations surrounding technology. Hence, this intervention to introduce a technology that composes language may also be understood as a demand for a language in which to think and speak about language, script, and typography.

Sasi Kiran Mallam's chapter (Chapter 13) can be read in conjunction with Thongam Bipin's chapter (Chapter 12) as both engage with the modernisation of cultural institutions—the institutionalisation of Telugu cultural production via Telugu textbooks during colonial rule and the contemporary standardisation of the Meetei script. It is important to note that Bipin discusses a border region that has fraught relations with the Indian State, and this tension informs his writing of its cultural history. De-Hinduising and detribalising cultural institutions and practices were strategies adopted in the Manipur nationalist movement. His analysis of the elaborate discussion around the modernising of the Meetei script with a non-Bengali version is sensitive to this history. Mallam's work on Telugu textbooks is primarily concerned with the Andhra region of the then Madras Presidency. The production of modern textbooks appears as a site of multiple contestations related to linguistic identity formation, language pedagogy, and the place of Telugu in the production of modern knowledge. This 'vernacular modernity', or vernacular-mediated modernity, was ushered in by the cultural elite, who had an ambivalent attitude towards social democracy and modernity. Both chapters deal with the multiple and heterogeneous components that act on the media object—be it policymaking, the choice of script, or the production of textbooks in the Telugu language.

We hope that these chapters will offer a fresh understanding of both historical and theoretical studies of the interconnections between heterogeneous elements such as media, technology, and communities, including caste and sexual identities. Affective arrangements and milieus require massive tweaking and displacing of established concepts such as nation, modernity, and globalisation, with transcultural perspectives and longitudinal views of cultural and technological pasts. This book is hopefully a humble step in that direction.

NOTES

1. See the UGC regulations (of February 2018) on the minimum qualifications for the appointment of teachers and other academic staff in universities and colleges, and measures for the maintenance of

standards in higher education. This new policy was approved in 2018 itself, but candidates were given a three-year window to complete their Ph.D. and thereby ensure that they were not disadvantaged by the immediate implementation.

2. The SITE Studies is based on an exemplary impact narrative framework. For more, see Eapen (1982).

REFERENCES

Alam, Muzaffar, and Sanjay Subrahmanyam. 2007. *Indo-Persian Travels in the Age of Discoveries, 1400–1800*.Cambridge: Cambridge University Press.

Appadurai, Arjun. 1998. *Modernity at Large: Cultural Dimensions of Globalization*. Minneapolis: University of Minnesota Press.

_____. 2015. 'Playing with Modernity: The Decolonization of Indian Cricket'. *Altre Modernità* 14, 1–24.

Bates, Crispin, and Subho Basu. 2005. *Rethinking Indian Political Institutions*. London: Anthem.

Bayly, C. A. 2012. *Recovering Liberties: Indian Thought in the Age of Liberalism and Empire*. New Delhi: Cambridge University Press.

Blackburn, Stuart. 2003. *Print, Folklore, and Nationalism in Colonial South India*. New Delhi: Permanent Black.

Blackburn, Stuart, and Vasudha Dalmia (eds). 2013. *India's Literary History: Essays on the Nineteenth Century*. New Delhi: Permanent Black.

Chakrabarty, Dipesh. 2000. *Provincializing Europe: Postcolonial Thought and Historical Difference*. Princeton, N.J.: Princeton University Press.

Chatterjee, Partha. 2004. *The Politics of the Governed: Reflections on Popular Politics in Most of the World*. New York: Columbia University Press.

Connolly, W. 1999. *Why I Am Not a Secularist*. Minneapolis: University of Minnesota Press.

Cox, W., and S. Sharma. 2024. 'India as Theory: Allusions, Poetry, Story Telling, and Translation'. *History of Humanities* 9 (1).

Eapen, K. E. 1982. 'Administrative and Critical Research: Notes on the Satellite Instructional Television Experiment'. In *AMIC Seminar on Priorities in Communications Research in Asia: Singapore*, 17–21. Singapore: Asian Mass Communication Research and Information Centre.

Eapen, K. E. 1995. *Communication: A Discipline in Distress*. Chennai: Department of Communication, Gurukul Lutheran Theological College and Research Institute.

Fielder, Sergio. 2002. 'Social Analysis'. *The International Journal of Social and Cultural Practice* 46 (2), 164–166.

Fraser, Robert. 2008. *Book History through Postcolonial Eyes: Rewriting the Script*. London: Routledge.

Gadamer, Hans-Georg. 2013. *Truth and Method*. London, New York: Bloomsbury.

Ghosh, Anindita. 2006. *Power in Print: Popular Publishing and the Politics of Language and Culture in a Colonial Society, 1778–1905*. New Delhi: Oxford University Press.

Ghose, H. P. 1952. *The Newspaper in India*. Calcutta: University of Calcutta.

Green, Nile. 2009. 'Journeymen, Middlemen: Travel, Transculture, and Technology in the Origins of Muslim Printing'. *International Journal of Middle East Studies* 41 (2), 203–224.

Gupta, Abhijit, and Swapan Chakravorty. 2004. *Print Areas: Book History in India*. New Delhi: Permanent Black.

——— (eds). 2008. *Moveable Type: Book History in India*. New Delhi: Permanent Black.

Harder, Hans (ed.). 2010. *Literature and Nationalist Ideology: Writing Histories of Modern Indian Languages*. New Delhi: Social Science Press.

Heidegger, Martin. 2008. *Being and Time*. New York: Harper & Row.

———. 2013. *The Question Concerning Technology, and Other Essays*. New York: Harper Perennial.

Huhtamo, Erkki, and Jussi Parikka (eds). 2011. *Media Archaeology: Approaches, Applications, and Implications*. Berkeley: University of California Press.

Ho, Engseng Ho. 2006. *The Graves of Tarim: Genealogy and Mobility across the Indian Ocean*. Berkeley: University of California Press.

Joshi, Priya. 1998. *Culture and Consumption: Fiction, the Reading Public, and the British Novel in Colonial India*. Baltimore: Johns Hopkins University Press.

Kant, Immanuel. n.d. 'What is Enlightenment?'. Available at www.columbia.edu/acis/ets/CCREAD/etscc/kant.html (accessed November 2024).

Kesavan, B. S. 1984. *History of Printing and Publishing in India: A Story of Cultural Re-awakening*. New Delhi: National Book Trust.

Krishnamurthi, N. 1966. *Indian Journalism: Origin, Growth and Development of Indian Journalism from Asoka to Nehru*. Mysore: University of Mysore.

Larkin, Brian. 2008. *Signal and Noise: Media, Infrastructure, and Urban Culture in Nigeria*. Durham and London: Duke University Press.

Latour, Bruno. 1996. 'On Actor-Network Theory: A Few Clarifications'. *Soziale Welt* 47 (4), 369–381.

Leonard, Dickens. 2020. 'On an Uncommon Association against a not-so-common Assemblage'. In Soumyabrata Choudhury (ed.), *Now it's Come to Distances*. New Delhi: Navayana.

Messick, Brinkley M. 1993. *The Calligraphic State: Textual Domination and History in a Muslim Society*. Berkeley: University of California Press.

Muniruddin, 2005. *History of Journalism*. New Delhi: Anmol Publications.

Natarajan, J. 1954. *History of Indian Journalism: Part II of India, Report of the Press Commission*. New Delhi: Publications Division.

Natarajan, Srividya. 2018. *The Undoing Dance: You Will Be Seduced Completely*. New Delhi: Juggernaut.

Nicholson, A. J. 2021. 'Review of Karl-Stéphan Bouthillette, *Dialogue and Doxography in Indian Philosophy: Points of View in Buddhist, Jaina, and Advaita Vedānta Traditions*'. *Sophia* 60 (3).

Orsini, Francesca. 2009. *Print and Pleasure: Popular Literature and Entertaining Fictions in Colonial North India*. Ranikhet: Permanent Black.

Pai, Gopalakrishna. 2017. *Swapna Saraswathe*. Manipal: Manipal University Press.

Palshikar, S. 2014. *Evil and the Philosophy of Retribution: Modern Commentaries on the Bhagavad-Gita*. New Delhi and Abingdon: Routledge.

Pollock, Sheldon. 2001. 'The Death of Sanskrit'. *Comparative Studies in Society and History* 43 (2), 392–426.

_____ (ed.). 2003. *Literary Cultures in History: Reconstructions from South Asia*. Berkeley: University of California Press

Proudfoot, Ian. 1997. 'Mass producing Houri's Moles or Aesthetics and Choice of Technology in Early Muslim Book Printing'. In Tonny Street and Peter Riddell (eds), *Islam: Essays on Scripture, Thought and Society. A Festschrift in Honour of Anthony H. Johns*, 161–184. Leiden, New York, Koln: Brill.

Rajadhyaksha, Ashish, and Paul Willemen (eds). 1994. *Encyclopaedia of Indian Cinema*. London: British Film Institute

Ricci, Ronit. 2011. *Islam Translated: Literature, Conversion, and the Arabic Cosmopolis of South and Southeast Asia*. Chicago: The University of Chicago Press.

Robinson, Francis. 1993. 'Technology and Religious Change: Islam and the Impact of Print'. *Modern Asian Studies* 27 (1), 229–251.

Soneji, Devesh. 2012. *Unfinished Gestures: Devadasis, Memory, and Modernity in South India*. Chicago: The University of Chicago Press.

_____. 2013. 'The Powers of Polyglossia: Marathi Kīritan, Multilingualism, and the Making of a South Indian Devotional Tradition'. *International Journal of Hindu Studies* 17 (3), 339–369.

Spivak, Gayatri Chakravorty. 2007. 'Religion, Politics, Theology: A Conversation with Achille Mbembe'. *Boundary* 34 (2), 149–170.

Srivatsan, R. 1993. 'Imaging Truth and Desire: Photography and the Visual Field in India'. In Tejaswini Niranjana, P. Sudhir, and Vivek Dhareshwar (eds), *Interrogating Modernity*, 155–198. Calcutta: Seagull.

Starke, Ulrike. 2008. *Empire of Books: The Naval Kishore Press and the Diffusion of the Printed Word in Colonial India*. Ranikhet: Permanent Black.

Thirumal, P., Narmada P., and H. Chintakunta. 2024. 'Notes Toward a Theoretical History of Indic Media: On Elite Comportment and Technological Affordances'. *Public Culture* 36 (2), 279–302.

Venkatachalapathy, A. R. 2012. *The Province of the Book: Scholars, Scribes and Scribblers in Colonial Tamilnadu*. Ranikhet: Permanent Black.

2

Telegraphy and Journalism in Colonial India, *c.* 1830s to 1900s*

Amelia Bonea

This chapter weaves together two distinct strands of Indian historiography: the history of technology and the history of journalism. Taken separately, technology and journalism have been two of the most prolific fields of inquiry for historians of colonial South Asia. However, attempts to examine the history of the press at the intersection with technology have been few and unsystematic. This holds true for older technologies like the printing press, which enabled newspapers and periodicals to assume the visual forms so familiar to their readers, as well as 'newer' technologies like steamers, railways, and electric telegraphs, which became indispensable mediators in the circulation of information and ideas from around the mid-nineteenth century onwards (Samaddar 1994).[1]

This absence in Indian historiography is all the more intriguing if we consider that technologies of communication have long been associated with transformations in media practices, not only in India but also globally.[2] Indeed, contemporary arguments about the impact of the internet on journalism echo nineteenth-century enthusiasm about the telegraph and its role in facilitating worldwide communication. Rudyard Kipling, well-known for his musings on technology, remarked at the end of the nineteenth

*First published as 'Telegraphy and Journalism in Colonial India, c. 1830s to 1900s', *History Compass* 12 (5), 7 May 2014. Reproduced with the kind permission of John Wiley and Sons.

century that electricity, Morse instruments, and submarine cables had brought the flutter of conversation to some of the most remote corners of the Earth and the recesses of the seas, subduing time and distance and making the world 'one'.[3] Such celebratory accounts of the technological 'marvels' of the Victorian age were not, however, devoid of tensions and contradictions. The narrative of progress, unity, and rapid communication frequently overlapped with the frustrating reality of new work and life rhythms. Kipling himself was not oblivious to this modern dilemma. One of his short stories offers a rare glimpse into the changing work routines of newspaper editors and composers in India, a scene probably inspired by his own experiences as a journalist with *The Pioneer* and *The Civil & Military Gazette* in the 1880s:

> A King or courtier or a courtesan or a Community was going to die or get a new Constitution, or do something that was important on the other side of the world, and the paper was to be held open till the latest possible minute in order to catch the telegram. I drowsed, and wondered whether the telegraph was a blessing, and whether this dying man, or struggling people, might be aware of the inconvenience the delay was causing. (Kipling 1994, 120)

These literary examples illustrate the moments of self-reflexivity that surround the emergence of new media (Thorburn and Jenkins 2003, 7), while also illuminating the manifold ways in which the use of telegraphy intersected with journalism, especially news reporting. The historiography of the press and telegraphy in colonial South Asia has so far shown little inclination to probe in greater depth the nature and extent of these interactions, besides occasional intimations that the new technology radically transformed the newspaper world. Krishnalal Shridharani's claim in the early 1950s that 'The whole newspaper industry [in India] was revolutionized [by telegraphy]' (Shridharani 1953: 61) was echoed two decades later by Mel Gorman's statement that the telegraph had created 'a veritable revolution in newspaper reporting' (Gorman 1971: 597). While Gorman failed to elaborate this point, Shridharani argued that the telegraph significantly reduced the amount of time it took news to travel between India and other parts of the world, and allowed newspapers to provide 'full coverage' of events at cheap transmission rates. According to him, 'the modern newspaper ... [was] almost exclusively the child of telegraph [*sic*] and telephone' (Shridharani 1953, 2, 60–62).

The historical context in which Shridharani's pioneering history of telegraphy was written is significant. The publication of the book anticipated the centenary of the Indian telegraph and coincided with the Government of India's First Five-Year Plan, with its strong emphasis on the development of transport and communications in the post-independence period. In fact, both Prime Minister Jawaharlal Nehru and the Minister of Communications, Jagjivan Ram, endorsed the book. Under these circumstances, it is perhaps not surprising that most of Shridharani's conclusions about telegraphy and the press pertained to the twentieth century. The first five decades of telegraphic communication—the period from around the 1840s to 1900—were glossed over with furtive statements about the telegraph being an instrument of British imperial domination that provided the colonial government with an 'added avenue of censorship', and was used primarily for the transmission of military and political news (Shridharani 1953, 61). Shridharani's treatment of the subject, in particular his focus on the twentieth century, is indicative of a general trend in the historiography of technologies of communications and media in South Asia. In this chapter, I would like to advocate a return to the relatively neglected nineteenth century and suggest that the 'moments of cultural and technological transition' it witnessed could help us rethink predominant narratives of media and technological revolution (Thorburn and Jenkins 2003, 1).

Later analyses of the history of telegraphy focused little on its use in the field of journalism but expanded on the idea of the telegraph as an imperial 'tool'. This was particularly the case with Daniel Headrick's work on technology transfer in the British Empire (Headrick [1981] famously referred to technologies as the 'tools of Empire') and D. K. Lahiri Choudhury's more recent work on British imperialism and telegraphic communication in colonial India (Lahiri Choudhury 2010). Both historians were preoccupied primarily with the use of telegraphy in domains of activity such as colonial administration, warfare, and business, where the exploitative nature of the colonial state was particularly visible. They also recognised that newspapers and news agencies like Reuters were among the first and most important beneficiaries of telegraphic communication in the Indian subcontinent, although this argument was left undeveloped. Headrick and Pascal Griset, for example, described the press and news agencies as the 'most important customers' of cable companies (Headrick and Griset 2001, 551), while Lahiri Choudhury highlighted Reuters' monopoly over the distribution of foreign telegrams in India and argued that the prices demanded by the agency were unaffordable for vernacular newspapers, who 'rel[ied] on digests of news and translations from papers with resources to afford Reuters' (Lahiri Choudhury 2004, 971).

Useful clues pointing to the role of telegraphy in the development of the newspaper press in the British Empire can also be found in other historical works that do not focus primarily on South Asia, but seek to understand the role of technology in processes of globalisation since the nineteenth century. One example is Dwayne Winseck and Robert Pike's work, which critiques classical theories of imperialism by highlighting the role of the capitalist enterprise in shaping international communications during this period (Winseck and Pike 2007). Their research documents the entanglements between cable businesses and news agencies and portrays Julius Reuter as an important proponent and beneficiary of telegraphic expansion. The significance of news agencies like Reuters, Havas, and Wolff in spearheading the development of telegraphic communication is also noted by Roland Wenzlhuemer, who points out that, in addition to geopolitical and commercial considerations, global flows of news were 'also shaped by the rationale of the network'. Thus, although London was the centre of telecommunications during this period, the telegraph could facilitate the transformation of 'geographic peripheries' into 'information centres', and *vice versa* (Wenzlhuemer 2012, 91).

This brief overview suggests that, for historians of telecommunications, Reuters has provided one of the few connecting links between the history of telegraphy and the history of the press in colonial South Asia. The same conclusion holds true for historians of the press in India and the British Empire more generally. Indeed, the conspicuousness of Reuters' telegrams in the pages of nineteenth-century newspapers seems to have been matched by the agency's own visibility as a topic of scholarly research. During the past two decades in particular, an important body of scholarship has set out to investigate the connections between news agencies, imperialism, and globalisation.[4] Such work is part of a broader attempt to recast the history of the press and journalism as 'media history', and has been strongly infused with the concerns of global historians to investigate connections and interactions beyond the traditional framework of the nation-state, which has held particular appeal for many historians of the press in India. These recent developments in media history and the global history of telecommunications provide the perfect momentum to examine anew the history of the press in nineteenth-century India.

So far, technology has played only a marginal role in explaining the development of the newspaper press in nineteenth-century India. This has been the case not only with technologies of communication such as steamers and telegraphs, but also with industrially produced printing presses like the Albion and the Columbian, used in India during the second half of the nineteenth century.[5] For the sake of convenience, histories of the press in India can be divided thematically into two broad categories: general histories, which trace the development of the press from the publication of the first English-language newspapers and periodicals at the end of the nineteenth century, and more specific studies that examine various aspects of press history. These include the role of newspapers in political mobilisation and the creation of regional and national identities, the press as an instrument of propaganda, the evolution of colonial press regulations and their impact on the vernacular press, and biographies of journalists.[6] In recent years, there have also been sporadic efforts to approach the history of the colonial press from less explored angles, such as that of advertising (Chaudhuri 2007; Sharma 2009).

The number of general histories of the press and journalism in India is indeed impressive. Many of them were published in the 1950s and 1960s, in the wake of the First Indian Press Commission and, more recently, in connection with the establishment of departments of Mass Communication and Journalism at numerous Indian universities. In the latter case, they often function as textbook introductions to the subject (for example, Basu 1979; Ghose 1952; Ghosh 1998; Krshnamurthi 1966; Moitra 1969; Munirrudin 2005; Natarajan 1955). Despite the sheer number of such publications, there has been little theoretical and methodological variation in their approach to the study of the press. Furthermore, many continue to draw on Margarita Barns' pioneering history of the Indian press (Barns 1940). Published more than seven decades ago, her study remains the main work of general reference for those interested in the history of the press during the colonial period.

Mirroring a line of argumentation well-established in the historiography of colonial South Asia, most general histories of the press adhere to a linear narrative of colonial transfer and national adoption and adaptation of the newspaper medium. Thus, the newspaper in its 'modern form' was introduced to India with British colonialism at the end of the eighteenth century, during a period when the government of the East India Company seemed little inclined to tolerate criticism of its actions and servants.[7] This is often demonstrated by appeal to familiar names such as that of James Augustus Hicky, editor and publisher of India's first printed newspaper, *Hicky's Bengal Gazette or the Original Calcutta General Advertiser*, who was notoriously imprisoned on account of his criticism of Governor-General Warren Hastings. Despite his association with a style of journalism that was often dismissed as 'scandalous' by his contemporaries, Hicky has been re-appropriated, particularly in nationalist historiography, as an early example of an 'Indian' journalist who fought for press freedom in colonial India (Naqvi 2007; Singh 2010).[8] This is an ironic pronouncement if we consider that one of the most striking features of press history in colonial India has been the insistence on the methodological and ideological separation of Anglo-Indian and Indian journalism. This trend was accompanied by a tendency to overlook the 'scandalous' dimension of Hicky's journalism and a failure to contextualise it historically. In a sense, then, for the purposes of nationalist historiography, Hicky had to be rescued not only from the constraints of his 'national background', but also from the particular style of journalism he practised. This resonated, rather uncomfortably, with the 'yellow journalism' of the early nineteenth century, of which both colonial and nationalist histories were equally dismissive.

There is no denying that colonial rule was responsible for the creation of 'invidious distinctions' between various sections of the press in India. These distinctions usually pitched the Anglo-Indian press against the vernacular one, but also operated within these two categories.[9] Much of the historiography of the post-independence period maintained this dualism while attempting to rehabilitate the Indian press from the derision in which it had been held during the colonial period. Hicky is, therefore, an exception in a historical meta-narrative which, by and large, posited the formal and ideological separation of Anglo-Indian and vernacular newspapers, with the former usually described as the mouthpiece of the colonial government and rhetoric, and the latter as a catalyst of anti-colonial resistance and regional or national mobilisation. For nationalist historians, in particular, shifting attention to the Indian press provided an opportunity to document the role of Indian newspapers in the fight for independence and the creation of a national identity.

Analytically, this also meant that newspapers were examined predominantly for what I would like to call their illustrative value—as records of past events and creators/moulders of public opinion, rather than as historical artefacts whose content and form were shaped by the political, socioeconomic, technological, and even aesthetic exigencies of their times. To put it differently, there has been a greater interest in the content of newspapers and their ideological pronouncements rather than in understanding how newspapers were created and functioned, how they acquired the information they published, what technologies enabled the transmission of this information, or the particular sociopolitical and information networks that connected them. While this methodological bias is hardly surprising, its implications are significant, not only for historians of the press but also for those whose primary interests lay outside this particular field, and yet who draw extensively on the surviving newspaper records in order to test and illustrate their arguments. This has been particularly so in the aftermath of Benedict Anderson's work on the role of printed matter in the creation of nations as 'imagined communities', as well as Juergen Habermas' equally impactful study on the importance of the printed medium in forging a bourgeois public sphere in eighteenth- and early nineteenth-century Europe (Anderson 2003; Habermas 1991).

Yet, in many historical contexts—colonial South Asia is no exception to this—the relationship between the content of the newspaper and the type of responses it evoked in its readers has been one of the most difficult to document aspects of press history. Causal connections have often been inferred on the basis of circumstantial evidence about the identity of the journalists who produced the newspaper and the identity of the newspaper itself, rather than empirical data about their actual readership and their reception of the message carried in the newspaper. Readers' responses to newspaper content have also been more heterogeneous than is usually assumed. Finally, as Robin Jeffrey has aptly pointed out in his discussion of print, newspapers, and politics in Kerala, scholars have often treated newspapers 'as if [they] were the same, and had the same effects, no matter the place or time' (Jeffrey 2009, 486). In the South Asian context, a good illustration of the pitfalls of this line of argumentation comes from Gerald Barrier's work on politics and press in Punjab, where he attempts to recover the complexity of newspaper and readership identity in nineteenth-century India. Using the example of the *Lahore Tribune*, a paper frequently portrayed by historians as a 'powerful voice of nationalism in Punjab', Barrier shows how the *Tribune*'s potential for political mobilisation was drastically circumscribed by the fact that it was run by Bengali editors and patronised by a small group of Hindu professionals. According to him, the paper assumed a clear pro-Hindu stance despite the editors' efforts to avoid involvement in factional and communal politics (Barrier 1985).

If we accept the proposition that the nature of news is to circulate, then it becomes increasingly evident that a framework of analysis limited by the geographical and ideological constraints of the nation-state cannot account for the complexity of news production and circulation in nineteenth-century India. It is here that a focus on technologies of communication, such as the telegraph, can be particularly helpful in overcoming some of the limitations and homogenising tendencies of nation-based analyses, by drawing attention to a different set of concerns that can enrich our understanding of press history in colonial India. Among these are the evolution of news reporting patterns and news values during the nineteenth century, the role of technology in transmitting news, in particular, the routes along which information travelled from its source to the pages of the newspaper, and the ways in which technology shaped the content and form of news, the differences between telegraphy-in-use and telegraphy-in-(colonial) discourse, and the colonial government's use of telegraphy as an instrument of censorship—all concerns that have received little attention in previous histories of the press in India. This is not to detract attention from the oppressiveness of colonialism nor to deny the role which many newspapers played in the fight for independence (with the essential qualification that anti-colonial is not necessarily synonymous with national). Rather, it is to recognise that newspapers in colonial India were complex and interconnected projects, even when they subscribed to opposing political projects and ideologies. They were part of formal and informal networks of communication that allowed news to be exchanged, sold, clipped, contested, refuted, or validated. The extent of these networks was shaped both by human agency and technologies of communication.

In recent years, there has been a growing appreciation of the extent and importance of these press networks, both formal and informal, among media historians. To my knowledge, Bryna

Goodman was the first to discuss the concept of 'press networks' in an Asian context in her study of the press in Republican Shanghai. She demonstrated the fluid and entangled nature of Chinese, English, and Japanese-language newspapers and the manner in which they resisted simplistic categorisations along national lines (Goodman 2004). In his analysis of English-language press networks in East Asia (1918–1945), Peter O'Connor also highlighted the dynamic and flexible nature of press networks, which he defined as an 'informal accumulation of commonalities of editorial line, worldview and commercial interest' (O'Connor 2010, 66). In the South Asian context, Chandrika Kaul's work on the reporting of the British Raj by British newspapers has also been instrumental in showing how human and technological networks combined to mediate a certain image of British colonial rule at 'Home'. Kaul, Juergen Wilke, and Peter Putnis have also edited a volume dedicated exclusively to the historical analysis of global news networks (Kaul 2003; Putnis, et al. 2011).

Recent developments in the history of the book in South Asia have also provided new avenues for exploring the history of the press in nineteenth-century India. Studies such as those of Anindita Ghosh (2006) and Francesca Orsini (2009) have made us more attentive to the mechanisms of print production and consumption in colonial South Asia, and opened up to inquiry a whole new world of popular literary production which did not comply with the canons and sensibilities of middle-class, elite literary forms (ibid.). Ulrike Stark's *An Empire of Books* (2009) is another excellent example of work in this vein, which also documents processes of news production at *Avadh Akhbar*, the first Urdu-language daily in northern India. Her study shows that this newspaper published a great variety of domestic and foreign news, including telegrams. News was often reprinted from English and Anglo-Indian papers, such as *The Times*, *The Pioneer*, and *Friend of India*, as well as Persian and Arabic newspapers. In addition, Munshi Naval Kishore maintained an extensive system of correspondents and enlisted the help of the reading public by offering free copies of the newspaper in exchange for items of intelligence of particular interest (ibid., 265).

To summarise, I have, through a review of existing literature on the history of telegraphy and the press in South Asia, so far argued that although telegraphy and journalism have received a fair amount of attention from historians as disparate areas of inquiry, attempts to connect the two have been sparse and unsystematic. This is particularly so for the period of technological transition represented by the second half of the nineteenth century. Furthermore, the nationalist bias in much historiography of the press has limited considerably the thematic repertoire of scholarship, which a recent theoretical and methodological shift in the global history of telecommunications, media history, and book history promises to unsettle. In what follows, I will briefly demonstrate how the historiography of the press in South Asia can benefit from an engagement with the history of technology by using examples from my own research, which has examined the use of telegraphy in English-language news reporting in nineteenth-century India. I have attempted to trace the use of technology, both from a long-term perspective by examining the evolution of news reporting in a number of newspapers at intervals of ten years from the 1830s until the 1900s, and by scrutinising specific instances of coverage of international and domestic events, such as the Austro-Prussian War (1866) and the murder at Poona in 1897 of two European officers associated with plague relief measures.

With regard to the argument that electric telegraphy generated a 'revolution' in newspaper reporting, an examination of English-language newspapers published in the Indian subcontinent during the nineteenth century reveals that this was a period of transition for the newspaper press, and that the changes which ensued from the use of telegraphy were gradual rather than abrupt and disruptive. The drive for regular and timely news was connected both to the demands of the colonial administration and those of the mercantile communities in Britain and India, with the telegraph being used to report predominantly political and commercial intelligence. In fact, the format of the telegraphic news follows well-established conventions of reporting shipping intelligence, which can be traced back to the appearance of serial publications in seventeenth-century London (Harris 1999, 39–63). Furthermore, it must be remembered that communication times between Britain and India decreased only gradually, following the expansion of the telegraph network and the construction of direct telegraph lines. In India, the first lines were opened for public use on 1 February 1855, by which time newspapers were already publishing telegraphic news. By 1865, communication between Britain and India was made possible by two lines to Karachi via the Ottoman Empire (Turkish Route) and Russia (Russian Route). In 1870, two additional routes were completed, one of which had the advantage of being under British control: the Indo-European line built by Siemens and the Red Sea route built by the famous cable magnate John Pender. For example, in 1866, the year of the Austro-Prussian War, the average transmission time for a message from Britain to India on the Turkish line was six days, eight hours, and forty-four minutes, while five years later, the average transmission time was six hours and seven minutes on the newly opened Indo-European line (Blondheim 1994).[10] By the end of the century, communication between Britain and India had become almost instantaneous.

During the nineteenth century, English-language newspapers in India drew on a variety of technologies to obtain their news. In the case of international news, the telegraph was used alongside steamers to obtain full reports of events from correspondents based in London and other European cities. The correspondence by the overland mail provided the 'flesh' to the skeleton of information transmitted with the help of telegraphy by news agencies such as Reuters, and occasionally by correspondents and short-lived telegraphic agencies like that operated by *The Times of India* in the early 1860s (Hirschmann 2008, 76). Similarly, telegraphs, steamers, railways, runners, and other means of communication were used complementarily during the nineteenth century to transmit domestic news. In the case of domestic news telegrams, the gradual transformation in reporting practices was clearly visible during the last three decades of the century, when domestic news telegrams began to make an appearance in the 'Latest Telegrams' section of the newspapers examined. This was connected to the introduction of price concessions for press telegrams by the Government of India in 1872 and 1880, which led to a gradual increase in the number and length of telegrams published, a trend also visible in the case of foreign telegrams (Bonea 2016, 179–82).

Thus, although the electric telegraph had been used in the transmission of domestic news since the 1850s, it was only during the last three decades of the century that newspapers could begin to explore the full potential of this technology. Even then, access to this technology continued to be circumscribed by the political and economic considerations of the colonial state, which actively discriminated between newspapers based on their perceived political stance, economic standing, or informal networks of patronage. For example, the press message privilege, which allowed newspapers in India to send and receive telegrams at concessionary rates, was initially extended only to English-language newspapers, with vernacular papers specifically excluded between 1872 and 1876. There is indication, however, that in spite of these restrictions, a well-known Gujarati newspaper like the *Bombay Samachar* was able to avail of the press rates, at least during part of the period when the restrictions were in force (Bonea 2016, 235). If we corroborate this information with the fact that official intelligence was communicated preferentially only to some Anglo-Indian newspapers, we can conclude that access to telegraphic news during this period depended not only on the 'national' background of an editor or newspaper, but also on that paper's socioeconomic standing and its relationship to the colonial administration.

A focus on technologies and routes of communication also helps us transcend nation-centric approaches by uncovering less obvious connections and exchanges. In a different context, I investigated the competition between Reuters and *The Times of India* Telegraphic Agency in reporting the Austro-Prussian War in India (Bonea 2010). In that discussion, I pointed out that this competition was reflected in the two types of telegrams which newspapers such as *The Times of India* and *The Englishman* of Calcutta published during the war, namely 'Reuters Telegrams' and 'Subscription Telegrams'. As the name itself reveals, the former category of news was transmitted by Reuters and was based on the newspapers' subscription to its telegraphic service. The latter category of news was sent from London to Bombay via the news agency operated by the editor of *The Times of India* and distributed from there to other subscribing newspapers like *The Englishman*.[11]

The range of circulation of both Reuters and 'Subscription Telegrams' extended beyond the geographical confines of South Asia. For example, *The Japan Times* of 26 January 1866 published 'Subscription Telegrams' delivered via Hong Kong by the Japanese steamer Fusiyama (*sic*).[12] Although the format of the news suggested timeliness, the intelligence was two months old by the time it was published in Japan, a clear reflection of the state of communication between South Asia and Japan at the time. The Fusiyama, a steamer built in the United States for the Japanese government, had set sail for Japan on 4 September 1865 via Rio de Janeiro, the Cape of Good Hope, and Hong Kong.[13] It was at this latter port that the steamer came in possession of the Calcutta newspapers containing the telegrams, which were delivered to Japan after passing Singapore on 11 December of that year, as *The Straits Times* testifies.[14] This glimpse into the channels of news circulation in South and East Asia reveals how newspaper form and content moved across the region, familiarising people with places, names, and styles of reporting, and creating a common base of knowledge to discuss and engage with.

In short, the introduction of telegraphy in nineteenth-century India did not translate immediately into revolutionary changes in the field of journalism. Change was incremental and the evolution of news reporting in the English-language press built on previous conventions of reporting intelligence, especially shipping intelligence, and was shaped by a wide variety of technological, socioeconomic, and political factors. The telegraph allowed information to travel much faster than previously possible, but it also created new distinctions and boundaries, as much as it facilitated integration and connections through the circulation of similar, sometimes identical, information to English-language newspapers in India and other parts of the world. Studying newspapers in colonial India through the lenses of technology allows us to question dominant narratives of media revolution in nineteenth-century India and to recover the diversity of newspaper interactions and connections during this period.

Acknowledgements

This is a revised version of a paper first published in *History Compass*. I would like to thank the journal for permission to reproduce it here and the two anonymous reviewers who refereed the original paper. I am also indebted to Robin Jeffrey for his constructive criticism on an earlier draft and his contagious enthusiasm for all things press related.

Notes

1. For the late twentieth century, one important exception is Samaddar (1994).

2. See Ahlers (2006); Carey (2009); Rantanen (2009); Thorburn and Jenkins (2003). For a Japanese perspective, see Akagi (2011). A recent example from India is Udupa (2011).

3. Kipling (1869, 9). The word 'Anglo-Indian', as employed in this essay, reflects the nineteenth-century usage and refers to British residents in India, not to people of mixed British and Indian descent. Similarly, 'Anglo-Indian newspapers' refers to newspapers published in India by British residents, usually in the English language.

4. For example, see Kaul (2006); Potter (2003); Putnis, et al. (2011).

5. I am grateful to Robin Jeffrey for bringing this point to my attention. Email communication with Robin Jeffrey, 24 July 2012.

6. Some examples of specific histories are Boyce (1988); Hirschmann (2008); Khare (1964); Narain (1998); Israel (1994); and Wagle (1999). For examples of general histories, refer to note 18 below.

7. This should encourage us to reconsider the very definition of newspapers. So far, 'modern' newspapers have been distinguished from their 'pre-modern' predecessors, such as newssheets, based on their ability to reach a broad audience, their regular publication, and the fact

that they were printed. Yet the limitations of this definition are readily apparent, even for the temporal frameworks associated with 'modernity'. For example, *The Kandahar News* began in 1879 as a handwritten newspaper produced for the benefit of a restricted audience, namely the garrison stationed in that region. The newspaper had a limited circulation in other parts of India as well, but it was only printed in 1880.

8. See, for example, Singh (2010, 7), who draws on Barns (1940) to support this argument, and Naqvi (2007, especially pp. 36–37). See also *Deccan Herald* (2011). Such articles, penned by academics and non-academics alike, commonly appear in contemporary media.

9. The expression is Somnath Roy's (Roy 1967, 748).

10. Simpson (1928). Here, Menahem Blondheim's argument that before the introduction of telegraphy, communication times had already shrunk considerably in the United States due to the use of steamers is valid in India's case as well. See Blondheim (1994, 11–12).

11. See, for example, *The Times of India*, 26 June 1866; *The Englishman*, 27 June 1866.

12. *Japan Times*, 26 January 1866.

13. *The New York Times*, 5 September 1865.

14. *The Straits Times*, 12 December 1865.

REFERENCES

Ahlers, D. 2006. 'News Consumption and the New Electronic Media'. *Press/Politics* 11, 29–52.

Akagi, K. 2011. 'Gijutsu to jānarizumu o meguru shimbun-kai no giron: 1950-nendaimatsu kara 1960-nendai ni kakete no gijutsukakushinki no kōsatsu' ('Discussions on Technology and Journalism in the Japanese Newspaper World: A Review of the Technological Innovation Period from the Late 1950s to the 1960s'). *Journal of Information Studies* 80, 71–83.

Anderson, B. 2003. *Imagined Communities: Reflections on the Origin and Spread of Nationalism*. London: Verso, 12th edn.

Barns, M. 1940. *The Indian Press*. London: George Allen & Unwin.

Barrier, N. G. 1985. 'Punjab Politics and the Press, 1880–1910'. In M. Case and N. G. Barrier (eds), *Aspects of India: Essays in Honor of Edward C. Dimock, Jr*, 118–33. New Delhi: Manohar.

Basu, J. N. 1979. *Romance of Indian Journalism*. Calcutta: Calcutta University.

Blondheim, M. 1994. *News over the Wires: The Telegraph and the Flow of Public Information in America, 1844–1897*. Cambridge, MA: Harvard University Press.

Bonea, A. 2010. 'The Medium and Its Message: Reporting the Austro-Prussian War in the Times of India'. *Historical Social Research* 35, 167–87.

_____. 2016. *The News of Empire: Telegraphy, Journalism, and the Politics of Reporting in Colonial India, c. 1830–1900*. New Delhi: Oxford University Press.

Boyce, M. T. 1988. *British Policy and the Evolution of the Vernacular Press in India, 1835–1878*. New Delhi: Chanakya Publications.

Carey, J. W. 2009. *Communication as Culture: Essays in Media and Society*. New York: Routledge, rev. edn.

Chaudhuri, A. 2007. *Indian Advertising, 1780 to 1950 A.D.* New Delhi: Tata McGraw-Hill Publishing Company Limited.

Deccan Herald. 2011. 'Hicky: A Pioneer Who Unleashed the Power of the Press', 29 January. Available at https://www.deccanherald.com/opinion/hicky-pioneer-unleashed-power-press-2389724 (accessed November 2024).

Ghose, H. P. 1952. *The Newspaper in India*. Calcutta: University of Calcutta.

Ghosh, A. 2006. *Power in Print: Popular Publishing and the Politics of Language and Culture in a Colonial Society, 1778–1905*. New Delhi: Oxford University Press.

Ghosh, S. 1998. *Modern History of the Indian Press*. New Delhi: Cosmo Publications.

Goodman, B. 2004. 'Semi-colonialism, Transnational Ties, and Press Culture in Early Republican Shanghai'. *The China Review* 4, 55–88.

Gorman, M. 1971. 'Sir William O'Shaughnessy, Lord Dalhousie and the Establishment of the Telegraph System in India'. *Technology and Culture* 12, 581–601.

Habermas, J. 1991. *The Structural Transformation of the Public Sphere: An Inquiry into a Category of Bourgeois Society*. Cambridge, MA: MIT Press.

Harris, M. 1999. 'Shipwrecks in Print; Representations of Maritime Disaster in the Late Seventeenth Century'. In Robyn Myers and Michael Harris (eds), *Journeys through the Market: Travel, Travellers and the Book Trade*, 39–63. New Castle, DE: Oak Knoll Press.

Headrick, D. R. 1981. *The Tools of Empire: Technology and European Imperialism in the Nineteenth Century*. Oxford: Oxford University Press.

Headrick, D. R., and P. Griset. 2001. 'Submarine Telegraph Cables: Business and Politics, 1838–1939'. *The Business History Review* 75 (3), 543–578.

Hirschmann, R. 2008. *Robert Knight: Reforming Editor in Victorian India*. New Delhi: Oxford University Press.

Israel, M. 1994. *Communications and Power: Propaganda and the Press in the Indian Nationalist Struggle, 1920–1945*. Cambridge: Cambridge University Press.

Jeffrey, R. 2009. 'Testing Concepts about Print, Newspapers and Politics: Kerala, India, 1800–2007'. *Journal of Asian Studies* 68, 465–489.

Kaul, C. 2003. *Reporting the Raj: The British Press and India, c. 1880–1922*. Manchester: Manchester University Press.

Kaul, C. (ed.). 2006. *Media and the British Empire*. New York: Palgrave Macmillan.

Khare, P. S. 1964. *The Growth of Press and Public Opinion in India, 1857 to 1918*. Allahabad: Piyush Prakashan.

Kipling, R. 1869. 'The Deep Sea Cables'. In *The Seven Seas*, 10. London: Methuen and Co.

———. 1994. *The Man Who Would Be King & Other Stories*. Hertforshire: Wordsworth Classics.

Krshnamurthi, N. 1966. *Indian Journalism: Origin, Growth and Development of Indian Journalism from Asoka to Nehru*. Mysore: University of Mysore.

Lahiri Choudhury, D. K. 2004. 'Sinews of Panic and the Nerves of Empire: The Imagined State's Entanglement with Information Panic, India c. 1880–1912'. *Modern Asian Studies* 38, 965–1002.

———. 2010. *Telegraphic Imperialism: Crisis and Panic in the Indian Empire, c. 1830*. Basingstoke: Palgrave Macmillan.

Moitra, M. 1969. *A History of Indian Journalism*. Calcutta: National Book Agency.

Munirrudin. 2005. *History of Journalism*. New Delhi: Anmol Publications.

Naqvi, H. 2007. *Upkar's Journalism and Mass Communication*. Agra: Upkar Prakashan.

Narain, K. 1998. *Press, Politics and Society: Uttar Pradesh, 1885–1914*. New Delhi: Manohar.

Natarajan, J. 1955. *History of Indian Journalism, Part II of India, Report of the Press Commission*. New Delhi: Publications Division.

O'Connor, P. 2010. *The English-language Press Networks of East Asia, 1918–1945*. Folkestone: Global Oriental.

Orsini, F. 2009. *Print and Pleasure: Popular Literature and Entertaining Fictions in Colonial North India*. New Delhi: Permanent Black.

Potter, S. J. 2003. *News and the British World: The Emergence of an Imperial Press System*. Oxford: Oxford University Press.

Putnis, P., C. Kaul, and J. Wilke (eds). 2011. *International Communication and Global News Networks: Historical Perspectives*. New York: Hampton Press.

Rantanen, T. 2009. *When News Was New*. Chichester: Wiley-Blackwell.

Roy, S. 1967. 'Repercussions of the Vernacular Press Act, 1878'. *Journal of Indian History* 45, 735–748.

Samaddar, R. 1994. *Workers and Automation: The Impact of New Technology in the Newspaper Industry*. New Delhi: Sage.

Sharma, M. 2009. 'Creating a Consumer: Exploring Medical Advertisements in Colonial India'. In Biswamoy Pati and Mark Harrison (eds), *The Social History of Health and Medicine in Colonial India*, 213–228. London: Routledge.

Shridharani, K. 1953. *Story of the Indian Telegraphs: A Century of Progress*. New Delhi: Government of India Press.

Simpson, M. G. 1928. 'The Indo-European Telegraph Department'. *Journal of the Royal Society of Arts* 76 (3928), 382–400. London, 2 March.

Singh, S. K. 2010. *Press, Politics and Public Opinion in Bihar, 1912–1947*. New Delhi: Manak Publications.

Stark, U. 2009. *An Empire of Books: The Naval Kishore Press and the Diffusion of the Printed Word in Colonial India*. Ranikhet: Permanent Black.

Thorburn, D., and H. Jenkins (eds). 2003. *Rethinking Media Change: The Aesthetics of Transition*. Cambridge, MA: The MIT Press.

Udupa, S. 2011. 'Informing News: Information Revolution and the Transformation of News Media in Bangalore'. Ph.D. dissertation, University of Bangalore.

Wagle, N. K. (ed.). 1999. *Writers, Editors and Reformers: Social and Political Transformations of Maharashtra*. New Delhi: Manohar.

Wenzlhuemer, R. 2012. *Connecting the Nineteenth-Century World: The Telegraph and Globalization*. Cambridge: Cambridge University Press.

Winseck, D. R., and R. M. Pike. 2007. *Communication and Empire: Media, Markets and Globalization, 1860–1930*. Durham: Duke University Press.

 3

Indian Films and Nigerian Lovers*
Media and the Creation of Parallel Modernities

Brian Larkin

God make him rich so he can go to India.
Mallam Sidi, husband of Hotiho.
Sidi's ambition is for God to make him rich so he can go to India.
Mallam Sidi, husband of Hotiho.
His ambition is to see Hotiho…
Mallam Sidi, husband of Hotiho.
He swears if he sees Hotiho then no problems can move him.
Mallam Sidi, husband of Hotiho.

Mamman Shata, '*Mallam Sidi, mijin Hotiho*',
'Mallam Sidi is the husband of Hotiho'[1]

The sight of a 15-foot image of Sridevi, dancing erotically on the screens of the open-air cinemas of northern Nigeria, or the tall, angular figure of Amitabh Bachchan radiating charisma through the snowy, crackly reception of domestic television have become powerful, resonant images in Hausa popular culture. To this day, stickers of Indian films and stars decorate the taxis and buses of the north, posters of Indian films adorn the walls of tailors' shops and mechanics' garages, and love songs from Indian films are borrowed by religious singers, who change the words to sing

*This chapter was previously published as 'Indian Films and Nigerian Lovers: Media and the Creation of Parallel Modernities', in *Africa: Journal of the International African Institute* 67 (3), 406–440. Reproduced here with the kind permission of Cambridge University Press.

praises to the Prophet Mohammed. For over thirty years Indian films, their stars, and fashions, music, and stories have been a dominant part of everyday popular culture in northern Nigeria. If, as Bakhtin (1981) writes, communication is fundamental to human life, that self and society emerge in dialogue with others surrounding them, then Indian films have entered the dialogic construction of Hausa popular culture by offering Hausa men and women an alternative world, similar to their own, but from which they may imagine other forms of fashion, beauty, love and romance, coloniality and postcoloniality.

Before I began my research, I read all I could find by Nigerian and Western scholars on media and film in Nigeria. For the most part, this scholarship dealt with the complex and continuing problem of cultural imperialism—the dominance of Western media and especially, Hollywood films. When I first visited Kano, the major city in northern Nigeria, it came as a surprise, then, that Indian films were shown five nights a week at the cinemas (compared with one night for Hollywood films and one night for Chinese films); that the most popular programme on television was the Sunday morning Indian film on City Television Kano (CTV); and that most video shops reserved the bulk of their space for Indian films (followed by Western and Chinese films, Nigerian dramas, and religious videos). The question of why Indian films are so popular among Hausa viewers has occupied much of my research since that time.[?] What pleasures do Hausa viewers take from films portraying a culture and religion that seem so dissimilar and are watched usually in a language they cannot understand? Why has such a prominent part of the popular culture of many African societies received so little attention from academics[3] (Ekwuazi 1987; Fugelsang 1994; Muhammad 1992; Sheme 1995a, b).

This chapter attempts to answer these questions by considering seriously the significance of Indian films in Hausa culture. It explores the influence of Indian cinema on Hausa social life through the medium of Hausa *littatafan soyayya* (love stories). This pamphlet-type market literature, which began as recently as 1989, has created a popular reading public for wilful, passionate heroes and heroines who mimic a style of love and sexual interaction found in Indian films. *Soyayya* books, and videos based on their plots, produce a world where the imagined alternative of Indian romance is incorporated within local Hausa reality.

The popularity of Indian film in Nigeria highlights the circulation of media within and between non-Western countries, an aspect of transnational cultural flows that has been largely ignored in recent theories of globalisation. Indian films offer Hausa viewers a way of imaginatively engaging with forms of tradition different from their own, at the same time as conceiving of a modernity that comes without the political and ideological significance of the West. After discussing reasons for the popularity of Indian films in a Hausa context, I account for this imaginative investment of viewers by looking at narrative as a mode of social enquiry. Hausa youth explore the limits of accepted Hausa attitudes to love and sexuality through the narratives of Indian film and Hausa love stories. This exploration has occasioned intense public debate, as *soyayya* authors are accused of corrupting Hausa youth by borrowing foreign modes of love and sexual relations from Indian films. I argue that this controversy indexes wider concerns about the shape and direction of contemporary Nigerian culture. Analysing *soyayya* books and Indian films provides an insight into the local reworking and indigenising of the transnational media flows that take place within and between Third World countries, disrupting the dichotomies between West and non-West, coloniser and colonised, modernity and tradition, foregrounding instead the ability of media to create parallel modernities.

PARALLEL MODERNITIES

I use the term 'parallel modernities' to refer to the coexistence in space and time of multiple economic, religious, and cultural flows that are often subsumed within the term 'modernity'. This formulation resonates with the term 'alternative modernities' used by Appadurai (1991; see also Abu-Lughod [1993a]),[4] but with a key difference. Appadurai links the emergence of alternative modernities with the increased deterritorialisation of the globe and the movement of people, capital, and political movements, across cultural and national boundaries. While deterritorialisation is important, the experience of parallel modernities is not necessarily linked with the need of relocated populations for contact with their homelands (Appadurai 1991, 192). My concern, by contrast, is with an Indian film-watching Hausa populace who are not involved in nostalgic imaginings of a partly invented native land, but who participate in the imagined realities of other cultures as part of their daily lives.

By stressing the importance of modernities that run parallel to the classical paradigm of the West, I want to criticise recent work in African studies and media studies that has been dominated by a focus on local 'resistance' to various forms of 'dominant culture'. Lila Abu-Lughod (1990) has warned that the 'romance of resistance' tends to focus on the creativity of resistors and fails to explore fully the effectiveness of systems of power. My concern is different, as I argue that concepts of resistance in African studies and elsewhere often depend on a reductive binary distinction between oppression and resistance. The effect of this is that phenomena that cannot be neatly organised within that binary distinction then fall out of view. In a recent review essay on African historiography, Frederick Cooper addresses some of these concerns:

> The difficulty [in contemporary Africanist historiography] is to confront the power behind European expansion without assuming it was all-determining and to probe the clash of different forms of social organisation without treating them as self-contained and autonomous. The binaries of coloniser/colonised, Western/non-Western and domination/resistance begin as useful devices for opening up questions of power but end up constraining the search for precise ways in which power is deployed and the ways in which power is engaged, contested, deflected, and appropriated. (Cooper 1994, 1517)

Cooper wishes to move away from what he sees as monolithic constructions of the civilised coloniser and the primitive colonised (and the related labels of modernity and tradition) by asserting the heterogeneity of both colonial rule and African resistances. While complicating the picture, he nevertheless remains wedded to a structural binarism that looks at the organisation of the African experience in terms of its response to Western rule and its consequences.

Recent theories of postcolonialism have also unintentionally tended to reify this distinction in that the term 'postcolonial', despite a variety of different definitions, connotes a historical periodisation based on the core period of colonialism.[5] Northern Nigeria, for example, was colonised by the British in 1903, and achieved independence in 1960. A history of over 1,000 years is divided into the period pre-colonial, colonial, and postcolonial, which centres less than sixty years of British rule at the heart of Hausa experience. Even while criticising the role of the West in postcolonial Nigerian life, theorists of cultural imperialism and postcolonialism often view Nigerian reality largely in terms of its relation to the West, with the resulting irony of reaffirming cultural imperialism at the same moment as critiquing it. It is as if the periphery could not have an experience independent of its relation to metropolitan centres. Ella Shohat and Robert Stam criticise this contemporary insistence on resistance for producing an 'inverted European narcissism' positing a monolithic West as the source of all evil in the world, which 'reduces non-Western life to a pathological response to Western domination' (Shohat and Stam 1994, 3). The widespread popularity of Indian films in Nigeria necessitates a revision of conceptions of global cultural flows that privilege the centrality of the West and refuse to recognise the common historical process of centres and peripheries engaged in contemporary cultural production.

The narrow conception of cultural imperialism has left little place for the study of phenomena such as Hong Kong or Indian film, which cannot be as easily tied to a wider economic hegemony as is the case with Hollywood film[6] (McNeely and Soysal 1989; Sreberny-Mohammadi 1991). This myopia is also the result of the disciplinary boundaries of contemporary scholarship, which has little ethnographic understanding of cross-cultural media environments. Recent groundbreaking works in African cinema, such as Diawara (1992; see also Ekwuazi 1987; Ekwuazi and Nasidi 1992; Ukadike 1994), deal largely with production by African filmmakers and are less concerned with what African film audiences are actually watching. Until recently, anthropologists, with their disciplinary focus on indigenous cultural production, have been suspicious of foreign mass-mediated cultural forms, no matter how popular they may be (*cf*. Abu-Lughod 1993b; Ginsburg 1991; Hannerz 1992). Karin Barber, for instance, in her seminal definition of African popular arts, argues that 'imported commercial entertainments ... symbolize Western culture (though they include Chinese Kung Fu movies and Indian romantic melodramas)' (Barber 1987, 25; her parenthesis). Along with reducing foreign media to a subset of Hollywood, Barber is reluctant to admit any real engagement by African audiences with these texts. Because they do not originate from an African reality, she suggests they have little meaning in African life. '[E]ntertainment films that are least mediated by African culture .... [she concludes] are also the most easily replaced' (ibid.). Barber's observations are probably influenced by her experience among the Yoruba, where indigenous videos have provided a popular alternative to imported cinema in recent years. She fails, however, to appreciate the complicated identifications that allow audiences to engage with media forms, no matter how superficially 'foreign'. The popularity of Indian films in Africa has fallen into the interstices of academic analysis, as the *Indian* texts do not fit with studies of African cinema; the *African* audience is ignored in the growing work on Indian film; the films are too non-Western for Euro-American-dominated media studies; and anthropologists are only beginning to theorise the social importance of media.

My intent is not to downplay the importance of the cultural struggle of Nigerians against foreign media, or to minimise the hegemony of Western culture, but to stress that this is only part of the cultural reality of many African nations. It is necessary to move towards a more ethnographic understanding of the range of media environments that offer Hausa youth the choice between watching Hausa or Yoruba videos, Indian, Hong Kong, or American films, or videos of Qur'anic *tafsir* (exegesis) by local preachers. In this, my work has been influenced heavily by participation in the Program in Culture and Media and its affiliates within the Department of Anthropology at New York University. Borrowing from media and cultural studies as well as from traditional anthropological theory, the Program is developing a variety of critical anthropological perspectives that examine the social relations within which media are embedded and enacted (Abu-Lughod 1993b, 1995; Ginsburg 1991, 1993, 1994; McLagan 1996; Sullivan 1993). Examining the significance of Indian films in an African context, and the processes of identification by which the ideas, values, and aesthetics of another culture are incorporated within an African quotidian, is a step further in this developing field. With other approaches to transnational cultural studies, such as that emerging from the journal *Public Culture*, this work is building a sophisticated and supple theoretical frame to deal with what Appadurai terms a 'new cosmopolitanism' that unites the cultural, financial, and political flows within and between Western and non-Western countries into a single conceptual whole. 'Modernity,' Arjun Appadurai and Carol Breckenridge assert, 'is now everywhere, it is simultaneously everywhere, it is interactively everywhere' (1995, 2).

Appadurai argues that the new cosmopolitanism brought about by movements of people and capital in the contemporary era has created a deterritorialised world that has new significance for the understanding of media and of imagination (Appadurai 1990, 1991). Media figure prominently in creating interconnections between different peoples who can now consider alternative lives based not on experiences in their own locality, but on a range of experiences brought to them through international mass media. As more people throughout the world see their reality 'through the prisms of possible lives offered by the mass media', Appadurai argues that contemporary ethnography must now expand to find ways of understanding the social reality of imagination: 'fantasy is now a social practice; it enters, in a host of ways, into the fabrication of social lives' (Appadurai 1991, 198).

The concept of imagination as outlined by Appadurai is helpful in gaining insight into the pleasures that Indian films offer Hausa viewers. (I shall discuss this further below.) It also provides a theoretical way to understand the complicated identifications of audiences and cultural forms that cross expected racial, cultural, and national lines. For Hausa viewers, Indian films offer images of a parallel modernity to the West, one intimately concerned with the changing basis of social life, but rooted in conservative cultural values. Characters in Indian films struggle over whether they should speak Hindi or borrow from English, and whether they should marry the person they love or wed the person their parents choose. In these and many other similar decisions, the narrative tensions of Indian films raise, consider, and resolve minor and major anxieties within contemporary Indian society, anxieties that are relevant to Hausa viewers. Moreover, when Hausa youth rework Indian films within their own culture by adopting Indian fashions (such as the headscarves or jewellery of Indian actresses), by copying the music styles for religious purposes, or by using the filmic world of Indian sexual relations to probe the limitations within their own cultural world, they can do so without engaging with the heavy ideological load of 'becoming Western'. The popularity of Indian films rests on this delicate balance of being situated between Nigerian 'tradition' and Western 'modernity', offering a mediating space for postcolonial Hausa viewers from which they may reflect on and consider the nature of contemporary social change.

Indian Films and Hausa Viewers

One result of the myopia regarding the presence of Indian films in West Africa is that hard data regarding their distribution and exhibition are extremely difficult to come by. Hyginus Ekwuazi, for instance, borrows from UN statistics to write that in 1978–1979, 86 per cent of all films imported into Nigeria were of American origin (Ekwuazi 1987, 121). Yet, earlier in the same book he acknowledges that many films come in through a grey market that escapes official notice, and unofficially 'the all-time favourite is the Indian, not the American film' (ibid., 44).[7] Whereas all American films were imported through the American Motion Picture Exporters and Cinema Association (AMPECA), later the Nigerian Film Distribution Company (NFDC), Indian films were imported by a host of entrepreneurs in different countries, including the Middle East, England, and India. British censorship records reveal that Indian films were first introduced by Lebanese exhibitors in the 1950s, who were eager to see whether the diet of American and English films could be supplemented by the odd Arab or Indian one.[8] These exhibitors speculated that Arabic films would be popular in the north because of the many religious links between northern Nigeria and the Islamic world. As the language of religious practice and debate, Arabic carried immense authority, but despite these links the films never became popular on northern Nigerian screens, while Indian films came to dominate them.[9]

The lack of information on the political economy of Indian film obscures the relation between the economic and symbolic reasons for its popularity (but see Pendakur and Subramanyam 1996). It seems likely that the disappearing presence of American films is related to the increasing cost of American film prints, which makes the cheaper Indian films more attractive. However, Hausa, Lebanese, and Indian film and video entrepreneurs I interviewed all accounted for the dominance of Indian film in symbolic and cultural, rather than economic, terms. In an interview with Michel Issa, manager of the Cinema Distribution Circuit, which owns cinemas throughout northern Nigeria, Issa argued that Indian films were popular because 'their culture is the same' as Hausa culture.[10]

One Indian video entrepreneur posited that it was the (allegedly) common linguistic roots of Hindi and Hausa that accounted for the sense of cultural familiarity (an argument supported by Muhammad [1992]).[11] Uninterested in my questions about why Indian films were more popular, Issa finally said he had no idea why Arab films had not been accepted. All he knew was that from the beginning, Indian films gained a massive popular following in the north. Even before American films stopped being distributed in Nigeria, he pointed out, they had been largely replaced by Indian films on northern screens.

Indian film fans and theorists refer to contemporary Hindi films as *masala* films. Referring to the blend of spices used in Indian cooking, popular Indian cinema often mixes the genres of romance, melodrama, action, musical, and comedy within the same film. For a considerable time, this eclectic mix was seen by both Western and Indian academics as evidence of the inability of Indian filmmakers to make 'proper' American-style films. More recently, Indian film scholars have come to view Bombay films not as poor imitations of American films, but as based on a distinct narrative style and structure (Chakravarty 1993; the special issue of *India International Centre Quarterly* 1980; Mishray 1985; Thomas 1985, 1995). Rosie Thomas argues that:

> A form has developed in which narrative is comparatively loose and fragmented, realism irrelevant, psychological characterization disregarded, elaborate dialogues prized, music essential and both the emotional involvement of the audience and the pleasures of sheer spectacle privileged throughout the three hour long duration of the entertainment. (Thomas 1995, 162)

Indian films, or at least the Hindi ones that are imported into Nigeria, are made for a pan-Indian audience, and the makers of the films are aware of the necessity of constructing a filmic style that crosses both linguistic and cultural boundaries. Even so, these films are embedded in a cultural specificity that presupposes familiarity with Indian cultural values, the Hindu religion, and a strong sense of Indian nationalism. They are also playfully intertextual, making constant reference to classical Indian mythology, folk drama and literature, and Hindu religious practice. Chakravarty (1993) argues that Indian films have created a 'communal' mode of address, a 'we-ness' of common cultural and national concerns that accounts for their appeal, but which is largely a fiction in a country as large and diverse as India.

Indian films are subtitled in English at Hausa cinemas, but the majority of those on television (which has the largest audience) are broadcast in Hindi only. This means that most Hausa viewers are watching Indian films in a language of which they have little understanding. After thirty years of watching Indian films, Hausa audiences are, of course, sophisticated enough to understand the narrative style of the films, and many families have several members who claim they can 'speak' Hindi, but inevitably there is a considerable cultural gap between the intertextual references to local cultural and religious values in Indian films and a Hausa viewing audience.

Despite the cultural gap between the (largely) Hindu Indian audience to whom the filmic text is being addressed and the Muslim Hausa one watching in northern Nigeria, what is remarkable is how well the main messages of the films are communicated. This problem is made easier by the narrative structure of Indian films, which is borrowed from the Indian religious epics, the Mahabarata and the Ramayana (Mishray 1985). The dependence upon the epics means that there is usually a fixed range of plots, with clear moral contrasts that make the outlines of Indian films familiar to their viewers. The regularity of character types whose actions fall within a limited range of behaviour, such as the hero, the mother, the comedic friend, or the evil boss, with many of the lesser roles (such as the boss or the mother) played by the same people in film after film, further aids the fixed parameters of plot structure within which the spectacle unfolds. This dependence on religious epics for narrative structure provides an easily comprehended moral guide for characters' actions and creates a limited set of narrative possibilities, facilitating the easy 'translation' of Indian films across cultural, linguistic, and national boundaries.[12]

Talking to many friends about their love of Indian films, I was struck by the common refrain that Indian culture was 'just like' Hausa culture. I found it surprising that staunchly Muslim Hausa should identify so strongly with Hindu Indian culture, but over time different cultural similarities became clearer. Most obvious are the many visual affinities between Indian and Hausa culture. Men in Indian films, for instance, often dress in long kaftans, similar to the Hausa *dogon riga*, over which they wear long waistcoats, much like the Hausa *palmaran*. Women are also dressed in long saris and scarves which veil their heads, and accord with Hausa ideas of feminine decorum. The iconography of Indian 'tradition', such as marriage celebrations, food, village life, and so on, even when different from Hausa culture, provides a similar cultural background that is frequently in opposition to the spread of 'Westernisation'. Indian films place family and kinship at the centre of narrative tension as a key stimulus for characters' motivations, to a degree that rarely occurs in Western films. They are based on a strict division between the sexes, and love songs and sexual relations, while sensuous, are kept within firm boundaries. Kissing is rare and nudity absent. These generic conventions provide a marked difference from Hollywood films, and many Hausa viewers argue that Indian films 'have culture' in a way that American films seem to lack.

More complexly, Indian films are based upon negotiating the tension of preserving traditional moral values in a time of profound change. Ashis Nandy argues, in terms as relevant for Nigerians as they are for Indians, that Indian films are successful with Indian masses because despite their spectacle and rich settings, they are based in a moral universe of action that is grounded in a traditional worldview. 'The basic principles of commercial cinema derive from the needs of Indians caught in the hinges of social change who are trying to understand their predicament in terms familiar to them' (Nandy 1995, 205). Nandy argues that commercial cinema tends to 'reaffirm the values that are being increasingly marginalized in public life by the language of the modernizing middle classes, values such as community ties, primacy of maternity over conjugality, priority of the mythic over the historical' (ibid., 202).

Characters in Indian films have to negotiate the tension between traditional life and modernity in ways that Hausa, in a similar postcolonial situation, can sympathise with. The choice of wearing Indian or Western-style clothes, the use of English by arrogant upper-class characters or by imperious bureaucrats, even the endemic corruption of the postcolonial State, are all familiar situations with which Hausa viewers can engage.

The familiarity that Hausa viewers experience when watching Indian films is reinforced by changes over time in the style and themes of Indian film. Contemporary films are more sexually explicit and violent, and borrow heavily from the styles of Western film genres. Nigerian viewers comment on this when they compare older Indian films of the 1950s and 1960s, which 'had culture', with newer ones, which are more Westernised. Older films were more often set among the rural poor than contemporary films. Characters, for instance, were more likely to wear traditional clothes, to keep animals, or to travel by oxen. Not only did visual iconography change, but musical styles, once based mainly on Indian classical forms, also began to incorporate disco beats and Western instrumentation. This perceived shift toward a growing materialism in Indian film echoed a similar shift in Nigerian society, brought about by the radical dislocations of the oil boom of the mid-1970s. For Nigerian audiences, the evolution of the Indian film style thus corresponded with developments within their own society, which brought home the similarities between the two. This has been a contentious process, and as difficult for Hausa viewers to accept in Indian films as it is to accept in their own culture. One young friend, who was a fan of Indian film, complained to me about this shift:

> When I was young and watching films, the Indian films we used to see were based on their tradition. You wouldn't see something like disco, going out to clubs, making gangs. Before, they didn't do it like that. But now Indian films are just like American films. They go to discos, make gangs, go out for picnics.[13] They'll do anything in a hotel and they play rough in romantic scenes where before you could never see things like that.

The perceived rise in violence, in sexual immorality, and in materialism are all represented in my friend's complaint. Clubs, hotels, and discos are symbols, in both Indian film and in Hausa popular culture, of corrupt immoral spaces frequented by the rich. They are emblems of Western life and stand in moral contrast to the Indian or Hausa social spaces, such as the temple, mosque, or village. Indian films depict an ambivalent attitude to such spaces, exploiting their use as spectacle while at the same time ensuring that the heroes and heroines are at some moral distance from them. Nandy argues that Indian films stand against the vicissitudes of the postcolonial State by grounding the shifts in materialism, urbanisation, and apparent Westernisation within a moral universe that is structured around familiar religious values. This is why, despite its apparent Westernisation, Indian films depict moral dilemmas that are strikingly different from Hollywood or other Western films.

The reasons why Hausa viewers recognise commonalities between their culture and Indian culture are many and varied. In an Islamic African society, the films are popular because they engage with the disjunctures of social change, elaborated in terms that are familiar to Hausa society yet also distinct from it. This coexistence between likeness and dissimilarity is important because it is in the gap that the narratives of Indian film allow the exploration of social relations. I now discuss in greater detail this aspect of narrative and offer suggestions as to why it has become so controversial in *soyayya* books.

Imagination, Narrative, and Social Change

The narratives of Indian films allow the exploration of attitudes and social possibilities that are still controversial in everyday Hausa social life. The psychoanalyst Sudhir Kakar has discussed this phenomenon in India, arguing that Hindi films are successful because they engage everyday fantasy. 'The power of fantasy …,' he argues, 'comes to our rescue by extending or withdrawing the desires beyond what is possible or reasonable' in the social order (Kakar 1989, 27). He defines fantasy as 'that world of imagination which is fuelled by desire and which provides us with an alternative world where we can continue with our longstanding quarrel with reality' (ibid.). My concern in this chapter is with the narrative tension between love marriages and arranged marriages, which is a dominant theme of both Hindi cinema and Hausa *soyayya* books. There is much more to Hindi films than this—the spectacle of beauty and wealth, the difficulty of reconciling responsibility to kin in a rapidly urbanising bureaucratic world, or the problem of operating with honesty and honour in a corrupt postcolonial world—but this one genre of Indian film offers an insight into a broader conflict between desire and responsibility toward a wider social order.

The romantic insistence on the potentially subversive power of imagination has been explored in two recent works on African oral literature and social structure. Thomas Beidelman argues that imagination has both an individual and a group importance. On the one hand, 'it relates to the ways that people construct images of the world in which they live ... a cosmology that ... presents a picture in which they measure, assess and reflect upon the reality of their experiences' (Beidelman 1993, 1). On the other hand, imagination offers a space from which to reflect upon the social order: 'In this sense imaginative exercise constitutes means for criticism, for distortion, even subversion of the moral social order' (ibid.). Michael Jackson, in his study of Kuranko oral literature, puts forward a similar picture of the power of narrative to explore ambiguities in social life. 'Kuranko narratives,' he argues, 'initiate a dialectic of doubt and uncertainty ... [that] promote ambivalence and exploit ambiguity as a way of stimulating listeners to resolve problems of choice' (Jackson 1982, 2). Jackson stipulates that narratives are a secure way to bring up ambiguous situations, allowing readers the imaginative space to explore multiple resolutions of narrative tensions, before resolving them (in the case of oral literature) safely within the limits of accepted norms.

What Jackson and Beidelman see as a function of oral literature Kakar views as part of the collective fantasy provided by the mass culture of Indian films. I argue that the engagement with themes of romantic love revealed in *soyayya* books and Indian films exemplifies precisely this desire to explore the limits of social norms during a period of rapid change. The tension between arranged marriages and love marriages is not new to Hausa society, nor is the idea that romantic love may be subversive of the moral order, as many Hausa folk tales exemplify. What is new, however, is the speed of contemporary social change that has placed the issues of love, marriage, and sexuality squarely at the forefront of social concern. The increase in conflicts over the style and nature of courtship, the appropriate age and conditions of marriage, and over what is seen as the increased materialism of marriage partners condenses fears about the pace of social change. As Indian films and *soyayya* books are the main mass cultural forms that provide a sustained engagement with these issues over a long period of time, it is unsurprising that they have become a topic of public controversy. To account for the intensity of this controversy, it is first necessary to outline the boundaries of social transformation in contemporary Hausa society.

Youth and Marriage in Contemporary Kano

The oil boom of the 1970s thrust Nigeria into the fast capitalism of an oil economy, transforming not only the economic basis of the country but also the pace of urbanisation, consumption habits, and the political system. Michael Watts and Allan Pred (1992) have borrowed from Benjamin to label this revolutionary change the 'shock of modernity'. As well as making the country dependent upon the imports of basic foodstuffs, the boom internationalised the consumption habits of the middle classes, creating the easy assumption that fast capitalism meant fast Westernisation. The economic crash which followed the oil boom exacerbated these transformations and contributed to a growing self-consciousness about the changing nature of Nigerian society, marked by Islamic revitalisation and criticism of secular Westernisation. The transformative impact of the boom and bust of the oil economy continues to affect all classes of Nigerian society, but the position of the youth has become an issue of considerable concern (Barkindo 1993; Dan Asabe n.d.; Said and Last 1991).

The 'problems' of contemporary youth are evidenced in different realms, from the perceived rise in violence to theft, drug-taking, disrespect for elders, and materialism. Even the rise in the Islamic participation of youth has been a key moral discourse by which youths have challenged the authority of the government and elders[14] (Lubeck 1987; Watts and Pred 1992) Important religious scholars such as Sheikh Isa Waziri in Kano preached regularly against the changing attitudes and behaviour of Hausa youth, and it is these social tensions that are indexed by the debate about *soyayya* books. At the forefront of this concern is the problem of changing marriage patterns in northern Nigeria, and more especially the concern over regulating female sexuality.

The collapse in the Nigerian economy has made the cost of the *lefe*, the gifts each man must give his wife before marriage, economically difficult for many young men. The *lefe* forms only part of the rising cost of marriage, and this inflation has been vehemently attacked as one of the most visible markers of the growing materialism in Hausa society. Religious leaders have complained regularly against the practice, and there have even been attempts by state governments to regulate the costs involved, but to little avail. The result is that young men are delaying marriage until a later age when they will have the income to afford the expense. Meanwhile, the marrying age of women has also been moving upward. The introduction of compulsory primary-school education in 1976 affected the traditional practice of arranging marriages for girls before the onset of puberty, at around thirteen years of age (Callaway 1987). Nowadays it is more common for parents to wait until a child has finished school, around the age of sixteen or seventeen, before choosing a marriage partner. Barbara Callaway, in her study of Hausa women in Kano, sees the rise in both Western and Islamic education as the source of potential change in the status of women (ibid.). As women become more enlightened about their rights as women under Islamic law, she asserts that there may be more room to resist Hausa cultural practices from the point of view of Islamic orthodoxy. One consequence is that increased education and the rise in the age of marriage mean that women may be more prepared to assert some measure of control over the choice of their marriage partners.

For parents and religious leaders, the increase in the number of sexually mature young people outside the bounds of marriage is not only contrary to a proper Islamic social order, but has also become an issue demanding public regulation. In 1987 the Kano state government set up state committees to find solutions to contemporary social problems. Along with the rise in crime, hooliganism, and begging, the 'problem' of unmarried women was the subject of state examination. Two years later, in his Ramadan sermon, Sheikh Isa Waziri, one of the prominent Islamic leaders in Kano, addressed the same issue when he sent out a call for rich men to marry more wives in order to solve what he termed the 'calamity' of unmarried women (Barkindo 1993, 96). A perceived rise in sexual activity before marriage, as well as in the growing number of prostitutes (seen as a moral rather than an economic problem), has neatly conflated the issues of Westernisation, materialism, the need to regulate sexuality, and the immorality of the secular Nigerian State for northern political and religious leaders.

In her discussion of Hausa female marriage and sexuality, Callaway points out that there is no acceptable space within Islamic society for a woman who is of childbearing age and unmarried. As more women occupy this 'unacceptable' space, relations between the sexes are seen to evolve. Callaway, for instance, describes traditional Hausa interaction between the sexes as extremely limited. Compared with the West, she argues, Hausa men live separate physical and emotional lives. She concludes,

> Thus, men and women live in two separate worlds, normally do not share their thoughts or their lives, and function fairly independently of each other in their different spheres. Even husbands and wives do not normally socialize together or with each other; in order to show respect in the home, they do not eat together, seldom interact and avoid addressing each other by name. (Callaway 1987, 44)

As a result of this sexual segregation, Callaway argues, 'The experience of romantic love is not normally part of an Islamic marriage'; '"Love" and "Romance" are Western concepts and have little real meaning in this [Hausa] culture' (Callaway 1987, 36, 40). Callaway's comments caricature and devalue the complex emotions of Muslim marriages[15] (Abu-Lughod 1986), but she does represent problems that many Hausa experience. Many *soyayya* authors discussed the issue with me as they talked of the massive changes in the way young men and women interact with each other in contemporary Hausa society. Ideally, both women and men in Hausa society are expected to exhibit *kunya*, a sense of modesty and shame. Adamu Mohammed,[16] author of the novel *Garnak'ak'i* ('Uncompromising'), explained what this meant in terms of sexual interaction. Traditionally, he said, all meetings between boys and girls would be chaperoned by older relatives. Frequently, the couple involved might be too embarrassed even to speak to each other, and women, especially, would communicate reluctantly, if at all. Another author, Dan'Azumi Yan Gurasa,[17] confirmed this. 'When I was young,' he said, 'and came across the girl I loved, I couldn't face her and tell her. Instead I would send someone who could talk to her about it.' Nowadays, both authors agreed, this sense of shyness has been transformed, and both men and women act in a manner that would have been unacceptable twenty years previously.

In their plots, *soyayya* authors examine some of the issues made contentious by the shift in gender interaction. The common narrative conflict between youth wishing to marry for love and parents who wish to organise marriage partners reveals how romance narratives allow a form of moral enquiry for Hausa youth. The fantasy encoded in fictional narratives succeeds, as Beidelman points out, 'by presenting a version of experience and things that is both less and more than what we ordinarily encounter', allowing, in part, 'a luxuriation of qualities and possibilities not encountered in reality' (1993, 5). For over thirty years Indian films provided a dominant forum for the creation of an imaginary space where real social tensions over love and responsibility, individual desire and social control, appeared, and various resolutions of these tensions were considered. Indian films could do this successfully only by engaging with issues that were meaningful to Hausa viewers, while at the same time providing enough of a difference for alternative resolutions to be possible. This engagement with the conflict of love and courtship in contemporary society is what has defined the plots of *soyayya* books for both their admirers and their critics. Examining these stories reveals the intertextual presence of Indian films and its appropriation within Hausa popular culture.

MARKET LITERATURE IN THE VERNACULAR: THE RISE OF *SOYAYYA* BOOKS

In the past few years, there has been a near-revolution in the publishing of Hausa literature. A whole new genre of *littatafan soyayya*, love stories, has emerged, published by authors themselves and sold through markets and small shops all over the northern region. During the time of the Structural Adjustment Programme (SAP), when the cost of imported goods (such as paper) had been soaring and the purchasing power of incomes had been collapsing, *soyayya* authors published over 200 books, and created a system of publishing and distribution that kept book prices within the range of ordinary people. Earlier books have achieved the status of 'bestseller', giving their authors a great deal of fame. Many of them are read out on the radio, on the extremely popular programme *Shafa Labari Shuni* (meaning 'a person exaggerates what he hears'), and adaptations of successful books form a significant proportion of the vibrant new market in Hausa videos. While the debate rages over whether *soyayya* books are a beneficial addition to Hausa culture, their great achievement has been to create a popular Hausa reading public for fiction.

In his major survey of Hausa literature, Graham Furniss argues that *soyayya* writers 'appear to owe more to the English language publishing of Mills and Boon, and James Hadley Chase ... than to any Hausa precedent' (Furniss 1996, 54–55). Furniss is correct in assessing the innovativeness of this new style of literature, but mistaken in seeing it as based solely on Western precedents. *Soyayya* authors and their critics cite many sources for their books, including English romances and Hollywood 'bestsellers', but they also admit the important influence of Arabian tales, Nigerian romance magazines, and Indian films. I concentrate on the influence of Indian films, not to ignore these other media, but as part of my larger point in analysing the flow of media within and between non-Western countries. The great appeal of Indian films across class, education, and gender, along with the recognised similarities in culture, make them a significant precedent for contemporary writers and readers.

Images 3.1a, b: *Soyayya* books on sale at Gidan Dabino, bookseller and publisher.

Image credit: Brian Larkin.

Kano *soyayya* books are pamphlets a little more than fifty pages in length. Many run to two or three parts in order to keep costs down. They are badly typeset, badly printed, and from the point of view of critics, badly edited and written. Furniss (1996) argues that authors adopted the practice of publishing their own work, using offset litho printers, following the example of religious *ajami*[18] poets. Print runs are typically small, running from 2,000 to 5,000, but successful books will go into multiple printings. Originally, *soyayya* books were sold from shops and through vendors selling school books. As they have become more established, it is not uncommon to see market stalls devoted solely to *soyayya* books, or to see hawkers wandering around markets and business districts balancing books on their heads. The authors, unlike earlier generations of Hausa writers, come from neither an elite nor even a well-educated background. Some have never received Western education, and most of those who have, left after primary level, remaining only in Islamic schools; consequently, their knowledge of English, and with it, their integration into existing literary culture, is often poor. Women make up a significant proportion of *soyayya* authors and some, like Hajiya Balaraba Ramat Yakubu (*Alhaki Kwikwiyo*, meaning 'Retribution is Like a Puppy, It Follows its Owner' [1990a], and *Budurwar Zuciya*, 'The Heart's Desire' [1990b]), are among the most famous *soyayya* authors. Secondary-school leavers make up a significant proportion of the readers (although perhaps not as great a proportion as people claim), and there is a strong association in the public mind between *soyayya* books and women readers. Despite this, many young men I knew were avid readers of the literature, and the high percentage of men who write fan letters to the authors suggests that there is a significant male relationship.

Soyayya books first emerged from Kano, the metropolitan centre of northern Nigeria. Originally, authors came together to organise writers' clubs modelled on the famous drama clubs organised by the heroes of independence in the north, Mallam Aminu Kano, Sa'adu Zungur, and Maitama Sule. The first and most famous clubs were Raina Kama ('Deceptive Appearances')[19] and Kukan Kurciya ('The Cry of a Dove'), created in order to exchange mutual aid and advice among neophyte authors. Since that time, new writers' clubs have appeared in many major cities and contemporary *soyayya* authors come from all northern urban centres. Many authors began by basing their first novel on a personal experience, or one that had happened to their friends, often an affair of love. *In da so da K'auna* I, II (meaning 'Where There's Love and Desire') by Ado Ahmad (1989) or *Garnak'ak'i* I, II by Adamu Mohammed (1991) are both examples of this. Many authors go on to write about other issues, whether it be politics, as in Bala Anas Babinlata's *Tsuntsu Mai Wayo* I, II ('The Clever Bird', 1993). or *'yan daba* (thugs) and crime in Dan'Azumi Baba's *Rikicin Duniya* I, II, III ('This Deceptive World', 1990). The dominant theme with which most books are identified remains the conflict over love.

Soyayya books dramatise the problems of contemporary sexual relations, criticising forced marriages and the increasing material demands of both lovers and parents. Many authors claim a didactic purpose for their writing, arguing that they are educating young people and their parents about the problems that beset contemporary youth. The fact that many authors begin writing as a direct result of a personal experience underscores the close relation between the stories and perceived social problems. Adamu Mohammed explained to me that he began writing books when the parents of the girl he loved married her off, against the wishes of both lovers, to a wealthier man. As a poor man, Mohammed argued, he had no means of fighting the decision except by writing his book, *Garnak'ak'i* ('Uncompromising'). This sense of outrage and vindication is common to many of the early *soyayya* writers. A similar event sparked off the career of Ado Ahmad. As Maigari Ahmed Bichi (1992) reports, the arrangements for Ahmad's first marriage had been broken off despite the fact that he and his fiancée were in love and her parents were happy about the marriage: 'a misunderstanding between their two families .... was caused by the grandmother of the girl, who ... had arranged for the girl to be given to one Alhaji[20] for marriage' (ibid., 7). As a result of this, Ahmad intended his first novel to 'show how love is played in Hausa society and the role of parents in marriage affairs' (ibid.). One fledgling author from Kaduna, Adamu Ciroma, who also began writing after a personal experience, argues that many, if not most, *soyayya* authors begin writing this way:

> Our writers today we share experiences which makes us start writing.... An experience happens to me and so I decide to write about it in order to enlighten people on what has happened.... Nine out of ten writers begin writing *soyayya* because they have experienced it. (Interview, Aminu Ciroma, Kaduna, March 1995)

For *soyayya* authors, a didactic and moral purpose informs their discourse on love, which gives their novels a sense of social responsibility. They argue that incompatibility in the choice of marriage partner leads daughters to run away from their parents to become 'independent women' (and hence prostitutes), or to attempt suicide, or to go through an unhappy marriage and early divorce—even if the partner chosen is wealthy. But as the author Dan'Azumi Baba argues, 'now everything has changed [and] because of reading such books [*soyayya* books], no girl agrees with forced marriage and parents understand that if they force their daughter to marry somebody, she will eventually go and become a prostitute' (interview, 28 June 1995). He continued, 'the main problem of marriage is lack of love', adding that most women now are wise to the fact that 'if there is love, they will not mind about any problems'. The concerns aired by Dan'Azumi and others over the increasing commodification of contemporary love and the iniquities of forced marriage are not just the province of *soyayya* books, but form the staple themes of Indian films as well. For over thirty years, Indian films have provided an extended narration of the problems of arranged marriages and of the place of materialism in a 'traditional' society that mimics real events in everyday Hausa lives. Before discussing *soyayya* books themselves, it is worth returning briefly to the concept of fantasy and imagination to give an example of the investment of viewers in Indian narratives.

The possibility of imaginative investment was brought home to me one day when I was talking to an older Hausa friend in his forties. Knowing that he liked Indian films, I was surprised to hear him say that they had a negative influence on Hausa culture. He cited the example of his own marriage.

Image 3.2: An illustrated cover of a *soyayya* book.

Image credit: Brian Larkin.

He said that when he was young, in the 1970s, he went to see lots of Indian films. Like many other men, he liked the commitment that Indian films showed to the family, the importance of marriage and children, and many other cultural values. The problem, he said, was that in Indian films, women are very supportive of their husbands. He explained that when an Indian man sees his love, they talk about their problems. He declares his love for her, she declares hers for him, and they embrace. In the 1970s, men who went to the cinema expected or wanted similar behaviour from their wives. It was what he had wanted himself when he got married. But when he returned home and tried to talk to his wife, she would turn away, answer as briefly as possible, and try to leave the room. He told me that women in Hausa society were taught that their husband is everything and they should be in awe of him. His wife was acting with the modesty expected of a good Hausa wife, whereas he wanted the sort of relationship he had seen in Indian films. As a result, he encountered many problems early in his marriage, and that was why, he argued, the films could be harmful. Indian films conveyed ideas about marriage and relationships that the local culture could not support.

Image 3.3: An illustrated cover of a *soyayya* book. Note especially the Indian features of Sumayya in this image.

Image credit: Brian Larkin.

Image 3.4: An illustrated cover of a *soyayya* book.

Image credit: Brian Larkin.

My friend's anecdote is a striking example of the complicated ways in which transnational media flows become incorporated into individual experience and affect larger social constructions such as gender. The fact that this is so clearly dated makes it even more fascinating. In the early 1970s, the screening of Indian films was largely restricted to the cinema. The practice of female seclusion (*kulle*) meant that women were absent (for the most part) from the male arena of the cinema, and it was not until the growth of domestic technologies such as television and video that women gained access to the popular culture of Indian films. Since then, Indian films have come to be identified as 'women's films' because of their huge popularity among women. The stereotype now is of women demanding that their partners act more like the lovers in Indian films, while it is men who complain that Indian films create demands that cannot be met. This complaint has become all the more controversial with people accusing *soyayya* authors of dramatising the Bombay melodrama style of love within a Hausa context.

All You Need Is Love...

To give some sense of the tone and structure of the texts I am dealing with, I will briefly outline the plots of the two *soyayya* books I discuss: *Inda so da K'auna* I, II by Ado Ahmad (1989) and *Kishi Kumallon Mata* (meaning 'Jealousy is the Nausea of Women') by Maryam Sahabi Liman (1993). The two-part volume *Inda* was abridged and translated into English as *The Soul of My Heart* in 1993. Its author, Ado Ahmad, calls it the bestselling of all *soyayya* books, having sold over 50,000 copies, and it has since been adapted into a three-part Hausa video. It remains one of the few *soyayya* books to have been translated into English[21] (Ahmad 1993a). *Inda*, as one of the earliest and most popular books, has been the subject of great attention and discussion, and exemplifies many of the major themes associated with *soyayya* books. *Kishi* is a more recent novel, published after *soyayya* books had received a great deal of public criticism. Because of this, Liman is careful to avoid many of the themes that have led to *soyayya* books being dismissed as a form of *iskanci* (immorality, loose living), and provides a good counterpoint to *Inda*.

Inda tells the story of Sumayya, a rich girl who falls in love with a much poorer boy, Mohammed. Unfortunately, Sumayya herself is the object of the affections of Abdulkadir, a wealthy young businessman. When Sumayya rejects Abdulkadir, he visits her grandmother, taking with him gifts and money, and persuades her to intervene on his behalf with Sumayya's parents. Accordingly, she threatens to withdraw her blessing from her son if Sumayya is not wed to Abdulkadir. Abdulkadir, meanwhile, arranges to have Mohammed beaten up by thugs to warn him off Sumayya. Sumayya and Mohammed are crushed by the news of the arranged marriage. As the wedding draws near, Sumayya throws herself down a well in a desperate attempt at suicide. She survives and is taken to hospital, where her life is saved by a timely blood transfusion from Mohammed. Her parents, seeing this, feel that the couple should be united and agree to the marriage. They are wed and Mohammed goes into business, becoming rich, while Abdulkadir, on his way back from a business deal in Abuja, is pursued by armed robbers who force his Mercedes off the road and rob him of all his money, leaving him a pauper.

Kishi describes the problems that arise from jealous co-wives. It tells the story of a rich man, Usman, who falls in love with and marries Ruk'ayya. They live happily together until they discover that Ruk'ayya cannot conceive. After consulting both Western doctors and religious teachers, Ruk'ayya selflessly advises her husband to take a second wife. Ruk'ayya persuades her good friend Saratu to attract the attentions of her husband so that he would marry her, arguing that if she has to have a co-wife, it should be someone she is friends with. Usman and Saratu marry and Saratu becomes pregnant. Immediately, though, she accuses Ruk'ayya of trying to poison her from jealousy. Usman comes to support Saratu's accusations of poison and witchcraft against Ruk'ayya. He moves Saratu to a different house and later, when he travels to America on business, he leaves his affairs in the hands of Saratu's grasping father. After his departure, Ruk'ayya discovers that she is two months pregnant. Months later, while Usman is still away, she gives birth and while she is in hospital, Saratu is admitted because of a miscarriage. Usman returns home to find that his and Saratu's baby has died, that Saratu had fabricated the accusations of poisoning and witchcraft against Ruk'ayya, and that her father has been ruining his business. Usman divorces Saratu and returns to Ruk'ayya, who accepts him lovingly and without recrimination.

Soyayya books create a utopian world where the norms governing sexual relations are inverted and transformed. *Inda* and *Kishi* recount the love stories of young people of a similar age. Unlike usual Hausa sexual relations, here, men and women not only share social space with each other, but they also spend recreational time together and lead a shared emotional life. The traditional sense of shyness that regulates social interaction is transformed. Men openly declare their love for women, and women, more shockingly, are equally vocal in expressing their love in return. In *Inda*, for instance, Sumayya is the first to look at Mohammed. She initiates contact with him through letters and when they finally meet: 'Mohammed,' she said shyly, 'I must confess that you are always on my mind. I love you very much' (Ahmad 1993a, 10).

Similarly, in *Kishi*, Usman and Ruk'ayya address each other in phrases that are new to Hausa lovemaking: in one scene, Ruk'ayya approaches a worried Usman and asks, 'O my lover, the milk that cools my heart, what is worrying you?' (Liman 1993, 20). Usman replies, 'There is nothing, light of my heart' (ibid.).

Soyayya books portray a field of sexual interaction that is very different from 'traditional' Hausa ideals. Open declarations of love, expressed in an elaborate and highly formalised manner, are one of the most visible markers of the shift in styles of love among Hausa youth. In fact, *Inda* represents a reversal of the norms governing the Hausa sexual hierarchy, with Sumayya, by virtue of her money and status, being narratively more active and passionate than Mohammed. This subversive link between materialism and sexuality is another common theme of *soyayya* books, and reiterates the fears of many Hausa youth about the difficulties of marriage. At the beginning of *Inda*, Mohammed's friends notice Sumayya eyeing him; this sets off an exchange among his friends, who dismiss Mohammed's concern that Sumayya is too rich for him. They make the claim familiar among male Hausa youth—that there are too many unmarried women—and they lament the fact that they cannot afford to marry: 'Husbands are hard to come by now, anyway.' 'Exactly,' Garba agreed. 'The table has now turned. It is the girls that now court. Men are extremely scarce you know' (Ahmad 1993a, 3).

Garba discusses the reason behind this unnatural state of affairs: 'The fault lies squarely on the parents. They try to commercialise marriages. It goes to the highest bidder…. [A]ll of us here crave marriage but it is the demands that scare us away' (ibid., 4).

The commodification of religious affairs such as marriage that Garba refers to is represented by the figure of the grandmother. Her age should represent the accrual of wisdom and authority, but she loses the respect she is due when she commodifies her authority by accepting bribes from Abdulkadir. Instead of representing what is best about tradition, she comes to stand for what is worst about the corruption in contemporary times. It is this illegitimate act that allows Sumayya's rebellion against parental authority to remain within the bounds of an ideal moral universe.

The tension between tradition and modernity that materialism represents in the story is mimicked in the conflict between individual desire and social responsibility. Early in the book, Mohammed points out to Sumayya that her parents are likely to view the possibility of their marriage negatively, owing to their unequal social status. Sumayya reveals her commitment to modern social values as she dismisses his argument:

> Please do understand that nothing is permanent, riches or otherwise. Are we the ones who determine our destinies? I assume that our creator has that singular quality. He gives to whomever he wishes and refuses whomever he wishes. Besides, talking about parental interference, I think that has by now been one of the bygones. They now accept what the boy and girl want. The evils of forced marriages are too clear for all to see. (ibid., 10–11)

Sumayya is overconfident in her belief that forced marriage is a thing of the past, and that parents will readily cede autonomy to their children. She makes the religiously acceptable argument that it is Allah who determines destiny, but she does so as she sloughs off concern for parental authority and asserts the right to control her own destiny.

While an overt rebellion against parental authority is missing, this sense of individual control also marks the storyline of *Kishi*. *Kishi* was overtly intended to avoid the criticism that surrounded early *soyayya* books such as *Inda*. The suicide attempt by Sumayya, for instance, was alleged to have inspired other young girls to follow her example, and critics accused Ahmad of teaching girls to rebel against their parents (Giginyu 1992). Liman is careful not to advocate rebellion and attempts to articulate the new subjectivity of youth, and the fascination of romantic love, within an accepted Hausa framework. *Kishi* is full of platitudinous statements about ideal behaviour, which are immediately contradicted by the logic and tension of narrative development. Unlike *Inda*, all the youths in *Kishi* respect and obey their parents and never contemplate rebelling against their decisions. But then Liman never puts them in a position where they have to. Usman and Ruk'ayya meet and court by themselves. When they fall in love they decide to tell their parents, who are delighted and pose no embarrassing obstacles. Significantly, though, control over the choice of marriage partner is left to the young people themselves. This is the case even with Usman's second marriage, to the devious but beautiful Saratu.

Liman creates a utopian world of rich and beautiful youth who fly to Europe for medical treatment, who act selflessly and love passionately, but always in the context of proper Hausa behaviour. It may be that the characters drive fancy cars, go to Western-style hotels for their honeymoon, and live in large houses filled with the latest in electronic consumer goods, but Liman accompanies this spectacle of material wealth with moral homilies referencing key Hausa virtues. When Alhaji Lawal, Usman's grandfather, instructs him that now is the time to be thinking of marriage and to begin looking for a bride, he tells him, 'Even though I won't prevent you from looking for beauty, you should make sure it's religion that leads you to marriage and not your heart' (Liman 1993, 2). Usman agrees to this obvious insertion of 'ideal' Hausa values, but in the next paragraph he sees a girl, their eyes meet, and he falls in love, asking himself if she will agree to marry him before he has ever said a word to her, let alone found out about her religious values. Similarly, Usman announces his wedding to his grandfather by saying: '"Grandfather, today something wonderful has happened to us." Then he told him the story from the beginning to the end. Fortunately Alhaji Lawal knew Mallam Haruna [Ruk'ayya's father] and knew him for an upright character who doesn't care about worldly things' (ibid., 9–10). Liman protects Usman's desire for control over his own life and Alhaji's concern for proper Hausa values, as individual desire and parental will coincide in a perfect world.

The dominant melodramatic tension in *Kishi* revolves around the moral of sacrifice. This theme constitutes part of the basic genre of Indian film and depends for its significance on the tension between modernity and tradition in postcolonial societies. Sacrifice, as it is mobilised in *Kishi* and many Indian films, depends upon a moral choice between individual desire and social responsibility, taking on a cultural as well as an individual resonance. Ruk'ayya, in *Kishi*, is the supreme example of the self-sacrificing wife. Not only does she accept the unjust accusations of her co-wife uncomplainingly, but the very fact of her insistence on her husband taking a second wife also reveals how willing she is to sacrifice her individual happiness for the good of the family. In Hausa, the name for co-wife, *kishiya*, derives from *kishi*, the Hausa word for jealousy, and is particularly identified with women (as the proverb and title of the book, 'Jealousy is the nausea of women', implies). Most Hausa readers I spoke to thought it highly likely that a husband and grandfather would look for a second wife if the first were barren (again reiterating the utopian nature of the book), but this device is necessary to highlight the individual nature of Ruk'ayya's sacrifice.

Jackson argues that narratives function by raising 'ethical dissonance' (1982, 2), situations of doubt and uncertainty through which the audience can reflect upon the nature of the social order. He argues that this is especially true in folk tales about love. In many societies, the choice of marriage partner is an important decision affecting the entire family, and so is rarely left to the individuals directly concerned. Love affairs, Jackson points out, are based on individual choices. 'Love,' he states, 'like all strong emotions, is difficult to control, and its course is unpredictable' (ibid., 202). As a consequence, love can be wild and a potential threat to the social order. To ensure that the passing fancies of men and women are regulated for the common good, love has to be reined in and controlled by the authorities, usually elder kin. Abu-Lughod makes a similar point in her discussion of the poetry of love and emotions among Bedouin. 'Succumbing to sexual desire, or merely to romantic love,' she asserts, 'can lead individuals to disregard social convention and social obligations', and threaten the social values of honour and the authority of elders (Abu-Lughod 1986, 147–148). Stories of romantic love raise questions about the importance of individual action *versus* familial obligation, but precisely how these stories are resolved varies. When, in *Kishi*, Ruk'ayya decides to regulate her emotions and sacrifice her desires for the good of the family, she makes a choice in favour of the social order. Conversely, when Sumayya decides to reject what she sees as the illegitimate decision of her parents, she refuses their authority in the form of an attempted suicide.

By presenting two radically different solutions to comparable problems, these books bear out Jackson's argument that narratives promote ambivalence and ambiguity as a way of allowing readers to imaginatively explore social tensions in their multiple connotations. Jackson argues that this process occurs in the development of a single narrative, but it is my point that the mass culture of *soyayya* books and Indian films develops the process of ambiguity by presenting various resolutions to similar predicaments in thousands of narratives extending over many years. By engaging with both individual stories and the genre as a whole, narratives allow for a social inquiry. Sacrifice is significant to postcolonial societies, negotiating the rapidity and direction of social change, because it is the readers and viewers who feel the conflict between parental authority and individual desire most keenly. This is one reason why the theme of sacrifice is so prevalent in Indian films and *soyayya* books, and why it is relatively absent in Western genres such as Hollywood films. Precisely because this theme has such relevance to Hausa society, the success of *soyayya* books has occasioned a powerful backlash against them—and even, by proxy, against Indian films, which previously was a relatively unremarked upon part of the Hausa cultural landscape.

To conclude my discussion of transnational media and social change, I now outline the contours of the public debate that surrounds the success of *soyayya* books. This controversy reveals how conflict over the direction of social change is condensed around issues of changing sexual relations among the youth, and the place of Indian films as a cultural third space situated between Hausa tradition and Western modernity.[22]

SOYAYYA BOOKS, YOUTH, AND SOCIAL CHANGE: THE CONTROVERSY

> Right from your book cover the design is sinful.... Similarly when somebody reads your books he will see that inside consists of sin and forbidden things. And when it comes to letters in the books to believe in them will make somebody deviate from the teachings of his religion. Quotations like 'my better half' [*rabin raina*], 'the light of my heart' [*hasken zuciyata*] and other lies makes you wonder whether the writer should not be lashed. (*Zuwa ga marabutan Soyayya*, 'An open letter to soyayya authors', from the Editor, *Gwagwarmaya* ('Struggle') 2, 19)

The strong moral lessons embedded in *soyayya* books have gained enormous popularity with a young Hausa audience. Yet it is often the youth who are the bitterest opponents of this new form of fiction. The success of *soyayya* books has created a public discourse that includes a profusion of articles in Hausa-language magazines and newspapers, letters to the authors themselves, and the everyday conversation of fans and critics. The tone and passion of this public discourse indicate the volatility of the response to the popular culture of romance. One letter to the editor of the Hausa-language newspaper *Nasiha* ('Advice') is typical of the debate:

> Dear Sir, I wish to take space in your widely read newspaper to appeal to the Federal Government and the State Government. In truth, it would be better if the Government took steps regarding the books that certain notorious elements are writing everywhere in Nigeria, especially in the north. (19 May 1995, 8)

The letter writer continues, 'These books only succeed in corrupting our youth, especially girls', and adds that it has become necessary for the government to take action.

When I was in Nigeria, the idea that the State government was about to take radical action 'against' *soyayya* books was widely believed by young men who were opposed to their continued distribution. Such youths had two main complaints against the books. The *first* was that the material world of fine clothes, expensive cars, and generous lovers that the books presented encouraged girls to demand presents from their boyfriends and lovers, which the latter could not afford. As a consequence, boys who may have been courting a girl for years, giving her small presents and supporting her education, lose out to a rich Alhaji who meets and marries the girl within just a few months. The *second* complaint is that girls demand a different style of behaviour from their lovers. In a reversal of the complaints made against Indian films cited earlier, girls both demonstrate and demand greater sophistication in the language and behaviour of love. One friend of mine who attacked *soyayya* books vehemently said that in the past, if you tried to kiss a girl before you were married, she would scream and call for her brothers. Now, he said, if you do not kiss her by the second time you meet, she will think you are 'bush' (backward), and this is the result of reading *soyayya* books. Along with calls for the government to intervene, some secondary school headmasters are said to have embarked on a campaign to expel any girls found with *soyayya* books in their possession. The discourse around the books, then, has touched on an issue of considerable public passion.

The press debate was sparked by the efforts of two journalists (both fiction writers themselves) working at the newspaper *Nasiha*: Ibrahim Sheme and Ibrahim Malumfashi. Sheme initiated a regular literary page in the newspaper which, soon after *soyayya* books began appearing in northern markets, published an interview with an author, Hauwa Ibrahim Shariff (6 September 1991). Thus began the public debate over the pros and cons of *soyayya* books, including a seminal exchange of articles between Ibrahim Malumfashi (then at Usman Dan Fodio University in

Sokoto) and Ado Ahmad. Malumfashi opened the debate with an attack on *soyayya* writers, 'On the need to change the style of Hausa literature' (November 1991, 7). In this article, he charged *soyayya* writers with dwelling on themes of escapism that had little or no relevance to the problems of poverty and deteriorating lifestyle that dominated everyday existence. He argued that the books borrowed shamelessly from other cultures, creating situations that could never possibly exist in Hausa society. Later, Malumfashi extended his critique of cultural borrowing in an article titled 'Between second-hand and original' (*Nasiha*, 7 August 1992, 4; 14 August 1992, 4), where he argued that *soyayya* books were 'second-hand' and that if Ado Ahmad 'watches Indian films he will realise that it is these films that are being translated into Hausa and claimed to have happened in Kano, Kaduna, Katsina or Sokoto. Most of these books are filled with rubbish' (14 August 1992, 4).

Ahmad responded to Malumfashi in his capacity as Chairman of the main *soyayya* writing group, Raina Kama. His article, 'Let's go with modern times!' (*Nasiha* 24, 31 July 1992), makes the powerful point that for the first time, Hausa markets are filled with books written in Hausa that, far from copying foreign cultures, represent an efflorescence of Hausa culture. Times have changed, Ahmad argues, and *soyayya* books call for the betterment of society, rather than corrupting it. Ahmad's argument stems from the fact that many *soyayya* writers who create stories from personal experience are writing about issues that are important to the contemporary culture, and which should not be ignored for the sake of more 'relevant' issues. It is a point of view echoed by Yusuf Adamu Mohammed when he asks why contemporary authors write love stories:

> The contemporary generation of readers are more interested in what concerns them: stories of ancient empires and jinns [spirits] are no longer appealing to them.[23] Second, many of these young authors are young and unmarried … [and they suffer] from the misdeeds of autocratic rich men in society…. Since the young novelists are also among the downtrodden, in real life they are virtually helpless. Yet they

> can use their pens to fight for their rights and the rights of the oppressed. (*Association of Nigerian Authors Review*, October 1994, 9, 10)

The debate between Ahmad, Malumfashi, and others sparked an outpouring in the pages of *Nasiha* and other Hausa-language magazines and newspapers. Sheme, who had initiated the debate, finally had to request for no further submissions because the paper was inundated (*Nasiha*, 28 August 1992), although the debate still continues regularly. The debate in the press was supplemented by letters to the authors themselves. Many *soyayya* authors include a postal address on all the books published, and popular authors such as Ahmad, Dan'Azumi Baba, and Adamu Mohammed get an enormous response. Ahmad has received more than 2,000 letters covering a range of topics, from requests for free copies, to expressions of love, to requests for advice on how to manage relationships, and compliments and criticism. One such letter from a recent (male) school graduate stated:

> Among all the writers of Hausa soyayya books you [Ado Ahmad] are the best of them. This is because you are aware of what is going on nowadays. And you are more devoted Islamically and culturally than all of them.... [Your popularity is] because of your struggle to educate youth on marriage and not only children but parents too. The books stop parents making arranged marriages for their children and give freedom of choice to each and everybody irrespective of tribe or culture. This is of course the major aspect of your books that impresses and encourages people to read more soyayya books. (3 November 1993)

It is interesting, and unsurprising, that the writer registers Ahmad's devotion to religion and to culture, as these are the grounds on which *soyayya* authors are attacked most strongly. Many other letter writers have praised Ahmad for his stand against materialistic parents. One said that contemporary youth were sick of the greed of money-mongers (*mai idon cin naira*) like Sumayya's grandmother, and grateful for the 'educative' nature of *soyayya* books. Another said that the books showed him the wrongs of forced marriage (*auren dole*) and the importance of individual choice. The books, he continued, 'teach us how to live successfully in the world ... how parents should take care of their children and be careful in letting their daughters choose the person they love and admire' (undated).

The insistence on individual choice over parental authority is cited by many critics as the prime reason for the pernicious effect of *soyayya* books. 'I swear, Mallam Ado,' wrote one youth in response to *Inda*, 'most of the crises that are occurring nowadays are caused by your writings. Our youths are spoiled by reading your books.' He continued:

> [Ado Ahmad] you are among those who mobilise our youth, especially our girls, to start feeling freedom of choice by force, and that they should start doing everything according to their own interest and to forget about their parents' interest, and that they should only marry the person they love. For example, mostly in your books you write about a girl running away from her parents, because of someone she loves and chooses to be with. And, as you see, this is a great deviation from the teachings of Islam and culture, as you forget that girls are under the thumb of their parents religiously and culturally. (29 January 1994)

The response of letter writers to Ahmad and other authors indicates how close, in people's view, the relation is between *soyayya* books and everyday life. One letter to Ahmad said the writer became a fan of Ahmad's books when his girlfriend insisted he read them, because there were so many things he could learn from them. Similarly, Baba and Ahmad receive many letters asking for advice in matters of love. It is unsurprising, then, that these books generate such passion, as fans of *soyayya* writers and their critics are both responding to the mundane concern about contemporary social change. *Soyayya* books effectively dramatise this change within the realm of romance and sexuality. The profusion of articles, both for and against *soyayya* books, in the press has taken what was mainly a controversy among young people (reading *soyayya* books would be considered too demanding for older men) into a wider public arena.

Conclusion

One Friday night I went with a friend to see the classic Indian film *Mother India* (1957, directed by Mehboob Khan) at the Marhaba. A Lebanese distributor had explained to me how, despite the fact that he had been screening the film for decades, it could still sell out any cinema in the north, and he made me curious to see whether it was true. Sure enough, on Friday night at the Marhaba, the busiest night (usually reserved for new films) at the newest and largest cinema in Kano, all the seats were full. As the film started, the friend I went with turned to me and said, 'Besides you, everyone in the cinema has seen this film at least fifteen times.' I relate this anecdote to give some sense not just of the pervasiveness of Indian film, but of the fan culture that surrounds it. This comes across strongly when you watch a film where everyone knows the songs, when people laugh at the comedy routines almost before they are finished, and where the dialogue, the narrative, and the emotions invoked carry the familiarity and comfort of a well-known and well-loved film.[24] When I returned home that night, another friend in his late twenties asked me where I had been. I told him and asked if he knew when the film was made. He laughed, saying, 'I don't know, but as soon as I knew film, I knew *Mother India*.' Just as I, growing up in London in a cinematic world dominated by American stars, incorporated American media as part of English popular culture, so it is for Hausa audiences. Indian films have been reworked and incorporated to form an integral part of contemporary Hausa social life.

The long struggle against cultural imperialism has not so much criticised the influence of Indian films as ignored it. While the politics of representation, and the effects of cultural imperialism, are highly politicised topics in Nigeria, Indian films, by virtue of their traditions and 'culture', have created a space that largely sidesteps criticism. This is because for Hausa viewers, Indian films are situated in a cultural space that stands outside the binary distinctions of tradition and modernity, Africa and the West, resistance and domination. The images of modernity they offer are mediated through a concern for maintaining traditional social relations, and so they run parallel to, and are similar yet different from, the modernity offered by Westernisation. Hausa viewers managed to engage with texts that showed a culture that was 'just like' Hausa culture, as long as it was also irreducibly different. It is no surprise that, when the difference collapsed through the rise of *soyayya* books, Indian films became controversial in a way they never were before. As one letter writer to Ado Ahmad put it, 'In truth, Ado, you are among those who spread this modern love to our young people, not the films they watch, because in those films they don't usually understand what they are about. But now you are telling us in our own language' (29 January 1994).

The tendency of many Africanists to see resistance as the underlying cause of a vast range of social and cultural phenomena led, in its reductionism, to the elision of other cultural flows that did not fit neatly into the pattern. How else do we account for the absence of Indian films from analyses of African popular culture? The understandable tendency of anthropologists and others to concentrate on the vibrancy of the popular arts produced by the people, while laudable, has elided some forms of mass-mediated culture from academic purview. Barber, for instance, asks,

> What exactly an African audience gets out of, say, a film in a foreign language, about culturally remote people who perform a series of actions almost invisible to the naked eye on a dim and flickering screen. Do these shows perhaps represent novelty itself in its most concentrated form? (Barber 1987, 25)

What audiences take from these films is considerable. Indian film has been a popular form of entertainment in urban West Africa for well over forty years, and commands viewers because it engages with real desires and conflicts in African societies. Instead of indulging in a blanket dismissal of these forms, it is necessary to take them seriously in their textual, cultural, and historical specificities. The task that remains is to theorise adequately the complexity and heterogeneity of contemporary national and transnational cultural flows. Why are Indian films more popular in northern Nigeria? Are the reasons for their popularity the same elsewhere in West Africa? Why have influential film genres such as Egyptian films had so little impact in Nigeria? These are questions that need to be answered, for, as Appadurai and Breckenridge (1988) observe, transnational cultural flows emerge from many centres and flow into many peripheries.

In this chapter, I have been concerned with articulating why one media form—Indian film—has resonance in the very different cultural environment of northern Nigeria. Indian films are popular because they provide a parallel modernity, a way of imaginatively engaging with the changing social basis of contemporary life that is an alternative to the pervasive influence of a secular West. Through spectacle and fantasy, romance and sexuality, Indian films provide arenas to consider what it means to be modern and what may be the place of Hausa society within that modernity. For northern Nigerians, who respond to a number of different centres—whether politically to the Nigerian State, religiously to the Middle East and North Africa, economically to the West, or culturally to the cinematic dominance of India—Indian films are just one part of the heterogeneity of everyday life.

ACKNOWLEDGEMENTS

Funding for this research was provided by the Wenner-Gren Foundation and a Dean's Research Grant from New York University. I am grateful to Faye Ginsburg, T. O. Beidelman, Lila Abu-Lughod, and Meg McLagan, who all commented on drafts of this article. I also thank Karin Barber and Murray Last for their editorial comments. The article relies heavily on the generous help given by the *soyayya* authors Dan'Azumi Baba, Yusuf Lawan, and Adamu Mohammed. I especially thank Ado Ahmad and Yusuf Mohammad Adamu, who initiated me into the world of *soyayya* literature. This article could not have been written without them. Ibrahim Sheme and Ibrahim Malumfashi added their critical view of *soyayya* books to the picture. Finally, I thank Usman Aliyu Abdulmalik and Abdullahi Kafin-Hausa for help with translation.

NOTES

1. Mamman Shata is one of the most famous Hausa singers. This song was written as a satire on his friend, Mallam Sidi, who 'fell in love' with an Indian film actress.

2. I use the term 'Indian film' throughout as it is how Hausa viewers describe what is, in actuality, the Bombay Hindi film. 'Indian film' should properly refer to the variety of Indian-language films.

3. To my knowledge, the only Nigerian film critics to discuss Indian films are Hyginus Ekwuazi (1987), who criticises them, and Bala Muhammad (1992), who praises them. For a journalist's view, see Sheme (1995a, 1995b). Fugelsang (1994) discusses the viewing of Indian videos by Lamu youth.

4. Lila Abu-Lughod (1993a) also argues for increased attention to global flows that do not originate in Euro-American centres.

5. My use of the term 'postcolonial' in this chapter is historical rather than theoretical, referring to the aftermath of the experience of colonialism for ex-colonised nations.

6. The success of Brazilian telenovelas in China, the Soviet Union, and elsewhere, and the regional dominance of Egyptian film and soap operas among Arabic-speaking countries are other examples of the phenomenon. See McNeely and Soysal (1989) for a discussion of this trend, and Sreberny-Mohammadi (1991) for a critique.

7. Ekwuazi, while admitting the widespread popularity of Indian film, argues that 'its impact on the cultural landscape is relatively minimal' (1987, 44). In an almost direct contrast to this chapter, he argues that the reason is that Indian films are unable to offer a 'feasible model for (teenage) dreams' (ibid.). That Ekwuazi comes to what I see as a mistaken conclusion is a marker of the devalued position that popular Indian cinema has among scholars. (See Thomas [1985] for a discussion of this phenomenon.) Ekwuazi views Indian film as a cheap copy of American film, and rather than considering Indian narratives, stars, or spectacles as governed by an alternative filmic style, he judges them by their failure to live up to Western standards: 'To anyone who has seen the real thing, the Indian imitation film is an aesthetic offense; it makes even the worst American film a sight for sore eyes' (ibid.).

8. History and Culture Bureau, Kano (HCB): Edu/14, Cinematograph and Censorship of Films, Exhibition of Films.

9. The reason why this is so is unclear. Arab films have long been successful internationally, and popular Egyptian films have a wide

audience outside their own country. Perhaps it was precisely because Arabic is a religious language that its association with such a profane domain as cinema (as it is seen in northern Nigeria) made it impossible to attract an early viewing public. The recent introduction of satellite television in Nigeria has made channels from Saudi Arabia and Egypt available. As this comes at the same time as a revival in Arabic-language learning, it may give Arab media a new popularity.

10. Interview, Michel G. Issa, Manager, Cinema Distribution Circuit, May 1995.

11. Many Arabic loan words are common to both Hindi and Hausa, which creates an oft remarked sense of linguistic similarity.

12. It is no accident that the two other popular genres of film in Nigeria are Chinese Kung-fu and gangster films, and American action films. Action films depend more heavily on visual sequences than on complex narrative development, which makes them easier to understand across linguistic barriers.

13. Going for picnics is a disreputable activity because it refers to increased mixing between unrelated men and women. This goes against the traditional norm of sexual segregation and is widely seen (and criticised) as an index of growing immorality.

14. The participation of youth in Islamic religious movements has been part of the history of northern Nigeria. Contemporary challenges, revealed in movements as diverse as the '*yan tatsine*' (see Lubeck 1987; Watts and Pred 1992) and the Muslim Brothers, illustrate how oppositional contemporary religious movements can be for the status quo.

15. Consider, for instance, that during the time Callaway was researching and writing, Indian films were already established as a common part of everyday female popular culture. Often referred to as 'women's films', the concentration of romance and melodrama was and is seen as the prime reason for female identification. Only two years after Callaway's book was published, the efflorescence of a Hausa romance literature, identified primarily with women readers (and with a significant number of women writers), makes her assertion that romance cannot exist in Islamic marriages untenable. Abu-Lughod (1986) provides a much more nuanced analysis of the romance, the poetry of love, and emotional attachments among an equally sexually segregated Bedouin society.

16. Interview, December 1994.

17. Interview, June 1995.

18. Hausa can be written in either Arabic or Latin script. *Ajami* refers to Hausa written in Arabic script, *boko* to Hausa written in Latin script.

19. For the sake of consistency, wherever possible I follow (as here) the translation of *soyayya* clubs and books as cited in Furniss (1996).

20. Strictly speaking, *Alhaji* means a man who has made the pilgrimage (*hajj*) to Mecca. In common Hausa usage, it refers to any person of wealth or status.

21. Ahmad abridged and translated his book into English in order to tap into a wider Nigerian English-speaking audience (interview, May 1995). Following its publication, he did begin to receive letters in English from fans belonging to many other Nigerian ethnic groups, indicating its success. In 1995, he abridged and published *Masoyan Zamani* I, II ('Modern Lovers', 1993) as *Nemesis*. The only other English-language *soyayya* book is *The Sign of the Times* (1994) by Tijani Usman Adamu. Adamu's book was written in English and no Hausa version exists.

22. Indian films present an alternative to both Hausa tradition and Western modernity in that, while they depict a culture 'just like' Hausa culture, their popularity resides in the fact that Indian culture is also precisely *unlike* Hausa culture. Indian films portray an alternative world where actions that would not be tolerated within Hausa social norms are raised without attracting widespread condemnation. A comparison with the Hausa reception of Yoruba or Igbo films is helpful here. Onitsha market literature, Yoruba and Igbo videos, and popular romance magazines such as *Hints*, all suggest how popular the theme of love remains in southern Nigeria. Clearly, many of the Yoruba and Igbo films are set in locations with cultural references that are familiar to, and have similarities with, Hausa audiences. Yoruba and Igbo films, however, are often sexually more explicit in their themes than either Hausa videos or Indian films. While many Hausa viewers watch and enjoy these videos, for others their themes are too explicit for comfort. The attitude of one Hausa video shop owner I talked to, who sold Igbo and Yoruba films but was reluctant to let members of his family watch them, is not exceptional.

23. Mohammed is here referring to the subject matter of stories which make up classic Hausa fiction, such as Abubakar Imam's *Ruwan Bagaja* (1934) or *Gand'oki* by Bello Kagara (1934). For further discussion of these works, see Furniss (1996); Rahim (1990); Sani (1990); Yahaya (1988).

24. This familiarity is one reason why *bandiri* singers have drawn on popular Indian film songs for religious music. These Sufi adepts will take

the songs from a popular film, such as *Mother India*, or *Kabhi, Kabhie* (1976, directed by Yash Chopra), and change the words to sing praises to the Prophet Mohammed.

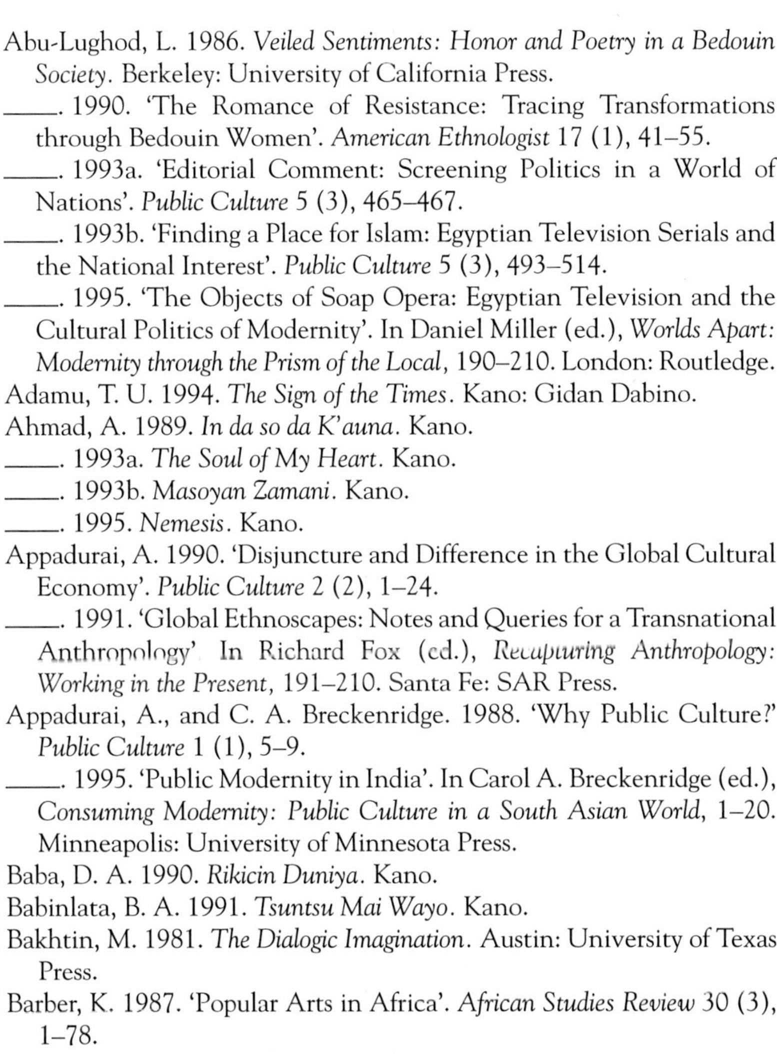

SELECT REFERENCES

Abu-Lughod, L. 1986. *Veiled Sentiments: Honor and Poetry in a Bedouin Society*. Berkeley: University of California Press.

_____. 1990. 'The Romance of Resistance: Tracing Transformations through Bedouin Women'. *American Ethnologist* 17 (1), 41–55.

_____. 1993a. 'Editorial Comment: Screening Politics in a World of Nations'. *Public Culture* 5 (3), 465–467.

_____. 1993b. 'Finding a Place for Islam: Egyptian Television Serials and the National Interest'. *Public Culture* 5 (3), 493–514.

_____. 1995. 'The Objects of Soap Opera: Egyptian Television and the Cultural Politics of Modernity'. In Daniel Miller (ed.), *Worlds Apart: Modernity through the Prism of the Local*, 190–210. London: Routledge.

Adamu, T. U. 1994. *The Sign of the Times*. Kano: Gidan Dabino.

Ahmad, A. 1989. *In da so da K'auna*. Kano.

_____. 1993a. *The Soul of My Heart*. Kano.

_____. 1993b. *Masoyan Zamani*. Kano.

_____. 1995. *Nemesis*. Kano.

Appadurai, A. 1990. 'Disjuncture and Difference in the Global Cultural Economy'. *Public Culture* 2 (2), 1–24.

_____. 1991. 'Global Ethnoscapes: Notes and Queries for a Transnational Anthropology'. In Richard Fox (ed.), *Recapturing Anthropology: Working in the Present*, 191–210. Santa Fe: SAR Press.

Appadurai, A., and C. A. Breckenridge. 1988. 'Why Public Culture?' *Public Culture* 1 (1), 5–9.

_____. 1995. 'Public Modernity in India'. In Carol A. Breckenridge (ed.), *Consuming Modernity: Public Culture in a South Asian World*, 1–20. Minneapolis: University of Minnesota Press.

Baba, D. A. 1990. *Rikicin Duniya*. Kano.

Babinlata, B. A. 1991. *Tsuntsu Mai Wayo*. Kano.

Bakhtin, M. 1981. *The Dialogic Imagination*. Austin: University of Texas Press.

Barber, K. 1987. 'Popular Arts in Africa'. *African Studies Review* 30 (3), 1–78.

Barkindo, B. M. 1993. 'Growing Islamism in Kano City since 1970'. In Louis Brenner (ed.), *Muslim Identity and Social Change in Sub-Saharan Africa*, 91–105. Bloomington: Indiana University Press.

Beidelman, T. O. 1986. *Moral Imagination among Kaguru Modes of Thought*. Bloomington: Indiana University Press. New Edition, Washington, D.C.: Smithsonian Institution Press, 1993.

Bichi, M. A. 1992. 'The Author's Imagination' II, *The Triumph*, 17 March, 7.

Callaway, B. 1987. *Muslim Hausa Women in Nigeria: tradition and change*. New York: Syracuse University Press.

Chakravarty, S. 1993. *National Ideology in Indian Popular Cinema, 1947–87*. Austin: University of Texas Press.

Cooper, F. 1994. 'Conflict and Connection: Rethinking African Colonial History'. *American Historical Review* 99 (5), 1516–1545.

Dan Asabe, A. K. n.d. 'The Way Youth Organise Themselves: A Study of Clubs in Kano Metropolis, Nigeria'. Unpublished manuscript, Kano.

Diawara, M. 1992. *African Cinema: Politics and Culture*. Bloomington: Indiana University Press.

Ekwuazi H. 1987. *Film in Nigeria*. Jos: Nigerian Film Corporation.

Ekwuazi, H., and Y. Nasidi (eds). 1992. *Operative Principles of the Film Industry: Towards a Film Policy for Nigeria*. Jos: Nigerian Film Corporation.

Fugelsang, M. 1994. *Veils and Videos: Female Youth Culture on the Kenyan Coast*. Studies in Social Anthropology, Stockholm: Gotab.

Furniss, G. 1996. *Poetry, Prose and Popular Culture in Hausa*. Edinburgh: Edinburgh University Press; Washington, D.C.: Smithsonian Institution Press, for the International African Institute.

Giginyu, N. M. 1992. 'A Little Knowledge is a Dangerous Thing: A Reply to Ado Ahmad Gidan Dabino'. *Nasiha*, 28 August.

Ginsburg, F. 1991. 'Indigenous Media: Faustian Contract or Global Village?' *Cultural Anthropology* 6 (1), 92–112.

_____. 1993. 'Aboriginal Media and the Aboriginal Imaginary'. *Public Culture* 5 (3), 557–578.

_____. 1994. 'Embedded Aesthetics: Creating a Discursive Place for Indigenous Media'. *Cultural Anthropology* 9 (3), 365–382.

Hannerz, U. 1992. *Cultural Complexity: Studies in the Social Organization of Meaning*. New York: Columbia University Press.

Imam, A. 1934. *Ruwan Bagaja*. Zaria: NNPC. Also in *India International Centre Quarterly*, Special Issue, 8 (1), 1980.

Jackson, M. 1982. *Allegories of the Wilderness: Ethics and Ambiguity in Uranko Narratives*. Bloomington: Indiana University Press.

Kagara, B. 1934. *Gand'oki*. Zaria: Literature Bureau.

Kakar, S. 1989. *Intimate Relations: Exploring Indian Sexuality*. Chicago: University of Chicago Press.

Lawan, Y. 1993. *Kamai Wahalar So*. Kano.

_____. 1995. *Mai Hakuri*... Kano.

Liman, M. S. 1993. *Kishi Kumallon Mata*. Gusau: Bushara Publishing House.

Lubeck, P. 1987. 'Islamic Protest under Semi-Industrial Capitalism: Yan Tatsine Explained'. In J. D. Y. Peel and C. C. Stewart (eds), *Popular Islam South of the Sahara*, 369–389. Manchester: Manchester University Press, for the International African Institute.

McLagan, M. 1996. 'Computing for Tibet: Virtual Politics in the Cold War Era'. In G. Marcus (ed.), *Connected: Engagements with Media at Century's End*, Late Editions 3. Chicago: University of Chicago Press.

McNeely, C., and Y. M. Soysal. 1989. 'International Flows of Television Programming: A Revisionist Research Orientation'. *Public Culture* 2 (1), 136–145.

Mishray, V. 1985. 'Toward a Theoretical Critique of Bombay Cinema'. *Screen* 26 (3–4), 133–146.

Mohammed, A. 1991. *Garnak'ak'i*. Kano: Kamfanin Kwabon Masoyi.

Muhammad, B. 1992. 'The Hausa Film: A Study of Slow Growth, Problems and Prospect'. In Hyginus Ekwuazi and Yakubu Nasidi (eds), *Operative Principles of the Film Industry: Towards a Film Policy for Nigeria*, 179–204. Jos: Nigerian Film Corporation.

Nandy, A. 1995. *The Savage Freud and Other Essays on Possible and Retrievable Selves*. Princeton: Princeton University Press.

Pendakur, M., and R. Subramanyam. 1996. 'Indian Cinema beyond National Borders'. In John Sinclair, Elizabeth Jacka, and Stuart Cunningham (eds), *New Patterns in Global Television: Peripheral Vision*, 67–82. Oxford: Oxford University Press.

Rahim, O. A. (ed.). 1990. *Essays on Northern Nigerian Literature* I. Zaria: Hamdan Express Printers.

Said, H. I., and M. Last. 1991. *Youth and Health in Kano Today*. Special issue of *Kano Studies*.

Sani, A. A. 1990. 'The Place of Rupert East in the Culture and Literature of Northern Nigeria'. In Oba Abdul Raheem (ed.), *Essays on Northern Nigerian Literature*, 12–21. Zaria: Hamdan Express Printers.

Sheme, I. 1995a. 'Indian films and Our Culture', *New Nigerian*, 13 May, 7.

_____. 1995b. 'Zagon k'asar da finafinan Indiya ke yi wa al'adanmu' ('The Danger of Indian Films to our Culture'). *Gaskiya ta fi kwabo*, 15 May, 5.

Shohat, E. and R. Stam. 1994. *Unthinking Eurocentrism*. New York: Routledge.

Sreberny-Mohammadi, A. 1991. 'The Global and the Local in International Communications'. In James Curran and Michael Gurevitch (eds), *Mass Media and Society*, London: Edward Arnold.

Sullivan, N. 1993. 'Film and Television Production in New Guinea: How the Media become the Message'. *Public Culture* 5 (3), 533–555.

Thomas, R. 1985. 'Indian Cinema: Pleasures and Popularity'. *Screen* 26 (3–4), 116–131.

_____. 1995. 'Melodrama and the Negotiation of Morality in Mainstream Indian Film'. In *Consuming Modernity: Public Culture in a South Asian World*, 157–182. Minneapolis: University of Minnesota Press.

Ukadike, N. F. 1994. *Black African Cinema*. Berkeley: University of California Press.

Watts, M., and A. Pred. 1992. *The Shock of Modernity: Capitalisms and Symbolic Discontent*. New Brunswick: Rutgers University Press.

Yahaya, I. Y. 1988. *Hausa a Rubuce: Tarihin Rubuce Rubuce Cikin Hausa*. Zaria: NNPC.

Yakubu, H. B. R. 1990a. *Alhaki Kwikwiyo*. Kano.

_____. 1990b. *Budurwar Zuciya*. Kano.

4

A Community in Print
Islam and Print Culture in Malabar, South India

K. A. Nuaiman

In 1898, Kuriyadath Kunhi Moosa published *Alif Laila Va Laila* (*The Thousand and One Nights* or *The Arabian Nights*), the popular Arabian story collection, from Mazzharul Uloom Press in Thalassery, a major port city situated on the Malabar coast of the Arabian Sea. The book, which had been published some five years earlier by one Kannambra Ramanunni Elaya Nair from Vidya Vilasam Press in Kozhikode, was already in circulation and widely available in the region. What made Kunhi Moosa's publishing venture unusual was the fact that publishing the same book by two different printers/publishers, that too from two nearby cities in such a short span of time, was rare in those times. Then why did Kunhi Moosa do it? This question sheds light on one of the crucial but often neglected aspects of print cultures in the region—the ways in which Muslims technically produced and represented their texts in print.

This chapter argues that many of the misconceptions about Muslim engagements with printing technology (and subsequent narrations about Muslim–media interactions with later information technologies) emerge precisely from the failure to understand questions such as the above one. Instead, media historiography in the context of Muslims has largely been focussed on questions such as why Muslims were late in accepting print or what it did to their religion/religious authority, etc. These questions are insufficient to grasp the meaning and significance of printing technologies in Muslim communities, precisely because such questions assume that technologies as well as communities are undifferentiated entities. Instead of asking such rhetorical questions, we need to look at what a specific community accepted from among the technological choices available to them, its precedence in their specific community histories, and the factors that might have shaped them to accept/reject certain technologies over others. Only such an inquiry can enable us to identify the discursive pattern through which communities historically negotiated with technologies. The challenge, then, is to identify the differentiations within technologies and the specific regional/religious aspirations they embody in the production and reception of the texts and traditions of a given community. For that, one needs to look in detail at the forms of media prevalent in a community and its specificities.

Unfortunately, the history of print in India was largely explored either in terms of the sociocultural and political changes it brought into a community, ascribing full agency to an undifferentiated technology and leaving the agency of the community and their textual cultures unattended to, or in terms of the content presented in the printed works. This emphasis on the normative promise of a technology or content does not allow scholars to focus on the form of the technology or to draw their analytical conclusions based on its characteristics in relation to other similar technological forms available in a given time. This is evident, for example, from the way we use terms such as 'book' and 'text' interchangeably. 'Book' being a form and 'text' being the content within it, this interchangeable use of the terms hides the difference between form and content. Thus, media forms carried little significance in most of the studies.

This chapter is an attempt to make sense of the technological forms that Mappila Muslims use to print, and the philosophy of knowledge they represent and aspire to reproduce. The chapter also looks at print as an object and analyses whether the forms it adopted in the Muslim context were incidental. To elucidate this line of inquiry, the study proposes to examine the forms of print adopted by Mappila Muslims in Malabar and locate them within the larger background of the textual cultures that preceded the advent of print. By doing so, I ask how the sociocultural and other specificities of a community are reflected in their choices of a particular form of technology. This will help us to understand not only how texts were mechanically produced, but also how their different forms emerged and conveyed meanings in the everyday Muslim life-world.

Mappila Muslim Printing: A Brief History

Archival evidences suggest that Mappilas, as Muslims in Malabar are popularly known, had extensively used printing technology and published widely. Their literary activities were on the increase in the early decades of printing and publishing itself. The Catalogue of Malayalam books in the British Museum for 1772–1961 (Gaur 1971) reproduce long lists of books printed and published by Mappila Muslims in Kerala.[1] 'The Reports on Publications issued and registered in the several Provinces of British India 1876–1898', kept in the Kozhikode regional archive, is another resource that documents the history of Mappila Muslim publications. Although these reports on publications issued and registered in several provinces of British India do not provide comprehensive details of the Muslim publications, this document, prepared on the basis of the books preserved under the virtue of the Indian Copyright Deposit Act (1867), definitely helps one to recognise some general characteristics of the history of printing in the region, with details such as the year and a community-wise number of publications.

To get a broad picture of the scenario, I look at the history of printing in the region from 1869 to the 1920s. A perusal of the Catalogue of Malayalam Books in the British Museum provides publication details for the period. Among the 311 books in the British Museum collection, put together under the virtue of the copyright deposit and donations from individuals, missionary societies, and university departments between 1876 and 1912, thirty-two are Islamic books. I call them 'Islamic books' because of their explicitly Islamic religious content, often prepared for didactic purposes. Brief descriptions of the content of each book provided in the catalogue suggest that most of them are either a translation or an interpretation/commentary of an earlier Islamic classical text rendered into Arabic-Malayalam. As evident from the names on the jacket, all these books were authored/published by a Muslim and printed in a Muslim-owned printing press. These thirty-two books were mostly published from the three major Muslim settlements in the region: Tellicherry (Thalassery) in Kannur, and Ponnani and Tirurangadi in Malappuram.

The first two (Islamic) books in the catalogue, according to the chronological order of publication, are the *Kachodappattu*, a metrical compendium of Muslim faith whose author is unknown, and the translation of Muhammad ibn Ibrahim Fakhr al-Din's *Kasd ul Sabil*, a compendium of Muslim faith and practice. Both books were published in Thalassery in 1879. It is interesting to note that in a catalogue of Malayalam books published from 1772, the first Muslim book appears only a century after the cataloguing was started, and a decade after the first Muslim printing press was established in Thalassery in 1869. This was three years after the Indian Press and Deposit Act (1876), which allowed the India Office Library and the British Museum the right to requisition a copy of every book printed in British India in any language, was implemented.

It is impossible to believe that the first Muslim printing press in Thalassery had not published any book in the first ten years of its operation or that there were no printed Muslim books till then. The catalogue itself lists the names of about eighteen Muslim printing presses functioning in Malabar between the years 1879 and 1912. But, according to the catalogue, all of them together had published only thirty-two books over a span of more than three decades. This throws up some important questions about the applicability of the British legal superstructure in monitoring Muslim printing and publication operations. The low rate of book registration under the Copyright and Deposit Act, according to Proudfoot (1994), has to do with the Muslim understanding of the book. Padwick (1961) also observes that one cannot make sense of Muslim publications from these periods using categories such as copyright, authoritative/original edition or printer, author, and publisher, as there were no such distinctions among them. The 'Reports on Publications issued and registered in the Madras Provinces of British India (1876–1898)' provides hints to understanding how these concerns might have worked out in Malabar. The report notes that the literary activities of the Mappila were on the rise, and most of the Mappila Muslims' books and pamphlets printed during this period were lithographed version of already existing popular texts in manuscript form. So it was obvious that Muslim books could have slipped through the British legal structures, which were primarily meant to monitor originally authored books and their authoritative editions.

Mappila Muslims as a Lithographic Community

The most explicit and striking information that this catalogue provides concerns the specific form adopted for printing by Muslims during this initial phase of Muslim printing in the region: lithography, as opposed to the then popular typographic printing methods. The descriptions given in the catalogue for each Malayalam book in the British Museum clearly show that early printing by religious communities in Malabar could be easily categorised along the lines of the specific forms of printing technologies they had used. While Muslim print is clearly marked by the lithographic form, non-Muslim printing escapes such easy categorisation. When they are described at all in the catalogues or bibliographies, they are marked by their typographic form. This categorisation is more explicit in the initial decades of the advent of print.[2] The 'Reports on the Publications issued and registered in several Provinces of British India 1874–1898' also notes that literary activities in the form of publications were not only present among Mappila Muslims during this period, but also that most of their publications were lithographed books and pamphlets. All books either published by Muslims or printed at a Muslim printing press were produced using lithographic printing presses. As the story of Kuriyadath Kunhi Moosa indicates, the same books published by non-Muslims using typography were printed by Muslims using lithography.

We also see that in *The Malayalam First Reader* in the Laccadive textbooks series published by MacMillan from Madras in 1899, the Arabic characters were printed separately using lithography, while the Malayalam texts were printed using typography. The only non-Muslim lithographic press mentioned in the catalogue is the Basel Mission Press in Tellicherry. Basel Missionaries established this lithographic press in Thalassery in order to expand their missionary activities in the Malabar, a region with a significant Muslim population. The details of the books they published reveal that most of their publications were actually meant for the Mappila Muslim readers. Although the number of Muslim books mentioned in the catalogue does not match with the number of printing presses functioning in Malabar during this time period, what is certain is that most of the Muslim-owned printing presses in the region were lithographic.

Another two factors that the catalogue reveals are that the Muslim printing presses and their technological forms can be easily identified from their Islamic names and the technological details mentioned in the very titles of the printing presses. These two characteristics take on importance because such details are not readily available for books published in non-Muslim contexts. To see how a typical Muslim printing press is named in the said period, look at these examples: Manba'ul-Hidayah Litho Press, Manba'ul-Ajaib Press, Mazhar al-ulum Press, Muhikk ul-Ghara'ib Press, Nur al Hidayat Litho Press, Ali Hajji, Amir ul Islam Litho Power Press, Mafatih al Huda Litho Press, Al Murshid Litho Press, and Mathba'thul Islamiyya Litho Press. This nomenclature informs us of the special status given to the lithographic type in Mappila Muslim contexts, as opposed to the movable typographic type. While print, with no additional descriptions, was used as a synonym for typography, lithography was never that. Does this mean, then, that lithography was treated as a minor phenomenon within print?

The above data explains how printing, in its early phase in the region, was clearly differentiated along the lines of community and specific forms of technologies, as opposed to being perceived as a monolithic phenomenon. Although such differences have been widely recognised, explored, and used today in mechanical engineering and related sciences to improve the technical qualities of printing (Bakshi 2006), it has seldom been used in media/historical studies to understand and reflect upon the sociocultural circumstances that shaped the arrival and popularity of different forms of printing technologies and their implications for specific communities.[3] Whenever such details are provided, they are mentioned in passing and describe the technical characteristics of a given printing press, without drawing any analytical conclusions from it.[4] The exceptions in this regard are Proudfoot's studies on early Malay Muslim printing (Proudfoot 1994, 1997) and Messick's study on printing in Yemen (Messick 1993).[5] It is surprising that historians working on print cultures in India paid so little attention to such details, despite the fact that archival evidence strongly suggests that clearly demarcated distinctions did exist in the early phase of printing technology.[6] Even then, print—both as an idea and as a practice—has been widely analysed, either as a homogenised transition from orality, which produced cracks in the relationship between literary cultures and oral traditions, or as a bridge between the two, without paying much attention to the differences within print itself.[7]

If lithographic usage was well-defined and popular among Mappila Muslims, as these records show, what is its analytical value for writing a history of Muslim negotiations with technology in general and with print in particular in the region? How are we to understand the ontological manifestations embedded in lithography? What insights can it provide for writing a history of the Muslim community in the region? To answer these questions, one needs to look at texts as well as the technological forms these texts adopted for their mechanical reproduction. The discussion that follows will seek to understand lithography's self-presentation as a particular way of reading, writing, thinking, and learning, and therefore of historical truth-making with regard to the orders of knowledge in Islam.

The book, in history as well as in the present, is considered an emblematic figure of civilisational growth and prosperity. As an important cultural product, books are not lifeless entities meant to present facts and figures; they themselves embody and express the aesthetics and the values of their time and space. Their very physical form and appearance in and of itself have been exploited to improve the quality of the interaction between texts and their targeted recipients (Pearson 2008). So the meaning of a book cannot be separated from its verbal content, visual imagery, font type, cover design, look and layout, and *vice versa*. Books have their verbal content supplemented by various kinds of visual imagery. Thus, the form a book adopts in its presentation of the content has an effect on the way it will be approached, touched, and consumed. Therefore the form of a book makes it difficult for its reader to read the text objectively (ibid.). Hence, the book and its formal characteristics are not meant to provide the contents alone; rather, they mediate the meaning of the content as much as the content shapes its form. While a great deal of information is indeed communicable, valuable, and measurable, without much opinion on the receivers' part as to how it is delivered, it remains that for the nature of that knowledge to be understood in its entirety, there must be some understanding of the platform through which it is delivered and of the interpretative limitations as well as potentialities that the medium offers to the text. Thus, we may have to assume that the preference for lithographic printing in the Mappila Muslim context is more epistemologically motivated than economic, ideological, or politically inspired. So a shift from manuscript to print or changes within print itself is more than just a change in the medium. But the emphasis usually placed on printing, both in the West and in non-Western literature, has not always been helpful in comprehending the nature of these changes. Indeed, many commonly held assumptions about print have been largely dictated by those for whom the process of printing was not only the most important form of reproducing their texts, but was also the first form of mass reproduction of these texts. The story of print and the impact it had has been told and disseminated from their perspective, rather than from those of people who were affected by—what was for several generations—only one (and often minor) aspect of the reproduction of texts and traditions. Before we go into any further discussion on understanding lithography as a way of epistemology—a way of conceiving, composing, constituting, and disseminating knowledge in the Muslim community, and as a discursive statement—let us delineate the differences between typography and lithography in the Muslim context.

Typography, Lithography, and the Authorial Presence

Although they share the basic features of mass reproduction, typography and lithography are two different modes of printing involving completely different sets of technical procedures and formalities. But they also differ in their very approaches towards language and printing, with far-reaching implications at every stage of the conceptualisation and production of printed materials.[8] The time gap between the invention of these two technologies also explains their differences in some detail. Invented in 1440, typography was widely used for the mass production of texts such as the Bible, dictionaries, and grammar books. But it was with the invention of lithography in 1796 that non-textual forms, such as maps, diagrams, etc., found a place in printed materials (Proudfoot 1997). So it can be assumed that the two technologies, at least in their initial stages, were used for two different purposes. Importantly, the latter was used to accomplish many of the tasks the former technology could not undertake.

Another way to locate the difference between typography and lithography is to look at how the inventors of these technologies conceptualised their mechanics. Johannes Gutenberg, who invented typography, was a goldsmith, and Alois Senefelder, who invented lithography, was an actor and playwright. Their respective professions not only contributed to their inventions, but also to the later use to which they were put. The technical skills required for the professions of goldsmith and playwright are clearly reflected in typographic and lithographic technologies, respectively. For example, Senefelder's initial thought while tinkering with lithographic technology was to see if it could be used to reproduce musical notations.[9] Providing a very detailed account of the invention of this new medium and a course on its application in his *The Classic 1819 Treatise*, Senefelder (2005) says:

> A page of wretchedly printed music from a prayer-book, which I accidentally met with at a shop at Ingolstadt, suggested to me the idea that my new method of printing would be particularly applicable to music printing; I, therefore, resolved on my return to Munich, to go directly to Mr Falter, a publisher of music, to offer him my invention. I learned that Mr Gleissner, a musician of the Elector's band, was just about to publish some pieces of sacred music. This was most welcome news to me. Without further delay, I called on Mr Gleissner, to whom I communicated my new invention, offering him, at the same time, my services for the publication of his music. The specimens of music printing which I showed him, obtained his and his wife's highest approbation; he admired the neatness and beauty of the impressions, and the great expedition of the printing; and, feeling himself flattered by my confidence, and the preference I gave him, he immediately proposed to undertake the publication of his music on our joint account. (ibid., 13)

Situating these differences in the Islamic context, Messick (1997) delineates and distinguishes typography from lithography at different levels. He argued that while lithography retained the oral qualities of manuscript texts, typographically printed text eradicated or further distanced such traces. At the level of composition of letters for printing, while the individual letters in a word are joined naturally in an unbroken script in lithography, the words in typography were joined mechanically. This difference in the way letters are placed in words made reading lithographically produced texts more comfortable in certain times and places. These two demarcations were crucial for Arabic letters. In typography, types for letters are independently arranged. Linguists note that this is a unique characteristic of European languages and their alphabetic system (Morison 1972). In Arabic, the very nature of the script does not allow letters to be arranged independently. So an easy transition from manuscript to typography was impossible. The standard universal type form employed in typographic printing blocs also posed a barrier for the conversion of the Arabic script into letter blocs as the calligraphic art, which was the predominant form of visual art in the Islamic world, was so diverse; their specificities from region to region had already given rise to distinct local ways of writing Arabic.[10]

Another major theme that Messick (1997) brings into his analysis is the issue of impersonality and regularity in typography. Since lithography is a technique based directly on a handwritten copy, traces of the personal characteristics of one's handwriting is maintained during its reproduction; typography, however, is a process of transforming handwriting into movable type characters, thus making the text impersonal. This process of mechanical impersonalisation in typography, according to Messick, causes the technique to embody a new stylistic and technical order, and thereby a new world of textual authority. Hence, at the very basic technical level itself, lithography and typography differ, where the former attempts to maintain the styles in manuscript production while the latter seeks to abandon it completely. Therefore, lithographed books were often considered printed manuscripts, 'which allowed the age of script to continue under the guise of print' (Khalid 1994, 192). This attempt to see writing as a form of deliberate and self-conscious orality that preserves a feeling for the book as a kind of utterance might be elaborated upon to understand the lithographic modality as a mediated textual culture between orality and print in communities like the Mappila Muslims.

The concept of fixity/certainty has been a major theme of debate in print history as the classical European historiography on print culture believed that the real strength of 'the textual overtures of modernity' lay in its ability to fix the text and its meaning, or what Elizabeth L. Eisenstein (1980, 113) famously calls the preservative power of print. It is this assumption that print fixes texts and its meanings in a homogenised manner, guiding readers to imagine collectively, that acts as the core basis for Benedict Anderson's idea of imagined communities (Anderson 1991). As already indicated, this idea of fixity has been questioned by many scholars, who argue that print afforded not just one culture but many cultures (Baron, et al. 2007; Johns 1998). The lengthy errata lists attached to typographically printed books as an annexure, particularly in the early phases of printing, to alert readers to the mistakes in the printed book and their corrected versions, clearly demonstrate the ambiguities of printing, as opposed to the certainty it hoped to bring in. For scholars like Messick, these lengthy errata lists in typographically produced books, while contributing to the unreliability of the printed word, also points to the potential perfectibility, finality, and closure of the printed word. But lithography reminded its reader of the imperfect qualities of the human script and the living presence of a particular calligrapher, thus dislodging the idea that print is comfortable only with the finality (Ong 1982). This invocation of pre-print manuscript cultures and the persona they embody in lithography invokes the pre-egalitarian hierarchies of scholars, and their textual cultures, according to Messick (2013), do not qualify lithography to be an appropriate medium for an emergent 'imagined community' of homogenous and interchangeable citizens.

The relationship between printer, publisher, text, and readers also changes based on the medium used for printing (Mckitterick 2003). While the printer in lithography was always identified with individuals because of the presence of their persona at various stages of the lithographic printing process, particularly the role of scribe, the printer in typography is often identified as machines. In Muslim lithographic printing, the scriber and the author get almost the same treatment, whereas in typography, the role of the composer is completely insignificant. In lithography, both authors' and scribes' names are prominently mentioned on the very first page of the text itself.[11] Another major difference is the way authors or their publishers physically visualise their texts in their final printed form. While lithography gives publishers a sense of the final appearance of the printed book before it is actually printed, typography does not offer such a possibility. Apart from all these, lithography also offered another possibility to its consumers. While typography was more like a territorially and linguistically bound technology, lithography, through the very nature of its technology, could overcome such limitations. As a result, a lithographic printing press in one region could potentially print in any language belonging to varied ethnicities and geographies.[12]

In order to situate the arguments developed so far in the Mappila Muslims' historical-ethnographic context, the attempt now is to understand Mappila Muslim lithographic print in *longue durée*. For that, I will lay out how the idea of the book originated, developed, and was practised among the Mappila Muslim community, and how lithography as a technology meant for mass reproduction embodied such historical experiences.

Book in Mālabār before Print

The history of media in general and that of the book in particular has often been written by identifying them with printing. As already indicated, this bond between print and media had been further strengthened through a historiography that privileged the experience of the people for whom printing was the first and the most important method of textual reproduction. But how are we to write it through the eyes of communities for whom printing had been only one aspect of reproduction for several generations? The history of the Mappila Muslim community provides an exciting case in point to write such a story.

It is believed that Islam was popularised through the activities of Malik b. Dinar (d.748) in the Malabar Coast. According to historical sources, he is the first copyist known to sell the premier Muslim book, the Qur'an. Malik b. Dinar took up scribal practices as a profession for his living (Grundler 2012, 2016). Considered one of the six Basaran scholars who were without equal from Kufa, Malik b. Dinar was interested in Qur'anic readings (Pellat

2012).[13] Although there is not much historical evidence of his activities in Malabar, it can be assumed that he continued his scribal practices here as well for two important reasons:

(*i*) After the introduction of Islam in eighth-century Malabar, the growing Muslim population, evidenced through the construction of mosques throughout the Malabar Coast, led to a huge demand for copies of the Qur'an. As a professional scribe, this demand for the Qur'an might have provided Malik b. Dinar with ample opportunities to make a living in a new land.

(*ii*) Apart from the demand aspect, as a propagator of Islam in the region, it would have been mandatory for Malik b. Dinar to make the Qur'an available to everyone. Additionally, writing the Qur'an was considered the noblest profession, which would bring *baraka*, blessings from God, into one's life, both here and hereafter.

Therefore, it can be assumed that Malik ibn Dinar, who belongs to the first generation of propagators of Islam in the region, was also its first publisher. His *da'wa* activities would have set the background and foundation for later developments in the field. The growth of an Islamic scholarly and writerly culture in the region in the following decades supports this assumption. The development of a unique Arabic script for writing Arabic in the region, later known as *Ponnani lipi*, demonstrates how strong the Muslim scribal culture in the region was.[14] Since the Qur'an is the first Muslim book around which Muslim scribal culture and book production practices flourished, Muslim conceptualisation of and approach to the book in Malabar have been shaped by their view of and approach to this sacred text, the arts that flourished from it, and their function within the domain of piety.

We do not have much material evidence to understand the introduction and development of Islam in the region, except a few epigraphs. There is also not much known about the forms of communication that Muslim scholars and their followers used in the early stages of their community-building efforts in Malabar.[15] Since reciting the Qur'an, the foundational book of Islam, is an everyday obligation for Muslims, it is evident that Muslims in the region, as elsewhere, were aware of the idea of *kitab*/book.[16] The strong Muslim presence in the region by the tenth century itself can be taken as irrefutable evidence of the fact that the idea of *kitab*/book was also prevalent amongst them. Whether they knew it in the book codex format as we see it today or not is uncertain. Since no physical specimens of such books survive from before the sixteenth century, it is also not known what exactly their form and structure were. But what is known for certain is that Malik b. Dinar, as a professional copyist, knew it in the book codex format. The literary sources in Arabic written by Muslim scholars, both native and foreign—who either visited the region or propagated Islam in Malabar from the early fourteenth century onwards—provide strong evidence for the flourishing book-centred teaching and learning cultures among Muslims as early as the eleventh century. Two of the early examples in this regard are the *Qissat Shakarwati Farmad*, an anonymous Arabic manuscript, and Ibn Battutah's *Rihla*.

On visiting the mosques in Malabar, Ibn Battutah noted that he met several students studying various religious subjects at different mosques in the region, which he lists out in the travelogue. Two examples he provides in his travelogue show how systematic the mosque-centred educational activities in Malabar were: stipends for students generated through revenue from assets belonging to the mosques and the extensive superstructures of the mosques, meant to provide infrastructural facilities for students to stay in and study. In Mangalore, he notes that all Muslims knew the Qur'an by heart because the town had twenty-three schools for boys and thirteen for girls. The list of Muslim religious specialists who acted as judges, preachers, and Imams, whom Ibn Battutah met in Malabar and mentions in *Rihla*, shows the extent of the thriving scholarly culture in the region.[17] The fact that most of these scholars were foreigners trained in the then important centres of Islamic learning in Mecca, Medina, Yemen, and Baghdad once again affirms that Malabar served as a knowledge hub in the thirteenth century. Apart from their training in religious education, their names and familial genealogy (*nasaba*) reveal that most of them belonged to scholarly families whose members had produced innumerable books on various subjects and disciplines. These scholarly exchanges were not unidirectional. We also see local scholars from Malabar travelling to foreign countries, spending long periods of time with reputed scholars, and mastering religious subjects.[18] Such scholarly exchanges are obvious from the legal queries Malabari scholars had sent to the then renowned scholars and religious education centres in the Arab/Islamic world, and the questions Malabari scholars in turn received from various Muslim societies across the Indian Ocean and beyond.[19]

The Makhdoom family's arrival in the Malabar Coast from Ma'bar of Coromandel, Tamilnadu, in the early fifteenth century had further strengthened these scholarly networks. Evident from the exceptionally popular books written by Makhdoomi scholars in various disciplines of the Islamic knowledge tradition, Makhdoomi scholars' career in the Malabari mosques in various capacities had renewed the Mappila Muslim orientation towards books. They assigned books a central role in their teaching and learning activities. Many historians identify this late medieval period in Islamic societies as an age in which the notion of religious authority had been largely explicated through writing texts, the dissemination of these texts, and through the development of pedagogical practices emphasising book-based learning (Bang 2011, 91–92). Among Mappilas, the 'textualization of religious authority'[20] took place through three related developments: (*i*) The initiative taken by Makhdoomi scholars in writing and disseminating books; (*ii*) the production of a systematic curriculum for religious education in the Ponnani mosque, the then higher centre for religious education, with a list of books and authors categorised according to disciplines; and finally, (*iii*) the development of book collections in both public and private libraries.

As already noted, most of the scholars Ibn Battutah met in the Malabar Coast were members of established scholarly traditions, either through their familial genealogy or institutional affiliations. But unfortunately, their writings are not available to us, except for a few anonymous Arabic manuscripts or passing references to them in secondary literature. In such a situation, *Hidayat al-Adhkiya' ila tariq al-Awliyya*, a late fifteenth-century Sufi text authored by Sheikh Zainuddin Makhdoom Kabir (d.1522), has to be considered the oldest surviving book written by a Mappila Muslim scholar in Malabar. Since then, a series of other books have been written and circulated not only within Malabar but also throughout the Indian Ocean regions, from the East African coast to the archipelago of Southeast Asia. Among them, *Fata al-mu'in* ('The Victory of the Helper'), composed in 1574/75 by Shaikh Zainuddin Makhdoom Sagir (d.1619), deserves special mention. *Fata al-mu'in* was an attempt to interpret Islamic religious law (Sharia) in the context of the Malabar Coast, addressing their socio-religious-economic and political needs.[21]

A bibliographical analysis of *Fata al-mu'in* and *Ajeebathul Ajwiba*, a collection of *fatwas* by the same author, reveal that a huge collection of books by scholars from across the world, belonging to different schools of law, had reached the Malabari scholars long before both these texts were composed.[22] The practice of acquiring old texts has a specific connotation in Islam, and they were copied several times and circulated even to faraway places. The way *Fiqh* (jurisprudential) literature has developed historically among the Islamic scholarly communities will explain this. Since most of *Fiqh* literature is either a commentary/super-commentary/abridgment or a poetical rendering of an already existing book, the very process of writing books in Islam demands acquiring already written books. This demand for old books in Muslim scholarly circles operates not at the level of intellectual exercise alone, but is also a material demand.

The actual process of writing commentaries was always carried out in the blank spaces of books from the past. This peculiar practice has even given birth to a genre in *Fiqh* literature called *Ta'leeq*, meaning 'writing in the margins'. These commentaries on an older book in the form of page-by-page notes/comments/footnotes are then published not as an independent/separate new book, but as part and parcel of an already existing book. Thus, the resulting text is a creative blend of both the old and the new writings. A cursory analysis of old Arabic manuscripts will show that their pages are designed in such a way that the blank spaces occupy a greater portion in the books, more even than the contents. The *Fiqh* literature employs scholarly Arabic language, which demands further explanations. These two elements—language and design—of Islamic books clearly demonstrate that books in the past were actually written and designed keeping future commentators in mind. Thus, writing a book or commentary in Islam, apart from being a scholarly activity, has also been a way of relating to the past and the future of Islam.

Fata al-mu'in also belongs to this long tradition of *Fiqh* literature, starting from Imam Al-Shafi'i's (d.820) *Kitab al Umm*, which is considered the authoritative guide and foundational text in the Shafi school of law (Ponmala 2015). This foundational text itself was written down by the students of Al-Shafi'i from their notes of his teaching sessions. Thus, this book was not a written text at first, but was orally transmitted.[23] *Fata al-mu'in* was an extensive commentary/*Hashiya* on Makhdoom's own *Fiqh* compendium, titled *Qurrat al-'ayn* and composed in 1567.[24] This textual relationship that Makhdoom builds up can be tracked from the full title of *Fata al-mu'in*: *Fata al-mu'in bi sharahi Qurrat al-'ayn*.

The books written in the Malabar Coast in the fifteenth and sixteenth centuries were widely available across the Indian Ocean region and invited many commentaries and super-commentaries from later scholars from different regions and languages, as stated above.[25] What we see then is how texts travel through time and space; both horizontal and vertical or what Ho calls 'travelling texts' in Islam (Ho 2006, 116). The comradeship thus formed through Muslim textual traditions and genres are vertical as well as horizontal. This was not a characteristic peculiar to Muslim books written in Arabic alone. *Muhyadheen Mala* (1607), the first known and surviving book written in Arabic Malayalam, states explicitly in the text that it is a poetic rendering of another book, titled *Bahjathul Asrar va Maadinul Anwar* and written by Sheik Abdul Hasan Ash Shettanaufi (d.1313) two centuries ago. Such experiences in the Malabar Coast questions the proposition that the writing of commentaries was made possible for the very first time in the Indian subcontinent only when increasing numbers of classical works were becoming available to the Ulema through print, and that it was through the wholehearted embracing of printing technology that religious scholars could effectively disseminate their ideas among their audience (Zaman 1999, 2007).

Apart from such writerly cultures, several decrees in *Fata al-mu'in* also provide details about the nature of book circulation among Mappila Muslims. The *fatwa*s by Sheikh Zainudheen Makhdoom Saghir, instructing readers to correct the mistakes they found in books kept in the public library collections established through religious endowments, highlight three key aspects: the existence of diverse systems of book circulation within the community, the flexible and dynamic nature of content in Muslim books compared to the more rigid and fixed nature of texts in many other contexts, and the accessibility of libraries, which were not exclusive spaces for scholars but were open to the general public.[26] At the same time, the fatwa forbids readers from making any alterations in the content if the book with errors they found or borrowed was from a private collection, thereby invoking the question of ownership. However, if the text in question is the Qur'an, the *fatwa* continues, it is obligatory for any reader to correct the mistakes, regardless of whether it was privately or publicly owned.

Another argument in the *fatwa* deserves special attention. *Fata al-mu'in* forbids the readers from correcting the mistakes found in the Qur'an if the reader's handwriting does not match the elegance of the calligraphy in the Qur'an. Hence, it is clear that scholars paid great attention to the aesthetic and material qualities of book production. This thriving culture of book production in Malabar was assisted by two other practices related to the traditional educational system: the invention of Ponnani ink and the introduction of the art/*jild* of book binding. Over the course of time, these two practices were developed into full-fledged professions in many traditional teaching and learning circles.

To compare this Muslim book experience with that of the Christian community in the region, which had introduced printing technology in early nineteenth-century Malabar as part of their missionary activities, let us look at Claudius Buchanan, an Anglican priest who visited Kerala in 1806. When Buchanan (as cited in Arunima [2006]) showed the Christian priests in Mavelikkara a copy of the printed Syriac New Testament, they were not only astonished to see it, but were also 'suspicious of whether he was a Christian at all and what his motivations are' (ibid., 64). Further conversation between Buchanan and the priests in Mavelikkara attest to the scarcity of Christian religious literature, including the Scriptures. This absence finally forced the Christian community to agree with Buchanan's request to introduce printing technology, to translate the Bible into Malayalam, and to establish schools in each parish for Christian instruction. Buchanan's visit to Kerala was in 1806, nearly five centuries after Ibn Battutah's visit to Malabar, where he was astonished to see not the scarcity of Islamic religious literature, but its abundance in systematically organised popular religious centres, and the networking of scholars and scholarship in the Malabar Coast within the wider Muslim community.[27] This means that, at least in its early stages of introduction in the region, as opposed to other communities, print did not have many things to offer to the Mappila Muslim community—or the Muslims did not perceive a lacuna that could have been filled through technological means.

LITHOGRAPHY IN *LONGUE DURÉE*

The extent of the Mappila Muslims' familiarity with book production at least two to three centuries before Gutenberg printed the first Bible in Europe in 1456, and the prevalent sociocultural practices associated with books among them, have been explained in the previous sections. Much before the first printing press reached the Malabar Coast in the 1550s with the establishment of a printing press in Ambalakkad in Cochin by

Jesuit missionaries, the first book in the native Malayalam language was printed from Rome in 1772, and the first Malayalam book was printed in Travancore/Kerala at the CMS Press, Kottayam in 1824,[28] Mappila Muslims had produced innumerable books written on paper sheets. These were bound by stacking the sheets, fixing one edge, and gathering in thick or differently designed cover pages, and there also developed a well-organised system for their circulation both within and outside the region.[29] The *fatwas* in *Fata al-mu'in* about the private-public book collections clearly underline these facts. Obviously, there was no particular reason for Mappila Muslims to get excited when they saw the printed book for the first time, because many of the things that print offered to other communities had already been achieved through manuscripts and related arts in Muslim societies. This demands that we situate Muslim book production and their encounters with print technologies within the specific context of the Islamic knowledge tradition. How, then, are we to locate the prominence that lithography gained over typography in the Mappila Muslim printing cultures? What are the epistemological ambitions it aspired to fulfil? What specific Mappila Muslim aesthetic values did lithography embody? What does this shift in focus from what Muslims wrote/published to how they wrote/published it achieve?

Makhdoom Zagir's *fatwa* in *Fata al-mu'in*, which explicitly forbade readers from correcting mistakes in the Qur'an if their handwriting did not match the magnificence and sophistication of the calligraphy in the Qur'an, points to the aesthetic investments that Mappila Muslims made in their manuscript tradition. Their long experience with the book as a material had already contributed immensely to the development of a strong aesthetic imagination. However, it was not merely an aesthetic investment, but a theological one as well; it was the search to develop a script worthy of God's word that laid the foundation for Arabic calligraphy. The theological base for these strivings was the Qur'an's own claim with regard to its form: 'And we have arranged it in the best form' (25: 33).[30] Although this particular *ayath* (verse) specifically refers to the form of revelation, in another chapter the Qur'an introduces itself as a text written 'on honoured, exalted and pure pages, by the hands of noble and virtuous scribes' (80: 13–16). Later Qur'anic scholars, in their *tafseers* (commentaries) on these verses, also warn Muslims of the care to be taken in beautifying their ways of writing God's words.

It is a general belief among Muslims, supported by Prophetic traditions, that writing God's word will bring *barka* (blessings) to one's life. Hence, the profession of a calligrapher was not only considered a noble one in Islam, but it was also believed that the money one made from this profession was the most virtuous source of income. So it was common practice among Muslim scholars to be trained in this art, and copy the Qur'an and other books for their livelihood. What primarily motivated scholars like Malik b. Dinar to work as a copyist was this reward from God that the profession could bring into the life hereafter. Thus, this profession brought income, fame, and blessings, all together. One of the stories that Muslim scholars in Malabar often cite in their *wa'z* (pious exhortation) to alert their followers to the importance of building a career related to the Qur'an and allied activities is that of the Mughal emperor Aurangzeb. Aurangzeb, despite being the emperor of a large kingdom, worked as a copyist to meet his daily living expenses. It was this piety attached to writing God's word that offered calligraphy a flourishing future among Muslim societies across the world.

In many respects, calligraphy was to Islamic learning what painting was to the European Enlightenment. The aesthetic investment that Muslim scholars, writers, and their rulers made in this regard is underscored by what Pablo Picasso, the twentieth-century European painter, had to say about the Arabic calligraphy of his time. He said that if he had known there was such a thing as Islamic calligraphy, he would never have started to paint. 'I have strived to reach the highest levels of artistic mastery, but I found that Islamic calligraphy was there ages before I was' (Picasso, as cited in Frembgen [2010, 136]).[31] If one can explain the history of Europe through its paintings, then one can narrate Muslim history through the development of Arab calligraphy (Murad 1999). The long and rich Muslim experience with letters in their most explicit physical form played a significant role in shaping complex and diverse styles in Arabic calligraphy, and through that their attitude towards the poetics of book production.

Roper (1985) notes that in Britain, which was a relative latecomer to Arabic typography, printing in Arabic was aesthetically less satisfying with regards to clarity, legibility, and its fidelity to the Arabic *naskhi* script until the mid-nineteenth century. The reason for the Muslim rejection of the first printed copy of the Qur'an (also known as Paganino's Qur'an) in Italy in 1537 was the poor quality of its production, especially the aesthetically dissatisfying type designs. The Arabic printing experience in Britain in the 1820s showed that the situation had not changed much in Europe even after three centuries. Therefore, it was not surprising that a huge number of typographically printed Islamic books from Europe, targeting Muslim readers in the Arab/Islamic worlds, remained unsold and piled up in book shops in the Muslim cities (Proudfoot 1997). This happened despite the Ottoman government's formal initiatives to import Arabic books from Europe. The absolute absence of typographically printed books in the local Mappila Muslim libraries attached to mosques and established at the crest of the printing revolution in the nineteenth and early twentieth centuries in Malabar is also clearly indicative of the aesthetic choice that Muslims made between typography and lithography.

The Muslim choice in favour of lithography was also motivated by technical reasons. Given the particular characteristics of the script, typographic printing presses were unable to print Arabic letters. Written in the cursive script with four different forms and numerous diacritical marks, as opposed to only two forms (upper and lower cases) in European languages, typographic printing in the Arabic language posed formidable challenges for publishers as they had to purchase a minimum of 625 characters, in contrast to less than half that for European languages. Even then, the result was unsatisfactory. This situation was further worsened in the case of printing in regional Arabic scripts, like the one in Malabar. Accommodating the local Ponnani Arabic script into the existing

Arabic typographic setting was almost impossible. The situation was even more difficult if one had to print in Arabic-Malayalam, as it accommodated sounds and vocabularies from several languages, including Arabic, Persian, Tamil, and Urdu, although written with an adapted Arabic script.[32] This required not only a greater number of types, but also multiple impressions in some cases. A comparable example in this case is the story of printing music. In the initial stages, staves and notes in music were not printed, but were added by hand. When they were printed for the first time, it was done either through double impression or notes were written over the printed staves. The diacritical marks in Arabic are reminiscent of the staves and notes in music. Scholars also note that compared to printing in other languages, Arabic typographic printing caused a huge financial burden as it required a greater number of types (Bentahila 1988).

Another major reason for the Muslim disinterest in typography was that it disrupted the human presence that manuscript traditions tried to retain. In the Islamic knowledge tradition, human presence is considered of enormous value and has been retained in the Muslim educational system through several means: face-to-face learning sessions, oral instruction, long stay with a teacher, and *ijaza* and *sanad* (authentication). The manuscript culture in Muslim societies could accommodate many such elements of human linkages. The manner in which the books had been written and pages organised reminded the reader of this human linkage and its presence. The way in which books had been conceptualised, written, produced, and circulated amongst Muslim scholars aimed at perpetuating the presence of a master. We have already discussed how commentaries, super-commentaries, or abridgment of an old text had become a major convention in Islamic scholarly tradition. But the typographic print either extracted this human presence completely or minimised its impact on texts. This is particularly visible in the way commentaries and super-commentaries from previous texts had been printed in typography. While commentaries were published in manuscripts and lithography as part of an original book, thereby making the book with the commentary an original one in turn, such ways of producing books were technically impossible in typography.

What we see then is the failure of typography to meet the Muslim aesthetic expectations cultivated through their centuries-old relationship with books on the one hand and typographic technical constraints to accommodating Arabic scripts on the other. In such a situation, the obvious conclusion was that the typographic printing press was not meant for Muslim writings, and manuscript traditions were continued until lithography was invented in 1796. This Muslim attitude towards typography and their continued relationship with the manuscript tradition are also underlined by the fact that many of the typographically printed religious books were republished and circulated in manuscript form. In addition, the typographically produced texts were later painstakingly copied and lithographed several times.

In Kerala, when the first Arabic typographic printing press, Coronation Memorial Press (CMP), was established in Edava, in the erstwhile Travancore in 1936, under the patronage of the Travancore princely state, they had to use both typography and lithography in order to complete the Arabic book printing projects. This use of a mixed medium, clubbing both typography and lithography in a much-celebrated Arabic typographic printing press, points towards the failure of typography in fulfilling Muslim concerns with textual reproduction. It is reported that CMP had received orders for Arabic book printing from places as far away as Punjab in present-day Pakistan. This brings to the fore the rarity of typographic printing presses, even in Muslim-majority regions in northern India. It is a curious coincidence that the first printing press established by Christian missionaries in 1845 in north Kerala, at Illikkunnu Bungalow near Thalassery, a region with a substantial Mappila Muslim population, was a lithographic printing press and the first Arabic typographic printing press in the region was established in (Travancore) Thiruvananthapuram, where the Muslim population was comparatively fewer. It is curious when we take into account the fact that almost all the printing initiatives of Christian missionaries in India were typographic.

CONCLUSION

It is obvious that in a community where orality was privileged over other forms of communication, lithography, a printing technology initially invented to reproduce sound, was welcomed wholeheartedly. This easy acceptance of lithographic printing among Muslim communities also sheds light on the Muslim apathy towards typographic printing when it was initially introduced. Earlier studies have explained this large-scale resistance of Muslim communities towards adopting typographic printing technologies in terms of Muslim conservatism (Hitti 1970), politically motivated hostility (Bayly 1996), the fear of sacred texts falling into the hands of infidels (Lane 1890), opposition from influential *khatibs* (the scribe class), the fear about *bid'a* (illegitimate religious innovation), and the fundamental scepticism of Muslim religious authorities towards the written word and the subsequent democratisation of knowledge (Robinson 1993). The assumption then was that the introduction of printing in the Muslim world would 'turn Islam upside down, Islamic empire ripped off, institutions of religious authority flattened' (Ayers 2004, 6). But the grand technical investments made in setting up an Arabic (typographic) printing press in the sixteenth century could not accomplish the textual perfection which a normal Muslim reader would naturally expect in their reading materials. Books printed from these presses were badly produced and aesthetically dissatisfying. In a society where fascination with manuscript production had even led medieval scholars to fear the over-production of manuscript books (Hirschler 2012), where books were painstakingly copied and decorated and the art of book production was highly sophisticated, the expectations of the reading Muslim public were naturally very high. Typographic printing was incapable of meeting most of these Muslim epistemological concerns and aesthetic expectations. But lithographic printing technology could. Just as the manuscript culture had preserved the feeling for a book as a mode of utterance, lithography retained the oral qualities of written texts, associated knowledge practices, and thus the feeling for the Muslim book.

Notes

1. Arabi-Malayalam book collections in various libraries suggest that Mappila Muslims had also printed and published from various cities outside present-day Kerala. For example, the book titled *Majma, Ahkam al-Nikah*, authored by Muhammad Kalikoothi, was published from Bombay in 1883. The Yale University Library Catalogue introduces this book as; 'A metrical compendium of the Muhammadan law relating to women, accompanied by a paraphrase in arvi, i.e., Malayalam in the Arabic character.' But such books published by Mappila Muslims outside the region are yet to be studied. Bombay Government Gazettes, which documented the details of the books published from the city, are a useful source in this regard.

2. The categorisation of printed materials along the lines of typography and lithography in the library/catalogues becomes all the more important because it took many centuries for libraries and catalogues in Europe to differentiate between print and manuscript (McKitterick 2003). This intermingling of print and manuscript in libraries and catalogues can be seen as a reflection of the continued relationship between manuscripts and print, which questions the basic assumption that with print, the world of the manuscript book came to an end.

3. None of the studies on book history in India has lithography as an entry in their indexes. One of the pioneering works on Indian book history is curiously titled *Moveable Type* (2006), which explains all types of printing, but in the name of typographic moveable printing without mentioning that other forms of printing existed in India. None of the chapters in the book even recognise that there existed other forms of printing that were very prevalent in the Muslim quarters of then India. The author does discuss books printed at the Muslim-owned lithographic presses, but without acknowledging its difference from other forms of printing and its analytical value in the Muslim context.

4. In her article, Ulrike Stark (2007) mentions the arrival of the book in Hindi and Urdu, stating that it was the introduction of lithography in India in the 1820s that opened up the realm of print to Indian agency. She also briefly discusses the impact of lithography on regional language printing in India. But she stops there without exploring further the affinity between lithography and the Indian agency she talks about, or its status in the Muslim context. This is very crucial, given that the first Indians to own lithographic presses were all Muslims; Fai'z Ali in 1830 at Calcutta, the Nawab of Avadh, and Munshi Wajid Ali Khan

in 1833 (Shaw 1994, 1998). In a recent article on early Qur'an printing in colonial India, Ulrike Stark takes up this issue and discusses why Muslims considered lithography a more appropriate technology for them (Stark 2022). We may also assume that someone like Francis Robinson (1993), whose works claim to map technology and religious changes in Islam in the context of India and print, may draw on these distinctions. He noticed that such distinctions existed, as he stated that he was 'not talking of Gutenberg movable type, but of lithography. Movable type for Islamic cursive scripts was not widely used in South Asia until the twentieth century, and to this very day has not succeeded completely in displacing lithography' (ibid., 239–240). However, this does not inform his analytical framework.

Christopher Pinney (2003) also discusses lithography, albeit briefly, to appreciate its relevance in photo printing. All this indicates that the analytical value of lithography was recognised by book historians, either for its technical specificities or for its commercial importance, as it was considered a cheap, portable technique that enabled mass production. What is equally surprising is that Sheldon Pollock, in his studies on Indian intellectual and literary history, does not recognise the sociocultural value of this technology in printing Indian languages, particularly Sanskrit.

5. There have been many studies on the relevance of lithography in printing Persian texts. While Marzolph's (2001) work discusses the role of lithography in printing illustrations in Persian texts, Nile Green (2010) discusses lithography only to trace the circulation of industrial commodities as a marker of Iran's integration into an industrialising global economy. Scheglova (1999) acknowledges that lithographic printing in Muslim contexts—as opposed to non-Muslim contexts—took a different turn, but without going into the details of its specific Muslim characteristics. His discussion is limited to Persian manuscripts lithographed in Indian presses.

6. However, emerging scholarship on Muslim print culture is now addressing this oversight. For instance, Amanda Lanzillo's (2019a, 2019b) recent works examine lithography as a crucial analytical category for understanding the relationship between aesthetic decisions and sociopolitical claims of lithographic publishers in Muslim-ruled princely states, as well as its role in consolidating vernacular literary cultures in late nineteenth-century colonial India. Similarly, Muntasir Zaman (Zaman 2024) discusses the implications of lithography for editorial activities in printing Hadith literature in colonial India. For further

reading, see Baig (2023), Bar Sadeh (2023), Sievers (2023), and Sobers-Khan, et al. (2023) for more recent works that explore Muslim literary cultures vis-à-vis lithography from Indian context.

7. Stuart Blackburn's (2003) work on Tamil print is a good example of this, where he takes printed folklore as an example to demonstrate the intersection of print and orality. He reads literary practices as being set in motion by the advent of colonial printing in Tamilnadu, in opposition to orality. It is precisely because of this categorisation that he does not differentiate between typographic and lithographic printing, or dwells on the conceptual differences between them.

8. For example, a flat surface is used in lithography, as opposed to a raised surface in typography.

9. The techniques for printing music varied from time to time, and included woodblocks, movable type, and engraving. All these techniques were not only expensive and time-consuming, but also produced messier results. Printing music typographically required multiple and separate impressions for staff lines, words, and notes.

10. As opposed to the Mashriqi-Ammiyya (Eastern dialect), there developed different varieties of spoken and written Arabic, such as the Maghrebi Darija (Western Arabic). I will discuss its implication in the section on the Muslim preference for lithography.

11. In some books I have seen in Malabar, the author's name is not provided. But the scribers' names are printed prominently. This indicates that in certain cases, the scribers gained more prominence than the actual author(s) of the books. For example, in *Mawahib Al Waliyyul Akhbar Ala Jami Manakhibhi shaikhi Ali Akbar*, a *mawlid* (panegyric poetry) printed at Bayaniyya Litho Power Press, Parappanangadi, in 1971, the author is unknown, but the name of the scriber, P. Muhammad Kutty, is printed on the last page.

12. It was this possibility offered by lithography that enabled the Mappila community to print and publish their texts from various cities outside present-day Kerala.

13. Kufa and Basara were two mjaor centres of Islamic learning in the classical period and two rival centres of the early Islamic legal controversy and language debate. See van Gelder (1996) and Melchert (2014) for more details.

14. Ponnani lipi is a distinct way of writing Arabic developed in the Malabar region. This was primarily used to write Malayalam in Arabic characters. In addition to the 28 letters in Arabic, Ponnani script uses many special characters to denote Malayalam phonemes which are not

available in Arabic. For an elaborate discussion on this, see Cheerangote (2012).

15. The reason for this lack of material evidence in Mappila Muslim history has always been alluded to as the colonial approach towards Muslim subjects in the region. Muslims believe that many historical traces of their early life had been either confiscated by the Portuguese, Dutch, and later British colonialists, or had been destroyed.

16. Reciting the Qur'an is a mandatory activity for all Muslims, as it is obligatory in all the *salat* (ritual of worship), one of the five basic pillars of Islam.

17. Ibn Battutah lists the following names of Imams, preachers, or Qazis in *Rihla*: Muhammad al-Naqawri, Nur al Din Ali, Dadar al Din al Ma'bari, Husayn, Said (from Maqdashu; he studied in Mecca and Medina), Al-Sarsai (from Baghdad), Fakhr al Din Uthman, Shihab al-Din al- Kazaruni (from Persia), Fakhr al-Din, and another judge and preacher from Oman.

18. Yaqut ibn-Abdullah al Rumi al Hamawi (d.1229), a twelfth-century Arabic biographer of Greek origin, notes in his *Kitab mujamal Buldan* ('Dictionary of Countries') that he had personally seen Ibn Asakir's (d.1175) *Tarikh Dimashiq* ('History of the City of Damascus') where he had written of a Malabari *Hadith* scholar who spent a long time in Damascus.

19. Ibn Hajar al-Haytami (d.1566/67) a renowned legal expert in the Shafi School of law was approached by someone from Malabar seeking his legal opinion on the status of a *talaq* [divorce], which was pronounced with incorrect Arabic words. Al-Haytami included this question and his legal opinion in his famous collection of fatwas called, *Al-Fatawa al-Hadithiyyah*, mentioning that the question was directed to him from Malabar.

20. 'Textualization of religious authority' is used in the sense that authority no longer rested solely in a person/s, but rather in particular person's ability to write or access texts. Here charisma came to be embedded in texts and their interpretation rather than 'routinized' in the sense Weber describes.

21. In a paper presented at the International Conference on Ocean of Law in Leiden University, Panakkal (2016) analysed this sixteenth-century legal text to illuminate how Zainudheen Makhdoom Saghir took a moderate stand in his legal formulations to befit the particular sociocultural and geographic contexts of his immediate audience in Malabar.

22. Studying the bibliographical entries in a book can reveal not only the key works and scholars that the author of a particular book deals with, but also his scholarly connections, imagination, and the scholarly network that the author is a part of, or envisions to be part of. Thus, it constitutes an important source of social history. In a bibliographical analysis of *Fata al-mu'in* and *Ajeebathul Ajwiba* presented at 'Kochi 1514', an international conference on the cross-cultural networks between Central Europe, South Asia, and beyond in the early modern period, Nuaiman (2014) explored Malabari Muslim scholars' global connections in the sixteenth century. For more details on the implications of bibliographical analysis for writing social history, see Tanselle (2009).

23. This idea of writing down the master's teaching sessions into a book form is a longstanding tradition in Islam. This is also important in the following discussions. In the modern idea of reading, the reading always comes after a book is published. But in the Islamic contexts, it is a common practice that the reading/reciting of a book comes before it is written. So one might have recited a book or learned/memorised it by heart through its sound form well before it was actually written. Lambek (1990) demonstrates this as the Islamic way of approaching the text as a form of copying/reproducing the text orally. Also see Makdisi (1981).

24. For a detailed discussion on *Hashiya* and its role in the development of *Shafi fiqh* literature, see El Shamsy (2013).

25. Kooria's (2016) Ph.D. work on the expansion of the Shafi School of Law in the Indian Ocean regions traces the circulation of *Fata al-mu'in* and its commentaries in Swahili, Arabic, Malay, Tamil, and Malayalam languages. His recent work on *Fata al-mu'in*, which looks specifically at the life of the text in Zanzibar-Tanzania, shows that many East African scholars were familiar with this Malabari text. Kooria (2017) also explains that Umar bin Aḥmad bin Sumayt, the famous chronicler from the Swahili Coast, learned this text from his father, who had studied the text in Mecca with Sayyid Bakrī, who in turn has written a famous commentary on *Fata al-mu'in* called *I'ānat al-ṭālibīn*.

26. This practice of making books available in public forums was facilitated by the idea of *waqf*, an Islamic act of endowment, under Islamic law, which typically involves donating an asset for religious or charitable purposes with no intention of reclaiming the assets. A *hadith* attributed to the Prophet establishes the history and meaning of *waqf* in Islam as follows: Umar b. Khatab, the second Khalif, once asked the Prophet about the most pious way to make use of a piece of land he

acquired in Khaibar. The Prophet asked him to devote it to the welfare of human beings, in a way that it could not be sold or made the subject of gift or inheritance.

27. The Mappila Muslim approach towards the book has also been demonstrated, as Kooria (2017) observes, in the celebrations and feasts organised in coastal areas in earlier times to celebrate the arrival of the first copy of a manuscript from a distant place.

28. Although the first printing press in the region was established in the 1550s, it was not used to print Malayalam, but to print Syriac and Tamil. The first book printed from Ambalakkad in 1578 was the Tamil translation of *Doctrina Christum*. The Malayalam script was printed for the first time in a Latin book printed in the Netherlands in 1678. The book, *Hortus Malabaricus*, documented the plants in Malabar. In order to give the local names of region-specific plants, their Malayalam names were printed in the Malayalam script. It is also believed that before the publication of the first Malayalam book in 1824, a Malayalam translation of the New Testament was printed from Bombay in 1811. For more details, see Chummar (1950) and Kesavan (1985).

29. As opposed to the Hindu community's use of *ola*, a palm leaf, for writing, Muslim manuscripts were mostly written on paper.

30. The word *Tarteel*, which is used here to describe the form of the Qur'an, indicates the putting together of parts to form a strong, integral, and consistent whole. In another verse (73: 4), the word is used to specifically mean the recitation of the Qur'an by its followers, who are instructed to recite the Qur'an slowly and distinctly.

31. Also see Gertrude Stein's *Picasso* (1938), where she discusses the influence of calligraphy on Picasso's paintings.

32. In Arabic Malayalam, many of the sounds not available in the Arabic language were accommodated in Arabic scripts by adding additional diacritical marks.

References

Anderson, B. 1991. *Imagined Communities: Reflections on the Origin and Spread of Nationalism*. New York: Verso.

Arunima, G. 2006. 'Imagining Communities Differently: Print, Language and the Public Sphere in Colonial Kerala'. *The Indian Economic and Social History Review* 43 (1), 63–76.

Ayers, Bryan, S. 2004. 'Early Muslim Printing: A Study of Early Muslim Experience/s with Printing Press from 1700–1900'. Master's thesis submitted to the Graduate Faculty of The University of Georgia, Athens.

Baig, S. 2023. 'Editing and Printing the Arabic Book: Perspectives from South Asia'. *International Journal of Middle East Studies* 55 (1), 139–145.

Bakshi, V. 2006. *EUV Sources for Lithography*. Bellingham: SPIE.

Bang, A. K. 2011. 'Authority and Piety: Writing and Print—A Preliminary Study of the Circulation of Islamic Texts in Late Nineteenth and Early Twentieth Century Zanzibar'. *Africa* 81, 89–107.

Bar Sadeh, R. 2023. 'Printing Islamic Modernism: Arabic Texts for Arab and South Asian Muslims in the Early Twentieth Century'. *International Journal of Islam in Asia* 3 (1–2), 43–67.

Baron, S. A., E. N. Lindquist, and E. F. Shelvin (eds). 2007. *The Agent of Change: Print Culture Studies after Elizabeth L. Eisenstein*. Amherst and Boston: University of Massachusetts Press.

Bayly, C. 1996. *Empire and Information: Intelligence Gathering and Social Communication in India, 1780–1870*. Cambridge: Cambridge University Press.

Bentahila, A. 1988. 'Aspects of Bilingualism in Morocco'. In Christina Bratt Paulston (ed.), *International Handbook of Bilingualism and Bilingual Education*, 329–344. New York: Greenwood Press.

Blackburn, S. 2003. *Print, Folklore and Nationalism in Colonial South India*. New Delhi: Permanent Black.

Chummar, T. M. 1950. '*Malayalam patra pravartanatilekku oru tirinjunottam*' ('A Retrospect of Malayalam Journalism'). In *Malayala Manorama Diamond Jubilee Souvenir*. Kottayam: Malayala Manorama.

Eisenstein, E. L. 1980. *The Printing Press as an Agent of Change*. Cambridge: Cambridge University Press.

el Shamsy, A. 2013. 'The Ḥāshiya in Islamic Law: A Sketch of the Shāfiī Literature'. *Oriens* 41 (3), 289–315.

Frembgen, J. W. 2010. *The Aura of Alif: The Art of Writing in Islam*. New York: Prestel Pub.

Gaur, A. 1971. *Catalogue of Malayalam Books in the British Museum*. London: The Trustees of the British Museum.

Green N. 2010. 'Stones from Bavaria: Iranian Lithography in its Global Contents'. *Iranian Studies* 43 (3), 305–331.

Grundler, B. 2012. *Book Culture before Print: The Early History of Arabic Media*. Beirut: The American University of Beirut, The Margaret Weyerhaeuser Jewett Chair of Arabic.

_____. 2016. 'Aspects of Craft in the Arabic Book Revolution'. In Jürgen Renn and Sonja Bentjes (eds), *Globalization of Knowledge in the Post-Antique Mediterranean, 700–1500*, 31–66. London and New York: Routledge.

Hirschler, K. 2012. *The Written Word in the Medieval Arabic Lands: A Social and Cultural History of Reading Practices*. Edinburgh: Edinburgh University Press.

Hitti, P. K. 1970. *Islam: A Way of Life*. Minneapolis: University of Minnesota.

Ho, E. 2006. *The Graves of Tarim: Genealogy and Mobility across the Indian Ocean*. Berkeley: University of California Press.

Johns, A. 1998. *The Nature of the Book: Print and Knowledge in the Making*. Chicago: University of Chicago Press.

Kesavan, B. S. 1985. *Origins of Printing and of Publishing in Karnataka, Andhra and Kerala*. New Delhi: National Book Trust.

Khalid, A. 1994. 'Printing, Publishing and Reform in Tsarist Russia'. *International Journal of Middle Eastern Studies* 26, 187–200.

Kooria, M. 2017. 'African Jurists in Asia: Premodern Afro Asia Cnnections'. *International Institute for Asian Studies News Letter* 76, 8–9.

_____. 2018. 'Texts as Objects of Value and Veneration: Islamic Law Books in the Indian Ocean Littoral'. *Sociology* 6 (1), 60–83.

Lambek, M. 1990. 'Certain Knowledge, Contestable Authority: Power and Practice on the Islamic Periphery'. *American Ethnologist* 17 (1), 23–40.

Lane, E. W. 1890. *An Account of the Manners and Customs of the Modern Egyptians*. Cairo: The American University of Cairo Press.

Lanzillo, A. 2019a. 'Printing Princely Modernity: Lithographic Design in Muslim Ruled Princely States'. *South Asian Popular Culture* 16 (2–3), 245–252.

_____. 2019b. 'Translating the Scribe: Lithographic Print and Vernacularization in Colonial India, 1857–1915'. *Comparative Critical Studies* 16 (2–3), 281–300.

Makdisi, G. 1981. *The Rise of Colleges: Institutions of Learning in Islam and the West*. Edinburgh: Edinburgh University Press.

Makhdoom Saghir. 1983. *Fatḥ al-mu'īn bi sharḥ Qurrat al-'ayn*. Thiroorangadi: Amir al-Islam Litho Power Press.

_____. 2012a. *Islam Niyama Samhita. Fath'h-ul-Muin*, Sadiq Anwari, K. C. Ali Madani, Siddiq Irfani, and Ayyār Mammuṭṭi (trans.). Calicut: Poomkavanan Publications.

_____. 2012b. *al-Ajwibat al-Ajibat an al-Asilat al-Gharibat*, Abd al-Nasir Aḥmad al-Shafi al-Malaybari (ed.). Kuwait: Dar al-Ḍiya.

Makhdoom Saghir, Sheikh Zainudheen. 2006. *Tuhfat-ul Mujahideen fi ba'd Akhbar al-Burtughaliyin*, S. Muhammad Husayn Nainar (trans.). Calicut: Other Books.

Marzolph, U. 2001. *Narrative Illustration in Persian Lithographed Books*. Leiden: Brill.

McKitterick, D. 2003. *Print, Manuscript and the Search for Order: 1450–1830*. Cambridge: Cambridge University Press.

Messick, B. M. 1993. *The Calligraphic State: Textual Domination and History in a Muslim Society*. Berkeley, California: University of California Press.

_____. 1997. 'Genealogies of Reading and the Scholarly Cultures of Islam'. In S. Humphreys (ed.), *Cultures of Scholarship*, 387–412. Ann Arbor: University of Michigan Press.

_____. 2008. 'Sharia Ethnography'. In Peri Bearman, Bernard G. Weiss, and Heinrichs Wolfhart (eds), *The Law Applied; Contextualising the Islamic Sharia*, 173–193. London: I. B. Tauris.

_____. 2013. 'On the Question of Lithography'. In Geoffrey Roper (ed.), *The History of the Book in the Middle East*, 299–318. Farnham: Ashgate.

Morison, S. 1972. *Politics and Script: Aspects of Authority and Freedom in the Development of Graeco-Latin Script from the Sixth Century BC to the Twentieth Century AD*. Oxford: Clarendon.

Murad, A. H. 1999. *The Sunna as Primordiality*. Available at http://masud.co.uk/ISLAM/ahm/sunnah.htm (accessed December 2024).

Nuaiman, K. A. 2014. 'Zainudheen Maqdoom and Malabar's Global Connections in the Sixteenth Century'. A paper presented at the international conference on *Kochi 1514–Cross-cultural Networks between Central Europe, South Asia and Beyond in the Early Modern Period*. Berlin: Institute für Asien -und Afrikawissenschaften.

Ong, W. J. 1982. *Orality and Literacy: The Technologizing of the Word*. London: Methuen.

Padwick, C. E. 1961. *Muslim Devotions: A Study in Prayer Manuals in Common Use*. London: S.P.C.K.

Panakkal, A. 2016. 'Moderate Methods and Measures Reflected in Islamic Law of Indian Ocean Coastline of Malabar: A Study Based on Fath'hul Mueen of Sheikh Zainuddin Makhdum II'. A paper presented at conference on *Ocean of law II Islamic Legal Crossings in the Indian Ocean World*, 12–14 Dec. Institute for History, Leiden University.

Pearson, D. 2008. *Books as History: The Importance of Books beyond Their Texts*. London: British Library.

Pellat, Ch. 2012. 'Mālik b. Dīnār'. In P. Bearman, Th. Bianquis, C. E. Bosworth, E. van Donzel, and W. P. Heinrichs (eds), *Encyclopaedia of Islam*. Leiden: Brill, 2nd edn.

Pinney, C. 2003. *'Photos of Gods': The Printed Image and Political Struggle in India*. London: Reaktion Books.

Ponmala, A. K. M. 2015. *Imam Shafi*. Kozhikode: SYS Book Stall.

Proudfoot, I. 1994. 'Malay Books Printed in Bombay: A Report on Sources for Historical Bibliography'. *Kekal Abadi* 13 (3), 1–20.

_____. 1997. 'Mass Producing Houri's Moles or Aesthetics and Choice of Technology in Early Muslim Book Printing'. In Tonny Street and Peter Riddell (eds), *Islam: Essays on Scripture, Thought and Society. A Festschrift in Honour of Anthony H. Johns*, 161–184. Leiden: Brill.

Robinson, F. 1993. 'Technology and Religious Change: Islam and the Impact of Print'. *Modern Asian Studies* 27 (1), 229–251.

Roper, G. 1985. 'Arabic Printing and Publishing in England before 1820'. *Bulletin of the British Society for the Middle Eastern Studies* 12 (1).

Scheglova, O. P. 1999. 'Lithograph Versions of Persian Manuscripts of Indian Manufacture in the Nineteenth Century'. *Manuscripta Orientalia* 5 (1), 12–22.

Senefelder, A. 2005. *On Lithography: The Classic 1819 Treatise*. Meneola, NY: Dover Publications Inc.

Shaw, G. 1994. 'The Introduction of Lithography and its Impact on Book Design in India'. *Vihangama the IGNCA Newsletter* II (2).

_____. 1998. 'Calcutta: Birthplace of the Indian Lithographed Book'. *Journal of the Printing Historical Society* 27, 98–111.

Sievers, G. 2023. 'Learning How to Print in Colonial North India: The Nizami Press in Budaun and the First Urdu Manual on the Art of Lithography'. *Philological Encounters* 8 (1), 73–109.

Sobers-Khan, N., L. Uddin, and P. Basu. 2023. 'Beyond Colonial Rupture: Print Culture and the Emergence of Muslim Modernity in Nineteenth-Century South Asia'. *International Journal of Islam in Asia* 3 (1–2), 1–20.

Stark, U. 2007. *An Empire of Books: The Naval Kishore Press and the Diffusion of the Printed Word in Colonial India*. New Delhi: Permanent Black.

_____. 2022. 'Calligraphic Masterpiece, Mass-produced Scripture: Early Qur'an Printing in Colonial India'. In S. Reese (ed.), *Manuscript and Print in the Islamic Tradition*, 141–180. Berlin/Boston: De Gruyter.

Stein, G. 1938. *Picasso*. London: Batsford.

Tanselle, T. G. 2009. *Bibliography Analysis: A Historical Introduction*. Cambridge, NY: Cambridge University Press.

Zaman, M. Q. 1999. 'Commentaries, Print and Patronage: "Ḥadīth" and the Madrasas in Modern South Asia'. *Bulletin of the School of Oriental and African Studies* 62 (1), 60–81.

_____. 2007. *The Ulama in Contemporary Islam: Custodians of Change*. Princeton. NJ: Princeton University Press.

_____. 2024. 'Editing and Printing Hadith Literature in Nineteenth-Century India: Aḥmad 'Alī Sahāranpūrī and the Maṭba'-i Aḥmadī Press'. *Philological Encounters*, 20 November. Available at https://doi.org/10.1163/24519197-bja10058 (accessed February 2025).

5

Listening to the Sonorous

Digital Archiving as a Political Practice*

P. Thirumal and Sai Amulya Komarraju

Introduction

'Stories can break the dignity of a people, but they can also repair that broken dignity,' states Nigerian author Chimamanda Ngozi Adichie in her renowned TED Talk, 'The Danger of a Single Story' (2009). She argues that a singular narrative can have harmful consequences, and reflects on her initial astonishment that people of colour could 'exist in literature'. While the necessity of libraries and books for African-American children was emphasised—particularly during the height of the civil rights movement—as education was essential to overcoming the legacy of slavery (Wheeler, et al. 2004), there was also a growing recognition of the importance of *stories* and *storytelling* that neither erased children of colour from narratives (Bishop 2012; emphasis ours), nor essentialised entire communities, as Adichie so eloquently articulates.

Padma Velaskar (2012) observes that Ambedkar's vision of liberation was fundamentally tied to education, viewing it as a crucial tool not only for freeing Dalits from oppression, but also for facilitating the reconstruction of a new social order. Following

*This chapter was first published as 'Listening to the Sonorous: Digital Archiving as a Political Practice', in *Summer Hill* XXII (1), Summer 2016, published by the Indian Institute of Advanced Study, Shimla.

the Mandal Commission report and the era of liberalisation, Dalit mobilisation extended beyond securing a presence in educational institutions; it also encompassed the establishment of Dalit study centres and the active production of knowledge.

It included political and cultural activism as well. As Mary E. Hancock (2008, 14) says, the goal was to make Ambedkar a part of public memory and create 'an explicitly Dalit social and geographical space' by putting up statues and busts of him. The rise of the neoliberal regime and the proliferation of new media coincided with the post-1990s Dalit movement. As Hancock observes, transregional, transnational, and associational networks of Dalits have become increasingly effective in the past decade, employing a range of strategies. One significant factor enabling these networks is the internet.

Historically, mainstream print media, dominated by capitalist interests, has remained largely inaccessible to the Dalit-Bahujan community. Numerous studies have highlighted the conspicuous absence of Dalit-Bahujan voices in contemporary mainstream media, as well as the inadequate coverage of issues affecting them (Balasubramaniam 2011; Martand 2016). While Dalit-Bahujan intellectuals across India have made several attempts to establish their own newspapers (Aminmattu 2016; Omvedt 2006), these efforts have not coalesced into a unified anti-caste movement on a national scale.

Against this backdrop, the presence of Dalit-Bahujan voices in new media must be empirically studied, and theoretically understood. Online platforms such as *Dalit Camera*, *Round Table India*, and *Savari* serve as spaces for Dalit activism, where the material they produce does not simply show the world, but actively textualises it. Their writings do not aim to reinforce abstract, reified philosophical ideas; rather, they serve as powerful narratives that demand to be heard. In this process, digital archiving emerges as a key strategy—one that is not passive but deeply political. By producing what can be termed 'anti-caste matter', these digital archives challenge dominant hegemonic narratives and contribute to a broader political project of resistance.

The coming together of various strategies to organise activities across spheres (not just limited to politics or cultural production) is what Agamben discusses in his piece, 'What is an Apparatus':

> I shall call an apparatus literally anything that has in some way the capacity to capture, orient, determine, intercept, model, control, or secure the gestures, behaviors, opinions, or discourses of living beings. Not only therefore, prisons, madhouses, the panopticon, schools, confession, factories, disciplines, juridical measures, and so forth (whose connection with power is in a certain sense evident), but also the pen, writing, literature, philosophy, agriculture, cigarettes, navigation, computers, cellular telephones and—why not—language itself. (Agamben, as quoted in Packer 2010, 92)

Image 5.1: 'Manemma', Water painting.

Source: Anonymous, 2 October 2017.

However, this 'apparatus' falls short in describing what these revolutionary online spaces can do. Although technology itself can reify caste and re-assert the hegemonic order, it also has the potential to spring a surprise. In his introduction to *Anti-Oedipus*, Mark Seem (1983) writes that revolutionary actions intended to create new social orders cannot be based on relations of exclusion and segregation; instead, groups must multiply and connect in 'ever new ways' to keep the momentum of the movement going. The ways in which the internet is used by the Dalit-Bahujan-Adivasi men and women, and how they operate to create relations of solidarity across groups of people straddling different spheres of activities (politics, educational institutions, cultural production in the form of movement media), can only be described as, in Oliver Marchart's (2011) words, 'counter-apparatus'.

Most Dalit literary works are measured against a social emancipatory project, but certain expressions of it are unhinged and cannot be contained by the project. Dalit Studies centres largely seem to provide a negative description by reading itself against an already given political programme, but a positive description should account for the surplus meanings that certain literary and artistic works have produced.

This chapter then tries to ask, not what is caste, but what is anti-caste, and in so answering the question, draws from scholarship that explores body and embodiment, caste, and new media, to look at digital archiving as a political practice, and how technology facilitates this archiving. We argue that digital media has a way of lending itself to both the sensible and the intelligible, in contrast to print media, which privileges the intelligible over the sensible. The general economy of the intelligible is to produce and preserve the being, while the economy of the sensible alerts us to the economy of expenditure and the annihilation of being—caste being by writing out[1] the body (not to be confused with writing the body out). This anti-caste archival practice presupposes the Dalit body as a thinking, agential, and form-imposing matter. Digitality as a contemporary technic presupposes contingency and does not respect hegemonic pasts and historicities. The haunting dream of the anti-caste project is to listen to the 'casted' body and the fragrance of the casteless body, where the dream is not considered an apposite of waking life. The new media theoretically offers this place to experiment with the excription of the caste body, and to secure a new set of civilisational apparel. What sometimes gets worked out as anti-caste matter is a nakedness of caste, its body, and its mind.

To think caste and to live caste are two different phenomena and conventional social science fails to provide an embodied understanding of caste, caste oppression, or caste experience. Lived experiences and lived bodies form the basis for a phenomenological understanding of caste, rather than a disembodied engagement with it. It is true that some critical work has demonstrated the mutual exchange between a disembodied, philosophic reading of caste and an embodied understanding of it. This chapter, while pursuing the latter proposition, seeks to highlight the acoustic somatic rather than the 'touch' variable integral to caste dynamics (see Guru and Sarukkai 2012). More expansively, the chapter has argued that the acoustic somatic encompasses touch as well. A reading of the Dalit-Bahujan digital archives, therefore, should be read as offering anti-caste material that destabilises majoritarian religious identity, or identities of any kind.

ARCHIVING THE BODY

As French historian Jacques Le Goff (quoted in Cook 1997) suggests, archiving and archival politics has typically been about those in power who therefore could speak, excluding those who were/are forced to remain silent not only in public life but also in archival records, thereby creating histories that offer only one part of the story. Textual archiving, amongst other things, is based on the male principle and is predominantly about preserving the manuscript, wherein the matter is seen as an inert container. This matter lacks what is referred to as *spontaneous morphogenesis*, or, to put it simply, there is matter, and form is then imposed on it. It is made to seem as though matter does not possess the ability to produce a form on its own, a thought that is inherent in Western philosophy. Minorities, in this context, have been viewed as matter, as incapable of speaking for themselves, and instead forced to remain voiceless. The archives of minorities are about unlocking this potential of matter and providing a synthesis of their creative impulse in the form of a literature replete with biographical accounts, their experiences and desires, as well as a rewriting of histories that have hitherto not been allowed expression or a place in the archives.

WILL TO ARCHIVE

Colonialism led to the growth of Indology. Nationalist discourses critically engaged with Indology and sometimes with a more nuanced reading of this archive, but they still limited themselves to a certain closed reading of the Brahminic texts. In recent times, scholars like Sheldon Pollock have tried to present a longitudinal intellectual history of the Indic civilisation. This effort has resulted in a variegated archive, and they tend to refer to textual sources that come from a tradition that dissents from the Brahminic kind and are suggestive of an embodied understanding of the world and the self. It is the force of this embodied understanding and conduct that was discussed by the Dalit-Bahujans during colonial times and, more recently, on social media. The ancient strictures on listening, speaking, and touching prove that the senses played a crucial role in both articulating and violating the natural distribution of senses across the space of the body. The caste body was organised around a particular regime of the senses.

How does one understand the embodiment of caste? Among other things, such a question raises the issue of caste as a sensibility, which works on the tension between viewing caste as sense and caste as intelligible. It refers to the presentation of caste, or how caste appears in the form of food, clothing, sexuality, religion, relationships, and aesthetics, including the orientation of caste subjects towards these objects, people, and ideas. Touch has been the most important and visible sense that scholars have foregrounded in their examination, but hardly anybody has looked at caste as a form of listening, which is both intelligible and sensible.

In this chapter, we focus, among other things, on how Dalit-Bahujans bring their sense of body and bodily sense to critically deconstruct the Brahminic-Savarna form of presentation and orientation of the self towards both itself and the world at large (for example, 'Just Savarna Things', a Facebook page, pokes fun at people who claim to be 'casteless'[2]). More specifically, this intervention focuses on the form of listening that orients Dalit-Bahujans towards a sonorous world that has a resonant structure, and shows how this form enables them to exit the caste world even as they remain disciplined and contained by the cultural category of caste. At certain historical junctures, the resonant structure is powerfully articulated through their performative arts. The *Dandora* or the drum played a crucial part, not in playing out its traditional role of alerting Brahminic ears to the approaching and polluting untouchable, but as a tool for widening the democratising of the Dalit movement itself.[3]

The impossibility of assigning a will or purpose to these performative cultures attests to their ability to unhinge themselves from historical and cultural contexts. The indeterminacy of sense and the determinacy of reason play upon each other and, more often, play into each other and produce the experience of caste—and occasionally, an exit from caste. Computability has the potential to engage with infinite phenomena, but the relationship is one of governing rather than knowability. Lack of knowability is what produces indeterminacy. This indeterminacy of sense, coupled with the indeterminacy of the medium, is what propels the will to archive among the Dalit-Bahujan English-speaking chatterati, who process minutely the Brahmin-Savarna presentation. Presentation refers to a spontaneous act of the Savarnas, whereas representation or content would point towards a deliberate form of action or expression.

Affective Disposition and the Will to Archive

It appears that cultural memory is fraught and unlikely to handle a hostile past. It is in this context that the will to archive among the marginalised goes deeper than merely creating a storage facility. After all, storing grains—vis-à-vis knowledge—requires technologies that keep it safe from hoarders, pests, smugglers, and the corrupt, as well as revenue officials and intemperate and impoverished peasants. The State is the final arbiter of producing, storing, and distributing grains. The market may be considered another name for the State. Dalit-Bahujan women have traditionally been associated with planting, harvesting, and storing grains, of building the edifice of the traditional and the modern State, of producing the conditions that enable the creation of monuments and texts, of building bridges between experience and thought. In modern times, the foundation of nation-building, in the form of massive dams, flyovers, railway lines, concrete cities, and industrial and physical infrastructure, has been laid down by these women. Both the Nehruvian dream of dams and bridges, which Jawaharlal Nehru referred to as the temples of modern India, and the neoliberal dream of gated communities and concrete jungles that form the phallic, capitalist, Savarna economy are based on these kinds of labour.

Dalit-Bahujan women's affective disposition towards procuring, storing, and retrieving experience as knowledge may also be addressed as the will to archive. Both the capitalist economy and the micro-physics of work become the disciplining and controlling structures of repressive representational regimes. Further, it denies the Dalit-Bahujan body the power to act and think in order to transform the past, present, and the future. This is why stories and dances are enacted. We are suggesting that any translations of Dalit-Bahujan poets, mystics, or literary figures must be read in a manner that opens up a temporality that is less alienating. This time that is produced may be what Georges Bataille calls the Sovereign, an unattached time that is not tied either to a burdensome Brahminic past or a projected emancipatory future (Irwin 1993). It speaks of the immediacy of the instant. Is there a moment which offers an intensity for exiting a 'casted' body and mind and surrendering oneself to the infinite randomness of the world? Needless to say, the distinction between ideas and objects, histories and enactments, techniques and technologies does not pose serious issues.

This processing of matter requires knowledge, skills, and an affective disposition. The will to archive is about the need to capture this imperceptible process, one that is transient, resonant, and poetic, and extremely difficult to capture because it is the will to archive the Dalit-Bahujan being herself. This will to archive entails listening to the process of materiality through which the Dalit-Bahujan self is created and continuously processed. This processed self reimages casteless horizons, even as it inhabits the oppressive, negating, dominant casted horizon and embodied Brahminic structures that regulate horizontal thinking (where vertical thinking is about the communion between humans and God or supreme authority, horizontal thinking is about the communication amongst humans).

The Nature of the Archive

Archives, by their very nature, offer the trace of an event; they do not speak of the perceiving senses but of the perceived meaning of the event. It is the presentation rather than the content that the senses concentrate on; the singing, rather than the song. The perceived meaning is a hegemonic Savarna construction which also fits the capitalist logic. The perceiving senses are unavailable for examination through these hegemonic meaning systems, as they work on the model of a sonorous structure where the shapes and sizes of sounds are not immediately available through the act of listening. A Savarna-capitalist logic works towards constructing an intelligible world, while the Dalit-Bahujan aesthetics work towards the foregrounding of the sensible. The sensible refers to the presentation of a thing, an object, or a people, whereas the intelligible refers to the content of a thing, object, or a people.

Modernity drives a wedge between presentation and content and the prevailing Savarna logic reinforces the conceptual over the embodied. Scientific rationality works alongside political rationality, including religious faith, to erode the search for an artistic world that is not based on exalted human purposes or actions.

Perhaps the will to archive on the part of the Dalit-Bahujan aims to disrupt this emphasis placed on the intelligible over the sensible, and the conceptual over the embodied. Issues like the affirmative policy do not always make economic or rational sense, but they do possess a social, ethical, and an embodied rationality. The caste system does not allow for some kinds of resonances: listening for, listening to (which the caste system allows, in certain instances), and listening with (which is one of the possibilities, but is disallowed by the Savarna regimes of listening). The promise or the hope of this will to archive, situated in the realm of the aesthetic and the sensible, is to allow for *listening* and *speaking* with, instead of the dominant disposition of the Savarna to merely hear a sound-object, as the Dalit is often thought of, and to *listen* to the other regimes of the senses.

Textual archives (which reduced minorities to matter incapable of expression), now available as *digital archives*, should be seen as spaces where matter can reveal itself, where matter and form are interlocked, and where one is not privileged over the other. Archives today cannot simply be read as a manifestation of the dominant order, but as spaces of transformation of matter which can be explosive. The differentiation between the online and the offline or '*real*' worlds, referred to as the online disembodiment thesis, has long been rejected by digital culture scholars. Research on cybercrime, illness forums, and rape survivor blogs are often cited as clear indications that one's body cannot be transcended in the 'online worlds'. Such literature, although relevant and important, is predominantly framed around crime and violence (we acknowledge that offline hierarchies are often played out online as well), and do not consider how crucial *body* and *embodiment* are for the (liberatory) politics of the marginalised, who are 'most commonly associated with bodies' (Dumler 2003).

Digital archives provide a platform for people to create and curate spaces for themselves, and need to be thought of in terms that go beyond just representation and content.

THE OCULAR AND THE SONOROUS

From colonial calendar art to postcolonial modern commercial cinema, public culture in mainland India has been heavily influenced by the ocular-centric media. In both colonial and postcolonial modernity, the cultural expression of elites has largely been visual, while that of the masses is aural and oral. For instance, Anindita Ghosh's (2006) work on the Battala press discusses the valorisation of the printed word, its silent reading, and the use of what was deemed *proper and high culture* by the *bhadralok* (upper-caste people of Bengal), as opposed to the *basar* songs that were considered low culture and associated with lower castes and Muslims. Similarly, as Farina Mir points out, it is impossible to miss the orality or the performative aspect of Punjabi literature, because genres like the 'quissa, var, dole, kafi … were not meant for silent reading' (Mir 2010, 91).

Interestingly, in Northeast India, musical traditions have been foregrounded as public culture rather than visually orientated cultural artefacts like cinema, painting, or sculpture. Aizawl has emerged as the transnational musical centre for the production and dissemination of Northeastern music to neighbouring countries like Myanmar and Bangladesh. But even the narrative of Indian cinema, as Sheila Nayar points out, finds itself moored in a 'non-writing' mindset that uses motifs and techniques that are specific to oral cultures and storytelling (Nayar 2004). Ajith Kumar (2013), in an interview, discusses how Nadan Pattu (which literally means local songs, and is therefore associated with low castes and culture) moved into the public and urban spaces because of the Malayalam cinema industry. Nayar's assertion, then, is that it is important to focus on invisible orality because the subaltern may find representation through it.

This focus on sonority in a public culture that is ocular-centric, the main thrust of this chapter, then begs the question: If the privileged or the upper caste can listen, and if they do listen, then what kind of listening is valorised and what is disallowed? This chapter is not an exhaustive study of the portal, its users/readers, or a scrutiny of its content or moderation of content. Rather, it will study, as an example of a digital archive, *Savari*—an online collective started in 2012 by Adivasi, Bahujan, and Dalit women to share their stories. Many of the translations carried in Savari testify to the aforementioned distinction. The Tamil Dalit colonial newspapers like Iyothee Thass' *Oru Paisa Thamizhan* spoke of an experiment with newspaper genres, a domain that was monopolised by (Savarna) public reason. This ambition of Dalits in colonial India to produce news and demand that it be read and heard by others was met with little success. Also, technology of print did not provide the possibilities that digital media allows for Dalits in contemporary times. Shaping the senses of the upper caste was an audacious claim; but the claim was nevertheless made. The Dalit digital archive may profit from the inclusion of these formal academic research materials (cited in the text). It need not see these materials as antagonistic just because they have been produced by caste Hindus.

Savari: A Brief Profile

Savari is a space for Adivasi, Bahujan, and Dalit women to share their stories, converse with men in their communities, and comment on current issues. To quote:

> We are adivasi, bahujan and dalit women. Here we share our thoughts about our lives and the society we live in, including conflicts with the self, family and community. These are perspectives from our history, and our dreams for the future. Here we are in conversations with each other, with the men from our communities, and others. Inspired by our foremothers, the free spirited, knowledge bearing,

community healers of the Saura people, this space is named Savari. (Savari group: Authors and Organizers)

As evident in their 'We Are' section, they describe themselves as the 'authors' of their stories and 'organizers' of the website, archiving and creating alternative web-histories that take into account a multitude of voices, including Dalit, Bahujan, Tribal, and other marginalised groups. They publish personal stories that are self-reflexive, film reviews, reflections on current news stories and laws, Dalit literature and poetry translated into English, republish pieces that originally appeared in *Round Table India* or *Countercurrents*, combining materials from *Dalit Camera* to supplement what has been written.

Recently, literary historians have touched upon some aspects relating to caste and gender issues, but they have rarely paid exclusive attention to anti-caste texts. *Savari* is a robust Dalit-Bahujan online portal and has varied content with a large number of committed contributors and users/readers, and their greatest strength perhaps lies in the readers' allegiance to source loyalty (an anti-caste disposition). Perhaps for the first time, technology has allowed Dalit-Bahujans to collect, process, and store information in the form of digital archives, but Indian scholars are yet to attempt a deeply theoretical study of this interesting development in cyberspace.

Savari is a repository of knowledge and can be read as a site of what Hugo Gorringe, et al. (2007) refer to as the theoretical 'transformative capacity of embodiment'. It can be extended further to include the *transformative capacity of caste*, because caste is embodied in specific ways, as will be seen in the next section.

Bourdieu and Foucault: A Gorringean Analysis of Embodiment of Caste

This section borrows heavily from Gorringe's works on the embodiment of caste and the transformative capacity of embodiment. To explain how this transformative capacity can be extended to caste as well, we go back and forth between two important texts authored by Gorringe. Gorringe and Rafanell (2007, 100), in their essay titled 'The Embodiment of Caste: Oppression, Protest and Change', suggest that Bourdieu's 'caste' habitus helps in understanding how caste is internalised, and agency in such a set-up is only a 'by-product of this structural internalization'. As William H. Sewell, Jr. (1992) notes, lack of agency is inherent to the concept of habitus, except perhaps in structural crises where reflexive agency is only a slip and not a permanent state. But Gorringe and Rafanell (2007) find it useful to understand how the caste habitus shapes both the physical and the psychological practices of respondents in their empirical research.

In addition, they write that Michel Foucault's *Political Anatomy* balances Bourdieu's caste habitus, and shows that both power and agency emerge 'in and through interaction'. There is a stark contrast between the two in terms of how they think of bodies: for Bourdieu, the body is unaware of itself as the site of power struggles and the rules of the game, while for Foucault, the body is aware of the rules of the game and how it is being manipulated by those who create truth regimes. This can explain how caste operates as the structuring force at the macro level—which is one's caste habitus, on the one hand—and how it is re-reproduced through interaction on the other, and therefore for Gorringe and Rafanell (2007, 102), a combination of the two helps to explain how individuals and their micro-level interactions ultimately 'sustain the macro-level phenomena' of caste.

While there are multiple instances of *Savari* women speaking about the way caste is internalised in the caste habitus, they also write:

> It is caste system that disciplines and socializes bodies. Thus, the different stereotypes for bodies for 'upper' and 'lower' caste people. Traditionally these bodies were bound by their assigned jobs which are considered to be their duties. When the boundaries are transgressed, when they are visible in spaces which are otherwise meant to be for 'upper' castes, violence is not always explicitly physical but rather perpetuated through symbols and actions that would assert

> the authority of 'upper' castes by constantly humiliating the 'lower' castes. This maintains the existing status-quo and power structure of caste. This is done by distinguishing US from THEM; 'upper castes' from 'lower castes' through various symbols, of which body and skin tone is an important one. (Meenu, *Savari*, 17 July 2015)

As Gorringe and Rafanell (2007) note, caste is not just 'a state of mind' but is constituted and reproduced through interactions. In the quote above, Meenu also directs us to think about how, even while the macro-level social institution of caste 'disciplines and socializes bodies', one is also aware of the actions that help those in power to reassert their authority and provide sanction to certain kinds of performances over others.

In one sense, sharing would mean 'having', and on another level, it is also being with, and not merely as a possession. One of the important characteristics of the new media is that it provides a dignified address to its participants. Many of the educated Dalits come from rural or ghettoised urban Indian pockets. The anonymity provided by the virtual address obscures the otherwise marked body or spatial/physical location that Dalits generally inhabit. Theoretically, digital media disallows humiliation on the basis of one's address—it is an unmarked body and an unmarked domicile. The new media has the potential to create a form of sharing that obscures formal possessions and entitlements and allows for sharing or being with. The Rohith Vemula movement was based on this kind of sharing.

The Transformative Capacity of Body, Embodiment (and Caste?)

Gorringe's essay, 'The Transformative Capacity of Embodiment' (2007), also makes visible how bodily practices can lead to 'resistant modalities of agency', and that bodies have the potential to subvert and transform power structures. Gorringe contends that the biological body does not just disappear in various contexts and that this recognition of the biological body need not necessarily be essentialist. It can lead to an awareness that the biological posits the social just as the social posits the body, co-constituting each other, where the biological and the social cannot be seen as separate and one is not privileged over the other.

While the social shapes these bodies in specific and marked ways, affecting both physical and psychological practices, the awareness of how certain disciplining happens can lead to acts of resistance that transforms the social, and therefore both the bodies and the social are always in a state of flux, always in the process of co-constituting each other, thereby offering an opening for transformation (theoretically, at least).

Bodies that Do Not Belong

Since the mainstream largely ignores alternative histories and systematically silences the voices of the 'others', women writing for *Savari* will themselves into being, thereby creating techno-corporeal (inter)subjectivities that are individual and, due to their identification with committed readers, also intersectional and collective in nature:

> These [mainstream] most often end up reinforcing the savarna hegemony by appropriating voices of the underprivileged. It is in this context that the internet and social media gave a scope for breaking away from such narratives and became influential in making heard multiple voices which were otherwise kept away from mainstream discourses. (Meenu, *Savari*, 17 July 2015)

Also, consider:

> … the step to share your lived experience with your community through the self-determined platform of Savari. This is such a powerful story that some of us can identify with as we intersectionally navigate caste, class, religion and the politics of identity, culture and economics in the broader frame of caste reservations and Indian social milieu. (Noel Didla comments on Favita Dias's post, *Savari*, 28 November 2015)

It is imperative for the Dalit-Bhajuan community to gather themselves in the cyberworld because the political economy of creation and dissemination of information in the virtual world does not present problems of production as seen in the capitalist print economy. Although it is critical to note that given the problems of access in a developing economy like India, only the educated, university dwelling Dalit (more men than women) have access to the internet and the possibilities it offers, spaces like *Savari*, though a rarity, provide Dalit-Bahujan-Adivasi women with a crucial platform to voice their opinions.

Their writings make evident the fact that their corporeality, 'embodiment of caste', and their voices are not taken into account by the mainstream, and that this becomes the very reason for their online presence. Therefore, as Richardson and Harper (2002) write, it is 'impossible to separate theories of technology from theories of embodiment', despite the insistence of disembodiment theorists that technology offers closure for the body and an opening into the infinite possibilities of the mind and virtual reality, re-asserting that the mind is separate and privileged than the body.

These archives are important

> [b]ecause the explosive pertinence of a remembered detail may challenge repressive or merely complacent systems of prescriptive inventory of history [typical archiving based on male principle is a part of such an endeavour], memory, like the body, may speak a language that reasoned enquiry will not hear. (Davis and Starn 1989, 5)

ANTI-CASTE ARCHIVES

'Anti-caste' refers to both being and becoming human (Guru and Sarukkai 2012). It refers to a transformation on two levels: at the level of a theoretical understanding of emancipation from caste (as given in the provisions in the Indian Constitution) and an embodied awareness and inner transformation (through expressive arts like literature, performative arts, and spatial arts).

Indeed, these are not mutually exclusive spheres; however, such a distinction makes us aware that anti-caste is not merely a product of the mind but has deeper embodied moorings (Wakankar 2010). *Savari*—and various other Dalit forums online—offer a space where discussions include all three overlapping categories, that is, the constitutional rights and legal provisions provided for the marginalised, their experiences of marginalisation, Dalit literature and art, and an effort to bring to light the scholarly contributions made by Dalit thinkers.

Spaces like *Savari* transport us into different worlds where the past and present intertwine, where there is space for the sensible (encompassing the intelligible) and the performative. The 'authors and organizers' bring with them the historicity of experience, which is at once about the past and yet about the present, and in many instances timeless, and therefore relevant at all times. For instance, consider Jupaka Subhadra's poem '*Kongu*' (the end of a sari), translated into English by Niren Biddie, and published on *Savari*, where she says:

> Kongu isn't just a rag; she's my silent companion, absorbing my sweat and grief, a shield against aggression, a cradle for my children, and a comfort in my labours. In the fields, she spreads out like a bed for my tired body, while at home, she absorbs the first touch when my husband reaches out in love or anger. She shields me from the elements, cradling my eye babies when in grief, and bears the weight of my daily grind. Yet, through all this, she never rests, never falters—my kongu, the quiet witness to my life's struggles and triumphs. (*Savari*, 3 March 2012)

How does one read the immeasurable life of Kongu through the finite perceiving senses of Subhadra? At a time when women from the upper castes were eager to burn their sarees as a feminist gesture (see Zare and Mohammed 2012), this Dandora poetess un-weaves the gift and the limitless giving of the Kongu to materially, socially, and culturally outcast women. Unlike Brahminic strictures that do not allow all the senses to participate in abandon, the Kongu produces a casteless sensibility that allows the Dalit woman to gather herself, her sense of self, and her sense of the world together. The Kongu allows the Dalit woman to touch herself in a sensuous and desirable way, to protect and care for her body through severe weather, it delays her hunger and communicates deeply with her flesh, which enfolds both the sensible and the intelligible.

The Kongu that wraps the personhood, like a mother, caring for the body and 'eye babies', and unwraps to carry a day's ration, is alive. Subhadra's poem is evocative; the Kongu is not merely an instrumental object used for representational purposes, but moves out of a world of subject and object dualism and enters a world where one can hope for a glimpse of things in their totality. Such a possibility can be suggested here because it consciously moves away from the culturally embodied arrangement that caste provides, and reveals a much more basic, primal arrangement.

The Kongu, described variously as 'a tool, companion, a comrade-in-drudgery', suggests an inexhaustibility to the kind of relationship one can experience with 'objects', but for that to happen, one needs to go beyond perceiving them as mere objects. Subhadra's Kongu, an object of ire for (upper-caste) feminists (Zare and Mohammed 2012) because the nationalisation of women was irrevocably tied with 'covering the female body in layers of discourse through layers of cloth' (Srinivasan 2011, 153), draws attention to the fact that these mundane objects have a history and a relationship with people that move beyond the objective-representational framework.

Isolation or alienation of the *things and objects* marks the caste arrangement, where objects are thought of in terms of their use-value and representation. Both the sacred and sacrosanct and the undesirable bodies that do not belong are, in a Brahminic tradition, not allowed to be experienced in a sensorial way. Curiously, the distance between objects and people is a consequence of its being either sacred or not. But this reading of Kongu effectively disrupts this sort of arrangement, where a distance-less reading of the Kongu implies that one can touch the life of the object and, at the same time, the object can touch your life as well. In doing so, it also redefines the Savarna understanding of use and reflection.

Distance is produced to keep away certain impurities connected with the biological functioning of the human being; but then, it is not limited to these impurities alone, but is a general mode of receiving the experience by the touched (Savarna).

It is an intimate relationship that Subhadra shares with her Kongu, a life-force that expands and shrinks as needed, but always touches the body, the way it extends itself into worlds of labour and caring, but always remains intimately connected with the body, as though, even while the life-hardened Kongu provides shelter and life to the wearer, it also derives its energy from the very body it hugs. This to and fro between the sensible and the intelligible (and it is important to note that one can never say which is more important) is to be listened to with the being. To see/read the archive is to listen with the being; it is not merely hearing. 'Speaking with' would require an openness to listen to an immeasurable other. It is not an individual response to Brahminical supremacy and caste, but an anti-caste thought geared towards a secular criticism of casteism; not caste as religious or spiritual but caste as deprivation, lack of access and rights; an anti-caste thought that can counter caste as a modern category that has been institutionalised in modern spaces such as universities and the media.

Such a reading of Kongu reveals to us that, although determined by caste, cannot be contained by caste alone.[4] Just as 'untouchability is always in excess of its description' (Guru 2009, 49), so is this reading of objects and things. The realm of the sensible (which is also intelligible, but not vice versa) offers us infinite possibilities. It cannot be understood through the intelligible alone, since it is, by its very nature, situated in the realm of the sensible and the performative, and can be experienced in all its rich, sensuous magnificence, disclosing to us that the sonorous precedes and exceeds caste. We are talking about a sense and an experience that not only determines, but also exceeds caste.

Conclusion

We began this chapter by emphasising the importance of stories—of increasing visibility through being heard—and the role of digital spaces in enabling the Dalit-Bahujan community to highlight their exclusion from mainstream media. We also stressed the significance of listening to the sonorous, the often invisible oral traditions. This chapter does more than discuss the Dalit-Bahujan presence online; it explores the interplay between the poetic and the prosaic. It examines the relationship between new media and the intelligibility of print textuality, as well as the tension between Dalit women's poetic, transformative projects and the Brahminic philosophical tradition. This struggle is not only a fight against dominant forms of knowledge, but also an effort to preserve the capacity for the sensible. The productive tension between the sensible and the intelligible perhaps best characterises the anti-caste digital archives.

Should we restrict the meaning of this presence—this poetic presence, rather—to the modern transformative project, or should it be treated as a project in itself? It is against this second and broader social project that we read 'Kongu'. Subhadra's 'Kongu' is simultaneously a project to address both the inscription and excription of the 'casted' body, and transgresses caste not through a deliberate act but through a non-coercive, non-categorical way of addressing and describing the world. It is a form of interpretation that is not confined to producing the meaning of the world.

Notes

1. Jean Luc Nancy theoretically posits a condition of not only inscription of the body but also the excription of the body in his work, *Corpus* (2008 [1992]).

2. See https://www.facebook.com/justsavarnathings/ (accessed December 2024). Their 'About me' section reads: *We, the casteless people*. They also have an X handle, @justsavarna, and often use #justsavarnathings

3. Sundar Sarukkai's (2009) interesting phenomenological work on the drum seems to posit a Brahminically orientated understanding of the sensible; however, this is an effort to read the Dalit-Bahujan sensibility from the bottom upwards.

4. The lived life of objects is in excess of the social, economic, political, or philosophical engagement with that object. Hence, caste or patriarchy cannot contain the diverse manifestations of things in the world—this approach to objects is generally referred to as the ontology of things. Digital media, as a contemporary technic of mediation, refuses to be reduced to the affects that it produces—political, economic, or cultural.

References

Adichie, C. N. 2009. 'The danger of a single story', TEDglobal. Available at https://www.ted.com/talks/chimamanda_adichie_the_danger_of_a_single_story (accessed December 2024).

Aminmattu, D. 2016. 'Where are the professional Dalits in the media?' *Round Table India.* Available at https://www.roundtableindia.co.in/where-are-the-professional-dalits-in-the-the-media/ (accessed December 2024).

Balasubramaniam, J. 2011. 'Dalits and a Lack of Diversity in the Newsroom'. *Economic and Political Weekly* 46 (11), 21–23.

Bishop, R. S. 2012. 'Reflections on the Development of African American Children's Literature'. *Journal of Children's Literature* 38 (2), 5.

Cook, T. 1997. 'What is Past is Prologue: A History of Archival Ideas Since 1898, and the Future Paradigm Shift'. *Archivaria: The Journal of the Association of Canadian Archivists* 43 (February), 17–63. Available at https://archivaria.ca/index.php/archivaria/article/view/12175 (accessed December 2024).

Davis, N. Z., and R. Starn. 1989. 'Introduction'. *Representations* 26, 1–6.

Dumler, N. L. 2003. 'The Harm of Neglecting Embodiment: How Biomedical Ethics' Neglect of Bodies and Context Hurts Women and Minorities'. Ph.D. dissertation, University of Tennessee-Knoxville.

Ghosh, Anindita. 2006. *Power in Print: Popular Publishing and the Politics of Language and Culture in a Colonial Society, 1778–1905*. New Delhi: Oxford University Press.

Gorringe H., G. Haddow, I. Rafanell I, E. Tulle, and C. Yuill. 2007. 'The Transformative Capacity of Embodiment'. *Edinburgh Working Papers in Sociology* 32, University of Edinburgh.

Gorringe, H., and I. Rafanell. 2007. 'The Embodiment of Caste: Oppression, Protest and Change'. *Sociology* 41 (1), 97-114.

Guru, G. 2009. 'Archaeology of Untouchability'. *Economic and Political Weekly* 44 (37), 49–56.

Guru, G., and S. Sarukkai. 2012. *The Cracked Mirror: An Indian Debate on Experience and Theory*. New Delhi: Oxford University Press.

Hancock, M. E. 2008. 'The Formal City and its Pasts', Part 1. In *The Politics of Heritage from Madras to Chennai*. Bloomington: Indiana University Press.

Irwin, A. C. 1993. 'Ecstasy, Sacrifice, Communication: Bataille on Religion and Inner Experience'. *Soundings* 76, 105–128.

Kumar, A. A. S. 2013. 'Caste in Cinema and Music: The Kerala Experience'. *Round Table India*, 22 June. Available at https://www.roundtableindia.co.in/caste-in-cinema-and-music-the-kerala-experience/ (accessed December 2024).

Marchart, O. 2011. 'From Media to Mediality: Mediatic (Counter-) apparatuses and the Concept of the Political in Communication Studies'. In L. Dahlberg and S. Phelan (eds), *Discourse Theory and Critical Media Politics*, 64–81. Basingstoke: Palgrave Macmillan.

Martand, K. 2016, 'Missing the Story: Lessons for Indian Journalism from Dalit Mobilization Online'. *Caravan*, 1 March. Available at http://www.caravanmagazine.in/perspectives/missing-the-story-lessons-indian-journalism-dalit-mobilisation-online (accessed December 2024).

Mir, F. 2010. *The Social Space of Language: Vernacular Culture in British Colonial Punjab*. Berkeley: University of California Press.

Nancy, J.-L. 2008 [1992]. *Corpus*, Richard A. Rand (trans.), *Perspectives in Continental Philosophy*, John D. Caputo (series ed.). New York: Fordham University Press. Available at chrome-extension://efaidnbmnnnibpcajpcglclefindmkaj/http://pdf-objects.com/files/INDICES-nancy_corpus.pdf (accessed December 2024).

Nayar, S. J. 2004. 'Invisible Representation: The Oral Contours of a National Popular Cinema'. *FILM QUART* 57 (3), 13–23.

Omvedt, G. 2006. *Dalit Visions: The Anti-Caste Movement and the Construction of an Indian Identity*. New Delhi: Orient BlackSwan.

Packer, J. 2010. 'What is an Archive?: An Apparatus Model for Communications and Media History'. *The Communication Review* 13 (1), 88–104.

Richardson, I., and C. Harper. 2002. 'Corporeal Virtuality: The Impossibility of a Fleshless Ontology'. *Virtual/information/digital*. Available at http://researchrepository.murdoch.edu.au/id/eprint/11765/1/Corporeal_Virtuality.pdf (accessed December 2024).

Sarukkai, S. 2009. 'Phenomenology of Untouchability'. *Economic and Political Weekly* 44 (37), 39–48.

Seem, M. 1983. 'Introduction'. In Gilles Deleuze and Félix Guattari (eds), *Anti-Oedipus: Capitalism and Schizophrenia*, xvii–xxvii. Minneapolis: University of Minnesota Press.

Sewell Jr, W. H. 1992. 'A Theory of Structure: Duality, Agency, and Transformation'. *American Journal of Sociology* 98 (1), 1–29.

Srinivasan, P. 2011. *Sweating Saris: Indian Dance as Transnational Labour*. Philadelphia: Temple University Press.

Velaskar, P. 2012. 'Education for Liberation: Ambedkar's Thought and Dalit Women's Perspectives'. *Contemporary Education Dialogue* 9 (2), 245–271.

Wakankar, M. 2010. *Subalternity and Religion: The Prehistory of Dalit Empowerment in South Asia*. New York: Routledge.

Wheeler, M., D. Johnson-Houston, and B. E. Walker. 2004. 'A Brief History of Library Service to African Americans'. *American Libraries* 35 (2), 42–45.

Zare, B., and A. Mohammad. 2012. 'Burn the Sari or Save the Sari: Dress as a Form of Action in two Feminist Poems'. *Ariel: A Review of International English Literature* 43 (2), 69–86.

 6

From Invisibility to Hypervisibility and Back? The Lost Same-sex Object in Media History in India[1]

Ashley Tellis

Introduction

How does one write a history of an object lost to history? How does one configure a figure without an easily lisible referent? How does one recuperate earlier media forms from the loud apparatus of modern media? This chapter will attempt to plot the contours of such a historical quest, even if it might never find, let alone retrieve, its object. This object is the same-sex loving subject of South Asian history.

The history of sexual minority representation in the media is necessarily seen as a history of the present. Yet sexual minorities were almost never in the consciousness of the modern Indian media till the neoliberal moment, which brought along with international capital an international language with which to talk of sexual minorities. This was in the context of HIV/AIDS and via NGOs, both international and national, who set up house here and later with the legal case for what was to become the reading down of Section 377.[2] From the 2000s, there has been an explosion of media representation of sexual minorities, in both electronic and print media and in TV and cinema and other forms of cultural media.

But is this all there is to a media history of the same-sex subject of South Asia? My argument is that it cannot and must not be. How does one avoid this jackboot teleology of the progression into a rainbow LGBTQI sunset, crushing all silence in its wake? How does one avoid the pitfalls of the sociological and the anthropological to delineate a psychic and philosophical (because the psychic is always already also the philosophical) account of the historical same-sex subject in Indian media history? How does one imbue this subject with historical and material density and excavate the media forms it took to shape itself?

Finally, how does one write a depth-based history of the present forms of media, rich in surfaces and superficiality but spurious on substance, in their depiction of the same-sex subject? How does one confound the multiple violences of visibility? How does one show that the hypervisibility of the same-sex subject in contemporary media is actually an erasure of same-sex subjectivity?

A history of the LGBTQI media in the present is necessarily a history of class (who gets a voice in the media, who does not?), caste (the caste of the same-sex subject is almost never articulated, apart from woke Brahmins trying to outdo each other on who is more de-Brahmanised, the better Brahmin on the internet, and class-privileged Dalits writing from their bungalows and cars in Bangalore, attacking unnamed and oftentimes named 'savarna' folk). Might the histories of the present—presentist, transparently available, endlessly communicative of a core sense of identity, soaked in a US-influenced language of globalised identity politics—be linked to more occluded, barely legible and lisible historical same-sex subjects?

In attempting to address these questions, I will *first* argue that the current hypervisibility of the same-sex subject in the Indian media has been counterproductive to any real meaningful articulation of the South Asian sexual minority subject's identity, not only for more obviously marginalised communities like the hijras, but also for any progressive form of middle-class sexual minority politics.

I will suggest that perhaps a learning from the past with its more occluded forms of media and identity, politics, and living might be more useful to the project of understanding a same-sex past and the project of a sexual minority organising in the present. I will not focus on contemporary media at all, not least because it is inimical to such a historical inquiry and is best left out of the story at any time. To put it another way, we might have to learn what constitutes the media and what real journalism means all over again through this historical inquiry. However, I will trace the possibilities of some links between the efflorescence of the present media explosion around LGBTQI subjects to historical media forms and same-sex subjects from the past.

Finally, my understandings of the historical and of the media are textual, not least because that is my training, but also because embodied forms of the subjects of this chapter—the same-sex subject and the various media of the past—are not available to us, not readily apprehensible even, and only present in the faintest textual traces, submerged often in various kinds of obscuring scaffolding. In this soaking of the textual to read its traces, I draw on a psychoanalytic-feminist mode of reading. The South Asian same-sex subject, historical or contemporary, is seldom a psychic subject. Indeed, the historical is seldom interested or invested in the psychic. Yet, how can one understand a subject's articulation or voice without an understanding of psychic motors? Once again, these psyches are far from readily available to us. I am merely using the psychoanalytic reading practice to touch the textual in ways that might open it up.

A History of the Vanishing Present

A cursory look at the media around us will convince us that India has never been more same-sex sexuality-friendly ever in history. To make an inventory of where you might find same-sex culture: newspaper articles, online articles on various websites, exclusively LGBTQI websites, more and more LGBTQI characters in popular cinema and TV soaps, so-called progressive judgements on LGBTQI populations that produce mass media hysteria, an ever-increasing slew of short films on Indian LGBTQI themes on YouTube and other OTT platforms, reports by civil rights and human rights organisations on LGBTQI issues and populations, blogs, *Wikipedia* entries, documentary films on LGBTQI icons and lives, fiction and non-fiction books on LGBTQI issues and lives, collections and anthologies of 'queer' poetry. This is far from an exhaustive list.

In many ways, this explosion is a new exemplification of Michel Foucault's repressive hypothesis in the first volume of his magisterial four-volume history of sexuality, *Volonte de Savoir* (*The Will to Know*). The more the Victorians and nineteenth-century Europe talked about sexuality, Foucault argued, the less they actually knew and the more repressed they were, the more homophobic. A similar situation obtains in contemporary India.

It is my contention that the more the media here talk about homosexuality, the less they actually engage with it and the starker is their homophobia and the resultant homophobia of society at large. This is not just because the dominant tropes of the same-sexual in the media are those of spectacle, horror, and freakshow but, more conceptually, my argument is that visibilisation is more harmful for same-sex populations as the increased visibility actually increases violence against them. This may seem counterintuitive, but I contend that the forms of visibilisation the media offers are often incitements to violence, especially when the makers of these media documents are actually convinced that they are being supportive and 'progressive'.

Of these documents, I want to concentrate on newspaper reportage, which has been explicitly the least progressive of the media since the earliest reports on same-sex stories, continuing into the present. In newspaper reportage, I will concentrate on one subgenre, that of the report: the grisly murder of older 'gay' men at the hands of young 'not-gay' men or boys.[3] In particular, I will focus on one case reported salaciously by *The Times of India* from Chennai on 21 October 2013.

N. Nagarajan, a 57-year-old bank employee from Velachery in Chennai, was murdered by a handful of young men, men who had started visiting the older man when they were boys. From the title of the report itself, 'Banker murdered by gay lovers', the newspaper's sensationalist intent and sexual illiteracy are both clear. The boys/men are clearly not 'gay' (indeed, the story goes on to establish that and alleges that the gay banker is the sleazy 'gay' predator—he has 'seedy relationships', 'clutches', 'threatens', and 'blackmails', is 'seedy' again, and 'lures' young boys 'into bed') (*The Times of India* 2013).

The poor young boys, on the other hand, 'too young to understand the consequences of their actions',[4] according to Velachery Inspector V. Muthuraja, hit him on the head, punched him repeatedly, and strangled him with a belt. N. Nagarajan died. They told the police that Nagarajan had paid them for sex. Subsequently, he allegedly began blackmailing them, threatening that he would inform their parents that they were having sex with him. This highly unlikely story (Nagarajan himself was a married man, and there is no plausibility to the idea of him blackmailing anyone over the question of gay sex) gives us a sense of how the boys/men, the police, and the media construct the homosexual and what they consider a plausible narrative.[5]

The last line of the report says, 'Nagarajan's wife Selvi was away in the US when the murder took place.' The irrelevance of the figure of this woman, her voice missing from the story, underscores the homosocial, exclusively male world of the Indian media and, more importantly, the irrelevance of women to men's lives, even, or perhaps especially, when they are married to them. Many silent and irrelevant women are strewn across the historical and contemporary expanse of this chapter, and they demand a different essay, if not a book.

Excavating Historical Densities from Static Media Forms

However, it is not just the virulent homophobia and twisted heterofascism of *The Times of India* reporter or the activists and journalists at the Asian College of Journalism (ACJ) Conference in which I am interested. I am more interested in this media typology of the older man-young boy/man which, I argue, points to deeper and longer histories of what Shad Naved, the exemplary scholar of this complex in Urdu poetry (specifically the ghazal form) calls 'boy-love' (*amradparasti* in Urdu). The ghazal, as

Naved reminds us, is the most de-historicised form, moulded 'to give it the illusion of traditional cultural continuity' (Naved 2012, ii).

In a ground-clearing exercise, Naved weeds out the dominant, conventional ways of constructing an LGBTQI history, offering useful warnings, which are equally applicable as advice against the pits into which a media historian of LGBTQI representation might fall. For example, he points to 'the broken machinery of precolonial/early colonial which cannot be mended simply by learning the languages better or anthropologically filling in the back story through lived practices in the past and the present' (Naved 2012, 5), or warns against producing 'a modular view of sexual identity politics if we view these figures as bearers of "traditional" identities who stand outside their definition in debates and contestations about sexual desire, erotic attachments and bodily intimacies' (ibid., 14).

Referring to what he calls the 'neat circle of premodern expressiveness, colonial occultation and postcolonial recovery', 'where no particular cultural identity or idiom, we are told, is at stake', Naved argues that 'the continuities of (same-sex) desire are supra-historical, supra-cultural and supra-national' (ibid., 18). Crucially, 'the representational strategies of particular literary forms are assumed to be shed along the way to their self-objectification in sexual identity categories' (ibid., 19).

On the ghazal, Naved writes: 'The unity of tradition is tethered to a contemporary social landscape in which queerness towers above class, caste, gender stratifications and prejudices in order to "read" its "own" tradition from what look like very dominant (nationalist hegemonic) literary historical means' (ibid., 21).

Queer historiography, Naved shows us, presses for:

> an object which is both lost and never fully lost. Whatever is found through this research is cleansed of traces of historical existence (because we already know the discovered object's political worth and signifying value) and therefore the much-vaunted continuities, which only appear as the persistence of trans-historical same-sex desires in it. The task of history, in this view, is to fortify present (postcolonial) social (queer)

> consciousness as the consummation of a history that has come to an end in it. (Naved 2012, 21–22)

I have quoted Naved at some length because not only does he point to the key problems (and does it in crystalline and poetic prose), but in concentric chapters that move between the more contemporary and the past—from Firaq to Yaqin, from Hali to Mir—he also disinters for us complex social and political histories behind the glassy, perfect surface of the ghazal and its conventions.

I read the ghazal as a media form, not least because of the conditions of its production and dissemination. It is, as Naved tells us, a constellation of conventions. It is disseminated across various sites: the performed text (in various contexts, from courts to roadside *addas*); the printed text; the *mushaira*, where it is recited and often sung in *tarranum* in dialogic relation with a live and interactive audience; the recording as voiced poetry and as song heard by distant listeners who might weep, recognising their own stories in them and reciting them to themselves and to others. What Naved does is to show that a throbbing world of social nerves and veins lives beneath the perfected skein of the ghazal as form. Naved's work is (and should be) the template for media studies practitioners searching for the social worlds of the same-sex subject in Indian history, media history, and all histories.

In his stunning chapter on eighteenth-century poet Mir Taqi Mir, whom even Mirza Ghalib had to grudgingly acknowledge as his superior, Naved gives us an account of Mir's ghazals about boy-love as media texts mired in social, religious, cultural, caste, gendered, and masculine formations, all suppressed by the trappings and conventions of the classical form. Equally dismissive of the club-footed reading of them (by LGBTQI historians) as he is of classicist evacuations of the homosexual and the social by critics like Shamsur Rehman Faruqi, Naved offers us an account of the sexual as a linguistic orientation and the homosexual as a rhetorical trope. Yet, in acknowledging this, he does not effect yet another erasure of the homosexual or the importance of homosexuality, but shows how both as rhetorical trope and referent, it is ordering reality in a particular way from a particular point of view.

A Textual Psyche

The burden of an LGBTQI media history, however, to my mind, cannot stop where Naved stops. It must necessarily attempt to excavate a psychic formation from the kind of deep historical and social excavation of media forms from the past and the present that Naved undertakes. We need a psychic account of Nagarajan as much as of Mir. Naved does not risk that, working as he does within the framework of Comparative Literature. Psychoanalysis is not one of his tools, but it is my argument that historians and LGBTQI cultural theorists will have to take the risk of using that tool because the media forms per se, as the ghazal and *The Times of India* report show, occlude the same-sex identified subject without any attempt at excavating the psyches behind them.

In this section, I attempt to do this with a contemporary figure who featured prominently in the media, but simultaneously was utterly erased: the poet and professor Shrinivas Ramchandra Siras, of Aligarh Muslim University (AMU). I choose this figure to show that it is not only the historical same-sex figure that is occluded from us and needs the delicate textual work of retrieval, but that even a figure from the present might also be lost to us, and our tools can be too blunt to disinter his voice from our alabasterisation of it.

In early 2010, Siras' campus residence at AMU was broken into; he was filmed having consensual sex with Irfan, a *rikshawala* he had picked up (the reality seemed to be that this *rikshawala* was a regular and Siras and he were in some kind of relationship, if not long-term lovers), and was suspended from the university. With the 'help' of activists from the 'movement', Siras filed a case challenging his suspension, won his academic position and residence back, but was found dead in his rented apartment within a week of the Allahabad High Court's decision in his favour (Sarkar 2021 [2010]).

Professor Shrinivas Ramchandra Siras became the unwitting gay icon of 2010. The Siras case is in many ways the clearest indicator of the limited nature of the Indian LGBTQI movement and the liberal Indian media, both of whose well-meaning murder of his voice we must analyse closely and learn from.

The AMU establishment gunned for Siras for two reasons: *one*, to take revenge, as Siras was part of the movement on campus to hold the corrupt Vice-Chancellor (VC) accountable, and *two*, to deflect from the real issue on campus, which was the increasing exposure of the VC's corruption. The real issue was, and is, as is often the case,[6] the corrupt VC. Siras had countered his corruption in the past, stood up to him, and this was payback time. What better way than a sensationalist story about sleazy gay sex with which to divert attention?

This becomes clear if we ask a few questions, like: How is it that AMU discovered Siras' homosexuality and the fact that he picked up *rikshawalas* only when there was one year left for his retirement and when he had been there (and presumably doing this) for decades? Who were these newspersons? How did the footage land on the VC's table and not actually on the office tables of any media house? Had the VC instituted an unconstitutional and vicious witch-hunt against Siras? The RTIs that University members like Siras had filed must be made public. All records of the VC must be made public. Predictably, none of this was explored or asked for by the media.

The media, the fourth pillar of Indian democracy, concentrated entirely on Siras' sex life, parading it on national television, not even bothering with the courtesy given to victims of assault (which is to blur their faces in the images), with no thought for the repercussions on this man's mental state and life. They did not even mention the structural issues of corruption in AMU, let alone reflect on the ethics of their own practices. There was not a word on the blatant invasion of privacy, which the media repeated itself. There was only a salacious interest in his sexual practices and his purported sexual orientation.

The 'queer movement' then rushed in, generating a wide media and internet-based championing of Siras as a gay icon. A team of professional activists met him, got a reluctant Siras to file a case, did a fact-finding, and left. To me, this is as insensitive as the earlier two invasions. As is clear from all the interviews and coverage, Siras did not conform to any stereotype of being 'gay', in any conventional sense of what that word is taken to mean. He was 'outed' as homosexual by this VC and the offensive invasion of Siras' privacy.

The media's abetting of this humiliation by beaming Siras across the country rendered him even more vulnerable. Siras looked bamboozled and disoriented through the sordid media episode. He spoke in many contradictory, dazed narratives. He said AMU and his family were his support systems. He said what was done to him was unfair and he would fight it. He said his life was half pleasant moments and half harshness and harassment. When he was reinstated, he said he was delighted to be back at his beloved AMU. The classic illustration of the disconnect between his being yoked to gay iconicity and his own sense of himself, which he was not even allowed the space to articulate, is his encounter with an NDTV journalist when the story just broke.[7]

NDTV was full of liberal, righteous rage and bombarded him with questions dripping with a passion that barely concealed their utter hypocrisy. The questions aimed to whip Siras into a frenzy of self-righteousness and indignation; Siras instead answered in monosyllables and short sentences that simply did not rise to the bait of the questions, to which he clearly could not relate. Siras spoke of his hope and belief that people would forget his homosexuality soon; he spoke of being ashamed; he spoke of loving AMU and feeling sad that they had rejected him only because of his sexual orientation. He stuttered through the NGO-ised lines he had been asked to repeat by the lawyers and LGBTQI activists who had visited him on a fact-finding mission. He was packing his bags; he did not think of protest, although he did speak of what happened to him as a conspiracy. The interview generated the most unwatchable bathos from a same-sex identified subjectivity in postcolonial India's history.

Siras went home, the Allahabad High Court stayed his suspension, and at the moment of his legal triumph, he was found dead. We still know almost nothing about what caused it. He had gone home for a court hearing on a property dispute, and his family members did not even disclose their names to the press.[8] His last public thoughts, as I have indicated, were his delight at being back at what he called his 'beloved AMU' (NDTV 2010a).

Now all of this might seem deeply objectionable and annoying to us as assured LGBTQI activists, but if we are really supportive of homosexual subjects in this country, then we have to respect this man for who he was and what he did not want to be. Support has to be offered on the terms of the subject, not on the terms of the media activist. Does the role of the LGBTQI movement stop at a fact-finding mission and organising a battle on the legal terrain? Should the activists not have been with him throughout, gone home with him, sustained interactions with him, and asked him what he wanted? Instead of simply marshalling him to a cause, a cause he clearly did not see as his own, should there not have been attention to the affective, internal world of this clearly alienated subject, thrown into a series of languages he did not speak? Should there not have been some quietness to listen and perhaps learn from his languages? Instead, every campaign, every petition, and the fact-finding report concentrated on his gayness. Neither the structural reasons behind the suspension nor the grammar of his self-definition was paid any attention. It died with him, even as he became a martyr of the LGBTQI 'movement'.[9]

What I have tried to show through an exploration of the social text of Siras is that the lack of a historical foundation of the largely upper-class, upper-caste, urban 'queer movement' prevents it from listening to a subject who does not speak in their language. It seems not only unaware of the structures in which it is enmeshed, but also simply unable to even see a subject not mirroring itself.

At the level of the subject, I am proposing psychic accounts of different same-sex identified subjects in India, both historically and in the present, which complicate the media and force it to build its ethical foundation on their difficult, often resistant socio-historical particularities. I am reading their resistance to the available languages for the expansion it might offer of the available vocabularies of self and identity as same-sex subjects, rather than the imposition of an identity politics foreign to these subjects' senses of themselves and their being in the world.

Siras opens his collection of poems, *Paaya Khaali Hirwal* (*Grass Beneath The Feet*), with a quote from Gerard Manley Hopkins about the smallness of the human and the vastness of the natural world, but that world is conceived by that very small human's mind: 'O the mind, the mind has mountains; cliffs of fall/ frightful, sheer, no-man fathomed, Hold them cheap/May who ne'er hung there. Nor does long or small/ Durance deal with that steep or deep.' Already, we get a sense of Siras' aesthetic. The imagination is like nature and the human mind cannot endure its sublimity (its steeps and deeps) for long. The grass beneath the feet of the title echoes that experience of the sublime: grass covers everything in the end. It is an anti-identitarian aesthetic if there ever was one.

Section 2 of the book, the eponymous title, opens with another quote (full of errors and typos) from Lionel Trilling on Sigmund Freud's *Interpretation of Dreams*, in which Trilling speaks of how dreams do not follow logic and instead rely on condensation and displacement,[10] the unconscious choosing the concrete over the general, the trifling over the abstraction.[11] It opens with the eponymous poem, which is an exemplar of a poem as Freudian dreamwork.

> *Grass Beneath the Feet*
> I want green grass beneath my feet and the smell of it all around
> I want spring breeze and a mess of a few dreams
> Let the bright sun sink slowly for a drink
> You travelled all the way through my dreams for the desires of the night.
>
> Sometimes everyone's dreams are much greener than reality
> But only he is fearful of dreaming than the dreamer
> No door is open for wind and for moonlight
> And yet, krrrrr, the kingdom of dreams opens its door.
>
> Even now sitting and listening to the clock tick
> I instinctively understand that time does not drip
> What about the hourglass? The sweat on the body?

> The desert of disappointment I walked through while smelling my own sweat
>
> I need a few birds who would help me fly with feathers in my beak
> Perhaps the roads of your unflinching eyes would keep walking for me.
> When you take the bend, you will find a big, strong door
> Perhaps it is unopenable, the threshold gives shades to everyone.
>
> When I try to open my half-shut eyes for twilight
> Instead on its own the broken corners of my mirror slip and shine
> The image that was broken re-forms on its own, speaks to me.
> And, while speaking, it is understood that there is always grass beneath the feet.[12]
>
> (Siras 2002, 41)

I read this poem as being about same-sex desire, but it has none of the identity markers to 'prove' it. It is a dream palimpsest, a dream work (it is a little-known fact that Siras was a trained and licensed psychologist)[13] that, apart from the social history embedded in its metaphors and images, re-writes the body of the Marathi poem, avoiding both the exteriorities of identitarian protest or the interior sickliness of romanticism (the two major afflictions of modern Marathi poetry). This is done through a psychic delineation of the poetic protagonist waking from and slipping into a dream.

CONCLUSION

Responding to the first draft of this chapter, P. Thirumal characteristically asked the most searching question and offered the most astute critique of it that I have received. He wrote:

> What I am not getting at through psychoanalytic engagement, or unable to understand, is the filters that one has to fabricate/imagine between collective and individual

> corporeality. It is in that sense, a history of (same sex) desire has to be excavated. While the collective is markedly historical, individuation as a psychic formation, as you are arguing, via Naved, cannot be nested in either history, nation or any formed entity. The formlessness of 'desire' is what unsettles media forms and representational content. If the genre of history in itself is construed as a form and it has to process material (desire) that lacks an apparent form, then what is that needs to be visibilized? Desire allows for system-making and disallows systematic analysis. In that sense, the method of media history should be sensitive to the force of the immaterial (desire).[14]

Thirumal gets at the central problematic of the chapter—the conjunction between the individual and collective psyche—which for Freud meant the same thing (even if not in the Jungian sense of the collective). He rightly locates Naved's claim that the sexual exceeds the nation and poetic-historical forms, but misreads Naved as arguing that that sexuality is formless. On the contrary, for Naved, the sexual is material and tied up with the histories of caste, class, region, and gender.

However, as I have pointed out, Naved does not engage with the psychic, and how the sexual, with all these material imbrications, forms the psyche and the sense of subjectivity or self. Thirumal's conception of the sexual as formless and immaterial is simply not Naved's or my conception of the sexual. Like Naved, I am arguing that the sexual is imbricated in various materialities, but it also has a psychic component that exceeds the materialities of caste, class, region, and gender. Sexuality in the Freudian (as opposed to Foucauldian) sense is disruptive, but not necessarily in an affirmative sense (as it, implicitly, is with Foucault). The (im)possible (?) demand I am making of the media today, and of our reading of earlier media forms, is that we learn to at least recognise the traces of the psychic articulation of the sexual in the textual sources available to us, even ones as seemingly ossified as the ghazal form and others as apparently palpable and clear to us as the figure of Ramachandra Shrinivas Siras.

The grass of Siras' poem is what we need to feel beneath our feet when we look for same-sex presence in Indian media history.

The lost object of the same-sex figure in Indian media history may not be readily transparent to us, but they are not lost altogether if only we learn to listen for, and feel them.

Notes

1. I would like to thank P. Thirumal for not only commissioning this chapter, but for also provoking its shape and form with his comments on an earlier essay I had written on the idea of a damaged subjectivity dealing with damage, contemplating escape as a psychic-political option, to which he had responded with a long and useful phone call. I also thank Antony Arul Valan G. for very useful feedback on this chapter in a long phone call and Dr Bhargav Nimmagadda for kind words about the chapter and for likening my reading to Fredric Jameson's engagement with narrative as a symbolic act with history at its core. See Tellis (2021).

2. The media has been consistently announcing this as the decriminalisation of homosexuality, but no such thing has happened. Homosexual is not a word or category the Indian State recognises, or even acknowledges. This is not mentioned in Section 377. It is not mentioned in the Indian Constitution, even as sexual orientation. The lawyers who have run the cases from *Naz* to *Navtej* want us to treat sex as sexual orientation, but this is an absurd conflation and a legally untenable one.

3. The category of the boy (as opposed to man) and the idea of child sexuality are important cultural complexes that need unpacking, but this is beyond the purview of this chapter. For an excellent start, see Vashist (2019).

4. At a panel on the reporting of sexual violence in the media at a conference at the Asian College of Journalism in Chennai in 2016, anti-child sexual abuse activist Vidya Reddy of the NGO Tulir, analysing the *TOI* report, presented the outrageous case that the poor boys were minors (even though the main absconding murderer at the time of the murder was twenty. Reddy followed the *TOI*'s timeline about Nagarajan having first met them in 2008), and therefore more clearly and simply abused. She went as far as to say that they did not quite murder him, but only 'pushed him', and he happened to fall and die.

What was even more shocking was that some of the more gender-sensitive journalists in Chennai on the panel (from *The New Indian Express*, *The Newsminute*, and *The Hindu*) had no problem with this interpretation and at least one of them (Ranjitha Gunasekaran of the *TNIE*, personal conversation) actually endorsed it. This, despite the fact that Gunasekaran is also an anthropologist who did her M.Phil in Anthropology and wrote her dissertation on The Banyan's male shelter in Chennai.

5. An essay might be written on the assumptions and implications of this report, but that is not my intent here. I have written elsewhere about Chandrashekhar Pushkin, Ramachandra Siras, and other older men subject to murder of different kinds at the hands of men and boys. All of these articles, now difficult to access, were commissioned by Ranjitha Gunasekaran, who ran India's first LGBTQI page in a mainstream national newspaper, *The New Indian Express*, under the editorship of the brilliant Aditya Sinha from 2008–2011. Sinha briefly ran such a page during his short stint at DNA, and started an LGBTQI Agony Aunt column at his almost equally short stint at *Deccan Chronicle* in Hyderabad. Sinha has been a pioneer in Indian media history in working with the LGBTQI community and guaranteeing them media representation.

6. In 2010, I was sacked from IIT Hyderabad because of a corrupt director. Instead, Nikhila Henry carried a report in *The Times of India* alleging that I had been discriminated against as a homosexual on the IIT campus (Henry 2010). There was no IIT Hyderabad campus at the time, I was not discriminated against as a homosexual, except by an administrative staff member posing as a student, and I was sacked because of my opposition to the director's corrupt practices. The twenty-five media channels that contacted me in the aftermath of Henry's article did not want to listen to the story of the VC. As a result, I did not speak to any of them.

7. For a part of the interview, see NDTV (2016). Also see Agha (2018); Tellis (2018).

8. This despite the fact that his sister-in-law is the well-known writer Asha Bage. We also do know that his long-divorced wife turned up for her share after his death.

9. No attention, of course, was paid to the *rikshawala*, Irfan, who was so harassed by the police that he set himself on fire. His wife said he was consistently harassed. What of the subjectivity of the man who has sex and relationships with men in India, flattened to the NGO category of MSM or Men Who Have Sex With Men? The case left his burnt body by Siras' dead body. Who can write the histories of these men's psyches? Who knows how to read them? See NDTV (2010b); see also

Agha (2018). The unfortunate film made on the story, Hansal Mehta's *Aligarh*, turned this *rikshawala* into a hipster cool dude and erased him from all but the sex scene. Welcome to progressive Hindi cinema! See Tellis (2016).

10. Condensation and displacement in Freud (which Jacques Lacan reinterpreted as metaphor and metonymy) are two elements of his analysis of dreams. Displacement is a form of dream distortion in which one substitutes an illusion for something real and a shifting of focus from something to something else. Condensation is what happens when two or more incidents of displacements are brought together. These are used in the dream as defence mechanisms to mask the anxiety around sexual impulses in the unconscious. See Freud Museum London (n.d.) and Rahimi (2009).

11. Lionel Trilling was an American literary critic and novelist. He wrote a book called *Freud And The Crisis Of Our Culture* in 1955.

12. The translation is mine. I thank Rahul Sarwate for looking over it and refining it for me, and for his deep knowledge of all things Marathi.

13. In his very interesting obituary on Siras' death, his publisher, Arjun Jakhade, mentions the fact of Siras being a trained psychologist, but also tells fascinating stories of Siras' relationship to poetry. Siras was never too keen on publishing his poems, said he often could take up to ten years to finish a poem, refused to let Jakhade drop a couple of unfinished poems as he spoke of the fears he had of the poems coming to beat him up, kill him, eat him, if he allowed that. Jakhade talked about how Siras eventually completed the poems, which involved going back to the places where he had written the first drafts, and re-inhabiting the moment and the landscape in which they were born. Siras was, by all accounts, a manic traveller across the length and breadth of the country. See Jakhade (2010). I thank Rahul Sarwate for bringing this obituary to my notice and, once again, refining my translation of it.

14. Email communication, 24 February 2021.

References

Agha, Eram. 2018. 'Now That Gay Sex Is Decriminalised Will I Get My Rights Asks AMU Prof Siras' Partner'. *News18.com*, 6 September. Available at https://www.news18.com/news/india/now-that-gay-sex-is-decriminalised-will-i-get-my-rights-asks-amu-prof-siras-partner-1869569.html (accessed December 2024).

Asian College of Journalism. 2016. 'Understanding Sexual Violence as a Public Health Problem'.

Freud Museum London. n.d. 'The Dream-Work'. Available at https://www.freud.org.uk/education/resources/the-interpretation-of-dreams/the-dream-work/ (accessed January 2025).

Henry, Nikhila. 2010. 'IIT-H sacks gay activist Ashley Tellis'. *The Times of India*, 11 June. Available at https://timesofindia.indiatimes.com/india/iit-h-sacks-gay-activist-ashley-tellis/articleshow/6034644.cms (accessed January 2025).

Jakhade, Arjun. 2010. 'Pausaaadheech Saakdun Gelele Abhaad' ('The Sky that was Drained Before it Could Rain'). *Loksatta*, 16 May.

Naved, Shad. 2012. 'The Erotic Conceit: History, Sexuality and the Urdu Ghazal'. Ph.D. dissertation, University of California, Los Angeles.

NDTV. 2010a. 'Back to my Beloved AMU, says relieved Siras', 2 April. Available at http://www.ndtv.com/video/player/news/back-to-my-beloved-amu-says-relieved-siras/135566 (accessed December 2024).

______. 2010b. 'Gay AMU Professor Siras' partner attempts self-immolation', 18 July. Available at https://www.ndtv.com/india-news/gay-amu-professor-siras-partner-attempts-self-immolation-424217 (accessed December 2024).

______. 2016. 'Last Words of AMU Professor who was driven to death for being gay', 2 April. Available at https://www.ndtv.com/video/news/news/last-words-of-amu-professor-who-was-driven-to-death-for-being-gay-401772 (accessed December 2024).

Rahimi, Sadeq. 2009. 'The Unconscious: Metaphor and Metonymy'. *Somatosphere*, 29 April. Available at https://somatosphere.com/2009/unconscious-metaphor-and-metonymy.html/ (accessed January 2025).

Sarkar, Urvashi. 2021 [2010]. 'Mystery Shrouds Death of AMU Professor'. *The Hindu*, 17 November. Available at https://www.thehindu.com/news/national/Mystery-shrouds-death-of-AMU-professor/article16364777.ece (accessed December 2024).

Siras, Shrinivas Ramachandra. 2002. *Payakhaali Hirwal* (*Grass Beneath the Feet*). Pune: Padmaganga.

Tellis, Ashley. 2016. 'How *Aligarh* and *Kapoor and Sons* Reaffirm that Homosexuality Is Acceptable Only When Made As Heterosexual As Possible'. *gaylaxymag.com*, 20 June. Available at https://www.gaylaxymag.com/blogs/aligarh-kappor-and-sons-reaffirm-gomosexuality-has-to-be-heteronormative/#gs.x64t2u (accessed December 2024).

Tellis, Ashley. 2018. 'When it comes to Homosexuality in India, liberal media is like Hindutva brigade'. *DailyO*, 15 January. Available at https://www.dailyo.in/voices/section-377-ramchandra-siras-gay-rights-lgbt-pride-parade/story/1/21747.html (accessed December 2024).

______. 2021. 'Rocks That Block the River' *The Indian Quarterly* 9 (2), January–March.

The Times of India. 2013. 'Banker murdered by gay lovers', 21 October. Available at https://timesofindia.indiatimes.com/city/chennai/Banker-murdered-by-gay-lovers/articleshow/24457334.cms (accessed December 2024).

Vashist, Latika. 2019. 'Age of Consent and the Impossibility of Child Sexuality'. *Seminar* 721 (September). Available at https://indiaseminar.com/2019/721/721_latika_vashist.htm (accessed December 2024).

7

Cast Out Worlds in Print

Iyothee Thass (1845–1914) and the Tamil Public Sphere

Dickens Leonard

There is an increasing concern about the absence of prominent Dalit journalists and the lack of Dalit media-practitioners in contemporary India.[1] This 'lack of diversity' in the newsroom has been rightly identified as 'biased and partial' against the Dalits (Balasubramaniam 2011, 21–23). For instance, Oxfam India, in collaboration with Newslaundry (Oxfam India 2019), examined English and Hindi newspapers as well as flagship debate shows in the Indian media, amongst others, to provide a comprehensive report on the representation of marginalised caste groups in the media. The report states that even today, 'three out of every four anchors of flagship debates on TV are upper caste'. Glaringly, almost 90 per cent of 'newsroom leadership positions'—including editors, executives, and bureau chiefs—across TV news channels, news websites, and magazines are 'occupied by journalists from the upper castes'. And ironically, 'over half of those writing on issues related to caste in Hindi and English newspapers are also upper caste', while 'no more than five per cent of all articles in English newspapers are written by Dalits and Adivasis'. This report provides tangible evidence to substantiate that today, 'vast sections of India's marginalised caste groups lack access to the media platforms and discourses that share public opinion', which leads to their unjust 'invisibilization' in the public sphere (ibid., 2–4).

While the injustice caused haunts the public sphere even today, not many have seriously studied this history of negligence (Thankappan 2015). Nevertheless, one may ask: What if this is a history of erasure, and the blame lies with the print histories of South Asia that may have historically collaborated to cast out the words of the outcaste world? This chapter responds to this history of invisibility and explores one of the earliest Dalit articulations in south India during the colonial period, and extends the studies on anti-caste thought by foregrounding the Tamil cosmopolis.[2] It attempts to understand how the most oppressed by caste engaged with print in the early twentieth century. This extends, but departs critically, from prominent works on histories of caste as well as print in South Asia, as one can foreground Pandit Iyothee Thass' work as a *movement* geared through journalistic-print activity—in the context of Dalit migration to presidential cities, industrial towns, railway quarters, and military cantonments, as well as the indentured labour migration to countries such as Burma, South Africa, Ceylon, and Southeast Asia—in the late nineteenth and early twentieth centuries (Balasubramaniam 2016; Basu 2011; Leonard 2020).

Just like the late 1990s and early 2000s, when the Tamil intellectual sphere was churned and changed quite drastically by the 'little magazine' movements along with the Dalit socio-political emergence across the subcontinent, the earlier century (1890s–1910s) in which Iyothee Thass worked was a politically vibrant time.[3] Dalits used writing and reading as acts for a caste-less community to come, which had resources in the past. Thass and his contemporaries' efforts in the long nineteenth and early twentieth century hence need a historical re-look. The Dalit intellectuals in the early twentieth century held counterviews on caste and religion that were relative and transformative explorations against any singular inscription. They inaugurate and constitute a millennial anti-caste imaginary of a kind, as creative opposition to and history against caste.

Print, Reading-Writing Practices, and Anti-Caste Publics

Modern print, as a subject of research enquiry, has kept many historians, philologists, media theorists, and linguists busy. As often theorised, slowly yet systematically, print paved the way to make language largely soundless (McLuhan 1962, 1–11). Printed truths privileged the eye, more than any other sensory organ. Besides, print inscribed languages, and therefore knowledge, into a visual bias (Ivins Jr 1969, 1–20). Hence, print capitalism in the nineteenth and twentieth centuries could evoke the idea of a nation as 'imagined political community', a derivative category, in many countries as languages and nations were simultaneously produced through print modernity (Anderson 1991, 1–8). In Indian languages, particularly, the complex relationship between orality, print history, and nation has been a subject of scholarly interest for some time now (Blackburn 2003, 1–15). Despite serious research in this field, recent studies do not have much to say about the marginalised regime of truths (Gupta and Chakravorty 2004, 2008, 2016). In India, what was print to those who were considered outcaste, whose senses were 'untouched' and 'unseen'? What does modern print mean to Dalits?

Three important edited books published on the 'Book History in India' series—*Print Areas* (2004), *Moveable Type* (2008), and *Founts of Knowledge* (2016)—do not even have one chapter that foregrounds the caste question and/or the Dalits' engagement with modern print. All these books, however, prioritise print and publishing history across the Indian subcontinent in the twenty-four chapters written by prominent scholars—with just one from south India on the Tamil Encyclopaedia. Although many anti-caste movements across India generally—and by ideologues such as Phule (1827–1890), Thass (1845–1914), Ramasamy (1879–1973), and Ambedkar (1891–1956), in particular—engaged with modern print for their movements against caste, serious academic scholarship on print seems to be largely silent on this phenomenon.

For instance, Tamil historian A. R. Venkatachalapathy's *Province of the Book* (2012), while recounting the history of reading practices in the colonial Tamil public sphere, studies the Tamil book history by attending to the ways in which the reading and learning practices changed, as palm scripts were converted into print. He traces how a particular mode of reading—silent reading vis-à-vis reading aloud—emerged as a dominant practice. He argues that the printed book turned silent reading into the dominant mode, which was a historical transition from learning by rote and reading aloud. Venkatachalapathy hence drew attention to the new publics that the printed book was creating, while erasing the older reading-writing practices (ibid., 208–242).

However, historian V. Rajesh claims, in his detailed study of print history in Tamil, that the social history of the recovery and publication of Tamil classics in the nineteenth and twentieth centuries was dictated by a conglomeration of upper-caste landholding communities. They were active participants along with institutions like the 'dominant land holding Saiva mutts and the Tamil language promotion associations under the collusive pact with hegemonic colonial economy' (Rajesh 2011, 65). These attempts, he states, brought the Tamil classical texts as books into the print form by the turn of the nineteenth century itself, in the context of a competitive environment under colonialism. The literary canon was henceforth transformed from a manuscript into the print form by an elite, landowning, upper-caste public sphere whose patronage networks were both the religious (Saivaite) and the colonial institutions.[4]

Recent historical research argues that the popularisation of Tamil and the publication of Tamil classical texts were indeed a culmination of three factors in the late nineteenth century. Rajesh argues that one of the primary factors that influenced the institutionalisation of Tamil literature, language, and nation in a continuum was 'the growth of journalism' (2013, 17). But research into the subaltern articulations of Tamil as a heritage of the most oppressed, and not just the concerns of the upper castes—that either contest the Brahmins in the public sphere, or critique the colonial State—has been inadequate.

Historians, while foregrounding such an analysis, did not adequately reflect on the role of the emergent journalistic practice that gained currency among the most oppressed in the 'provinces' that 'the book' created,[5] nor is there a serious reflection on the Tamil public spheres and its anti-caste counter-publics that journalistic print brought forth. There is hardly any account of how an embodied anti-caste public had to work on alternative epistemological practices using journalistic print, rather than the book as a dominant print form which the caste public practised profusely.[6] And very few works highlight Thass' industrious work as an organic intellectual as his contribution to Tamil journalistic print and creative knowledge practice that prioritises an anti-caste point of view.[7]

Iyothee Thass and *Tamizhan*

The Tamil intellectual Pandit Iyothee Thass[8] (1845–1914) ran the magazine *Tamizhan* (1907–1914), which revived interest in Buddhism as an anti-caste religion. A man of anti-caste ideas, he was a major leader, intellectual, and activist whose life, work, and legacy have regrettably remained neglected by historians until recently.[9] In many ways a precursor to towering anti-caste figures like Periyar E. V. Ramasamy (1879–1973) and Babasaheb B. R. Ambedkar (1891–1956), Thass was the first to develop an anti-caste narrative by espousing and writing on Buddhism. He was a practitioner of *Siddha* medicine, and during the 1881 British-India Census, appealed that the *panchamas* (ex-Untouchables) were not Hindu and must be recorded as original Tamils—*Adi Tamizhar* (Aloysius 2015, 69). He used Tamil literary resources and palm scripts to field an anti-caste Tamil literature and folklore-based explanations on Buddhism.

Iyothee Thass was born Kathavarayan in the year 1845. In admiration of his teacher, Tondai Mandalam Vallakalatinagar Vee. Iyothithaasa Kavirayar Pandithar, he changed his name to Pandit C. Iyothee Thass (coincidentally, B. R. Ambedkar was to do the same five decades later).[10] Thass ran the Tamil journal *Oru*

Paisa Tamizhan (later, *Tamizhan* or *The Tamilian*) from 19 June 1907 to 29 April 1914; incidentally, just a year later Mohandas Gandhi returned to India from South Africa while Ambedkar was in the middle of his research at Columbia University, New York. Compared to other radical anti-race African-American magazines such as *The Chicago Defender* during the same time, *Tamizhan* published similar radical content against caste, health columns, and local and international news, and also had a wide reach among the marginalised (Ayyathurai 2011, 21–22).

Thass pioneered a Buddhist movement in cities where Dalits migrated as coolies, such as the Kolar Gold Field, Bangalore, Rangoon, and Durban. He devoted time to starting separate *vihars*, worship practices, festivals, libraries, schools, burial places, and marriage customs. These were done to reconstruct Dalit history through a Buddhist framework in the vernacular. He worked not only for the religious identity of the Dalits, but also for their political, social, and economic needs. This figure, when placed within the Dalit discourse, goes beyond both 'the *desi* and the derivative national discourse' (Guru 2011).[11] Although Thass' claims are based on a negative and oppositional language, he transcends into a normative form of thinking. In other words, Thass does not construct an anti-Brahmin discourse as a negative and oppositional stance alone. He talks about the Brahmin as an 'other' to imagine the self, but also transcends it to create an ethical imaginary in Tamil Buddhism. Thass's writings can be treated as part of a longer cultural legacy written against caste oppression, and by reading and remembering them, the oppressed can embody and practice anti-caste values.

Hence Thass' agenda, and his search for an alternative, were characterised by an 'anxiety to challenge yet transcend the given situation as an indispensable condition for Subaltern emancipation' (Aloysius 2010, 241). Thus, political and cultural idealism—which erupted within his astounding knowledge of history and culture—characterises Thass' writings. This was made possible not only by the historical context in which the Tamil Dalits emerged as a community during the early twentieth century, but also because the emergent public sphere proved to be a backbone to Thass' writings on Buddhism. It will be instructive to discuss the emergence of the Dalits as an anti-caste public sphere in the early twentieth century.

As stated earlier, Thass began *Oru Paisa Tamizhan* (later *Tamizhan* or *Tamilian*, 1907–1914), the Tamil journal, on 19 June 1907 from his Royapettah office in Chennai. The journal, printed at Gautham Press of Thiru Adimoolam, was a collective effort of 'philosophers, natural scientists, mathematicians, and litterateurs' (Aloysius 2010, 239). It served as a mobilisational tool of the new Buddhist movement among the subaltern communities against caste. The intention behind publishing the journal was 'to teach justice, right path, and truthfulness to people who could not discriminate between the excellent, mediocre and the bad' (Aloysius 1998, 61). The newspaper was published on every Wednesday for the rest of Thass' life, and carried a wealth of information on current events and interpretations of Tamil history, religion, literature, and politics, against the dominant and oppressive religio-cultural discourses of the time, to create an alternative discourse.

Thass' *Tamizhan* explores the myriad ways to articulate a novel critique associated with hierarchy as imagined by early twentieth century caste society, in which the entire system of signs and meanings were re-evaluated. Thass simultaneously rejected the nationalism propounded by the predominantly upper-caste Congress party and their demand for *swadeshi* by using the print space to articulate an alternative imaginary. At the same time, he challenged the caste-Hindu domination of the Tamil print public sphere.

Thass used journalism to register serious critiques and discussion, especially on literature and history. He possessed, in his personal collection, a plethora of palm scripts to which he referred profusely. He was an expert reader, trained in using print technology. His collection of materials in Tamil included epics, literary texts, as well as commentaries, which very few in the early twentieth century even accessed. These palm texts were circulated, he clarifies, amongst his community members as a legacy. This gives an entirely different idea about how the oppressed engaged with and produced knowledge during the colonial period with the emergence of print modernity (Balasubramaniam 2016, 2017; Rajangam 2008).

Thass' proficiency in languages such as Tamil, Pali, Sanskrit, and English helped him to refer these texts and derive a speculative etymology with which to constitute a creative historiography in his journal commentaries. His Tamil prose was relatively new. His use of an epic-style, narrative-based, historical investigation makes it difficult to differentiate historical references from images of the text. The style of writing is experimental as it rebels against an external resource-based historical writing that clarifies, verifies, and is evidential. The oral traditions of the oppressed castes were presented in a journalistic form as commentaries, through which he subverted the existing practices of historical writing. In many ways, his writings inaugurated a millennial narrative about the relationship between language, literature, and nation.

Through speculative etymology, Thass creates an imaginary (or imaginaire) of a resistant community. He becomes the sole mediator, an author/ity of/on a textual practice that is being transferred into anti-caste print cultures. As an intellectual hailing from a subaltern community, identified as untouchable by the technologies of governance in the nineteenth century, Thass used journalism as a tool to gain inroads into the emergent public sphere that altered the practice of knowledge so as to leave an anti-caste trace. He was of the belief that a sovereign nation does not only emerge, but is also contested tooth and nail, first in the language zone, through print journals—contested by both the colonial power and hegemonic caste nations within a language zone. *Tamizhan* provided explanations largely from literary sources and derived historical interpretations and perceptions from 'within' the community, which tried to steer clear of Orientalist, Brahminical, and casteist extrapolations of the marginalised communities.

Tamizhan also created a space where 'the voice of women remained concomitant and inseparable' (Ayyathurai 2011, 196) from Thass' hermeneutics of Tamil Buddhism. Apart from carrying an exclusive 'ladies' column' in the issues, the contributors particularly problematised the role of the dogmatic Hindu marital code. They rejected Brahminical patriarchy, the four *varnas* mirroring the Hindu doctrines, questioned their insensitivity to male and female sexuality, and brought to light the practice of female foeticide and the tragedy of women's collusion in child marriage. Thass, as one of the earliest feminists of his times, constantly appealed for a greater spread of women's education, which he argued would enhance the quality of their lives and reduce their dependence on men. He highlighted the core problems faced by women in India and their inseparability from the problems of caste.

Apart from sparking off a multifaceted feminist criticism of Indian society, the intellectual use that Thass made of journalistic print for anti-caste purposes became an important part of his legacy. But sadly, this was also a historical event of erasure. The prolific participation of scholars such as Thass imprinted their erasure in history, as they are conspicuously absent in the visible and legible historiographies today. These historical moments must be recovered to bring to light not only a valid answer to the question of Dalit absence in journalism, intellectual practice, and public sphere today in the present, but also as a pre-history resistant to caste and Brahminism itself (Leonard 2017; Ravikumar 2007).

Thass' Writings

Anbu Ponnovium (1923–2002), an early follower of Tamil Buddhism who had preserved the *Tamizhan* archives,[12] states that Thass and his work must be understood in the context of the Adi-Dravidar's contribution to Tamil in the nineteenth century.[13] He claims that many poets, artists, spokespersons, and writers were present among the Adi-Dravidas, and emphatically contributed towards society, religion, literature, politics, history, work, rationality, and reformation in that context. Ponnovium argues that Thass belongs to a continuum of Dalit intellectuals that included Rettaimalai Srinivasan, M. C. Rajah, and N. Sivaraj (1999, xxiv). Hence, he believes that the emergence of Adi-Dravida can be viewed as a revolt, and that it was foundational to the Dravidian movement that followed later. Thass belonged to the nineteenth-century anti-caste public sphere long before the Non-Brahmin movement even started in 1916 where the *Adi-Dravidas*, he claims, ran countless *sanghas* and *sabhas* (ibid.).[14]

Ponnovium also records that the subalterns worked with both a single leader and as collectives, expressing their requests, problems, and petitions through running journals. *Adi Dravida Maha Vigada Thoodhan*, *Poologa Vyasan*, *Paraiyan*, and *Adi-Dravida Mitran* were some of the journals run by the Adi-Dravidas from 1860 to 1910.[15] Poems, essays, and plays written in these journals are now completely lost. Although the activities of the anti-caste subaltern public sphere were not historically documented, Ponnovium states that not only *Tamizhan*—run under Thass from Madras, by G. Appaduraiyar from Kolar, and later by P. M. Rajarathinam—but also books such as *Madurai Prabhandham* and *Rangoon Pravesa Thirattu*, published by Pulavar Pudhuvai Seyyappa Mudhaliar in 1896, had carried information about the Adi-Dravida anti-caste public sphere (Ponnovium 1999, xxv). This is supported by Aloysius, who suggests that the subaltern classes of northern Tamil Nadu, particularly Dalits, 'showed definite signs of awakening and incipient mobilization in the last quarter of the nineteenth century' (Aloysius 2010, 240).

Aloysius also suggests that apart from their emergence during the colonial period, 'the Parayars also constituted an important segment of the population and they wielded power in the pre-modern culture and knowledge spheres', particularly in their access to 'Tamil literature, medicine, and traditions that practice several forms of asceticism' (Aloysius 2010, 239). Dalits in the late colonial period took to the printed word as a means of sociopolitical as well as religio-cultural awakening and mobilisation. Hence, it could be argued that through their activities in the public sphere, Dalits indeed belied the timeless 'depressedness' attributed to them through their sheer production of the word (Perumal 2000).

It is also suggested that the Adi-Dravida intellectuals who created this public sphere debated and countered each other.[16]

Thass in particular had problems with Rettaimalai Srinivasan, as well as with the poet Gangadhara Navalar, Advaidananda Swamigal, Omprakash Swami, Reverend John Rathinam, and the poet Velayutham.[17] 'All of them researched in Tamil,' Ponnovium states, and created a 'contesting Dalit public sphere', where they 'differed with each other' and yet were very 'productive in their writings' (1999, xxvi). As they were critically different from each other in their claims and research, it is also to be noted that Thass' research and thoughts were largely based on literature, history, and ethics in the Tamil language. He treated the Tamil language as an embodiment of thought and practice, using it as an archive for an anti-caste intellectual production of religion.

Using Tamil resources and oral practices, Thass claimed that the indigenous/original Tamils (*poorva/aadhi Tamizhar*) were those who, in contemporary times, were abused as untouchables. These are the same people, he claims, who came to work for the transformation and well-being of the land. Hence, he claims that Hinduism, in the form of Brahminism and Aryanism, is a foreign import that had particularly deceived the original truth of the land (Ponnovium 1999, xxviii). Thass claims that caste is untruth, and a religion that spreads such an untruth is unethical. He hence fought an epistemological war against Brahminism. This is embodied through Buddhism in Tamil as an ethical practice of life. It could be argued that Thass was proposing Buddhism as envisioning a communitas at hand, which treats caste and Brahminism as immunitas.

Thass extended this critique to the emergent Indian National Congress as well in the late nineteenth century. For instance, he contested the self-rule movement of the swadeshis in 1885, spearheaded by A. O. Hume's National Congress, by stating that the so-called 'backward and oppressed' people do not believe in swadeshi reform. He stated that 'these Hindu *swadeshi* reformists only talk about unity despite caste differences. They do not want to eradicate caste at all. They talk about caste differences only to bring together the *brahmin*, *kshatriya*, *vaishya*, and the *shudra* together' (Thass, cited in Ponnovium 1999, xxix). According to him, in this immunisation project transformation is impossible, as the upper caste would not treat the oppressed or lower castes equally, as their own elevation or protection is based on the elimination of the others. Hence, the Adi-Dravida intellectuals claim a distinctive civilisation as their own, which to them is much more egalitarian and humanistic than the caste-immunitas of Brahminism. The claims for such a civilisational community were made through the creation of *sanghas* and *sabhas* against caste and Brahminism.

On further research, it is indeed very clear that through his grassroots movement, Thass maintained that *swadeshi* reform was destructive as it was initiated by the Brahmanical civil society in India. Thass viewed it as a self-centred initiative that maintained and perpetuated a sacralisation of caste. He therefore asked the Adi-Dravidas to keep themselves 'away from the nationalist movement represented particularly by the nationalist congress in its inception' (Thass, cited in Ponnovium 1999, xxix). He stated that the nationalist movement was against education and against thought; it had no compassion, discipline, unity, or integrity. Thass used the violent metaphor 'impalement' (*kazhuvu etrudhal*), through which, he claimed, the Buddhists and Jains had been exterminated from the Indian subcontinent. He warned the Adi-Dravidas that 'the *swadeshis* would in fact impale them if they go along with them' (ibid.).

Thass further asked 'how the people who protected the texts from being accessed by others, by rejecting access to read and write can have compassion for *an other*' (Ponnovium 1999, xxxiv). He viewed the swadeshi reform as deceptively pulling one back to a violent immunisation, and towards the ultimate impalement of the masses in the country. Hence, as a contestation against the 'selfish *swadeshis*', he suggested that the 'untouchables' and the 'lowered' communities would fare better 'if they remain working in English man's houses, administration, industries, and plantations' (ibid., xxxiii). He warned: 'How could a political community that intends to impale people through an idea of eternal law (*sanatana dharma*), and through unchanging concepts of God that were produced to create, protect, and destroy can invariably lead everyone towards ethical action' (ibid., xxxv).

Interestingly, Thass used Tamil as a field to reclaim ethics as a way of life. He countered the religionist and extremist caste assault on the language during nineteenth-century Tamil scholarship, stating that 'by using the resources in Tamil languages, scholars have multiplied their caste-masks, spoken lies, professed religious shops, and have earned their wealth' (ibid., xxxvii). Accordingly, his argument was that not only should 'important memorials of caste-less historical material such as the *viharas* were destroyed', but also that 'knowledge resources such as the palm scripts were appropriated' (ibid.). Hence, he suggested that even Tamil, along with Sanskrit and Pali, languages that were used to propagate ethics, had been appropriated in the service of caste and Brahminism—towards unethical falsehoods.

Moreover, Thass argued that those who were most oppressed and discriminated by caste—the untouchables—have still preserved the literature, art, and medicinal knowledge. These earlier forms of anti-caste intellectual properties that were based on ethical action, he suggests, must be taken back and reprinted. The law texts, wisdom books, and astronomical texts that the Adi-Dravidas claimed possession of could be read as a civilisational memory that counters violation as a process. In many ways, this claim for a civilisational relationship with the Tamil language was a unique claim during the colonial period from a Dalit intellectual in the early twentieth century.[18]

For instance, his writings on literature, *Ilakkiyam*, begins with his commentaries on Valluva Nayanar's *Thirikural* (*Thirukkural*) and Auvaiyar's *Thirivasagam* (*Thiruvasagam*), *Kundalakesi*, *Thenbavani*, *Manimegalai*, and *Siddhar Padalgal*, along with a discussion on their publication history (Aloysius 1999, Vol. 2, 455, 456, 537, 566–779, 556–557). These literary criticisms in *Tamizhan* provide an alternative attempt at historical method itself. It will be worthwhile to study the intermediary space that Thass was exploring while commenting and writing on *Thirukkural*, which was first published in print by Francis Whyte Ellis in 1831. The print history and subsequent commentaries on *Kural* opened a vociferous public debate over literary historiography. Thass, in *Tamizhan* (from June 1908–1914), and until his death, continuously published articles on the *Kural* by retrieving material, interpreting the verses, giving references, deriving etymological meanings, introducing new texts, commentaries, and figures to recover *Kural* and Valluvar from the caste biography that had been published as print history.

In this attempt, Thass countered and discussed the biographical details of Valluvar and argued his case for a retrieval. Thass cross-refers verses from texts such as *Munkalaitivagaram*, *Pinkalai Nigandu*, *Manimekalai*, *Sivagasindhamani*, *Sulamani*, among others, to explain and construct an alternative reading of the given caste history. For instance, Thass rejected the title *Thirukkural* (The Holy Voice'—*Thiru* + *Kural*; *Thiru* is an honorific affix which may mean divine). Instead, he provides a Buddhist interpretation of the *Kural*. He explained this as *Thiri Kural*, where *thiri* means the three *pitakas* of the *Dhamma* doctrine, namely ethics (*Arathupal*), material (*Porutpal*), and love (*Kamathupal*). *Kural* is hence divided into three parts, called *Muppal*. This explanation gives Thass an opportunity to demonstrate with resources the Buddhist origins of Valluva Nayanar, the author of the *Kural*. Thass was apparently waging a single-handed intellectual battle with the Saivaite pandits of his times, countering their claims over Valluvar as well as Auvaiyar. Hence, through the poetic references and quotations, Thass literally weaves an intellectual project of retrieval, contestation, re-reading, and imagining an anti-caste (political) legacy (tradition), through journalistic prose.

Thass suggested that the texts which the most oppressed possess generate the practice of knowledge (*vithai*), rationality (*butthi*), generosity (*eegai*), and the right path (*sanmarkam*) amongst everyone. Brahminism and caste society have only celebrated falsehood, violence, and ignorance, not only by destroying this legacy but also by classifying these people as untouchables and *panchamas* (Ponnovium 1999, xIi). Thass claimed that the most oppressed were indeed 'killed without killing' by the caste extremists, who just generate falsehood. He termed 'the national congress as fake and dominated by caste-masked reformists' (ibid.). In this endeavour, Thass suggested that the most oppressed had found a better life by migrating out of their places of origin. Thass unveiled and remembered a casteless community in Tamil civilisation through non-violence, compassion, and following the right path. He researched and wrote about this Buddhist communitas to field it against (and outside) caste, which merely sanitises life and 'kills it without any kindness and thoughtfulness' (ibid.).

WRITING A WORLD OUTSIDE CASTE

For Thass, the objective behind critiquing caste and creating an anti-caste community imaginary was not just to portray the Brahmin as a figure of scorn with an appropriated ideal status. It was also a subversive attempt to create a textuality that refutes, so as to give rise to a religion and culture against caste. Stating that the metaphysics of caste as an enforced hierarchy remained largely intact in Thass' work and reading his discourses as merely underscoring the continuing power of the Brahmin in the Tamil context can be viewed as vindictive.[19] Renowned scholarly work on the 'Non-Brahmin' movement (Geetha and Rajadurai 1998; Pandian 2007) did not foreground Thass as foundational to an anti-caste critique that has a long historical significance, albeit a discontinuous one, while also ignoring the fact that various Dalits were indeed among its active participants.[20]

Thass engaged with Tamil print in the early twentieth century as he ran the magazine *Tamizhan*, which revived interest in Buddhism as an anti-caste religion. The magazine was instrumental in creating an anti-caste vernacular cosmology at the time. Thass was an intellectual—an expert reader, referee, writer, polyglot, publisher, and organiser—and he initiated a resistant knowledge practice by using journalism as a tool to gain inroads into the print public sphere, which was undeniably caste-ridden. Forty-two such Tamil journals—by Dalits—were run from 1850 to 1947 in the Madras Presidency (Balasubramaniam 2017). Why such an event in print history has been erased from public memory calls for a serious enquiry. In particular, the role of academics and history-writing in India needs to be viewed from a critical anti-caste perspective. Hence a re-evaluation of that historical moment of erasure is imperative to capture the prolific Dalit participation in and contribution to emancipatory knowledge practice in print language.

Not only did Thass write about a specific Parayar community's possession of cultural material, but he also refuted the socio-political principle of mass exclusion of any community. He especially refuted the Brahmanical assertion that untouchability as a religious practice was sanctioned for eternity (*sanatana*). Hence, Thass simultaneously deconstructed and reconstructed identifiers for an anti-caste community, as he rejected the terms *panchamas* and untouchables outright. Thass' chosen methodology was historicisation, where he contextualised the history projected by the dominant community as meta-historical or culturally essentialist. However, one should add that this historical interpretation was also aided by multi-level critical hermeneutics and textual exegesis. In fact, Thass primarily deconstructed the new socio-political identification that had emerged in the public domain during the late nineteenth century. He critically deployed his own arguments and established his own concerns by drawing upon Orientalism (although without imitating the Orientalists). Hence, he brought to the surface many hidden tensions inherent in the very conditions of subalternity.[21]

In a sophisticated manner, Aloysius suggests that the basic forces underlying the construction of Thass' Buddhism are *Sramanic* in nature—and different from the Brahmana tradition—where Buddhists attained the pinnacle of achievement. This set up an ideal in the social life of the people that was fundamentally against the antagonistic Brahminical socio-religious ideology. Aloysius suggests that 'cultures' developed around this basic force in a multidimensional sense, working around the *Sramana* ideal of a cluster of social relational values embodied in the Buddhist prescriptions. This led to the flourishing of arts and crafts until an alien counter-force identified as Aryan and Brahminical sectarian power and privilege initiated a long drawn-out war of ideals and ideology. Hence, he categorises the *Sramanic* as 'achievement based, rationalist, and humanist' (Aloysius 2010, 247–248). Thass practised both historical deconstruction and reconstruction to arrive at the truth through a moral critique.

For instance, Thass contested the category Parayar, which was floated to create the binary with the Brahmin in the Orientalist as well as the nationalist discourse. He argued that the Brahminical way of life is deceptive and despicable, and alien to both a historically genuine and legitimately political life. Hence, he asks: 'How could Tamil savants, Siddha practitioners, and advisers to royalties of old, current teachers, engineers, magistrates, *rai bahadurs* and *srestadhars* be contemptuously called as Parayars?' This, he clarifies, must be a contest against 'the pretenders and defenders of falsehood' (Thass, cited in Aloysius 2010, 249–250). Hence Thass even read the category 'untouchable' as referring only to those who were ill (lepers, cholera patients, those suffering from poisonous poxes), traitors, backstabbers, and murderers. He therefore asked: Why were decent and dignified people considered untouchable? On the contrary, he considered the Brahmins and casteists as being untouchable and unapproachable, and hence, their practice of untouchability was plainly selfish and opportunistic. In this deconstruction, Thass debunks the narrative that produced the Parayar as an untouchable; instead, he turns the gaze back on the caste-supremacist narrative of the Brahmin as the centre of socio-political and religio-cultural space in the subcontinent.[22]

Turning it around, Thass interestingly asks who could be an Iyer and transfers an oppositional gaze on the most dominant figure of aspiration. He rhymes the word 'Iyer' with the 'higher' class and professes that only those who can protect all life as their own, attain knowledge, excel in discernment, be generous and moral, transcend caste discrimination and jealousy, and promote human unity can be called 'Iyer/higher class'. He mandates that only those who become compassionate, inclusive, and selfless through self-discipline, good conduct, and universal compassion, while renouncing particularly the despicable distinctions of caste through long years of practice, can be termed higher human beings. He stated that 'the Buddhist moral qualities of an exalted human life were based on achievement' (Thass, cited in Aloysius 2010, 253), and not on one's birth.

He ultimately declared that identification is about what one does, and not one's birth, accusing those who have bought into the caste ideals as being mere imitators, *paarpaar*. Thass uses this term with a tinge of sarcasm to refer to those who call themselves Brahmins. He goes on to suggest that 'Hindu' and 'Hinduism' are merely alternative terms for 'Brahmins' and 'Brahminism', which sacralise the authority of Brahmins and their practice of caste through the act of imitation. Aloysius claims that the term *paarpaar* is the 'contribution of Thass to the lexicon of modern Tamil social history' (Aloysius 2010, 253). Thass counters the meaning of the word caste—*sathi*—by emphasising its verb form and not its noun form. In its verb form, he derives the meaning from Tamil; *sathi* means to achieve, to articulate, and to act. Hence, he states that one must be known only by what one achieves and articulates, and the way one acts. Thass states quite clearly, and very differently, that there is 'nothing natural, given, or divine about caste' in this subcontinent (Thass, cited in ibid., 254–255).

Thass constructs *Tamizhan* (Tamilian) as a casteless identification of the subaltern, where one neither believes in nor practices the caste way of life (*sathi aacharam*). Hence, he propounded that 'the casteless Tamil is the genuine and original Tamil (*aadhi Tamizhan*) and a caste Tamil is only a *paadhi Tamizhan* (*half Tamil*)' (Aloysius 2010, 254–255). The rest, therefore, is only '*meethi* (*residual*) Tamil' (ibid.). The Dravidian, which is another name for Tamil according to Thass, carries an oppositional socio-political meaning to the Aryan (which is nothing but a justification of caste as birth), which upholds human worth according to one's deeds. Hence, Thass' Dravidian is a positive non-caste political principle of egalitarian and inclusive unification, which Aloysius claims was 'an ideal that was based on congruence between power and culture' (ibid.).

Thass' counter emerged through the re-imagining of a history of language—Tamil—that rationalises a casteless sociality. Thass' counter-throw on history through his writing is a pedagogic act;

it desires a meaningful transformation of life at the heart of its thought. He wove together an alternative social and religious world that defied the ascriptive discrimination resulting from the Brahminical congruence of power and culture, and redefined the subcontinental history, culture, and tradition. Thass' writings insisted on a rationalised community while imagining a new language. Numerous pieces of historical and linguistic evidence were mobilised to build a logically coherent caste that had a continuity with and an identity similar to that of the *purva/ sakya* Buddhists. This anti-caste community, constituted through the lens of out-caste experience, provided an open-ended and inclusive identity that was based on castelessness and universal compassion as ethical principles.

Writing a world outside caste, the Tamil Dalits forcefully imagined a 'coming community' which is not transitory and liminal, but 'looks back' insistently at the past. The freedom to conceptualise this anti-caste community in Tamil is not dissociated from political practice. For people on the threshold such as the Dalits, 'alterity' is creatively explored to understand what community is. One may argue that the caste of the individual and the presence of caste are deconstructed, but the singularity of the self opens itself to alterity through writing, in the words of Nancy (1991). And the Tamil Dalits wrote and published extensively in the nineteenth and twentieth century.

Taking a cue from this significant critique, it is instructive to study Thass' efforts to create an anti-caste vernacular cosmopolitan in the Tamil print public sphere during the early twentieth century. His writings must be treated as words on a world outside caste. In particular, his journal carried writings on literary and cultural material, historical, and social analysis, and his ethico-religious commentaries were hermeneutically rich, interpretatively complex, and ideologically refreshing. Those most oppressed by caste used journals to create a language of a casteless world, so as to belong and communicate through a critical interpretative practice. Hence, the Dalits used the reserves of language to explore print modernity for an anti-caste exploration. But they were also experimental in their practice of knowledge. This was, as demonstrated, never recognised by even thoughtful historians of Tamil print history.

Hence, it could be argued that even before print gained momentum towards a print capitalism of the nationalist kind, Tamil Dalits used print journals to create an anti-caste community imaginary. They often contested and debated the nationalist aspirations of the dominant castes. This early period is least researched or documented. Many Dalit-subaltern intellectuals attempted to ingeniously create a reading community by using the emergent print reading-writing practice. For instance, C. Iyothee Thass, A. P. Periyasamy Pulavar, T. C. Narayanaswamy Pillai, T. I. Swamykannu Pulavar, Pandit Munusamy, Rettamalai Srinivasan, John Rathinam, Muthuvira Pavalar, K. Swappeneswary Ammal, among others, were pioneers in such a participation in journalistic print (Velmangai and Kumarasami 2013, 2). This helped in carving out not only a political but also an anti-caste cultural community that reads and writes in public.

Some of the journals run by these figures during the latter half of the nineteenth century were—*Suriyodhayam* (1869), *Panchama* (1871), *Sugirdavasini* (1879), *Dravida Pandian* (later *Dravidian*, 1885), *Dravida Mithran* (1885), *Anror Mitran* (1886), *Mahavikatathoothan* (1888), *Paraiyan* (1893), *Illara Ozhukkam* (1898), *Buloga Vasagan* (1900), *Dravida Kokilam* (1907), and *Oru Paisa Tamizhan* (later *Tamizhan*, 1907). The idea of 'Dravidian'[23] as a political imaginary, where anti-caste consciousness was first constituted, was also initially mooted by the Dalit-subalterns in the journalistic public sphere.

Raj Gowthaman (2004) supplements this by stating that texts on medicine, astrology, mathematics, astronomy, and grammar, which had a genealogical link with casteless Dravidian languages and Buddhism, were seen as a textual heritage possessed by the Dalits of north Tamil Nadu. Hence, texts such as Markalinga Pandaram's *Kumara Samiyam*, *Manikanda Keralam*, *Sodhida Alangaram*, *Varu Shadhi Nool*, and *Kanidha Nool* were published and circulated during the early nineteenth century. F. W. Ellis's assistant and the manager of Tamil Sangam, Muthusamy Pillai, a Dalit from north Madras, published Nayanar's *Thirikural*, *Naaladi*

Nanooru, and *Aranerith Theebam* with the help of the college at Fort St. George in Madras in the early nineteenth century. Besides, Mayilai Kuzhandhaivelu Pandaram published the *Siddhar Padalgal* and Pudhupettai Thiruvengada Sami Pandithar published *Vaidhya Kaaviyam*, *Sivavaakiyam*, and *Rathina Kaandam*. V. Ayothee Thassa Kaviraja Pandithar, who was apparently Thass' teacher, published *Pogar Ezhunooru*, *Agasthiyar Erunooru*, *Simuttu Rathinach Surookam*, and *Paalavagadam*. This production of texts by Dalits not only created a textual tradition in print that contested the Vedic Brahminic lineage of Tamil texts—both Vaishnavaite and Saivaite—but it also created a public sphere that was textually embodied and laid claim to a casteless civilisation in print (ibid., 116–138).

Hence, reading as an embedded activity was going through a tremendous modification. Print cultures introduced a mediatory effect, particularly through journals. Along with book-reading communities, print enunciated 'political imaginaries' of different kinds (Anderson 1991, 6). The Dalit-subalterns were active agents in such a transition, as participants of an emergent 'sensorium' that was being modulated not only as emancipatory—beyond being considered untouched—but to also lay claim to a civilisation that is much more open.

Thus, Aloysius points out and confirms that there were many reasons for the emergence of a Buddhist movement in northern Tamil Nadu in the second half of the nineteenth century. Primarily, he states, it was 'the relative low-level Brahmin impact on colonialism' (Aloysius 2010, 238) that created a multifaceted awakening among 'the colonially subalternized castes in South India'. He also claims that those who were called Adi-Dravidars and Parayars wielded some access to Tamil literature, medicine, and many sacral traditions based on several forms of asceticism, and suggests that the institutional modernity produced by colonialism provided the content for members of this community to resuscitate themselves, both individually and collectively. One of its manifestations, he claims, is that 'they took to the printed word' as a means of socio-political and religio-cultural awakening as well as mobilisation (ibid., 238–274).

Therefore, the emergence of print journals in the Tamil public sphere can be understood as having triggered debates and discussions on authority, interpretation, different versions of the palm scripts that were converted into print texts, literary historiography, religious and community claims over literary texts, referencing, and literary criticism in a heterogeneously politicised Tamil public sphere. The journalistic practice apparently crafted community as a political force that could emerge through print journalism, especially for the Dalit-subaltern constituencies in the late nineteenth and early twentieth century. But importantly, it was also fashioning new subjects who could sense—read, touch, smell, and cultivate tastes—a research area that is largely omitted and under-studied.

CONCLUSION

The Dalit community, in this context, arguably experiences its own communication as a political signification. This thrust on being-political exposes the community as being-in-common. It could also be understood that writing and communication constitute the 'political' moment in the self-definition of the community. It opens the community to itself, and to its limits. It enjoins its own dissemination, as Nancy argues, through its own writing by opening out to itself, with its own alterity forming a 'unique convergence' (Nancy 1991, xxxvi). Hence, community is brought into free play for a political purpose. Writing is political and gives the community a specific existence—of being-in-common—which gives rise to the existence of being-self. This mode of exposition is also posed towards an alterity—an appeal to the other. Therefore, Dalits cannot think of an anti-caste community as essence; in fact, they must counter it. 'Community is a matter of existence, not of essence, being-in-common without being absorbed into a common substance' (ibid., xxxvii).

Thus, the Tamil Dalits used print journals to create an anti-caste community imaginary in the late nineteenth and early twentieth century. They not only rejected the nationalism propounded by the predominantly upper-caste print-public sphere, but also laid out an alternative knowledge practice. This prioritised the oral traditions present among the oppressed communities. For Thass, journalistic print was used intellectually to retrieve, contest, re-read, and re-evaluate an anti-caste legacy. In short, his search for an anti-caste descent fundamentally transformed what was previously considered immobile and static. Not recognising his efforts is, ironically, to embrace the colonial discourse and high-caste apologetics aimed at erasing more than a century of Dalit attempts to make their own lives visible and legible. Increasingly, thus, Dalits use social media and the internet as alternative technological tools in their fight against caste today. This works against the media giants who structure the globalised regime of power that does not voice the violence of caste loudly.

Dalit intellectuals seem to conceptualise community as moving beyond the traditional model of the social bond, that is, caste. They interrogate community to undo caste and Brahminism. They provide an opportunity for a political to emerge, which would otherwise remain foreclosed. They question, using an ethical-ontological register, the philosophical suppositions of a caste society through a deconstructive understanding of community. Consequently, this provides a deconstructive opening, in an essential way, for the possibility of a casteless community.

Acknowledgements

Comments on an earlier draft by M. T. Ansari, Rupa Viswanath, Gajendran Ayyathurai, Thirumal P., Sumeet Mhaskar, Nathaniel Roberts, Werner Menski, Manju Edachira, and the anonymous reviewer are gratefully acknowledged. Earlier drafts were presented at conferences in Hyderabad and New Delhi, as well as in Berlin and Göttingen; the ideas expressed here owe a great deal to the responses at these forums. This chapter is dedicated to the memory of Professor Gail Omvedt (1941–2021), who relentlessly sought to re-vision *Begumpura* through her actions and words.

NOTES

1. Koppula Nagaraju, a budding journalist and Dalit activist from Hyderabad, who worked in *The Indian Express*, passed away in April 2015 due to a lack of institutional support for his cancer treatment. A discussion on the lack of supportive structures for Dalits and caste discrimination in the media spaces grew into a national debate. This prompted many to articulate the questions of caste in premier English media spaces. Questions about food and social cultures were openly discussed. English media houses in India were branded Brahminical and casteist. Earlier, in a three-part investigative report titled 'The untold story of Dalit journalists', senior journalist Ajaz Ashraf explained in *The Hoot*, a media monitoring website, the reasons behind the poor participation of Dalits in media and their low presence as journalists in India.

He also referred to an earlier article written by journalist B. N. Uniyal, in 1996, titled 'In search of a Dalit journalist', where Uniyal's answer, 'none', triggered Ashraf to start his investigation from the Indian Institute of Mass Communication, which is arguably among the best media institutes in the country. Ashraf interviewed twenty-three Dalit journalists to provide a clear picture of their presence in the Indian mediascape. Ashraf's investigation intended to study how media is imagined by the Dalit respondents' statements vis-à-vis the community's aspirations, while experiencing discrimination in all walks of life. He also turned it into a heterogeneous collective of voices on the mediascape as a spatial imaginary, to be used for the welfare of the oppressed community (Ashraf 2013; Sheth 2015).

2. 'Dalit', as a self-identificatory category of ex-untouchables, has come to indicate and mean a particular kind of realisation and politicisation of outcaste people, who form one-third of the human population in India, as 'broken subjects' in their fight against caste power, especially after the late 1990s. But one is also aware that there are tensions inbuilt in these attempts to conceptualise such a politicised identification. While many have sincerely attempted to converse with and criticise, but never readily reject, Dalit as a category for not reflecting on, if not referring to, the intrinsic differences and omissions that are constituted within, some have reductively treated it as a formation of identity that is essentially birth-based and therefore foreclosed. Nevertheless, one must be acutely informed that historically, Hindu Brahmanical caste practice, while violating the fundamental rights of a Dalit existence, have determinately

heaped humiliations by stigmatising Dalits as Chandalas, Antyajas, Panchamas, and Asprushyas in Brahmanical texts. And in everyday parlance, within specific regional contexts, Dalits are also identified and abused in Tamil as Pallan, Parayan, Chakkiliyan, and so on. Besides, the colonial State, in its collaboration with Hindu Brahmanical imposition, had produced and rigidified equally demeaning nomenclatures as State categories. Thus, even the Gandhian appellate 'Harijan' has a layered patronage that is inbuilt within the larger project of caste humiliation, which Dalits have readily rejected over time. It is in contrast, thus, that ideas and identities are continuously deconstructed, envisioned, and reconstructed by Dalits themselves, which are open-ended and not enclosed (Bathran 2016; Guru 2000; Ilaiah 1998; Jangam 2015; Leonard 2019; Margaret 2010; Muthukaruppan 2014; Nanda 2001; Nigam 2000; Pandian, 2002; Rawat and Satyanarayana 2016).

3. It is generally understood that Dalit writing—as a political act—emerged during the late 1990s, particularly during the 100th birth anniversary of Babasaheb Ambedkar, the unparalleled leader and icon of the oppressed across post-independent India. Dalit politics also emerged, particularly in the Tamil political sphere, with the rise of the *Viduthalai Chiruthaigal* (*Liberation Panthers*) and *Puthiya Tamizhagam* (*New Tamil Nadu*). This was ably supported by the rise of 'little magazines' in the publication field, especially with the circulation of *Dalit Murasu* and *Nirapirakai*. This promoted writers, particularly Dalits, to express and study anti-caste history and thought that had politically a Dalit foregrounding. Many writers explored Dalit poetry, prose, intellectual thought, and history, where figures like Iyothee Thass, Rettaimalai Srinivasan, L. C. Gurusamy, M. C. Rajah, N. Sivaraj, Meenambal, Appaduraiyar, and others were rediscovered.

4. Rajesh lays out three phases of patronage and its networks for the print and publishing industry in Tamil during the nineteenth and early twentieth centuries. The first phase, he states, started in 1812 with the establishment of the college Fort St. George through active patronage from the Madras government. The second phase, from the 1830s to the 1880s, consisted of the editorial and printing activities associated with the Saiva revival movement inaugurated by Arumuga Navalar in Jaffna, which was ably supported by the zamindars of Ramanathapuram and Tiruvavatuturai Atinam in Tirunelveli. The Tamil pandits played a dual role as printers and editor/publishers. And the third phase, from the 1880s to the 1920s, was dominated by C. W. Damodaran Pillai, U. V. Swaminatha Aiyer, and others who published the Sangam epics such as

Silappadhikaram, *Sivakasinthamani*, and *Manimekalai* in the 1880s for the first time. This third phase produced enormous numbers of Tamil classical texts as books by scholars who were all invariably Brahmin, such as U. V. Swaminatha Aiyer, Rajagopala Aiyangar, Pinattur Narayanasamy Aiyar, and Sowriperumal Aranyan. An intense competition continued between Damodaran Pillai from the Saiva mutt and Swaminatha Iyer to produce the maximum number of books from the antique Tamil past. Aiyar also maintained his link with very rich patronage networks, so much so that Rajesh clearly states that a conglomeration of upper-caste landholding communities such as *Smartha* Brahmins, Chettiars, Mudaliars, Vellala Pillais, and Maravars, in alliance with dominant Saiva mutts and colonial officers, actively participated in the transformation of the Tamil classics from the manuscript to its publication in printed book form (Rajesh 2012, 64–91).

5. It can be argued that Dalits largely countered the emergent dominant caste public sphere through print, so as to carve an anti-caste movement. Perhaps different kinds of nations as political imaginaries would have competed against each other—with respect to the caste question—within the same language, in the context of the changing reading practices that modern print enunciated in the twentieth century.

6. In recent years, attempts have been made to investigate the articulations of oppressed communities in the sphere of printing and publishing in colonial Tamil Nadu. Works such as Rajangam's *Theendapadatha Noolgal* (*Untouchable Books*, 2008) and Balasubramaniam's *Suryodhayam Mudhal Udhayasooryan Varai* (*From Suryodhayam to Udhayasooryan*, 2017) provide an excellent account of Dalit engagement with Tamil print in the nineteenth and twentieth century.

7. Ramaswamy's *Passions of the Tongue* (1997), a definitive book on the sociocultural history of modern Tamil Nadu, covering the period 1891–1970, does not even mention Thass in so much as a footnote. After more than two decades, Venkatachalapathy's *Tamil Characters* (2018), a book on Tamil political, cultural, and literary history, dedicates a chapter to Thass. But he acknowledges Thass as a cultural and literary figure who only anticipated Ambedkar, and not as a political personality in his own right—even in comparison to 'old guard' personalities such as the journalist 'Cho' Ramaswamy. Besides, the Dalit questioning of Dravidian politics is often viewed with contempt in the third part of his book on 'cultural questions'. A certain 'brushing aside', if not erasure, 'of the life-long efforts of Dalit intellectuals and activists who recovered

Dalit history, and challenged Dravidian politics', seems to be the general tone of such historians on Tamil Nadu (Azhagarasan 2019).

In contrast, works by Aloysius, Gowthaman, Dharmaraj, Ayyathurai, and Rajangam study Tamil history through different modes of enquiry—sociological, religious, cultural, historical-anthropology, and literary—by particularly foregrounding Thass as an anti-caste organic intellectual, who worked on an epistemology against Hinduism by engaging with print, towards a social movement.

8. Pandithar Iyothee Thassar (1845–1914) was born a Dalit from the Parayar community; nevertheless, he contested the category Paraya throughout his life. He floated alternative open identities such as *Poorva Bouddhar* (ancient Buddhist), *Jaadhi pedha matra Tamizhar/Dravidar* (casteless Tamils/Dravidians), and *Tamil Bouddhar* (Tamil Buddhist). Pandithar Iyothee Thaasar is also called Iyothee Thass and Thass in this chapter.

9. Likewise, many such figures seem to have worked like Thass during the same period in the vernacular regions. Narayana Guru (1856–1928) from Kerala, Bhima Bhoi (1850–1895) in Orissa, Poikkayil Yohannan (1878–1939) in Kerala, and a little earlier, Jyotirao Phule (1827–1890), had created a hermeneutic of anti-caste community in writing.

10. It is important to note the similar realm in which anti-caste intellectuals treat re-naming as a political act. Bhimarao Ramji Ambavadekar changed his name to B. R. Ambedkar in memory of his teacher. And later, in 'Away from the Hindus', Ambedkar explored a very interesting theory of names in the wake of the resolution passed in the 1936 Mahar conference in Bombay, where the community decided to abandon Hinduism and convert to some other religion. Ambedkar argued that:

> The name matters and matters a great deal. For, the name can make a revolution in the status of the Untouchables. But the name must be the name of a community outside Hinduism and beyond its power of spoliation and degradation. Such name can be the property of the Untouchable only if they undergo religious conversion. A conversion within Hinduism is a clandestine conversion which can be of no avail. (2014, 420)

11. Gopal Guru's 'The Idea of India' (2011) categorises the dominant nationalist thought in India as 'derivative' and 'desi'. He understands Chatterjee's work on nationalist thought as 'derivative', in the sense that it fashions itself on a modular form of nationalism as developed in the West, and is quite selective about its sources, at least for political

reasons. He argues that the derivative as a methodological language is necessary, but not sufficiently capacious to unfold the differential nature of nationalist thought in India. Guru presents a sharp contrast to the 'derivative' and 'desi' discourses governing nationalist thought and the 'idea of India' by studying the Dalit discourse in India. He demonstrates that the Dalit discourse—especially B. R. Ambedkar's work and life—goes 'beyond' the two in offering an imagination that is based on a 'negative' language which, however, transcends into a normative form of thinking. One can see similar creative impulses in much earlier anti-caste works, such as Iyothee Thass' writings on religion, particularly Tamil Buddhism.

12. Ponnovium was born in Penang, Malaysia in 1923. He settled down in Tindivanam near Madras, and along with his family, was one of the earliest followers of Tamil Buddhism. He worked for the Archaelogical Survey of India. Thass' quotations from the *Tamizhan* archives, including those cited by Ponnovium and Gowthaman, have been translated into English by me. The references from the *Tamizhan* archives are taken from Aloysius' edited volumes (see Aloysius 1999).

13. It is understandable to equate such attempts by subaltern thinkers to their immediate (out)caste identities, such as the Pallar, Parayar, or Chakkiliar, and so treat them as icons of these particular communities alone, even if they had continuously offered identifications such as Adi-Hindu, Adi-Dravidar, or Adi-Tamizhar in the twentieth century. This chapter, however, provides a departure from such a trajectory of descriptions that tacitly interpret, if not refute, these icons and their movements as 'problems and anomalies' (Geetha 2014). As Thass openly refuted such humiliating identities and called for open-ended casteless identifications and/or ideas, such as the *Jathi Betha Matra* (casteless) Tamilian and Buddhist, it is important to foreground these ideas as being iconic in history because they significantly bear an anti-caste signature and content, envisioning casteless pasts and futures for everyone. Thus, Dalit can be a creative yet critical position that recuperates an anti-caste tradition for their own emancipation from different sources. This is perhaps an exposition of the Dalit category to its outside, and to its other, so that anyone could ex-casteise themselves in their attempt to go 'beyond' any enclosures (Aloysius 2010; Guru 2011).

14. Ponnovium recounts that the Adi-Dravida Jana Sabhai, which was registered in 1892, was first run even before the Non-Brahmin conglomeration started. Thereafter, it was followed by the Adi-Dravida Maha Jana Sabai in 1916 and the All India Adi Dravida Maha Jana

Sabai in 1928. They were mostly run as grassroots organisations that worked not only for civic and social rights, but also for the right to political representatio (1999, xxiv).

15. For the first time, countering the lack of historical accounts of the Dalits and the print public sphere in the colonial period, historian Balasubramaniam (2017) highlights the 74-year-old history (1869–1943) of Dalit engagement with modern print in the Tamil country in his book (written in Tamil).

16. In 1891, Rettaimalai Srinivasan started the Paraiyar Mahajana Sabha and Thass started the Dravida Mahajana Sabha. Although they were related to each other, Thass filed a petition against Srinivasan's journal *Paraiyan* for using the term in contempt and for hurting the sentiments of the people. Aloysius argues that 'a very debatable Parayar-political emerged, and that a possible rivalry between both the leaders' also began along with it. Srinivasan was the foremost critic of Iyothee Thass, as '*Tamizhan* carried on a relentless hermeneutical battle against Paraiyar as a word to collectively identify the Subaltern communities' (Aloysius 2010, 241).

17. It is important to note the emergence of the first generation of leadership within the Dalit community in the early twentieth century—R. Srinivasan, Swami Sahajananda, M. C. Rajah, Veeraiyan, L.C. Guruswamy, Madurai Pillay, V. G. Vasudev Pillay, Appaduraiyar, Annapoorani Ammal, V. I. Munusamy Pillai, Periyasamy Pulavar, N. Sivaraj, Meenambal Sivaraj, and B. M. Rajarathinam. This crop of subaltern leaders and their organisation preceded the Non-Brahmin movement that produced a different kind of leader, and the former advocated a much more inclusive identity (Aloysius 2010, 259).

18. Thass claims that his grandfather Kandappan who worked as a butler to George Harrington, who was a close friend of F.W. Ellis, had given the palm-scripts of *Thirukural* and *Naaladi Nanooru* from *Sangam* literature around the year 1812 for the college at Fort St. George's work on the 'Dravidian proof' (*ibid*). Besides Thass highlights that the *Adi-Dravidas* contributed to this Tamil legacy, and therefore, suggesting that this was in continuity to the work of the Dravidian scholarship and the *Adi-Dravidas* relationship with the British in this front. Thass also wanted the Tamil letters to be reduced to make it pragmatically useful for print which eventually happened during the Dravidian movement after 1930s.

19. Belittling the Dalit movement's trenchant activities against caste, V. Geetha and S. V. Rajadurai, in *Towards a Non-Brahmin Millennium*,

suggest that leaders from the Dalit communities who possessed political power had a truncated political imagination (1998, 504). They find no use for them in their utopian or millenarian thought, which remains a staple of all anti-caste discourses in the modern period. This is also true of M. S. S. Pandian's seminal work, *Brahmin and Non-Brahmin* (2007), where he studies Thass along with Maraimalai Adigal (1876–1950) instead of a comparison with the more radical Muthu Kutty Swamigal and the *Ayyavazhi* movement, only to conceptualise how the new voice of the 'Non-Brahmin' speaks of the other and makes their own self. Pandian acknowledges that a network of associational life in the Madras Presidency during the late nineteenth and early twentieth centuries was run by the oppressed, who sought to air their views and grievances by publishing tracts and setting up organisations. However, just like Geetha and Rajadurai, he also sees them as articulating their views about only the Brahmin. Perhaps there is more to this 'talking', which may be interpreted as 'voicing' for a community of freedom to come, which is a self-becoming. As these expressions find their 'voice' in the emergent print public sphere for the first time, they cannot be just identified as narratives of identity, or that they merely celebrate their existent beings as 'untouchables, Sudras, neo-Buddhists, Saivaites, and rationalists'. (ibid., 102–143). He observes that Thass had to talk about the Brahmin to speak of one's emancipatory self. This is an inadequate reading as it does not account for—if not actively denies—the role of the oppressed communities' fight against caste in history.

20. To exaggerate and extend this a little bit, it is not hard to notice that Ambedkar and his followers claimed Jyotirao Phule as their precursor and guide for the movement against caste in Maharashtra and elsewhere, while no such claims were made by either Periyar or his followers. Ayyathurai thus argues that Dalits never presumed an egalitarian treatment within the non-Brahmin consciousness that the Dravidian movement propagated; in fact, they were ambiguously placed in the non-Brahmin discourse. They were ambiguously placed, he claims, in the Non-Brahmin discourse, which led to 'the *retention* of a dichotomy between the Dalits and non-brahmins unsurprisingly, as it was between the non-brahmins and brahmins' (Ayyathurai 2011, 25). He concludes that while Thass' articulations precede Periyar's critique of caste and Brahminism 'by more than three decades' (ibid., 219), what remains unexamined and acknowledged is the connection between their palpable resonances.

21. Orientalist discourse created the Brahmin as having an affirmative congruence with power, while identifying the Paraiyar as having a negative congruence with that same power. However, Thass consistently pointed out and relentlessly challenged the real-life Brahmin resistance to subaltern emergence in the new spheres of land allotment, education, employment, and political representation (Aloysius 2010, 245–246).

22. In *Tamizhan*, for instance, Thass deconstructs the narratives on *panchamas*, untouchables, and depressed classes that were circulated in the late nineteenth-century public sphere in Madras, through a thorough hermeneutic exploration of the word to reject the construction of the same. About the *panchamas*, he asks wittily: 'Are these the remnants of *pandavas* (*pancha pandavas*) of old, or victims of a famine (*pancham*), or constituted from the five elements (*panchaputham*) or are they indeed thrashed and scattered as cotton (*panchu*) or do they live along the five rivers (*pancha nadhi*)' (Aloysius 2010, 252)? He also states that the discourse changed from *panchamas* to depressed classes, only to dispense with the notions of pity, condescension, and welfare engagement for the dominant groups. He claims that this was a form of contempt, connoting that the so-called depressed classes lacked ideological and cultural resources, and hence an absence of human dignity. In this narration of the oppressed and the depressed, it appeared that the dominant Brahmin would be both the centre and the subject. Hence, he believed that all the talk about upliftment and welfare was merely opportunistic, adding that it was the best method for self-empowerment and employment. This was, he accused, a strategy deployed by the dominant players to curb the initiative of the so-called oppressed and restrict them to their present degraded status. As a counter to that, Thass proposed the identity of the true Buddhist to contest the idea of uplift by the other. Thus, he rejected identifications such as Paraiyar and lower castes as counter opposites to the self-identifications of the Brahmin and the upper caste.

23. The magazine *Dravida Pandian*, started by Rev. John Rathinam and Thass in 1885, was the first magazine to use the term 'Dravidian'.

References

Aloysius, G. 1998. *Religion as Emancipatory Identity: A Buddhist Movement among the Tamils under Colonialism*. New Delhi: New Age International.

Aloysius, G. 2003. *Iyothee Thassar Cinthanaikal (Thoughts of Iyothee Thassar)*. Vol. 3. Palayamkottai: Folklore Resources and Research Center, St. Xavier's College.

_____. 2010. 'Vicissitudes of Subaltern Self-Identification: A Reading of Tamizhan'. In Michael Bergunder, et al. (ed.), *Ritual, Caste, and Religion in Colonial South India*, 238–274. Halle: Neue Hallesche Berichte 9.

_____. 2015. *Iyothee Thassar and Tamil Buddhist Movement: Religion as Emancipatory Movement*. New Delhi: Critical Quest.

_____. (ed.). 1999. *Iyothee Thassar Cinthanaikal (Thoughts of Iyothee Thassar)*, 2 vols. Palayamkottai: Folklore Resources and Research Center, St. Xavier's College.

Ambedkar, B. R. 1993. 'Waiting for Visa'. In Vasant Moon (ed.), *Dr. Babasaheb Ambedkar: Writings and Speeches*, Vol. 12, 661–691. Bombay: Education Department, Government of Maharashtra.

_____. 2014. 'Away from the Hindus'. In Vasant Moon (ed.), *Dr. Babasaheb Ambedkar: Writing and Speeches*, Vol. 5, 403–421. New Delhi: Dr Ambedkar Foundation.

Anderson, B. 1991. *Imagined Communities: Reflections on the Origin and Spread of Nationalism*. London: Verso.

Ashraf, A. 2013.'The Untold Story of Dalit Journalists'. *The Hoot*, 12 August. Available at http://asu.thehoot.org/media-watch/media-practice/the-untold-story-of-dalit-journalists-6956#:~:text=To%20study%20their%20negligible%20presence,and%20their%20disenchantment%20with%20journalism.&text=None%20knew%20of%20a%20Dalit%20journalist (accessed December 2024).

Ayyathurai, G. 2011. 'Foundations of Anti-Caste Consciousness: Pandit Iyothee Thass, Tamil Buddhism and the Marginalized in South India'. Ph.D. Thesis, Columbia University, New York.

Azhagarasan, R. 2019. '"Tamil Characters—Personalities, Politics, Culture" Review: Politics and Social Justice'. *The Hindu*, 31 May. Available at https://www.thehindu.com/books/books-reviews/tamil-characters-personalities-politics-culture-review-politics-and-social-justice/article27376124.ece (accessed December 2024).

Balasubramaniam, J. 2011. 'Dalits and a Lack of Diversity in the Newsroom'. *Economic and Political Weekly* 46 (11), 21–23.

_____. 2016. 'Migration of the Oppressed and Adi Dravida identity Construction Through Print'. *Contemporary Voice of Dalit* 8 (2), 1–6.

Balasubramaniam, J. 2017. *Suriyodhayam Mudhal Udhaya Sooryan Varai: Dalith Idhalgal, 1869–1943 (From Suriyodhayam to Udhaya Sooryan: Dalit Journals, 1869–1943)*. Nagercoil: Kalachuvadu.

Basu, Raj Sekhar. 2011. *Nandanar's Children: The Paraiyan's Tryst with Destiny, Tamil Nadu 1850–1916*. New Delhi: Sage.

Bathran, R. 2016. 'The Many Omissions of a Concept'. *Economic and Political Weekly* 51 (47), 30–34.

Blackburn, S. 2003. *Print, Folklore, and Nationalism in Colonialism South India*. New Delhi: Permanent Black.

Chatterjee, P. 1986. *Nationalist Thought and the Colonial World: A Derivative Discourse*. London: Zed Books.

______. 1993. *Nation and its Fragments: Colonial and Postcolonial Histories*. Princeton: Princeton University Press.

Geetha, K. A. 2014. 'Unified Tamil Dalit Identity: Problematics and Anomalies'. *Prose Studies* 36 (2), 130–140.

Geetha, V., and S. V. Rajadurai. 1998. *Towards a Non-Brahmin Millennium: From Iyothee Thass to Periyar*. Kolkata: Samya.

Gowthaman, R. 2004. *Ka. Iyotheethassarin Aaivugal* (*K. Iyothee Thass' Research*). Nagercoil: Kalachuvadu.

Gupta, A., and S. Chakravorty (eds). 2004. *Print Areas*. New Delhi: Permanent Black.

______. 2008. *Moveable Type*. New Delhi: Permanent Black.

______. 2016. *Founts of Knowledge*. New Delhi: Orient BlackSwan.

Guru, Gopal. 2000. 'Dalits in Pursuit of Modernity'. In Romila Thapar (ed.), *India: Another Millenium*, 123–137. New Delhi: Viking.

______. 2011. 'The Idea of India: "Derivative, Desi and Beyond"'. *Economic and Political Weekly* 46 (37), 36–42.

Ilaiah, K. 1998. 'Towards the Dalitization of the Nation'. In Partha Chatterjee (ed.), *Wages of Freedom*, 267–292. New Delhi: Oxford University Press.

Ivins Jr., W. 1969. *Prints and Visual Communication*. Massachusetts: MIT Press.

Jangam, C. 2015. 'Politics of Identity and the Project of Writing'. *Economic and Political Weekly* 50 (40), 63–70.

Leonard, D. 2017. 'One Step Inside *Tamilian*: On the Anti-Caste Writing of Language'. *Social Scientist* 45 (1–2), 19–32.

______. 2019. 'Towards a Casteless Community: Dalit Experience and Thought as *Movement*'. *Economic and Political Weekly* 54 (21), 47–54.

Leonard, D. 2020. 'Anti-caste Communitas and Outcaste Experience: Space, Body, Displacement and Writing'. In Kaustav Chakraborty (ed.), *The Politics of Belonging in Contemporary India*, 101–125. New Delhi: Routledge.

Margaret, S. 2010. 'Dalit Feminism'. *Round Table India*, 3 October. Available at https://www.roundtableindia.co.in/dalit-feminism-23642/ (accessed January 2025).

McLuhan, M. 1962. *The Gutenberg Galaxy: The Making of Typographic Man*. Toronto: University of Toronto Press.

Muthukaruppan, P. 2014. 'Dalit: The Making of a Political Subject'. *Critical Quarterly* 56 (3), 34–45.

Nancy, J.-L. 1991. *The Inoperative Community*, Peter Connor (ed.) and Peter Connor, et al. (trans.). Minneapolis and London: University of Minnesota Press.

Nanda, M. 2001. 'Hitching Dalit Modernity to Anti-Modernist Wagon'. *Economic and Political Weekly* 36 (17), 1480–1483.

Nigam, A. 2000. 'Secularism, Nation and Modernity: Epistemology of the Dalit Critique'. *Economic and Political Weekly* 35 (48), 4526–4568.

Oxfam India. 2019. 'Who Tells Our Stories Matters: Representation of Marginalised Caste Groups in Indian Newsrooms'. *Oxfamindia.org*, 2 August. Available at https://www.oxfamindia.org/sites/default/files/2019-08/Oxfam%20NewsLaundry%20Report_For%20Media%20use.pdf (accessed December 2024).

Pandian, M. S. S. 2002. 'One Step outside Modernity: Caste, Identity Politics and Public Sphere'. *Economic and Political Weekly* 37 (8), 1735–1741.

_____. 2007. *The Brahmin and the Non-Brahmin: Genealogies of the Tamil Political Present*. New Delhi: Permanent Black.

Perumal, S. 2000. *People's Movements and Tamil Publications, 1850–1950*. Vellore: Megalai Publications.

Ponnovium, A. 1999. 'Iyothee Thassar: Oru Kannottam' ('Iyothee Thassar: A View'). In G. Aloysius (ed.), *Iyothee Thassar Sindhanaigal* (*Iyothee Thassar's Thoughts*), Vol. 1, xxiii–xlvi. Palayamkottai: Folklore Resources and Research Centre.

Rajangam, S. 2008. *Theendapadatha Noolgal* (*Untouchable Books*). Chennai: Azhi Pathipagam.

Rajesh, V. 2011. 'Patrons and Networks of Patronage in the publication of Tamil Classics, c1800–1920'. *Social Scientist* 39 (3–4), 64–91.

Rajesh, V. 2013. *Reproduction and Reception of Classical Tamil Literature: Textual Culture in Colonial Madras*. New Delhi: Cambridge University Press.

Ramasamy, S. 1997. *Passions of the Tongue: Language Devotion in Tamil Nadu, 1891–1970*. Berkeley: University of California Press.

Ravikumar, D. 2007. 'The Unwritten Writing: Dalits and the Media'. In Nalini Rajan (ed.), *21st Century Journalism in India*, 61–77. New Delhi: Sage.

Rawat, R., and K. Satyanarayana. 2016. 'Dalit Studies: New Perspectives on Indian History and Society'. In R. Rawat and K. Satyanarayana (eds), *Dalit Studies*, 1–30. Durham: Duke University Press.

Sheth, A. 2015. 'The Death of a Dalit Journalist and the Question of Casteism in Indian Media'. *The News Minute*, April. Available at https://www.thenewsminute.com/flix/death-dalit-journalist-and-question-casteism-indian-media-32336 (accessed January 2025).

Thankappan, R. 2015. 'Dalit (In)visibility and Journalism as Site of Caste Violence'. *Anveshi: Broadsheet on Contemporary Politics* 2 (10–11), 24–26.

Velmangai, K., and L. Selvamuthu Kumarasami. 2013. 'Iyothee Thass and Depressed Class Intellectuals' Print and Press Media in Liberation Struggle in Tamil Nadu'. *Indian Streams Research Journal* 2 (12) (January), 1–6.

Venkatachalapathy, A. R. 2012. *The Province of the Book: Scholars, Scribes and Scribblers in Colonial Tamil-nadu*. New Delhi: Permanent Black.

———. 2018. *Tamil Characters: Personalities, Politics, Culture*. New Delhi: Pan Macmillan.

 8

'Reality Must Improve'

The Perversity of Expertise and the Belatedness of Indian Development Television*

William Mazzarella

Sometimes I wonder whether it would have been better if we had no image of what TV is ... if we had just started here and nobody else had TV.

Yash Pal, quoted in Agrawal and Sinha (1986, 6)

Television came to India late, although the facts would seem to suggest otherwise. The very first small-scale telecasts took place in Delhi in 1959. The Satellite Television Instructional Experiment (SITE) of 1975–1976, an India–US joint venture, was the most ambitious attempt of its time to harness satellite TV to rural development. But television did not become a standard, taken-for-granted part of the fabric of Indian everyday life until the mid-1980s. Still, this chapter suggests that some of the most interesting and important questions arising out of India's experience with television had effectively been effaced by the time the medium caught on.

To that end, I will be making a double argument. On one level, I argue against reducing the story of Indian television to an oversimplified transition between 'statist' and 'consumerist'

*This chapter was previously published as '"Reality Must Improve" The Perversity of Expertise and the Belatedness of Indian Development Television', *Global Media and Communication* 8 (December), 2012, 215–41.

dispensations. As two apparently irreconcilable ideologies of television, the statist and consumerist models represent two ways of imagining the relation between the deployment of media and the project of modernity. Despite their surface differences, I will propose that both share a tendency to imagine television in primarily 'representative', rather than 'constitutive', terms. In other words, they both evaluate television according to its ability to represent or address supposedly pre-existing publics, as opposed to its power to help constitute those very publics. On another level, this privileging of the representative over the constitutive functions of media also helps to lend a dubious sense of historical inevitability to the transition between statist and consumerist dispensations.

On both counts, I will show how these assumptions can be called into question by revisiting a period in Indian television history—the decade stretching from the mid-1970s to the mid-1980s—that is too easily dismissed as little more than a transitional phase. My purpose certainly exceeds the antiquarian; I argue that the particularities of this apparently transitional period offer materials for a rethinking of both earlier and later phases of India's television experience. And while this chapter is empirically located in India, I hope that its categories might open onto comparative explorations of the relation between media and modernity in an age of globalisation.

Living Fossil

Today, India lives and breathes television. Until the early 1990s, Indian television was a government monopoly, embodied in the much-maligned state-run service, Doordarshan (DD). Currently, there are more than 500 different television channels, broadcasting in a dizzying variety of languages, styles, and formats. By the mid-2000s, India's television market was the third largest in the world, behind only the United States and China (Mehta 2008). Where once journalists and activists debated the functions, futures, and potential of television as an instrument of social transformation and/or entertainment, we are now left with little more than a story of how 'the market' rescued the medium from 'the State'. As Nalin Mehta writes: '[P]rivate industry broke down the barriers of statist control' (ibid., 7). Thanks to the market, apparently, the consumer-spectator wins: '[I]t is an entirely different world for Indian viewers today. [No longer] condemned to the so-called "have-it-or-leave-it" syndrome of the government-controlled Doordarshan, the audience can now have the last laugh by shuffling the channels around for the viewing of their choice' (Saksena 1996, 10).

Certainly, there is little reason to wax nostalgic about the bad old days of Doordarshan. Infamously bureaucratic, technically inept, corrupt, and directionless, the government television service and the ministry that controlled it were staffed by political appointees who often had little understanding of the medium and even less incentive to learn. Doordarshan's fawning coverage of the ruling Gandhi-Nehru dynasty's every movement prompted a survey by the market research company, Pathfinders, to remark in 1983 that '[d]uring the Emergency [Prime Minister Indira Gandhi's experiment with dictatorship in 1975–1977], Doordarshan promoted "youth leader" [Mrs Gandhi's younger son and heir apparent] Sanjay Gandhi with a fervour that even Kim Il Sung would have found embarrassing' (*Imprint* 1983). Little changed in this respect even after the Emergency. Despite Rajiv Gandhi's occasional attempts to make Doordarshan look more 'professional' and 'credible' during his tenure as Prime Minister (1984–1989), the State broadcasting operation, which in earlier years had been satirised as All-Indira Radio, now gained the sarcastic nickname, Rajiv Darshan[1] (Farmer 2003; Jeffrey 2008).

> [A]s the years passed, [Doordarshan] degenerated into nothing more than a propaganda machine for the government, carrying boring programmes on different development schemes, on what was happening abroad and in the country as given to them by the Ministry of External Affairs and the Ministry of Home Affairs, and broadcasting 'cultural' programmes that someone influential wanted shown, irrespective of how disgracefully shoddy and cheap they were. (Ghose 2005, 213)

These are not an outsider's easy potshots at Doordarshan, but the considered summation of a former Director General.

Throughout the 1970s and 1980s, the recurring assertion was that Indian television remained creatively and organisationally stunted because the government refused to grant Doordarshan the kind of formal autonomy enjoyed by a public broadcaster like the British Broadcasting Corporation (BBC). Concerted pushes to make Doordarshan autonomous occurred at moments of political transition in the late 1970s and the late 1980s, only to be frustrated each time by the collapse of fragile coalitions. By the time a watered-down version of the autonomy bill was finally enacted in 1997, the private broadcasting revolution had already occurred. In effect, the commercialisation of Indian broadcasting—the emergence of a kind of 'market autonomy'—had superseded the pursuit of an autonomous public broadcaster.[2] Apparently, by embracing an irreverent, entertainment-based appeal to Indian audiences, the market had brought about what the State never quite achieved: a vibrant televisual field comprising mass-mediated versions of the living manifold of Indian life ways (McMillin 2003; Mehta 2008).

Clearly, the cultural effects of a consumerist globalisation in world media have been far more complex than the prophets of cultural imperialism imagined in the 1970s and 1980s (Mazzarella 2003, 2004; *cf.* Tomlinson 1991). Until the 1990s, critics of the commercialisation of Indian television were certain that privatisation would bring only cultural homogenisation; Indians would be forced to watch whatever second-rate American soap operas had already maxed out their earning potential in First World markets. By the mid-1990s, however, it was clear that the new crop of globalisation theorists' predictions were coming true with respect to Indian television as well. If anything, the proliferation of private channels had led to a dizzying diversification of content, with the fastest growth being not in foreign content, but in Indian language shows.

At the same time, we should not forget that the story of the dismal mismanagement of television committed by successive Indian governments between the late 1950s and the early 1990s—a litany of missed opportunities (Farmer 2003)—continues today to shore up the legitimacy of market solutions. Of course, laments about the displacement of serious social issues by light entertainment and tabloid prurience still appear on the op-ed pages of Indian dailies, but it has become difficult to call the reigning market populism into question without coming across as dourly nostalgic for an outmoded paternalist-statist vision of the purpose of television.

Perhaps there is still room to shift the terms of the debate? Perhaps something about the earlier developmentalist dispensation has been effaced in this triumphant story of neoliberal liberation? My aim in this chapter is to revisit a fascinating period in the development of Indian television: the late 1970s and early 1980s, the years between the monumental statism of SITE in the mid-1970s and the consolidation of consumerist television in the mid-1980s. The coming of a new era—in this case, the 'opening up' of media markets and the breakdown of Doordarshan's monopoly—does not simply mean the redundancy of the old days. Rather, the apparently surpassed moment has been preserved as a kind of living fossil, alive enough to remind us of the undesirability of its time—the corruption, the tedium, the incompetence—but by the same token, trapped in a single, repetitive gesture: the gesture of obsolescence. Walter Benjamin once remarked that nothing was as unerotic as the recent past.[3] Constrained to bear witness, again and again, only to its own repulsive outmodedness, the living fossil of the recent past does the ideological work of underwriting the desirability and necessity of the present.

In histories of Indian television, the period comprising the late 1970s and early 1980s tends to be overshadowed by what came before, the soaring ambition but uncertain returns of SITE, and by what followed, the popular triumph of sponsored soap operas, mythological serials, and, in the 1990s, the explosion of satellite channels. Others have written compellingly on the rise of consumer spectatorship from the mid-1980s onward (Mankekar 1999; Rajagopal 2001), and SITE usually gets a mention in overviews of global TV history. But was the period that intervened just a kind of indeterminate grey zone between statist and commercial television paradigms? Not at all. Infused with the political energy of having defeated Indira Gandhi's Emergency and its top-down legacy of authoritarian communication, but at the same time not yet completely convinced of the inevitability of a commercial entertainment model for Indian television, broadcasting policy debates during these years were unusually energetic and open-ended.

Between the end of the Emergency in 1977 and the rapid expansion of Doordarshan as a commercial network starting in 1983, the emphasis of official policy certainly did shift from rural development to middle-class entertainment. Arvind Rajagopal argues that the Emergency was the crucial turning point between statist-developmentalist and market-populist dispensations in India, 'the high water mark of the developmental era' (Rajagopal 2011, 14). Victoria Farmer (2003) notes that SITE, which was supposed to inaugurate a whole new era of developmentalist broadcasting, in retrospect marked at once its pinnacle and its last hurrah. This is no doubt correct, but it seems to me that what makes the period between the Emergency and the commercial revolution so interesting is that the paradigms had not yet settled. While the commercialisation of Indian television might in retrospect appear to be a foregone conclusion, the debates that were still live during the decade stretching, roughly, from the mid-1970s to the mid-1980s problematised the relation between statist and market communication models more directly than at any point before or since. Or, to put it more simply, this was a time when it was still just about possible to imagine television as being something other than *either* 'what the State wants you to see' *or* 'what you, the consumer, want'.

Freeze Frame

One might say that this transitional moment is analogous to a lap dissolve between scenes in a movie. By freeze-framing the transition in the middle of the dissolve, I hope to arrest the retroactive sense of inevitability with which one era passes into another, and to dwell for a moment on an image that is curiously and inconclusively doubled, where figures supposedly belonging to completely different times and places blend and overlap in an ambiguous chronotope. My wager here is that we will remember something that has been conveniently forgotten in the history of Indian television. By revisiting this largely forgotten period, I am also trying to unsettle the complacency with which a simplified version of the televisual past has come to serve as an ideological alibi for the necessity of our neoliberal present.

At the most general level, I offer an argument about the relation between media and the particular conception of non-Western modernity invoked by the post-World War II global development paradigm. The European ideal of modern subjectivity, as crystallised in Enlightenment thought, rested on the proposition that the uniquely human capacity for reflective reason offered 'an "exit," a "way out"' from what was seen as a merely animal servitude to nature (Foucault 1997, 305). In Europe, this modern subjectivity was from the beginning tied to the political discourse of democracy, whether in its republican or its monarchical forms. The political freedoms of modern mass society were, in other words, imagined as coeval with the philosophical freedom of the modern subject.

Non-Western societies were, from the very beginning of this philosophical discourse of modernity, wheeled into service as exemplifications of lack—either as entirely deprived of the illumination of reason, or as stuck in a civilisational limbo between superstition and emancipation. After World War II, the colonial white man's burden shifted into a commitment to the socioeconomic development of a postcolonial world, now organised into independent nation-states. Consequently, the much-desired, ever-deferred condition of modernity, as viewed from what was now the 'developing world', became curiously split. Political freedom had already been attained in the form of national independence, but postcolonial elites within those new nations tended to legitimate their own custodianship of the development ideal—the urgent *need* for development—on the grounds that the vast majority of their less privileged compatriots had so far failed to manifest the forms of modern consciousness that had purportedly been achieved in the developed West. Postcolonial modernity, then, itself appeared as a kind of freeze-framed transition—a condition that had both *already* and *not yet* been achieved. Development was, one might say, the process through which the already achieved and the not yet reached aspects of postcolonial modernity might be brought together.

But herein lay another tension. Modernity was, by Enlightenment definition, the outcome of a process of autonomous self-fashioning: the rigorous cultivation of an inherent human capacity for reason with a view to the realisation of rational social forms. And yet, modernity as a universalised form of consciousness seemed to exist only in the developed West, and as such, to stand as a foreign example to be mimetically—and urgently—emulated by developing countries (Chakrabarty 2000; Chatterjee 1986, 1993).

This is where the electronic mass media entered the picture. The Enlightenment ideal of the modern subject rested on a conception of what Immanuel Kant (1970 [1784]) identified as 'public reason', a self-constituting autonomous space of public deliberation made possible by a literate print-based public sphere (Habermas 1989 [1962]). Given the absence of mass literacy in the post-war developing world, audio/visual mass media like cinema, radio, and television seemed to offer an efficient alternative. But the one-to-many, top-down broadcast structure of these media in their national avatars, together with the prevailing sense of urgency about 'catching up' with forms of modernity imagined as already existing in the developed world, tended to push the deployment of these media away from what I would call their *constitutive* possibilities and toward a more *representative* function. In a constitutive mode, media provides a public space in which to actualise social potentials, a context in which new collective self-understandings can emerge. In a representative mode, conversely, media either didactically stages aspirational ideals (for example, a 'modern way of life', etc.) that have been centrally pre-decided (the statist model), or communicate messages that are intended to 'fit' their audiences' pre-identified 'cultural values' (the consumerist model).

I suggest this distinction between constitutive and representative functions not as a description of empirically available pure forms, but rather as a heuristic for identifying emphases and tendencies. Clearly, any given media situation contains elements of both. But the distinction is useful for my argument here because it allows us to move beyond the over-determined state *versus* market reading of media histories. The question that runs through this chapter is: Why, despite constantly invoking a more actively constitutive potential for development television, has the critique of top-down statist media strategies, as articulated in countless editorials beginning in the early 1980s, nevertheless consistently tended to fall back on a representative ideal of cultural 'fit'? In the Indian context, one important reason for this consistent return to a representative ideal is the largely unacknowledged affinity between the discourse of cultural fit—in which development television 'caters to' the specific values and needs of a given population—and the kind of liberal-consumerist market orientation toward media policy ('give consumers what they want') that started becoming hegemonic in India in the mid-1980s. But I also want to argue that the very notion of state-coordinated development depends on a model of authority and expertise that wants media to be socially transformative, while refusing to grant them the open-endedly constitutive role that such transformation would require. Here, too, a representative reading of mass mediation remains the default position.

BOREDOM AND PLEASURE

Television was formally inaugurated in India in a very modest way on 15 September 1959. The Government of India, leaning heavily on money and equipment donated by UNESCO to promote television as a tool of community education, set up a 500-watt transmitter in New Delhi with a broadcasting range of 2.4 km.

There were seventy-one receiving sets. The official approach to broadcasting was distinctly top-down:

> [T]he state's communication policy rested on the axiom that information, rather than structural change, was the most essential ingredient required for India to modernise: disseminating development information would lead to a change in the attitudes of Indians, and this attitudinal change would, in turn, lead to a change in their practices. (Mankekar 1999, 59)

From the First Five-Year Plan in the early 1950s through the next thirty years, television was primarily conceived as an official mouthpiece of the government, the purpose of which was to facilitate the alignment of India's population to Plan policy.[4]

Still restricted to the Delhi area, television underwent a very slow expansion throughout the 1960s, supported by Ford Foundation grants and imported technology from the United States and Germany. In 1962, the Delhi transmitter's range was boosted to 40 km. It was not until the early to mid-1970s that Indian television moved beyond the capital: to Bombay in 1972, Srinagar and Amritsar in 1973, and Calcutta, Madras, and Lucknow in 1975. Personal importation of television sets was so heavily taxed as to discourage all but the very wealthiest from acquiring TVs abroad, and domestic production (or rather, assembly) of televisions was tightly regulated through a system of government licensing that imposed quantitative caps on each participating manufacturer. The distribution of sets was split between private purchases at high prices, and government-installed 'community sets' in rural areas.[5]

The idea that television could play a central role in Indian rural development really only started to gather momentum in 1964 when Indira Gandhi, as Minister of Information and Broadcasting, appointed the Chanda Committee to review the national broadcasting policy.[6] The Committee's report was published in 1966, and a weekly show for farmers (*Krishi Darshan*) was launched in 1967; meanwhile, the conversations that would in 1969 lead to a deal between the United States' National Aeronautics and Space Administration (NASA), All India Radio

(AIR), and the Indian Space Research Organisation (ISRO) to set up SITE were underway.[7] At the same time, the expansion of the terrestrial television network was driven by a dual desire to achieve urban middle-class coverage and a propaganda advantage in sensitive border areas, particularly in the northwest (Farmer 2003).[8]

As soon as Indian television expanded beyond its very earliest experiments with schools and community-based 'teleclubs' in the Delhi area, its profile and purpose bifurcated into a sharp opposition between didactic developmentalist programming aimed at the disadvantaged, and entertainment catering to the urban middle class. Actual audiences were not necessarily divided this way; indeed, anecdotal evidence suggests that film-based entertainment was by far the most popular type of programming across all viewer categories. Rather, and despite repeated expert appeals for more engagingly entertaining content, it was as if official programming ideology remained constitutionally unable to reconcile 'development' and 'entertainment' in the production of what the Joshi Report could still just about call 'a people-oriented TV in a society which is constitutionally committed to equality, freedom, democracy and socialism' (Government of India 1985, 91).

Rustom Engineer's ironic description captures the curious sense of uncertain and ineffective address that had already come to characterise Indian television by the early 1970s and that would persist until the commercial revolution of the mid-1980s:

> Evening after evening, and soon day in and day out, the affluent few who can afford sets will be treated to a mindless medley of song and dance, maybe news that could be mistaken for an official hand-out, the usual array of 'youth' programmes, dry as dust interviews and discussions, educational programmes that educate no one since the educators have not troubled to educate themselves, sports round-ups, programmes for women and children, and the lot. And, since these days we are all committed to *garibi hatao* [Indira Gandhi's 1971 electoral slogan: 'abolish poverty'], and since our long-sleeping social consciences are much

> aroused, we will no doubt see rows and rows of slums, and taps without water, as though we never saw these with our own eyes and must be convinced of their existence through the magic screen. (Engineer 1972, 2058)

Engineer's satire captures the sense of doubling and disjuncture that characterised this period: television that consisted of entertainment without substance and substance without entertainment. On one side, lightweight film fare, and on the other, boring didactic stuff about fertilisers and family planning.

This disjuncture between pleasure and propaganda was often interpreted as a reflection of a public divided between desire and need: an urban middle class that wanted to be entertained and a rural mass that needed to be educated. Certainly, such a notion structured many of the most influential policy papers of the time. Even the visionary Vikram Sarabhai, in his oft-cited 1969 appeal for development through satellite television, the manifesto for what would become SITE, remarked:

> I have no quarrel with those who wish to provide entertainment through media of mass communication for society certainly needs entertainment. But, I cannot see the same people determining policies and programming content related to education or instruction through the same medium. (1991 [1969], 97)

Between the end of SITE in 1976 and the launch of a coordinated, prime-time National Programme in August 1982, the *de facto* drift of Indian television, then, was toward a bifurcated system: urban broadcasting that sought to cater to middle-class consuming desires and a continuation of strongly paternalistic didactic broadcasting through a series of dedicated rural 'post-SITE' transmitters (Bhat 1987). Commercials (mostly still slides) were allowed on the urban Doordarshan stations starting in 1976, but not during the rural broadcasts.

Development television was all about *activation*. The 1978 Verghese Committee report summarised the task of Indian broadcasting policy in terms of a strenuous string of imperatives:

> In the Indian situation, the objective ... must be to *awaken* the people, *inform, mobilise*, and *educate* them to be democratic citizens since eternal vigilance is the price of liberty, *ensure* equity and equality of opportunity, *safeguard* national values, *preserve* both unity and diversity, and *promote* development and accepted national goals. (Government of India 1978, 17)

But for all that the visceral power of television was constantly invoked, Doordarshan's producers never quite seemed able to harness it. For them, TV remained a kind of 'radio with picture added on' (Kale 1973, 1256). Given that, as the Joshi Report pointed out, Indian radio was itself largely modelled on the press, it was not surprising that Doordarshan's production style tended 'to narrate utterances rather than depict happenings' (Government of India 1985, 75). According to one (perhaps exaggerated) 1981 claim, 99 per cent of DD producers were appointed without ever even having *seen* a TV programme (Raja 1981).

The result was, quite simply, that development TV was *boring*, 'as dry and drab as bones', consisting of shows that utterly failed to manifest a sense of 'urgency and necessity ... within the mental framework of viewers' (Vidyasagar 1980, 267). All available research testified to audiences' desire to be entertained, rather than instructed. A 1983 survey by the advertising agency (then called) Ogilvy Benson & Mather suggested that film-based programmes enjoyed viewership figures of between 76 and 84 per cent, whereas educational and social programming scored a miserable 2–4 per cent (*Imprint* 1983; Shah 1997). A survey such as this was of course largely based on data from urban, middle-class viewers and was designed to demonstrate the need for a more consumerist broadcast policy, but many advocates of development TV were also conscious of the pleasure deficit. Advertising methods developed to sell consumer products to those with disposable income were not, as many leading lights of the Indian advertising industry found out the hard way, necessarily suited to either the aims of rural development or to the bureaucratic culture of government. But surely more could be done to make

Doordarshan's reporting on matters of public concern less tedious and alienating? As the Verghese Report urged:

> The whole concept of news and current affairs must change from being ministerial, governmental and political to being newsworthy, relevant and interesting. India's development story and the process of social change—or impediments to it—constitute news, big news, and news of infinite variety and human interest. (Government of India 1978, 115)

Or again, elsewhere: 'If entertainment is one of the best liked items by the viewers, why should entertainment not be provided to them *interlocked* with the message to be imparted?' (Singh and Shingi 1975, 1437). As the Joshi Report declared: 'Our ancients knew that education need not and should not be joyless. How far Doordarshan is from this integrity of sound and sense, of beauty and truth, of form and content!' (Government of India 1985, 160).

Despite such nudges in the direction of what today might be called 'infotainment', development TV seemed largely stuck in a rut of humourless tedium. A former DD station director complained:

> [T]he 'do-gooders,' of whom there is no dearth within government and outside, fail to recognize that the lack of entertainment is one of the important problems of rural life. There is nothing to show that so-called urban entertainment such as film songs, drama and classical music are not enjoyed by rural folk. The overemphasis on an 'uplifting message' in every programme, very evident during the Emergency [the time of SITE] and ever lurking in the wings, is self-defeating and constitutes a danger which has to be guarded against. (Chatterjee 1991, 120)

Why was it so hard to make informative shows for the underprivileged that were also fun to watch? One of the policy establishment's most unshakeable beliefs was that development television meant, first and foremost, information transfer. Vikram Sarabhai wrote:

> In any developing country, one of the prime ingredients of development is the dissemination of information. The process of education is basically related to an information dissemination/transfer process. For the rapid and sustained growth of developing countries, the urgent need to disseminate information to the masses is obvious. Mass media are clearly the main components in this system of information transfer. (Sarabhai 1991 [1969], 96)

This basic assumption proved curiously durable, even in the face of repeated post-SITE suggestions that the problem with the development TV experts was that what they knew best was that they knew best.[9] The Verghese Report, for example, tried to marry an information transfer model with an ideal of reciprocity and—perhaps—the mutual transformation of the leaders and the led. Communications policy was, it stated, primarily supposed to 'facilitate the transmission of informational, educational, and cultural messages not merely from government to people but from people to government ... a circular flow with switches for cross-cultural exchange' (Government of India 1978, 18). And a few years later, the Joshi Report spent many pages extolling the virtues of interactivity, decentralisation, and collective participation, observing that '[s]ome of the most serious *distortions* in development have arisen from this *one-way* communication from the "uninformed" expert to the people below whose real conditions, needs, difficulties and perceptions remain alien to the decision-makers above' (Government of India 1985, 121; emphasis in the original). The Joshi Report waxed eloquent on the need not only to communicate with the 'real' India, the India of half-a-million villages, but to also take creative inspiration from the traditional cultures of its people, cultures in which the pleasures of play had not yet been separated from the utilities of work in the name of indolent, consumerist leisure.[10] And yet the authors *still* felt the need to reaffirm the old vision of information transfer, modulated only by a call for differentiated content:

> The process of developmental communication is basically an information dissemination/transfer process. For the rapid growth of developing countries, the urgent need to

> disseminate information to the rural masses is obvious. The difficulty is that there can be no uniform information package valid for the whole country. (ibid., 120)

Effort and Ease

Apparently, diversity was not such a pressing concern for prime-time urban entertainment. Coming at the same time as the introduction of colour in August 1982, the unified National Programme announced the displacement of television as a didactic tool for rural development in favour of a policy of 'national integration' that synthesised consumer marketing with aggressively centralised cultural nationalism (Rajagopal 2001).[11] This was the beginning of the commercial revolution in Indian television, consolidated in 1983 with the announcement of a Rs 680 million 'Crash Plan' to expand the national broadcasting infrastructure,[12] and in 1984 with the coming of sponsored serials and soap operas.

The new dispensation absorbed what had, for the last few years, functioned as a parallel rural broadcasting system into a coordinated nationwide network driven by sponsorship and advertising revenues. Doordarshan did its best to sell the new commercial dispensation to advertisers. The Controller of Sales at its Bombay Commercial Service declared to a meeting of advertising executives: 'Amongst the great inventions of the electronic age, TV is the most beguiling. A sound and light show, appealing to the prepotent senses of vision and hearing, it draws attention like a magnet' (Shroff 1983). The ad men and women were of course only too happy to pass on the good news to their clients, who were, in turn, prepared to pay top rupee for this unique combination of efficacy and reach.

In retrospect, it is easy to overestimate the inevitability and 'naturalness' of Doordarshan's commercial revolution; in fact, sponsors were initially reluctant, the Hindi-heavy National Programme met significant resistance in the non-Hindi-speaking south, and blockbuster serials like the pioneering *Hum Log* (Das

1995; Mankekar 1999) were, in the beginning, greeted with scepticism in many parts of India. But what the new consumerist dispensation did achieve was an impression of natural ease. To read the documents coming out of the heyday of Indian developmentalist television policy debates today (that is to say, official reports and activist critiques written between the early 1970s and the mid-1980s) is to be ceaselessly exhorted toward ever-new levels of *effort*—above all, the enormous labour required to forge a language of television that would be both substantial and entertaining, uplifting and engaging. Social scientists and policy mavens continuously stress the need for more 'holistic' approaches to communication research, with an eye to making television that would not just speak from the sky, but rather activate the organic transformational potentials embedded in the myriad life-ways of India's villages. One gets the sense at times of a research project whose ultimate, impossible desire is to overcome the distancing effects of mediation altogether, to reflect India at a 1:1 scale, to achieve a form of television that would in a sense *be* India, the better to transform it from within.[13]

Compared to the pleasurable ease invoked by the liberalisers, development television discourse seemed, forbiddingly, to be all about danger and difficulty. One former SITE producer reflected: 'Depiction of typical male/female roles in a variety of programmes has an everlasting and damaging effect on the mind of the growing child whose day-today experience already confirms what he sees on the TV screen' (Kalwachwala 1986, 97).[14] Compared to the ease with which television seemed able to affirm reactionary values, its ability to bring about progressive social change seemed like a drop in the ocean of a much larger set of practical challenges:

> Much has been done and quite a bit has been achieved and yet one is left with a gnawing feeling in the heart. What can television alone do? … [W]hat can television do to bring about change—[e]specially when the infrastructural facilities and the social system reflects an abyss of poverty in thought as well as action? (ibid., 95)

The commercial paradigm replaced policy-oriented communications studies with advertiser-oriented market research. The ideology of consumer aspirations as a transformative mediator between the world as it is and the world as it could be increasingly came to look like a dynamic and—crucially—a *democratic* way to tap into a dormant reservoir of 'natural' and universal desires (Mazzarella 2003). By contrast, the development experts' ceaseless straining to come up with a communications policy that would ignite the masses seemed both contrived and paternalistic. The unbeatable selling point of the commercial revolution was its ability to give the sensuous pleasures of consumerism a populist face, while at the same time pushing development TV into the thankless position of a stern parent humourlessly rattling on about duty and deferred desires.

By the mid-1980s, the standard complaint against the commercialisation of television was that Doordarshan and, more broadly, the Government of India, had let the lure of easy advertising revenue divert them from their duty to the 'real India'. Nowhere was this position more clearly articulated than in the Joshi Report: '*Software* [that is content] *planning must be a conscious attempt to prevent the appropriation of television by the emerging forces of commercialism and consumerism*' (Government of India 1985, 19; emphasis in the original). Instead:

> Doordarshan must reflect the changing life pattern and problems of the basic social categories of the Indian society—the village-dwelling working *peasants*, *artisans* and *labourers*, the town-dwelling workers, lower middle classes and the intelligentsia, the other half of Indian humanity comprising women, [e]specially those belonging to the villages and small towns with their real problems, conflicts and aspirations; the tribals of different parts of India at different stages of evolution with their colourful heritage but their insecure future; and India's children with their complex problems of growth and development in a changing society looking both backwards and forwards and embodying the hope and promise of India's future. (ibid., 50; emphasis in the original)

By the time the government agreed to release the Joshi Committee's report in 1985, the ideological train had already left the station. New transmitters were going up across the subcontinent at a furious rate[15] and the spate of commercially sponsored serials and soap operas had ushered in a new and extremely lucrative programming paradigm. The old 'progressive' argument that India's poor needed television that was more carefully tailored to their needs than a generic diet of soap operas and *masala* films now increasingly came off as a paternalistic unwillingness to cede control over the masses' newfound 'right to entertainment'.

Pushed into a defensive position vis-à-vis the new market populism, the advocates of development television were reduced to insisting, over and over again, that the kind of programming that advertisers would support was unrepresentative of the cultures and values of a vast majority of the Indian population, particularly its rural poor. Whether or not this was in fact the case is a moot point; certainly, the private sector found it easy to counter this two-tier model of Indian audiences with the claim that everybody, regardless of their social location, had a right to the same aspirations. As a leading Mumbai advertising professional told me in the late 1990s:

> I have always believed that it is not that the beggar on the road dreams of being the most well-off beggar. He has the right to dream of being a king.... So everyone wants the sun and the moon and the stars. It's not that people dream in segments—that I will only dream this much because I am here. Everyone has the right to dream. (Quoted in Mazzarella 2003, 89)

Critics of Doordarshan's commercial turn busied themselves in lamenting the many opportunities the state network was losing by becoming a more or less passive renter of airtime: the lost opportunity to set up a truly autonomous public broadcasting corporation, the lost opportunity to produce world-class programmes, and, above all, the lost opportunity to make Indian television an inclusive medium of Third World development. But perhaps equally, if not more, important was the lost opportunity to think seriously about television as a *constitutive*, rather than just a *representative*, medium. That is to say, to move beyond a critique in which the problem is always that programmes do not adequately 'fit' the existing social and cultural 'values' of their audiences, and toward a serious consideration of the ways in which television can actively help to constitute and transform the ways in which those 'values' come to be publicly expressible and intelligible.

Already—and not unreasonably—accused of paternalist condescension, the advocates of development television may have felt that any invocation of the constitutive work of television had become an ideological liability, redolent as it was of elite claims to expertise vis-à-vis the Indian 'masses'. But in tactically distancing themselves from this crucial issue, they played into the hands of the liberalisers and effectively foreclosed the one profound problem that development TV had at once posed and disavowed: What happens when television becomes not just a locus of pedagogy—whether of a consumerist or a developmentalist stripe—but an active and open-ended medium of self-making? That is to say, what happens when the constitutive potential of television is not only acknowledged, but also unleashed?

Close Distance

The debate on development television during the transitional period was marked by a dynamic that I have elsewhere called 'close distance' (Mazzarella 2003). In this case, close distance meant the pursuit of a kind of programming content that would at once be 'close' enough to resonate with the existing concrete life ways of audiences and 'distant' enough to prompt a desire for progress, as understood within the discourse of development. Not every intervention in the debate contained both elements; indeed, often the emphasis was laid squarely on one side or the other. The voluminous evaluative literature that followed SITE, for example, tended to argue that SITE had been too standardised and too distant from the live concerns and idioms of its audiences.[16] But even those critics who argued for maximal decentralisation and localisation of programme content tended to accept that the fantasy of a 1:1 'fit' between audience and programme content was, if not an ontological misunderstanding of mass mediation, then at least a practical impossibility (Agrawal and Malek 1986; Dhawan 1973, 1974).

Of course, the very experience of SITE marked a radical shift away from what had been—and would, after the introduction of the National Programme in 1982, be again—a strongly Delhi-centric bias in television content.[17] After SITE, Doordarshan did seem in principle to have accepted that more localised programming was desirable. There were plans to set up new production facilities in provincial cities such as Hyderabad, Cuttack, Gorakhpur, Nagpur, Rajkot, and Ranchi (Srivastava 1986). But in practice, the lure of advertising and sponsorship revenues, coupled with the centralised bureaucratic inertia of a hierarchical government department like the Ministry of Information and Broadcasting, scuppered any sustained decentralisation of production beyond the main metropolitan centres.

The experience of SITE also, as we have seen, cast doubt on the 'information transmission' model of development television, raising the question of what kind of active engagement with the medium would mobilise viewers to improve the circumstances of their lives. The push for localised programming against the centralising drift of Doordarshan found its strongest formal articulation in the Joshi Report,[18] where it was stated in strongly sensuous terms: 'Decentralisation is necessary because it alone assists in ensuring the integrity of things, the opportunity to touch each other, to feel the smells and sounds, to involve your total being and to ensure what is called true interaction' (Government of India 1985, 25). Such close television would draw for its content on 'traditional' cultural idioms, which the Joshi Report romantically valorised against the deracinated lifestyles of urban consumerism:

> All the positive elements in folk art—its beauty and simplicity, its vitality and vigour, its intense humanism and profound sense of justice, its love of nature, its materiality and emphasis on this-worldliness, its power of fun, its derision of the acquisitive instinct, its belief in the power of

> love and human brotherhood where Gods can co-exist with human beings—must find proper place [*sic*] in the software of Doordarshan. These are forms that by their very nature are not only forms of entertainment and artistic expression, but also of purposive social communication. (ibid., 170)

Against this ideal of a close television rooted in existing Indian life-worlds, many pro-liberalisation voices stressed the aspirational power of the distant, the as-yet-unrealised:

> A glamourised [*sic*] image of a middle class home in a TV serial is not a direct representation of a poor man's dwelling in a slum, nor is it meant to be; it stands in an antithetical relationship to his actual position in life and for that reason can become a strong object of desire. (Dhawan 1985)

Indeed, even former SITE producers remembered their own attempts to conjure closely authentic village settings sheepishly:

> In the initial stage of making science education programmes, all productions were studio-based. It was a whole new world of simulated huts, painted backdrops and characters dressed in *dhoti-kurta* (loincloth and long shirt) and *topi* (cap) hired from Maganlal Dresswala (costume rentals). Somewhere in the back of my mind banged the thought: 'Look! The child out there in Sambalpur or Chattisgarh or wherever is going to believe in this simulated reality just as much as you believe in the reality of the model village often depicted in Hindi cinema, with its mascaraed and lipsticked village belles, and its clean blue water pond with shocking pink lotus flowers. Six different regions—Karnataka, Andhra Pradesh, Bihar, Orissa, Gujarat and Rajasthan. Each with its own culture, traditions, language and geography. And my studio-village had to represent all of them and my studio-characters were to convince them of strange new concepts through a strange new medium! Were we creating a new myth? The myth of "the revolution in communication media"?' (Daswani 1986, 83)

For liberalisers, such a confession was simply evidence of the fundamental misunderstanding that informed development television, materialised here in a strenuous and ultimately pointless effort to create a televisual simulation of the 'real world'. The decentralisers, in turn, argued that the problem lay not in the ambition to make television lifelike for village audiences, but rather in misguided attempts to do so from the distance of a Bombay studio. The basic opposition remained: closeness or distance? Cultural fit or aspiration?

Impressionistic evidence from the official reports of that period suggests that audiences actually wanted it both ways at once. 'A group meeting in Assam' provided the Joshi Committee with a familiar protest against the Delhi-centrism of Doordarshan: 'We do not always want to see Delhi. We also want to see ourselves—programmes based on our life, our culture, our language, our creativity' (Government of India 1985, 11). And yet the Report also quotes 'a group of village-folk' (apparently their location was considered unimportant) making what would appear to be the opposite point:

> Why should a programme for the village show only the village to us? Take us beyond the village. We also want to know about the world, about other countries or even about people in other parts of our big country: how they live and work, what is common and what is different among us. Can we never be like the town-folk? (ibid., 10)

How are we to make sense of these utterances as anything other than mutually exclusive desires? Again, I would suggest that the key lies in considering television from the point of view of its constitutive potential, rather than merely its representative adequacy. To put some flesh and blood onto this rather abstract proposition, I want to revisit a unique television experiment that started under the auspices of SITE and continued into the mid-1980s: the Kheda Communication Project. I will suggest that the Kheda Project, precisely because it was the one sustained attempt to localise television production, discloses both the limitations of the representative understanding of mass mediation and the reasons for its ideological tenacity.

Playing Themselves

Vikram Sarabhai, who died before SITE could be implemented, had argued for the importance of conducting pre-production research in the parts of rural India that the project hoped to reach. In the event, his advice was largely ignored. Many SITE producers, complacently convinced of the ignorant inertia of rural life, only learned their lesson when it was already too late:

> Touring in the clusters, the viewing centres, in three states—Rajasthan, Bihar, and MP [Madhya Pradesh]—took me round 86 villages. Once I got to know the children and women, the erroneous picture I had held till then began to fade. Instead of finding motley crowds of mentally dull and bored people, they (the children) were lively, vibrant specimens full of enthusiasm for the TV shows. They exhibited the eagerness to learn, react and could even decide as to what suited them most. [B]y the time the true picture registered, it was too late to make any radical changes in the programmes. (Shukul 1986, 112)

One might ask: If the villagers really were 'full of enthusiasm for the TV shows' (and most other contemporary research suggested such enthusiasm was at best intermittent), then why was the producer's late arrival in the village a missed opportunity? Perhaps this is what the planner most fears: not so much plans leading to bad outcomes, but evidence of *unplanned* enthusiasm—audience excitement that cannot be traced back to a policy decision. In this case, the SITE team did not arrive too late for the villagers to enjoy television; rather, it arrived too late to be able to know whether their enjoyment was a result of the team's expertise.

This was not, of course, how the matter was usually framed. Most post-SITE evaluations argued that the project could have been much more socially effective with less distance between production and reception. The only real exception appears to have been the Kheda Project, often described as an experiment within the larger experiment that was SITE.[19] Kheda ran on a 1-kilowatt transmitter located in the village of Pij in Kheda District, which broadcast programming received by microwave from nearby Ahmedabad across an area of 3,000 square miles to 558 community television sets in 358 villages. Transmission lasted for one hour every evening, comprising thirty minutes of SITE programming in Hindi (which most villagers did not understand) and thirty minutes produced by the Space Applications Centre (SAC, a division of ISRO) in Charautari, the local dialect of Gujarati. The content was part 'hardcore' instructional development fare, mainly courtesy of SITE, and part 'softcore' commentaries on social issues, often dramatic or comedic entertainments addressing 'problems that form an integral part of rural existence in India: untouchability, exploitation, and discrimination' (Banerjee 1981). Staying on air after SITE closed down at the end of July 1976, the Kheda Project lasted until Doordarshan took over the Pij transmitter for commercial broadcasting in 1985.

What set the Kheda Project off from the rest of SITE was the close cooperation that developed between SAC's production team and the local villagers. Kheda District was then, and is now, home to a large number of affluent and successful Patels, many of whom have joined a global entrepreneurial diaspora (Joshi 1978). Mass media penetration was spotty at best.[20] To a significant extent, the dominant castes were able to regulate information exchange between the district and the wider world. SITE was an opportunity to leapfrog those entrenched privileges by setting up a direct line between the national development effort and the underprivileged. In part, this immediating[21] ambition rested on the prevalent hope that television would not only bypass the barrier of illiteracy, but also work a kind of subliminal sensory magic on its audience:

> Television works directly on the deeper regions of the mind.... The pictures on the TV screen, delivering the message, take the mind off the brain effort, and, with the lulling rhythm of the vibrating voice as an auxiliary aid, helps the message sink into the subconscious mind. (Banerji 1983)

SITE was planned in the pre-Emergency period, but its top-down orientation and promise to bypass established social hierarchies sat perfectly with the authoritarian populism of Mrs Gandhi's experiment with dictatorship. In that sense, it also prepared the ground for the televisual politics of the 1980s, which, while ostensibly consumerist, also involved 'a plan to circumvent party politics by appealing directly to the electorate' (Farmer 2003, 117).

Within the larger top-down context of SITE, the Kheda Project was alone in soliciting viewer responses on an ongoing basis and, ultimately, involving lower-caste and Dalit (formerly Untouchable) villagers in the actual production of shows. SAC Director Yash Pal saw in the Kheda Project an ideal blend of close concerns and distant connections:

> [W]e felt that mere reach may not be enough, that intimacy mattered. We have here a possibility of using communication technology in an intimate milieu, with close kins [*sic*] and near neighbours, and the daily business of growing up, learning and living with local sounds and smells. Simultaneously the satellite link-up can provide a window to the rest of the country and the world to ensure that we do not end up creating parochial cultures. (Pal 1978, 14)

Just as other SITE producers had harboured doubts about the simulated village sets they had constructed in their Bombay and Ahmedabad studios, so also the Kheda Project team soon found that middle-class urban actors were simply not able to capture and express the texture of the kind of village-based dramatic situations they were trying to stage. By taking their portable cameras to a village in Kheda, and moving past an initial sense of awkwardness in the gap between the script and the local setting, the producers soon found their show seemingly writing itself, emerging spontaneously out of the space of possibility created by the camera, a set of dramatic prompts, and the real-life concerns of the non-actors who were both creating and enacting the show:

> The whole rehearsal [with the villagers] was allowed to develop with no holds barred as to the techniques of acting, technology of shooting or equipment constraints. It started dawning on many of us that the problem was theirs and the

> performance was theirs and finally whatever was captured on the video tape was going to be theirs. One got the feeling that 'social relevance,' 'credibility,' 'identification' and 'comprehensibility' all existed—almost waiting for the camera to capture them and the video tape to record them.... In Bazin's[22] words the aim is to let 'reality lay itself bare'.... (Vishwanath 1978, 30)

This, perhaps, was the culmination of the 1:1 dream of decentralised, localised television—media without mediation.

> These Harijans [that is, Dalits], from a village which is extremely backward, has no electricity and from where very few people had even seen movies, came up with brilliant performances. The force and ingenuity of their performance, the nuances they brought in were really excellent. The programmes had no problems about authenticity or credibility because their 'acting' was almost reliving their own experiences. (Joshi 1978, 40)

Of course, the 'almost' here is crucial—it is the mark of the distance involved in the 'false illusion' generated when villagers 'played themselves' (Karnik 1978). Kheda television was, after all, not simply meant to represent local reality, but also to remediate it in such a way as to transform it:

> The purpose is not showing things as they are but also showing how they ought to be, or could be. [T]hese programmes will go a long way in optimising positive viewer response and helping them to acquire the status of 'praxis,' the process of reflection and action. (Raina 1986, 107)

Villagers were quick to reject shows in which there was '[a]ny glaring discrepancy of dress and address between drama characters and real characters' (Agrawal and Malek 1986, 52). And yet programmes that lacked a sense of hope—even if that hope was not strictly plausible—also ran into trouble: 'Most women want that programmes should take up "real" incidents/situations or issues relevant to them, but want to see a positive end, even if it is "unreal"' (Joshi and Joshi 1986, 29). The poorest villagers flocked eagerly to early episodes of the Kheda serial, *Chatur Mota*, even though it dealt with what the SAC production team soon realised were 'middle-class problems', rather than issues of direct concern to the rural poor. Worried that audiences were settling into a regressive pattern of passive consumption, the producers re-jigged the show so as to feature issues pertinent to the most disadvantaged: 'Skeptics were surprised to see that the new series was as popular as the earlier one, while simultaneously creating a major stir on many burning issues (untouchability, minimum wages, cooperating to fight exploitation, etc.)' (Karnik 1978, 17).

Villagers were simply thrilled to see themselves and their villages on television: 'Whenever a programme showed [Kheda Project village] Dadusar, the whole village was astir with enthusiasm and they braved rain and inclement weather to see it' (Agrawal and Malek 1986, 53). But the producers also found themselves involved in more self-consciously recursive remediations of local life. For *Daad Fariyad*, villagers would write to the producers about a problem, the producers would shoot an episode about it—often featuring villagers in real-life roles—and the episode would, in turn, trigger some kind of engagement from the authorities, which itself would then be filmed. Of course, the producers soon ran up against the limits of what television shows could do in the absence of infrastructural change—and this would become a standard lament in development television circles after SITE.

As much as the Kheda Project prized an intimately localised form of realism, the producers soon found that publicising villagers' problems carried its own risks and dangers. If the problem with SITE had often been the distance between the producers and the viewers, then the Kheda Project occasionally found itself dealing with the dilemmas of excessive proximity. An investigative series on illegal discrimination against Dalits, *Hawe Na Saheva Paap*, led to economic and physical threats against the Dalits involved with the show, and consequently, their refusal to continue collaborating with the producers. Suddenly, painfully, action and reaction seemed short-circuited. The Dalits had expressed strong pride in their participation in the shows, '[y]et when [they were] projected back to them they became an endless series of humiliations. "We felt as if somebody has thrust a dagger in our hearts," they said' (Banerjee 1981).

One member of the production team reflected:

> It is all very well for Ibaruri [*sic*][23] to say that '... it is better to die on one's feet than to live on one's knees ...' but is it correct for righteous producers (who have neither died on their feet nor lived on their knees) to convey this message? (Karnik 1978, 20)

Some kind of distancing device became necessary, a fictional alibi that would allow criticism of reality. The production team embarked on experiments with 'recording the real-life, factual situation up to the maximum possible "safe" point. Beyond this, the factual situation would be presented as "fictional" drama' (ibid., 18), either through a humourous device like the donkey puppet, Hun, who would ventriloquise social criticism in dialogues with a human actor, or in the adaptation of local 'folk' theatre idioms like *bhavai* to contemporary concerns.[24]

It was all very well, then, to proclaim that '[r]ural telecast has to return the community to itself. The common villager has to be heard and seen on the air' (Singh and Shingi 1975, 96). But in fact, this returning of the community to itself by means of community television necessarily involved a detour, a fictional displacement, a mediation that—paradoxically—would allow 'reality to lay itself bare' by doing something more than merely 'showing' it. One might say that this displacement was a pragmatic response, as in the case of *Hawe Na Saheva Paap*, to a potentially dangerous situation. But it also represented the recognition that any effective—that is to say, transformative—communication was by definition a constitutive intervention into local social relations and expectations. So of course were the few regular SITE transmissions, remotely controlled though they were, that had some small impact on farming practices. But the fact of the Kheda Project's grassroots engagement with its audience made the ethical stakes of such constitutive televisual remediation unusually palpable.

Even as the Kheda Project was awarded a UNESCO prize for effectiveness in rural communication in 1985, Doordarshan's

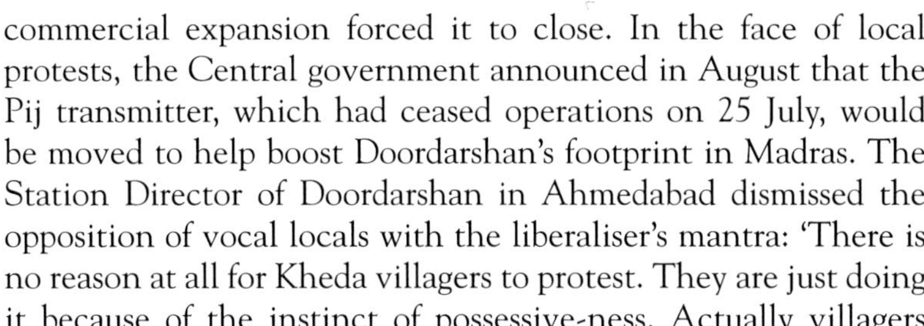

commercial expansion forced it to close. In the face of local protests, the Central government announced in August that the Pij transmitter, which had ceased operations on 25 July, would be moved to help boost Doordarshan's footprint in Madras. The Station Director of Doordarshan in Ahmedabad dismissed the opposition of vocal locals with the liberaliser's mantra: 'There is no reason at all for Kheda villagers to protest. They are just doing it because of the instinct of possessive-ness. Actually villagers want entertainment' (Menon 1985, 98).

The Kheda Project is nowadays remembered, if it is remembered at all, as the one Indian development television initiative that really tried to 'fit' its programming to the needs of a specific rural constituency. As such, it stands as a corrective to the oft-repeated trope with which I began this section: the official expert arriving too late among the people his plans are supposed to benefit. The Kheda experience illustrates the ethical complexities that arise out of a situation in which the expert (in this case, the production team) arrives on time and is engaged, face-to-face, with the open-ended outcomes of the kind of constitutive remediations that such a project necessarily involves. It is no accident that one of the producers describes handing the microphone to the villagers as a 'provocation' (Vishwanath 1978, 29)—an apt term for the unpredictably potentiating effect of 'returning the community to itself' via the detour of television (pro-vocation: literally, a calling forth). In practice, the production team tended to oscillate between a stance of total non-intervention that would respect the villagers' cultural integrity—'it is better to have a worse choice which is theirs rather than to have a better choice that is ours' (ibid., 32)—and intervening to disallow practices it could not help but consider irrational, as when villagers insisted on a causal connection between animal sacrifice and human conception.

We might say that the Kheda Project was unique because it truly brought television close to its public. But the importance of this closeness was, paradoxically, a heightened attention to distance—that is to say, to the constitutive, self-making distance involved in any mediation, any effort to (for better or for worse) 'return the community to itself' by means of public broadcast. This constitutive distance that dwells at the heart of mass publicity is the element effaced by both the top-down 'information transfer' model of development TV and by the market-populist discourse, both of which present efficacy as a problem of producing content that will seamlessly 'fit' or 'cater to' an audience whose values and preferences are imagined as always already constituted, and whose relation to the communication is imagined as one of belief and/or consumption. Unprotected by the distance granted to those experts who remained at the 'commanding heights' of the Planning Commission or in the simulated village of a Bombay television studio, the Kheda team had to deal with the constitutive work of distance right up close.

TENDERLY RECEIVED

More than a quarter of a century after the demise of the Kheda Project, 'entertainment' has now achieved the ideological status of a universal good, a direct line to the 'real' desires of television viewers everywhere. Nowadays anyone (with a certain minimum of disposable income) can expect to find their interests and aspirations represented on television. In many ways, as I have suggested here, development television dug its own grave. Its tendency toward substance without pleasure, its tedium, its complacency—all of these were no match for the blandishments of commercial entertainment. But I think what really sealed the historical fate of development television in India was the unwillingness of policy experts at the level of the state and its auxiliary institutions to let the emergent potential of an experiment like the Kheda Project call into question their claims to inviolably pre-constituted authority—even as this refusal was helping to make them obsolete.

Development television, geared as it was toward deliberate social change, could not help but generate the question of constitutive, rather than representative, mass mediation. And yet, almost as soon as the question arose, it was disavowed, either by falling back on some variant of the 'information transfer' model or by insisting that development TV was about the preservation of cultural diversity against the supposedly homogenising onslaught of the market.[25] For example, even at the point when the Joshi Report stresses the importance of making television more interactive, the old logic persists, effectively reducing interactivity to representational diversity:

> [A]ny software which does not evolve out of some form of public participation is weak in authenticity and appeal. Further, television software is at its best when it represents uniqueness and diversity. It is at its worst when it offers uniformity and homogenisation. The former is tenderly received while the latter is brutally imposed. (Government of India 1985, 13)

No wonder that development TV fell such easy prey to the commercial revolution, which, by the mid-1990s, could certainly claim to be both much more diverse and much more 'tenderly received' than Doordarshan ever was.

In one of its most striking formulations, the Joshi Report appears to acknowledge the postcolonial gap between a modernity that has both already arrived and not yet been achieved, asserting: 'One of the basic weaknesses of the [Indian] freedom struggle was that the anti-colonial task got precedence over the task of evolving a critical consciousness. This task has to be undertaken today with the aid of the mass media' (Government of India 1985, 100). But, as Srirupa Roy notes, Indian national planning split this 'critical consciousness' into two. On one side was an expert elite whose scientific authority was unquestionable, and on the other side the vast majority of ordinary Indians, in whom this expert elite was supposed to cultivate Jawaharlal Nehru's cherished 'scientific temper'. In practice, this meant not so much producing autonomous, self-legislating subjects, but rather citizens manifesting an 'active commitment to agendas of change and to a vision of the future unburdened by the dead weight of custom and superstition' (Roy 2007, 125). The state was imagined as the source of scientifically authoritative information that broadcast media might then disseminate, thus transforming both the practices and the mentalities of Indians in the direction of the collective project of national development. One might perhaps turn the Joshi Report's proposition around and suggest that if the freedom struggle did in fact delay the evolution of a 'critical consciousness', then the deficit was to be found not among ordinary Indians, but rather among official experts whose self-satisfaction rested on a claim to authority that could not, within the statist-developmentalist paradigm, be called into question.

This, finally, is what I take to be the real meaning of television arriving 'too late' in India. Recall the SITE producer who laments arriving too late in a village full of enthusiastic viewers. Behind the apparent regret lies the true perversity of expertise: the expert would secretly rather arrive too late to put his expertise into practice than arrive on time and have to contend with the unruliness of an open-ended social engagement. Having perpetually arrived too late, Indian development television could thus allow itself to be rudely ejected from the historical stage in the 1980s, preserving its dignity even as it shuffled off into obsolescence with mutterings about missed opportunities and neoliberal blackmail. The price of preserving its dignity was, in turn, the preservation of the entire complex experience of Indian development television as a living fossil, a simplified foil that allowed the commercial dispensation to look like an authentic and spontaneous expression of popular desire.

ACKNOWLEDGEMENT

The research for this chapter was made possible by grants from the Committee of Southern Asian Studies and the Lichtstern Fund at the Department of Anthropology, University of Chicago.

NOTES

1. 'Doordarshan' literally means tele-vision, as in 'seeing at a distance'. But the term *darshan* also signifies the kind of auspicious seeing that joins devotees to deities, and, by extension, political leaders

(Eck 1981). From a secular-critical standpoint, then, the name Rajiv Darshan implied a kind of slavish devotion unbefitting a critical public sphere.

2. Robin Jeffrey neatly summarises the sad history of the effort to create an autonomous Indian broadcasting authority:

> The journey to legislate such a body, which began in 1966, was unfinished until [the time of writing in] 2006. Once they are securely in power, Indian governments have failed to carry through legislation begun by shakier, more idealistic predecessors. 'No government,' a former Director-General of Doordarshan concluded, 'is ever going to let go of the electronic media' (Ghose, 2005: 223). A bill to create an autonomous corporation was introduced in May 1979, just before the fall of the Janata government [1977–79] and the return to power of Mrs. Gandhi. She let that bill die. Ten years later another minority government, this time succeeding Rajiv Gandhi and his Congress, passed a similar Prasar Bharati Bill, but the government fell before it could have the bill proclaimed as law. The new Congress government allowed the bill to lie in limbo, happy to pull the ancient levers of media control. Keep it in 'very cold storage,' Prime Minister Narasimha Rao instructed officials in 1994.
>
> Only with the return of another shaky coalition government in 1997 was the Prasar Bharati Act of 1990 finally proclaimed by the President ... But it was a diluted version of the original intentions. The new 'independent' authority has limited funds and 'lives on handouts from government' (Ghose 2005: 219). Doordarshan and AIR [All-India Radio] remain, in effect, responsible to the Minister of Information and Broadcasting. (Jeffrey 2008: 25)

3. 'A definitive perspective on fashion follows solely from the consideration that to each generation the one immediately preceding it seems the most radical anti-aphrodisiac imaginable' (Benjamin 1999, 64).

4. India's post-independence broadcasting philosophy was articulated as follows in 1951 at the time of the First Five-Year Plan:

> A widespread understanding of the Plan is an essential stage in its fulfillment. An understanding of the priorities of the Plan will enable each person to relate his or her role to the larger purposes of the nation as a whole. All available methods of communication have to be developed and the people approached through the written word no less than through radio, film, song and drama. (quoted in Chatterjee 1991, 117)

5. By 1972, when television expanded beyond the Delhi area for the first time, there were around 50,000 sets in use. At that time, a private consumer buying a set could expect to spend about Rs 2,500. In the early 1970s, the Indian government was pursuing a policy of economic self-reliance that meant that it refused permission to several foreign TV manufacturers who wanted to set up shop in India. Instead, it licensed a handful of large and forty-odd small Indian companies to assemble televisions, even as India remained dependent on imported picture tubes. At this point, the economic conundrum was to balance pressure from manufacturers, who wanted to increase their production quotas so as to be able to make cheaper sets, and policy planners, who were, in a manner almost unimaginable today, committed to actually *restricting* middle-class consumption (Dhawan 1973; Vohra 1972).

6. B. D. Dhawan (1973) argues that the 'hard' economic planners—for whom television had been at best a marginal consideration—started suffering a legitimation crisis in the early 1960s as a series of economic crises started to undo the monumentalist optimism of the immediate post-independence period.

7. The technical innovation that made SITE imaginable was NASA's invention of the geostationary satellite in 1965. Initially planned for 1972–1973, SITE finally got underway during the Emergency in August 1975, borrowing an American satellite (ATS-6) 36,000 km above Kenya, and beaming programming to villages in six states.

8. 'Towns in the Punjab are being given priority, since there are roughly 700 TV sets tuned in to Pakistan TV, although Pak TV does not deliberately beam programmes onto Indian territory. Anti-Indian propaganda is limited. During the [1971 India-Pakistan] war, we had jammed the Pak station' (Vohra 1972, 22).

9. I am paraphrasing Thomas Richards here (Richards 1990, 191).

10. Doordarshan, the Joshi Report insists, '*must not romanticise the empty life of the non-labouring elites in whose case play is divorced from work*' (Government of India 1985, 59; emphasis in the original). In the 'real' India, by contrast,

> [p]eople's life is a peculiar blend of the useful and the beautiful. There is no distinction here between craft and art, the entertainer and the entertained, and work and play. In tribal or peasant life, people work while they sing and dance and they sing and dance while they work. (ibid., 58)

11. The introduction of the National Programme, which ran in Hindi and English, led to lively protests in south India, where there is a

longstanding tradition of opposing northern attempts to impose Hindi as a national language.

12. The so-called Crash Plan was announced in July 1983, more than halfway through the Sixth Five-Year Plan. Broadly interpreted as a desperate bid on Mrs Gandhi's part to use television as a way of bypassing a critical press, the Plan led to a frantic period of expansion during the mid-1980s, when, it was frequently claimed, a new transmitter went up every day. Of course, Mrs Gandhi, assassinated in October 1984, would not live to reap the fruits of the new policy. That ambiguous privilege passed to her older son, Rajiv Gandhi, who had already been established as a media-friendly technocrat through his leading role in overseeing the colour broadcast of the Asian Games from Delhi at the end of 1982.

13. It is no accident that anthropologists and other social scientists played key roles in the research process before and after SITE. Binod Agarwal, an Anthropology Ph.D. from the University of Michigan, headed the Kheda Communication Project research group, of which more below (Agrawal and Malek 1986; Agrawal, et al. 1986).

14. New media, particularly when their appeal rests on the sensuous pleasures of entertainment, typically prompt a barrage of moral panic. So it was that the commercialisation of Indian television in the mid-1980s unleashed a storm of protest from leftist critics, whose commitment to social justice was inseparable from a puritan cultural politics. Praful Bidwai, for one, reached heights of excoriation at which even an Adorno might have blushed:

> These contextless and culturally counterfeit [television entertainment] images are rapidly internalised by the viewer, thanks to the mesmerising power of the television screen; it is difficult to resist watching it, however mindless, cretinizing and disorienting the experience might be. Fake images and stereotypes are integral to the new aesthetic that Indian television represents. This is an eclectic mixture of common commercial vulgarity and cannibalization of all manner of aesthetic modes. But at its core is a photographic enlargement of certain aspects of real life and a series of stereoscopic illusions that are calculated to produce a devalued sense of pleasure, fake euphoria, cheap thrill, titillation, a sense akin to that of being drugged. (Bidwai 1985)

15. The cliché from these years is that the Rajiv Gandhi administration presided over an expansion of transmitters that was equivalent to one a day. Certainly, the growth was dramatic. In 1983, around the time that the expansion plan was announced, there was a national total of forty-three transmitters. By the end of March 1985, there were 173, and by

the end of 1989, there were 400. At the time of writing (June 2011), the number is around 1,400.

16. SITE did try to localise somewhat: the transmissions came with different audio channels for different linguistic regions.

17. Purnima Mankekar notes that Doordarshan's attempts to incorporate regional diversity into its national programming during the mid-1980s invariably came off as ham-fisted and patronising:

> [I]t tried to compensate for its north Indian bias by awkward insertions of 'Bengali' and 'Tamilian' characters in its serials. Although these insertions aimed at 'approaching a national outlook' the amateur and clumsy ways in which these characters were portrayed only perpetuated regional and ethnic stereotypes. (Mankekar 1999, 62)

18. The Joshi Report was strongly influenced by the 1980 UNESCO report on global media policy, *Many Voices, One World*, popularly known as the MacBride Report. In particular, the Joshi Report borrowed from the MacBride Report a critique of cultural imperialism and an insistence that media policy be oriented toward the preservation and nurturing of national and regional cultural integrity.

19. The Indian Space Research Organisation was, in the lead up to SITE, sometimes criticised for pushing satellite technology when India's extraordinary linguistic and sociological diversity required something more decentralised (Dhawan 1973, 1974). And yet it was a wing of ISRO, the Space Applications Centre (SAC), that oversaw the most decentralised television project of all in Kheda (Kale 1973).

20. '36 percent of males and 66.5 percent of females reported that they never listened to radio broadcast[s]. In spite of the fact that radio was available in villages, it had not "reached" a vast majority. Similarly, SITE survey[s] show that 64 percent of rural men and 88.4 percent of the women had never been to a cinema show. 92.8 percent [of] men and 95.2 percent [of] women had never read newspapers' (Joshi and Joshi 1986, 23).

21. By 'immediation', I mean the hypermediated pursuit of an impression of immediacy (see Mazzarella 2006).

22. Vishwanath is referring here to French film theorist Andre Bazin (1918–1958), best known for *What is Cinema?*.

23. The reference here is to Spanish Communist leader and activist Dolores Ibarruri (1895–1989).

24. Apparently, Hun the donkey, originally made by a student from the National Institute of Design, became so popular in Kheda that he regularly received invitations to village weddings (Chitnis 1978).

25. The Verghese Report, for example, moves from the suggestion of a constructivist approach to a simple diversity position:

> Each event or development is subjectively seen and just as much as truth lies in the beholder's eye, it has been well said by Wilbur Schramm that 'news exists in the minds of men' in so far as it is not necessarily the event itself but the larger perceptions seen around it after the event that make the 'news.' It is therefore of cardinal importance that the subjective truth as seen or experienced by a particular person, party or ideology should be filled out by different images of that same reality as seen or experienced by others so as, perhaps, to arrive as near the objective truth as possible. (Government of India 1978, 107)

REFERENCES

Agrawal, B., and M. R. Malek. 1986. *Television in Kheda: A Social Evaluation of SITE*. New Delhi: Concept.

Agrawal, B., and A. Sinha (eds). 1986. *SITE to INSAT: Challenges of Production and Research for Women and Children*. New Delhi: Concept.

Agrawal, B., S. R. Joshi, and A. Sinha (eds). 1986. *Communication Research for Development: The ISRO Experience*. New Delhi: Concept.

Banerjee, S. 1981. 'Why Kheda Succeeded where SITE Failed'. *Business Standard*, 19 April.

Banerji, B. K. 1983. 'Role of Press in Educating Public'. *The Economic Times*, 9 September.

Benjamin, W. 1999. *The Arcades Project*. Cambridge, MA: Harvard University Press.

Bhat, V. 1987. *Mind Managers and Defiled Doordarshan*. Jalandhar: ABS.

Bidwai, P. 1985. 'TV's New Bazaar Culture'. *The Times of India*, 4 October.

Chakrabarty, D. 2000. *Provincializing Europe: Postcolonial Thought and Historical Difference*. Princeton, NJ: Princeton University Press.

Chatterjee, P. 1986. *Nationalist Thought and the Colonial World: A Derivative Discourse*. Minneapolis, MN: University of Minnesota Press.

———. 1993. *The Nation and its Fragments: Colonial and Postcolonial Histories*. Princeton, NJ: Princeton University Press.

———. 1991. *Broadcasting in India*. New Delhi: Sage, 2nd edn.

Chitnis, E. V. 1978. 'Participatory Software'. *Seminar* 232 (December), 22–28.

Das, V. 1995. 'On Soap Opera: What Kind of Anthropological Object Is It?' In Daniel Miller (ed.), *Worlds Apart: Modernity through the Prism of the Local*. London: Routledge.

Daswani, A. 1986. 'SITE Experience: Questions and Lessons—A Personal View'. In Binod Agrawal and A. Sinha (eds), *SITE to INSAT: Challenges of Production and Research for Women and Children*, 81–85. New Delhi: Concept.

Dhawan, B. D. 1973. 'Television in India: Retrospect and Prospect'. *Economic and Political Weekly* 8 (28), 1247–1255.

———. 1974. 'Satellite TV Revisited'. *Economic and Political Weekly* 9 (16), 634–640.

Dhawan, Y. P. 1985. 'Eroticism Strikes Roots: No Threat to Indian Way of Life'. *The Times of India*, 20 November.

Eck, D. 1981. *Darsan: Seeing the Divine Image in India*. Chambersburg, PA: Anima.

Engineer, R. 1972. 'Opportunities Despite the Constraints'. *Economic and Political Weekly* 7 (41), 2058–2060.

Farmer, V. L. 2003. 'Television, Governance and Social Change: Media Policy through India's First Half-century of Independence'. Ph.D. thesis, Department of Political Science. University of Pennsylvania.

Foucault, M. 1997. 'What is Enlightenment?' In P. Rabinow (ed.), *Michel Foucault: Ethics, Subjectivity, and Truth*, 303–319. New York: New Press.

Ghose, B. 2005. *Doordarshan Days*. New Delhi: Penguin/Viking.

Government of India. 1978. *Akash Bharati, National Broadcasting Trust: Report of the Working Group on Autonomy for Akashvani & Doordarshan*, Vol. 1. New Delhi: Ministry of Information and Broadcasting.

———. 1985. *An Indian Personality for Television: Report of the Working Group on Software for Doordarshan. Vol. 1*. New Delhi: Ministry of Information and Broadcasting Publications Division.

Habermas, J. 1989 [1962]. *The Structural Transformation of the Public Sphere: An Inquiry into a Category of Bourgeois Society*. Cambridge, MA: MIT Press.

Imprint. 1983. 'Rulers of the Air'. *Imprint* September.

Jeffrey, R. 2008. 'The Mahatma Didn't Like the Movies and Why it Matters: Indian Broadcasting Policy, 1920s–1990s'. In N. Mehta (ed.), *Television in India: Satellites, Politics and Cultural Change*, 13–31. London: Routledge.

Joshi, S. R. 1978. 'Mode of Operation'. *Seminar* 232 (December), 36–40.

Joshi, S. R., and H. Joshi. 1986 'Women and Television: ISRO Experiences'. In Binod Agrawal, S. R. Joshi, and Arbind Sinha (eds), *Communication Research for Development: The ISRO Experience*, 22–33. New Delhi: Concept.

Kale, P. 1973. 'Developing a Tool for Development: Television in India'. *Economic and Political Weekly* 8 (28), 1255–1257.

Kalwachwala, D. 1986. 'Portrayal of Women in India: A Viewpoint'. In B. Agrawal and A. Sinha (eds), *SITE to INSAT: Challenges of Production and Research for Women and Children*, 89–97. New Delhi: Concept.

Kant, I. 1970 [1784]. 'An Answer to the Question: "What is Enlightenment?"' In H. S. Reiss (ed.), *Kant: Political Writings*, 54–60. Cambridge: Cambridge University Press.

Karnik, K. 1978. 'A System Approach'. *Seminar* 232 (December), 16–21.

MacBride Commission. 1980. *Many Voices, One World*. Paris: UNESCO.

McMillin, D. 2003. 'Marriages are Made on Television: Globalization and National Identity in India'. In Lisa Parks and Shanti Kumar (eds), *Planet TV: A Global Television Reader*, 341–359. New York: New York University Press.

Mankekar, P. 1999. *Screening Culture, Viewing Politics: An Ethnography of Television, Womanhood, and Nation in Postcolonial India*. Durham, NC: Duke University Press.

Mazzarella, W. 2003. *Shoveling Smoke: Advertising and Globalization in Contemporary India*. Durham, NC: Duke University Press.

_____. 2004. 'Culture, Globalization, Mediation'. *Annual Review of Anthropology* 33, 345–367.

_____. 2006. 'Internet X-ray: E-governance, Transparency, and the Politics of Immediation in India'. *Public Culture* 18 (3), 473–505.

Mehta, N. 2008. 'Introduction: Satellite Television, Identity and Globalization in Contemporary India'. In N. Mehta (ed.), *Television in India: Satellites, Politics and Cultural Change*, 1–12. London: Routledge.

Menon, R. 1985. 'Fading Out: Kheda Project'. *India Today*, 15 October, 98.

Pal, Y. 1978. 'The Crucial Decision'. *Seminar* 232, 12–15.

Raja, M. 1981. 'Mental Torture'. *Industrial Times* June, 1–14.

Rajagopal, A. 2001. *Politics after Television: Hindu Nationalism and the Reshaping of the Public in India*. Cambridge: Cambridge University Press.

Rajagopal, A. 2011. 'The Emergency as Prehistory of the New Indian Middle Class'. *Modern Asian Studies* February, 1–47.

Raina, V. N. 1986. 'Strategy for Making Video Programme Packages on Health, Nutrition and Family Welfare for Transmission as well as Non-transmission Use'. In Binod Agrawal and Arbind Sinha (eds), *SITE to INSAT: Challenges of Production and Research for Women and Children*, 103–108. New Delhi: Concept.

Richards, T. 1990. *The Commodity Culture of Victorian England: Advertising and Spectacle, 1851–1914*. Stanford, CA: Stanford University Press.

Roy, S. 2007. *Beyond Belief: India and the Politics of Postcolonial Nationalism*. Durham, NC: Duke University Press.

Saksena, G. 1996. *Television in India: Changes and Challenges*. New Delhi: Vikas.

Sarabhai, V. 1991 [1969]. 'Mass Media and Development'. In G. S. Bhargava (ed.), *Government Media: Autonomy and After*. New Delhi: Concept.

Shah, A. 1997. *Hype, Hypocrisy and Television in Urban India*. New Delhi: Vikas.

Shroff, A. 1983. 'Update on Doordarshan: Its Plans, Opportunities for Advertisers and Agencies'. Presentation given at the Madras Advertising Club's 'Workshop on Media', 24 February.

Shukul, G. D. 1986. 'From SITE to INSAT'. In Binod Agrawal and Arbind Sinha (eds), *SITE to INSAT: Challenges of Production and Research for Women and Children*, 109–115. New Delhi: Concept.

Singh, N. P. and P. M. Shingi. 1975. 'Rural Telecast for Development: An Impressionistic Model'. *Economic and Political Weekly* 10 (36), 1433–1438.

Srivastava, J. S. 1986. 'Rural India is Not in the Picture'. In Binod Agrawal and Arbind Sinha (eds), *SITE to INSAT: Challenges of Production and Research for Women and Children*, 151–155. New Delhi: Concept.

Tomlinson, J. 1991. *Cultural Imperialism*. Baltimore, MD: John Hopkins University Press

Vidyasagar, M. 1980. 'Television Needs Audience'. *Vidura* August, 265–267.

Vishwanath, K. 1978. 'Case Studies'. *Seminar* 232 (December), 28–32.

Vohra, B. 1972. 'The TV Story'. *Illustrated Weekly of India*, 24 September, 20–25.

9

CITY AS A CONTINUUM

Cinematic Geography of Kochi in Malayalam Cinema

CARMEL CHRISTY K. J.

Cinema, as a production and capital-intensive art form, has been associated with urban centres—be it Los Angeles (Hollywood), Mumbai (Bollywood), or Madras (Tollywood, which used to be the hub of all south Indian cinema earlier). The emergence and growth of cinema and cities are associated with the processes of industrialisation and urbanisation. Scholars have pointed out the mutually entangled production of the city of cinema where major film studios are located, and the city that appears in cinema (Brunsdon 2007). In other words, cinema is informed by where it is produced from, whether a city (which it is, most of the time) or elsewhere, while the city is also shaped by cinema in several ways. Then, to analyse and understand cinema, one may also look at the city from which it is produced and how the city figures in cinema. Recently, city and cinema have been studied beyond the framework of representation to understand the co-constitution of both. Spanish scholar Ivan Villarmea Alvarez (2015) points to Edward Dimendberg's *Film Noir and the Spaces of Modernity* (2004) as an example of understanding film not just as text, but as part of the evolution of sociality itself. Dimendberg demonstrates the connections between the history of film noir and the growth of American urban planning from 1939 to 1959. Alvarez quotes Richard Koeck and Les Roberts (2010, 10) to explain this framework further: 'one that moves towards seeing film not only as a genre-dependent text, but also as a rich map of socio-cultural, political, economic and, of course, architectural discourses'.

It is in the context of these emerging analyses of the co-constitution of the city and cinema that this chapter studies the links between the growth of the city of Kochi and Malayalam cinema. Located in the southwest corner of India, Kochi is a comparatively small port city (with a population of 6.77 lakhs in an area of 94.88 km^2), with skyscrapers looming amidst the wetlands.[1] As a medium, cinema is always set in a specific spatiality; for example, indoor spaces such as the home or office, or the outdoors. This chapter traces the evolution of urban spatiality as it is a missing point in discussions about the socioeconomic context of Malayalam cinema. To do so, the chapter lays out a connected reading of the city in/of Malayalam cinema by highlighting how Kochi and Malayalam cinema are mutually shaped in relation to social, economic, and geographical specificities. A contextual analysis of cinematic frames and the affects they evoke leads me to identity three distinct cinematic geographies of Kochi in Malayalam cinema.

The city has been a part—through either its absence or its presence—of the cinematic frames of Malayalam cinema from the very beginning. As ideas of development, nation-making, and citizenship changed, so too did the city and cinema, contributing in their turn to these transformations. The first section of this chapter introduces some of these connected transformations, contextualises the move of the Malayalam film industry from Madras to Kochi, and explains how this move was reflected in a new technical and creative crew along with other changes. As a cumulative outcome of these various changes, the second section identifies three distinct cinematic geographies of Kochi that Malayalam cinema produced from the 1990s. The third section, comprising four elaborate parts, examines the Malayalam cinema of the 1980s and then identifies these three embodied geographies that captured the affective formation of the city and the cinema from the 1990s onwards.

Until the 2000s, Malayalam cinema was mostly produced in Madras (now, Chennai). From the 2000s, enhanced by greater connectivity and technological expertise, Kochi started attracting Malayalam cinema into its own linguistic and cultural territory.[2] Interestingly, this period also witnessed a surge in the number of Malayalam films that featured Kochi as a significant character, and where various parts of the city played a central role in the plot. This does not mean that the city was not present in Malayalam cinema earlier; however, one distinct aspect of recent cinema in and about Kochi compared to the earlier films is the foregrounding of multiple spatialities within the city, and the diversity of characters specific to spaces. Before embarking on a detailed discussion on why and how these changes came about, we will explain the dynamic linkages between the city and the cinema.

Cities, as spaces where capital, people, and resources are concentrated, have long attracted scholarly attention.[3] Like cinema, cities have also undergone major transformations in tandem with larger socioeconomic changes, such as the introduction of liberalisation policies in the 1990s. With developing countries adopting neoliberal policies since the 1990s, the boundaries of cities and their scope for an exchange of resources became seamless. Dutch-American sociologist Saskia Sassen (2005) identified 'Global Cities' such as Tokyo, New York, and London, which saw a transnational flow of resources, as spearheading the global economy. However, cities across the world have widely differing trajectories, and therefore they need to be analysed beyond the framework of renewed capital flows in the wake of economic restructuring (see Abu-Lughod 1999; McKinnon 2011). For instance, postcolonial cities need to be understood vis-à-vis their historical and geographical specificities rather than merely having their neoliberal experience compared to a Western city.

Despite studies about the increasing uniformity of cities in the neoliberal world, cities in developing countries still retain multiple valences, except for some similarity in their upscale neighbourhood markets. While cities do have streets and pockets that look alike, they also consist of spaces and people that are endemic to those specific regions. Similarities between the built environments in some sections of a city do not mean that we can understand all city spaces as being uniform and identical. This is because the built environments in a city are not inert, but are enlivened by the way people imprint their lives on such spaces. Cultural anthropologist Nadia Seremetakis (2019, 69) discussed the animated life of city structures:

> [T]he built environment and architectural space has to abandon much of its monumental aspirations and tendency for petrifaction and permanence, that the built environment has to become more of a living membrane and empathic skin upon which citizens can write and capture the flux, immediacy and indeterminacy of everyday life.

These structures live through a rhythm and a flow, and acquire meanings in relation to the people who inhabit these spaces. This becomes clearer in times when public spaces appear deserted and desolate, for example, during the Coronavirus lockdowns.[4] Urban spaces also acquire meaning from the way they are embodied by 'citi'zens. This chapter takes off from this premise in which affective spaces and dynamic technologies merge into each other in cinema, as well as in the city space of cinema.[5]

VIBRANT CITIES, CHANGING CINEMA

India's agricultural economy and Gandhi's vision of villages as being at the centre of the nation's development resonated in cinema after the 1950s, with its focus on rural landscapes and questions of economic and social development. Aspects of cities were often juxtaposed with village scenes in Malayalam cinema. For example, in *Anubhavangal Palichakal* (1971), the hero flees to an urban landscape, which can be identified as Kochi from the visuals, to escape his political and family problems. The city provides anonymity to the character, until he gets into a scuffle. He is later arrested for murder and sentenced to death by hanging. In some ways, the city provides a contrast to the village, where life unfolds calmly.

From the 1980s, city spaces became pronounced and significant in Malayalam cinema. Films such as *New Delhi* (1987, Director: Joshiy), *Irupatham Noottandu* (1987, Director: K. Madhu), *America America America* (1983, Director: I. V. Sasi), *Deshadanakkili Karayarilla* (1986, Director: Padmarajan), and *Gandhinagar 2nd Street* (1986, Director: Sathyan Anthikad) are examples of this trend. *New Delhi* and *Irupatham Noottandu* are political thrillers that unfold in New Delhi, the national capital, and Thiruvananthapuram, the state capital, respectively. In the other three films, Malayali characters come to cities in America and to Kochi. While much of the plot is set in the city, at the end they either leave the city or die in it.

From the 1990s, many more Malayalam films were set in Kochi: *In Harihar Nagar* (1990, Dir: Siddique Lal), *Dany* (2001, Director: T. V. Chandran), *Stop Violence* (2002, Director: A. K. Sajan), *Pothan Vava* (2006, Director: Joshiy), *Chotta Mumbai* (2007, Director: Anwar Rasheed), *Big B* (2007, Director: Amal Neerad), *Kutty Srank* (2010, Director: Shaji N. Karun), *Chappa Kurishu* (2011, Director: Sameer Thahir), *Honey Bee* (2013, Director: Lal Junior-Jean Paul Lal), *Annayum Rasoolum* (Anna and Rasool, 2013, Director: Rajeev Ravi), *Kammattipadam* (2016, Director: Rajeev Ravi), *Action Hero Biju* (2016, Director: Abrid Shine), *Parava* (2017, Director: Soubin Shahir), *Ee Ma Yau* (2018, Director: Lijo Jose Pellisseri). In films such as *Annayum Rasoolum*, *Honey Bee*, *Chotta Mumbai*, *Kammattipadam*, and *Big B*, the city becomes a prominent 'character', with a specific part of it being integral to the plot.[6]

In the 2000s, equipped with increased connectivity and availability of technology, Kochi slowly became the base for Malayalam cinema production. The lack of an international airport had been a hurdle, but the new Cochin International Airport became operational by mid-1999. One of the first film studios in Kochi, Lal Media, was started in Kaloor in 2001. Twenty years on, there are several film studios, some of them owned by film directors and actors themselves. This shift resulted in an increase in the number of Malayali technical crew in production in the place of Tamils, who were earlier among the majority in the film crews. This change is noticeable in the increasing number of noted film directors, cinematographers, and writers from Kochi, such as Siddique and Lal (actor, director, screenplay writer, producer; first film: *Pappan Priyappetta Pappan*, 1986); Benny P. Nayarambalam (screenwriter; *First Bell*, 1992); P. F. Mathews (screenplay writer; *Puthran*, 1995); Ashiq Abu (director; *Daddy Cool*, 2009); Sameer Thahir (cinematographer, director; *Big B*, 2007; *Chappa Kurishu*, 2011); Shyju Khalid (cinematographer, director: *Traffic*, 2011; *Anchu Sundarikal*, 2013), Soubin Shahir (actor, director; *Annayum Rasoolum*, 2013; *Parava*, 2017), among others. Some of the directors own film studios in Kochi, where most of their production work is carried out these days. Several Malayalam actors, such as Mammootty, Sreenivasan, and Mohanlal, have shifted their base from Madras to Kochi, and a new set of actors from Kochi found space in Malayalam cinema during this period as well.[7]

A confluence of the technological, economic, and shifting social dynamics of cinema and the city reflected itself in each other. In cinema, these diverse aspects can be understood not in a linear manner, but as dramatised depictions of multiple times, people, and spaces. Film studies has outgrown its earlier approach of studying a city with reference to its representation (Mazierska and Rascaroli 2003), that is, the city reproduced as text through the medium of film. Instead, the film is increasingly understood as 'a technology of place', 'as a medium able to produce spatiality through the set of its creative tasks—namely, location filming, mise-en-scene, framing, lighting and editing' (Brunsdon 2010, 94, quoted in Alvarez 2015). Taken together, each aspect mentioned above constitutes both a polyphonic history and present of the city, its inhabitants, and the cinema.

Cities such as Delhi and Hyderabad have areas known as the 'Old City', which is historical in nature and inhabited largely by religious minorities. These cities within cities challenge many studies that discuss the uniformity that characterises networked cities in the globalised world. Kochi, too, harbours a diversity of people and geographies. Multiple geographies of the city are socially produced by the people inhabiting them, and vice versa. In this sense, a city is not composed of tracts of disembodied spaces, but is made up of embodied entities. How do these embodied geographies inform cinema and, in turn, how does cinema create this polyphonic being of Kochi?

Cinematic and Multiple Geographies of Kochi

The geographical peculiarities of Kochi are inseparably linked to the city's emergence and growth. For instance, the earliest port in Cochin took shape in the late fourteenth century and was the result of a major flood.[8] This flood also created a cluster of islands such as Vypeen, Kadamakkudi, and Varappuzha in the backwaters. Currently, ships enter the port through the channel between Vypeen and Fort Kochi. These islands, though separated from the mainland by backwaters, are therefore an important geographical formation, and led to the development of Kochi as it is today.[9] These islands symbolise the seamless continuity of port cities beyond closed borders and boundaries. These continuities shape a port city like Kochi in its multiplicities at all levels—geographically, historically, and aesthetically.

These multiplicities, which have themselves been repeatedly constituted through mediatised images, narratives, and visuals, form part of the lived realities of the people inhabiting these spaces. As I will demonstrate, this constitution is consistent with the social production of the geography of the region, as circulated through developmental and cultural narratives. Malayalam cinema encapsulates three distinct embodied geographies of Kochi from the 1990s, in which the city is inseparable from the plot: *first*, the central zone of the city, the nerve centre of business activities, also known as Ernakulam. This is often referred to as the heart of Kochi in cultural representations (as seen in an advertisement in *Malayala Manorama*, *Metro Manorama*, 31 December 2014, 1), and has a thriving business population who settled in the city from the 1960s. The *second* zone includes areas such as Fort Kochi and Mattancherry, which were part of Dutch, Portuguese, and

British conquests and now form the centre of tourist activities. Yet, the larger area here remains underdeveloped and is home to religious minorities such as Muslims and Christians. The *third* cinematic-geographic zone is the cluster of islands in the backwaters, in north-central Kochi, on the border of the Arabian Sea. The population of these islands mostly comprises Christian communities such as Latin Catholics and Anglo-Indians (*Parangis*),[10] Dalits, and fishing communities.[11] Some of these spaces had appeared in cinematic frames even before the 1990s, but in a quite different manner.

TRANSIENT URBAN SPACE/LIFE OF THE 1980S

In Malayalam cinema of the 1980s, scenes of joyriding in the backwaters or at Bolgatty palace (built by the Dutch in 1744 and a major tourist attraction today) add beauty to song sequences, such as those in *Shyama* (song: *Poonkatte*) and *Deshadanakkili Karayarilla* (song: *Vaanampadi Etho*). The cinematic visuals and narrative allude to a tourist, as the protagonists briefly visit these urban landmarks. These sequences are filmed in brighter colours using wide shots, revealing the beauty of this 'new' space in the frames.

The song sequence *Poonkatte* in *Shyama* invokes a romantic past through colourful shots taken by the Vembanad lake, with anchored ships in the harbour forming the backdrop. The sequence is replete with scenes of the couple riding in the backwaters, with the Kochi skyline and islands visible in the distance. Crisp editing and fast-moving shots energise the scenes. In sharp contrast, it is the lack of drinking water facilities and infrastructure in this part of the city that makes the news in real life (see *Malayala Manorama* 2014, 1).

Vypeen was in the news in 1982 and even afterwards for the infamous hooch tragedy in which seventy-seven people died, sixty-three were blinded, and fifteen crippled after they consumed spurious liquor sold by a government-authorised liquor shop. Most of the victims were poor fishermen and labourers living in and around Vypeen. The film *Eenadu* (1982; Director: I. V. Sasi) was based on this tragedy. However, in the film, the location of the plot is not clearly foregrounded. In earlier films, too (as discussed above), the city beyond the mainland was represented as a mere tourist addition. In this sense, there was a certain disembodied geography of the region which appeared alluring to the protagonists seeking to explore the city. These islands were not the beneficiaries of postcolonial development schemes, and the politically and socially disadvantaged population remained disconnected from the mainland until 2004, when the Goshree bridges connecting the islands to the mainland were constructed. Despite being geographically significant for the port, the islands remained socially underdeveloped areas, lacking basic facilities such as hospitals, higher educational institutions, and proper roads. They—and their inhabitants—did not feature in colourful visuals of the city in 1980s Malayalam cinema, other than as distant greenery in scenes shot in the backwaters.

The film *Deshadanakkili Karayarilla* is about two girls, who are also close friends. They elope to the city of Kochi in search of a better life, compared to their schooldays in a non-urban milieu. Popular city spots highlighted in the film include the centrally located Subhash Park and the earlier Marine Drive walkway, which are also some of the markers of city planning. The two girls are shown to be living a happy and lively life in relative anonymity. The city's spaces are evoked through brighter shots, fast music beats and background score, and the fast pace of the narrative.[12] Sadly, the girls ultimately commit suicide, which may be read as a comment on the transient nature of happiness offered by the city.

Shyama depicts a similar experience of Kochi. In a song sequence ('Poonkatte…'), the heroine recalls a happy, romantic time with her lover in the city. Most of the city spaces featured in this song are the same ones highlighted in *Deshadanakkili Karayarilla*. Soon after this sequence, the hero dies in an accident and the heroine moves away from Kochi, to the mountains. The city's allure does not seem to last long in these films; the glitter it offers is fleeting and momentary before life ends. Is this an acknowledgment of the socio-political moment of the 1980s, when the nation was thinking beyond an agriculture-based economy? The Gandhian imagination that visualised a village-based development as the path to national growth was losing its sheen, and the country was on the verge of economic liberalisation. The national moral ethic was being extended beyond the village, and the city was becoming more than a grey, unattractive alternative to the village. In the 1980s, the city was beginning to be considered a vibrant place of movement on its own terms, albeit one that merited caution. In both films, the characters move to the city and dwell in it for a while, before meeting an untimely death. Life begins, and is lived, in a non-urban milieu; the city is merely a site to be visited, a place 'out there', away from one's 'own' place. The 'citi'zen is located elsewhere, and the city is only a space one passes through as life fades.

INHABITING THE CITY AFTER THE 1990S

The 'citi'zen becomes more visible in Malayalam cinema from the 1990s. The central part of the city features integrally in both the plot and the depiction of characters in this period. *In Harihar Nagar*, written and directed by Siddique and Lal, both of whom hail from Kochi, revolves around four young men in a middle-class colony. The film was mostly shot in Girinagar residential colony,[13] one of the first commercial residential colonies constructed in the mid-1960s. The park-cum-recreation club, locally known as Mammootty Park, provides the meeting place for the four friends.[14] Several local and city markers of urban planning form the backdrop to the plot. *In Harihar Nagar* introduces specific urban localities into the urban imagery of Kochi, compared to earlier films in which the city was synonymous only with Subhash Park, boat rides in the backwaters, beaches, and the walkway along the shores of Vembanad Lake. All local spots in the movie are middle-class spaces and the characters, too, come from the middle class. All four friends seem to be unemployed; they just hang out, riding their bikes and harassing young women. They are depicted as young urban men joyfully pursuing life in the colourful, burgeoning Kochi, and at the end, they come in possession of a suitcase full of money.

Chappa Kurishu (*Head or Tail*, 2011; written and directed by Sameer Thahir, who hails from Kochi) is also shot in commercially vibrant parts of the city such as Menaka, Broadway, M. G. Road, Pallimukku, and Marine Drive Walkway. By this time, Subhash Park had lost its novelty; instead, the roads, busy with people and traffic, corporate offices, and the house of one of the protagonists, situated in an upper-class locality, frame the city, which is visually created through several of these urban architectural markers. Arjun, a young, wealthy man engaged in the construction business, is involved with Ansari, a lower-class Muslim migrant working as a salesman in a supermarket. Ansari rides the bus daily from his dwelling in a slum to (and from) his workplace in the commercial heart of the city. Arjun is in command of the city and his spaces of operation, till he becomes embroiled in a tricky situation with Ansari. Arjun, the playful, successful young man of the city, is set against Ansari, with his lower-class status, Muslim identity, and rented room in a distant slum. The cinematic frames associate the central part of the city with individuals who are not bound by their religious identities, but who are shown as entitled and aspire to immerse themselves in the joys that the urban spaces offer.

Limitless Water, Confined Shores

In contrast to this, Malayalam films set in the islands and in Fort Kochi offers a social production of the region by etching out religious identities. Among the films set in the islands are *Dany* (2001), *Pothan Vava* (2006), and *Annayum Rasoolum* (2013), and some parts of *Kutty Srank* (2010). *Dany* was written, directed, and produced by acclaimed filmmaker T. V. Chandran, who comes from Telicherry, north Kerala. The film tells the story of a poor saxophone player Daniel ('Dany') Thompson, juxtaposing his life along with major historical events occurring in the world. While historical time is built into the narrative, space—Dany was born in a village near the sea in Kerala—finds only passing mention. The Malayalam dialect spoken by Dany and his friend Freddy is that of the Christian shore communities in Kochi. Their names, social background, and dialect suggest they could be either Latin Catholics or Anglo-Indians. Dany and Freddy's boat ride in the calm backwaters, a contrast to the strong waves of the sea, on their way back from Chavaro, home of the wealthy landlord, as well as Dany's hut near the beach indicate that the place is bordered by the sea on one side and the backwaters on the other. Vypeen fits these geographical specifications better than any other place in Kochi. However, this is never clearly articulated in the film; my deduction is based solely on the cinematic visuals provided. (It has to be noted that *Dany* was made in 2001, three years before the Goshree bridges were built. The islands and their inhabitants were yet to get their space in cinematic visuals.)

A wealthy landlord asks Dany to marry his pregnant daughter, whose boyfriend has died in an accident. Dany agrees after Freddy convinces him that doing so will save him from his poverty-stricken life. After marrying Margaret, Dany leaves his hut by the seashore to live with her, leaving behind everything related to his earlier life, including his saxophone, upon her insistence. Dany is reduced to an unwanted presence in the house, and faces constant humiliation at the hands of Margaret and her son. As he grows older, he is sent away to a hospital, where he becomes friendly with Bhargavi Amma, who had been similarly left behind by her family. They travel together to meet Dany's daughter from his first marriage, and Dany dies on their way back. Bhargavi Amma gives him a decent burial according to Christian rites, against the wishes of her family. Thus, Dany finds solace in death, despite being away from his home and family.

Annayum Rasoolum, directed by Rajeev Ravi, narrates the tragic love story of Anna from Vypeen (a Latin Catholic) and Rasool, a Muslim who lives in Mattancherry. This film is remarkable for the manner in which it captures the embodied geography of Vypeen and its connection to the mainland through the metaphor of boat journeys. Visuals of church festivals and the lower-middle class life of Christian shore communities in the islands, and of the lives of Muslim characters in the lower-class milieu of Mattancherry create a well-crafted blend of people and places. Although a love story, the film captures the flow of people who move from the islands to the city for work, shopping, and everything in between. Geographic context and human existence complement each other through the visuals, and technical details such as the editing and background score. Every day, Anna travels by boat to her workplace in the city with her friends. The alternating disconnect with and link to the city, and the differences and similarities between the two geographies are brought out through these boat journeys along the backwaters. Anna's life at home is dull and gloomy. Her family, including her aggressive brother, oppose her desire to marry Rasool. Anna tragically commits suicide after realising the impossibility of a union with Rasool. In the finely etched geography, the silence of Anna and her family members (other than her brother) is juxtaposed with the vibrancy around them. In both *Dany* and *Annayum Rasoolum*, the lower-caste Christian hero and heroine from the islands do not outlive the cinematic climax. The expanse of water surrounding the islands and its people, who are inseparable from this geography, enter Malayalam cinema through these films, but fail to survive the challenges of a cinematic geography.

Cinematic Geographies of Difference

Films like *Chotta Mumbai* (2007; Director: Anwar Rasheed, screenplay and dialogues by Benny P. Nayarambalam. Both are from Kochi), *Honey Bee* (2013; Director: Jean Paul Lal, also from Kochi), and *Big B* (2007; Director: Amal Neerad) are set in yet another part of the city—Fort Kochi, Mattancherry, and adjoining areas, which were sites of Dutch, Portuguese, and English colonial rule, but have been largely neglected in postcolonial development endeavours. Since 2012, however, this region has marked itself on the world art map as the venue of the Kochi-Muziris biennale, and now sees considerable tourist activity.

Chotta Mumbai, a box-office hit, revolves around Vasco, a small-time goon, and his friends who idle away their time in drinking and fighting. They live in a lower-class colony and most members of this group can be read as belonging to the Latin Catholic community (from cultural signifiers such as the Portuguese-origin names and social backgrounds). The geography of this part of the city is established in the beginning with an aerial shot of Fort Kochi, with the Arabian Sea to its west. The voiceover accompanying this shot, presumably of the main protagonist Vasco, says that he grew up in this city with the wind blowing from the west.

Proximity to the sea and a life woven around its possibilities and cultural associations are recurrent themes in the film. In one of the scenes set in Vasco's father's street hotel, his younger sister, making fun of a man who goes on ordering food, jokingly asks her elder sister: 'Is his stomach the Arabian sea?'[15] There are numerous visuals of ships docked in the background as the four friends meet to plan their next move; whether it is to pay Vasoottan, Vasco's friend, in the hope that he would find jobs for them in Malaysia, or just to hang out together. Even amidst their dire economic and social situation, the image of ships, both moving in the sea and docked in the harbour, signals possible movement and hope.

Big B, released in the same year as *Chotta Mumbai*, is also a popular Malayalam film set in Fort Kochi. The film garnered praise for its technical aspects, especially cinematography and editing. Houses and garages, especially the old Portuguese-style windows, are reminiscent of colonial architecture. The seashore and backwaters form the background, mostly during fight sequences. This is in contrast to *Chotta Mumbai*, where the seashore frames the meetings of friends, and their shared hopes and tensions. This difference in tone informs some of the crucial scenes in *Big B*, especially the last fight scene, which hints at who is the more rightful native of the land. The narrative also references the foreign invaders who came through the sea, and how some locals became their henchmen and enforced the colonisers' interests on their fellow natives. Assi, a Muslim character played by actor Vinayakan, tells Saayippu Tony, the villain: 'You forgot that our *baappas* (fathers) were already here when your forefathers started arriving in ships.'[16] The main protagonist Bilal, played by prominent actor Mammootty, also uses a degrading term to refer to the villain's mother, whom he accuses of having relationships with foreigners who came in ships to Kochi.[17] The images and references in the film suggest that the open waters, and the people they brought in, posed a cultural and material threat to the people of the land. Several dialogues in *Big B* stress the limits of the cosmopolitanism associated with open shores.

Big B and *Chotta Mumbai*, set in different areas of Fort Kochi, diverge in genre and spectator experience. However, in both films, the sociocultural background of the protagonists is clearly foregrounded. In *Big B*, the protagonists are lower-class Muslim, Latin Catholic, and Anglo-Indian youth, many of them engaged in various criminal activities.

Chotta Mumbai's protagonists are Latin Catholics, lower-caste Hindus, and Muslims. In these films, the central characters are native to Fort Kochi and their social backgrounds are well-etched. They are not just engaged in individualistic pursuits in the city, which vend(s) a 'dream of a total freedom for the individual' (Nandy 2001, 10); their communities are woven into the cinematic worlds of Fort Kochi and the islands, which are so unlike the imagination informing the central part of the city. Spatiality and religious communities are bound together in the cinematic imagination of Fort Kochi and the islands on different levels.

The diverse urban spaces of Kochi presented in recent Malayalam cinema have created an embodied cinematic geography informed by already existing narratives about these spaces. All the spaces and the people inhabiting them exceed these emerging cinematic presentations; however, once on film, these visuals are preserved forever. They will remain until new images circulate, created by more diverse people.

Cinematic Histories, Multiple Cities

Malayalam cinema and the city of Kochi complement each other's developmental trajectories in many ways, as shown in this chapter. The chapter foregrounded the methodological possibilities of combining Urban Studies and Media Studies to weave a linked narrative of the city and the cinema. It also calls for further research into cinematic geography, which can open up new avenues of analysis in the future,[18] not only because of technology's irreducible valence, but also for how the camera individualises a specific part of the city, frozen in the moment from several other possibilities, and makes it available for indefinite circulation. All the geographies discussed in the chapter are far more than what was chosen to be filmed. And this 'choice' in itself is socially constituted.[19] Historical time facilitates the capture of some spaces and people, leaving many others behind. Much more remains for Malayalam cinema to capture, in terms of the layered multiplicities of space and people thriving on the open shores of Kochi.

Notes

1. Kochi is a more recent name of the city of Cochin. I retain the use of Cochin in historical references and use Kochi for contemporary works. See, for details about the population, https://web.archive.org/web/20190408173504/https://cochinmunicipalcorporation.kerala.gov.in/documents/10157/32ef97a6-beb2-45ab-b6c1-20c0759023fd (accessed February 2025).

2. Cinema played an important role in shaping a national and linguistic identity after independence. Malayalam media, including cinema, actively participated in cultivating a Malayali identity vis-à-vis other linguistic state identities. For instance, there are numerous instances in Malayalam cinema and public space where Tamil culture is pitted against a 'Malayali' culture. Despite such a prevalent cultural discourse, it took almost half-a-century after independence for Malayalam cinema to find a complete production base in Kerala. Although there were several film studios such as Udaya Pictures (1947),

Navodaya Studio (1976), Chithranjali Studio (1980), etc., in Kerala, full-fledged production of a greater number of Malayalam films began in the state only in the 2000s (Krishnakumar 2013).

3. I have used both 'place' and 'space' in this chapter, following Michel de Certeau's differentiation between place and space. According to de Certeau (1984), place indicates a more stable site while space consists of mobile elements.

4. Several natural calamities have shown how cities and their structures render themselves empty when uninhabited. Nadia Seremetakis (2019), in her chapter about the destruction of the Greek city of Kalamata when an earthquake struck, notes,

> The skeletal building, in one of the photos, struck me as an ironic image. It was a spontaneous historical monument documenting the action of the seismic violence. It is also the petrified image of the impermanence of human achievement and effort, of its erasure by nature and the vanquishing of modernity. (ibid., 59)

The world witnessed how empty cities look without people when they were shut down due to the contagious Covid-19 scare across the globe (Knoll 2020).

5. American political geographer Edward Soja explains the complex relationship between the human body and geography:

> This process of producing spatiality or 'making geographies' begins with the body, with the construction and performance of the self, the human subject, as a distinctively spatial entity involved in a complex relation with our surroundings. On the one hand, our actions and thoughts shape the spaces around us, but at the same time the larger collectively or socially produced spaces and places within which we live also shape our actions and thoughts in ways that we are only beginning to understand. (2000, 6)

6. Ratheesh Radhakrishnan (2019) identifies films such as *Big B*, *Chotta Mumbai*, *Stop Violence*, and *Annayum Rasoolum* in which Kochi has a substantial part as a niche segment, and categorises them as a genre he terms 'Kochi cinema'.

7. Vinayakan (*Maanthrikam*, 1995), Vinay Forrt (*Ritu*, 2009), Srinda Arhaan (*Four Friends*, 2010), Sudhi Koppa (*Sagar Alias Jacky Reloaded*, 2009), Soubin Shahir (*Da Thadiya*, 2012), and Bineesh Bastin (*Porinju Mariyam Jose*, 2019) are actors who began appearing in Malayalam movies after the 2000s.

8. Robert Bristow (1959, 37), the engineer in charge of building a modern port in Cochin in the early twentieth century, notes in his book:

> Muziris, now known as Cranganur, lies at or near the mouth of the Periyar River some eighteen miles north of what is now Cochin. The famous backwaters, at the turn of the pre-Christian era, were still in process of formation and limitation by the gradual advancement of two strips of land, one from the north and one from the south.

9. Goshree Bridge, connecting mainland Kochi to Vallarpadam, Bolgatty, and Vypeen, was inaugurated in June 2004. Till then, boats were the main form of transport between the islands and the mainland.

10. The Malayalam word 'Parangi' literally refers to Portuguese lineage. For instance, the cashew nut is called *Parangi Maanga* (Parangi mango) in some parts of Kerala, probably because it was introduced by the Portuguese colonisers. Today, Parangis are an Anglo-Indian minority whose rituals and customs show a greater Portuguese influence. They are categorised under Other Backward Classes (apart from being Latin Catholics) to avail of affirmative action under the Kerala state list.

11. Kadamakkudy region, comprising fourteen islands, has a population that is 66.63 per cent Christian, 33.24 per cent Hindu, and 0.06 per cent Muslim, according to the 2011 census (Population Census 2011).

12. There are several readings of *Deshadanakkili Karayarilla* that discuss the queer undertones of the plot. The girls' suicide may be seen in the context of several suicides by lesbian couples in Kerala. The dominant heteronormative sociality suffocates sexual minorities, ultimately pushing them towards death, as shown in the film (see, Bharadwaj 2015; Mokkil 2019).

13. Girinagar residential colony is named after former Indian President and Kerala state Governor, the late V. V. Giri. K. V. Joseph, an early resident of Girinagar, remembers that the construction of the colony was inaugurated by V. V. Giri himself in 1967, after the wetland had been levelled for a Kerala Pradesh Congress Committee meeting in the 1960s. Panampilly Nagar residential colony, an upper-class locality today (where several of the Malayalam film crew reside), was built later, in the 1970s.

14. Malayalam actor Mammootty used to live in Girinagar housing colony in the early 1990s. Mammootty Park must have been named after him, since his house was close by.

15. All dialogues from Malayalam films have been translated by me.

16. 'Saayippu' refers to a white male foreigner in Malayalam. 'Baappa' means 'father' among the Muslims of Kerala.

17. Bilal John Kurishingal is one among the four adopted sons of Mary John Kurishingal. He has brothers whose names suggest a multi-religious background—Eddy John Kurishingal, Murugan John Kurishingal, and Bijo. Despite growing up in such an unconventional family, Bilal's character uses the same sexist tropes of paternity, sanitised motherhood, and nativity in these dialogues.

18. Another trend to be noted, but which does not fall within the purview of this chapter, is the manner in which different places other than Kochi have been foregrounded in Malayalam cinema in the past ten years. For instance, *Maheshinte Prathikaram* (2016; Director: Dileesh Pothen) is set in the mountainous region of Idukki, which is integral to the plot. So is *Vellimoonga* (2014; Director: Jibu Jacob), which is set in Shanthipuram, a mountainous village on the border of Kannur district. *Iyyobinte Pusthakam* (2014; Director: Amal Neerad) is set in Munnar and the geography of the high ranges blends with the plot. *Salt N' Pepper* (2011; Director: Ashiq Abu) unfolds in the backdrop of Thiruvananthapuram and several markers of the city, such as V. J. T. Hall, Palayam, Shanghumugham beach, M. G. Road, and Palayam, form the spaces in which the plot develops. *Njan Steve Lopez* (2014; Director: Rajeev Ravi) is also set in Thiruvananthapuram, and the city spaces figure as a significant backdrop to the plot.

19. In all the films discussed above, Dalit geographies did not make it into the frames. However, *Kammattippadam*, directed by Rajeev Ravi (2016), foregrounds the cinematic Dalit geography of Kochi. The film constitutes another micro-region of Kochi and introduces its people, who are ultimately killed after their bodies are marked on the Malayalam cinema screen. P. K. Ratheesh (2016) notes that the Dalit characters in *Kammatipadam* are made appealing to a liberal *savarna* audience by an amplification of their Dalitness, achieved through a mix of an added layer of 'blackness' to their complexion, prosthetics such as protruding teeth, and criminality, to showcase them as hyper-Dalit bodies.

References

Abu-Lughod, J. L. 1999. *New York, Chicago, Los Angeles: America's Global Cities*. Minneapolis: University of Minnesota Press.

Alvarez, I. V. 2015. *Documenting Cityscapes*. New York: Columbia University Press.

Bharadwaj, R. 2015. *Mithyakalkkappuram: Swavarga Laimgikatha Keralathil* (*Beyond Myths: Homosexuality in Kerala*). Kottayam: DC Books.

Bristow, R. 1959. *Cochin Saga*. Cochin: Bristow Memorial Society.

Brunsdon, C. 2007. *London in Cinema*. London: Bloomsbury.

_____. 2010. 'Towards a History of Empty Spaces'. In R. Koeck and L. Roberts (eds), *The City and the Moving Image: Urban Projections*, 91–103. London: Palgrave Macmillan.

de Certeau, M. 1984. *The Practice of Everyday Life*. Los Angeles: University of California Press.

Dimendberg, E. 2004. *Film Noir and the Spaces of Modernity*. Boston, MA: Harvard University Press.

Knoll, C. 2020. 'New York Was Not Designed For Emptiness'. *The New York Times*, 30 March. Available at https://www.nytimes.com/interactive/2020/03/30/nyregion/photos-of-new-york-coronavirus.html (accessed January 2025).

Koeck, R., and L. Roberts. 2010. *The City and the Moving Image: Urban Projections*. London: Palgrave Macmillan.

Krishnakumar, G. 2013. 'Mollywood comes home to Kochi'. *The Hindu*, 4 March. Available at https://www.thehindu.com/news/cities/Kochi/mollywood-comes-home-to-kochi/article4472387.ece (accessed January 2025).

Krishnan, R. and M. S. S. Pandian. 2006. 'The Brahmin and the Citizen'. *Economic and Political Weekly* 41 (27–28), 3055–3060.

Malayala Manorama. 2014. '*Vyppinil Venalilum Vellappokkam*' ('Vypeen Flooded Even in Summer'). *Metro Manorama*, 30 December, 1.

Maruthur, N. M. 2010. 'Sexual Figures of Kerala: Cultural Practices, Regionality and the Politics of Sexuality'. Ph.D. Dissertation, University of Michigan.

Mazierska, E., and L. Rascaroli. 2003. *From Moscow to Madrid: Postmodern Cities, European Cinema*. London: I.B. Tauris.

Mazumdar, R. 2007. *Bombay Cinema: An Archive of the City*. Minneapolis: University of Minnesota Press.

McKinnon, M. 2011. *Asian Cities: Globalization, Urbanization and Nation-Building*. Copenhagen: NIAS Press.

Mokkil, N. 2019. *Unruly Figures: Queerness, Sex Work and the Politics of Sexuality in Kerala*. Washington: Washington University Press.

Nandy, A. 2001. *An Ambiguous Journey to the City: The Village and Other Odd Ruins of the Self in the Indian Imagination*. New Delhi: Oxford University Press.

Population Census. 2011. 'Ernakulam District Religion Data—Hindu/ Muslim'. Available at https://www.census2011.co.in/data/religion/district/278-ernakulam.html (accessed January 2025).

Radhakrishnan, R. 2019. 'Urban/the City: An Experiment called the "Kochi Film"'. *Positions* 25 (1), 173–194.

Ratheesh, P. K. 2016. 'Kammattippadam, Athidalitham, Aaswadanam, Aaghosham' ('Kammattippadam: Hyder-Dalitness, Appreciation, Celebration'). *Utharakalam*, 7 June. Available at https://utharakalam.com/2016/06/07/14981.html (accessed January 2025).

Sassen, S. 2005. 'The Global City: Introducing a Concept'. *The Brown Journal of World Affairs* XI (2), 27–43.

Seremetakis, N. 2019. *Modern Cities of Silence: Disasters, Nature and the Petrified Bodies of History*. New York: Routledge

Soja, E. W. 2000. *Postmetropolis: Critical Studies of Cities and Regions*. Oxford: Basil Blackwell.

Filmography

Sthanarthi Saramma. 1966. Dir: K. S. Sethumadhavan, Jaya Maruthi.

Thulabharam. 1968. Dir: A. Vincent, Supriya.

Anubhavangal Palichakal. 1971. Dir: K. S. Sethumadhavan, Manjilas Films.

Shyama. 1986. Dir: Joshiy, Jubilee Productions.

Deshadanakkili Karayarilla. 1986. Dir: Padmarajan, Burton Movies.

Gandhinagar Second Street. 1986. Dir: Sathyan Anthikad, Kottayam: Casino Films.

In Harihar Nagar. 1990. Dir: Siddique-Lal, Ernakulam: Mohsin Priya Combines.

Roja. 1992. Dir: Maniratnam, Chennai: Kavithalaya Productions.

Dany. 2001. Dir: T. V. Chandran, Ernakulam: Film Commune.

Stop Violence. 2002. Dir: A. K. Sajan, Ernakulam: Vrindavan Pictures.

Pothan Vava. 2006. Dir: Joshiy, Ernakulam, Produced by Lal.

Chotta Mumbai. 2007. Dir: Anwar Rasheed, Ernakulam: Sree Bhadra Pictures.

Big B. 2007. Dir: Amal Neerad, Ernakulam: Marikar Films.

Kutty Srank. 2010. Dir: Shaji N Karun, Mahesh Ramanathan, Reliance Big Entertainment.

Chappa Kurishu. 2011. Dir: Sameer Thahir, Ernakulam: Magic Frames.

Da Thadiya. 2012. Dir: Aashiq Abu, Ernakulam: Anto Joseph.

Honey Bee. 2013. Dir: Lal Jr., Jean Paul Lal, Ernakulam: SJM Entertainments.

Annayum Rasoolum. 2013. Dir: Rajeev Ravi, Ernakulam: D Cutz Film Company.

Kammattipadam. 2016. Dir: Rajeev Ravi, Ernakulam: Global United Media.

Action Hero Biju. 2016. Dir: Abrid Shine, Ernakulam: Pauly Jr. Pictures—Full On Studios.

Parava. 2017. Dir: Soubin Shahir, Ernakulam: Anwar Rasheed Entertainments—The Movie Club.

Ee Ma Yau. 2018. Dir: Lijo Jose Pellissery, Ernakulam: OPM Cinemas—RGK Cinemas.

Kumbalangi Nights. 2019. Dir: Madhu C. Narayanan, Ernakulam: Fahadh Faasil and Friends—Working Class Hero.

Driving Licence. 2019. Dir: Lal Jr., Jean Paul Lal, Ernakulam: Prithviraj Productions—Magic Frames.

Maheshinte Prathikaram. 2016. Dir: Dileesh Pothan, Ernakulam: OPM Dream Mill Cinemas.

Thondimuthalum Driksakshiyum. 2017. Dir: Dileesh Pothan, Ernakulam: Urvashi Theatres—Kalasangham Films.

Salt n' Pepper. 2011. Dir: Ashiq Abu, Ernakulam: Lucsam Creations.

10

Lampooning the Raj

The Cartoon in Pre-independence Tamil Journalism*

A. R. Venkatachalapathy

Nowadays, people are raving about Mali and his cartoons. But I have observed the reception to his caricatures in the early days. Very few relished them. Many of the musicians who were caricatured used to take fright like undomesticated cows.... Only after repeatedly looking at his cartoons did people get used to them and shed their fright. Slowly this became a habit. Then a custom. Finally, as withdrawal of coffee causes headache, many eyes yearned for Mali's cartoons.

Thi.Ja (1952, 39–40)

It is perhaps appropriate to begin a chapter on cartoons and caricaturing in Tamil journalism with this observation from a popular and perceptive Tamil writer, Thi. Ja. Ranganathan (1901–1974). Writing in the 1940s, he drew attention to how the new art forms of cartoon and caricature had become entrenched in Tamil society, and how Tamil readers had been socialised into appreciating them. Further, Mali (T. R. Mahalingam, ?1906–1946),[1] the cartoonist referred to, first made his name in the *Free Press Journal* in Bombay before being immortalised in the pages of *Ananda Vikatan*, the first popular Tamil periodical, thereby underscoring the all-India context in which cartooning in Tamil journalism originated and flourished.

---

*First published as 'Lampooning the Raj: Subramania Bharati and the Cartoon in Tamil Journalism, 1906-1910', *CCTR Journal* V (1–2), 1996. Reproduced with permission.

ORIGINS IN INDIA

The earliest cartoons in India were published in the British-owned English periodicals. Kamal Sarkar states that the *Delhi Sketch Book*, published from Delhi in 1850, was the first to publish cartoons in India. Unfortunately, it folded up when the rebels took over the city in 1857 (Sarkar 1971).

However, as Partha Mitter has pointed out, 'no single humorous publication made a deeper impression in colonial India than the English magazine, *Punch*. A riotous procession of its offering greets us in the second half of the last century' (Mitter 1994, 138). It is perhaps from here that one should begin a history of cartoons in India. A series of journals, evidently inspired by *Punch*, proliferated across India: *The Delhi Punch*, *The Punjab Punch*, *The Indian Punch*, *Urdu Punch*, *Gujarati Punch*, *Hindu Punch*, *Parsi Punch*, *Hindi Punch*, and even a *Purnea Punch* (Khanduri 2009).

It is not clear which Indian-language newspaper was the first to publish cartoons. Partha Mitter suggests that the *Avadh Punch*, published in Urdu, was a pioneer in this regard (Mitter 1994, 158). In Bengal, the *Amrita Bazar Patrika* began to publish cartoons in 1872 (ibid., 137). In a monograph on wit and humour in colonial north India, Mushirul Hasan has reproduced a large number of cartoons from *Avadh Punch*, with English translations (Hasan 2007). It is likely that cartoons in Bengali followed soon thereafter, and proved the most influential. Bonny Thomas wrote that the first cartoons in the Malayalam press were published only in 1919, by P. S. Govinda Pillai in *Vidushakan* (Thomas 1994). The spread of cartoons in the Indian-language press has been necessarily uneven, stretching across a considerable temporal span.

The first iteration of this chapter—in the form of a Tamil book and then as various essays—was arguably the earliest attempt to explore the history of cartooning in India (see Venkatachalapathy 1994).[2] However, subsequent explorations have not referred to this work, despite the recent interest in the history of cartoons, largely spurred by the 2012 controversy around the cartoon of B. R. Ambedkar in an NCERT textbook.[3]

Ritu Gairola Khanduri's monograph studies the production and reception of political cartoons in colonial India at considerable length and in detail (Khanduri 2014). Unnamati Shyama Sundar's angry book on the Ambedkar cartoons is of great interest, not only for its marshalling of the caricatures of Ambedkar in the mainstream English-language press, but also for its incisive analysis (Shyama Sundar 2019). As such, it strikes a balance with compilations of cartoons focused on M. K. Gandhi and Jawaharlal Nehru, such as *Gandhi in Cartoons* (Das 1970) and *Don't Spare Me Shankar* (2009).

Understandably, writing the history of cartoons is fraught with difficulties. Sources continue to remain a problem. As yet, the history of the cartoon in India remains to be teased out from the footnotes, asides, and digressions in the histories of journalism. A full-length study awaits; this chapter is a modest attempt to chronicle the rise of cartoons in Tamil.

Bharati, the Pioneer

The pioneer of cartoons in Tamil was C. Subramania Bharati (1882–1921), the great modern Tamil poet.[4] This fact was completely missed by Partha Mitter in his otherwise admirable and pioneering work (Mitter 1994). Even Abu Abraham, in his brief introduction to *The Penguin Book of Indian Cartoons* (1988), shows no awareness of Bharati's work.

Considering the fact that the cartoon has been seen as a powerful tool for airing opinions, 'a unique visual which combines to make a strong commentary' (Hung 1994, 124), it is not at all surprising that Bharati should employ it during the Swadeshi period (1906–1911), which was the first time that the Indian nationalist movement showed signs of acquiring a mass character. The following notice in *India* testifies to Bharati's genuine pride in his innovation.

> **A New Development in *India*:** Readers would know that ours is the only magazine in Tamil which publishes cartoons. However, from the coming week onwards, we propose to add another adornment. Apart from the cartoon on the title page, we propose to publish other drawings and pictures to illustrate important news items. Such an arrangement is unknown in the Tamil, English, Telugu and Kannada language journals of South India. It is we who are introducing this novelty. Initially, we can proceed only little by little. But in the coming days further embellishments will be made. (*India*, 13 March 1909)

Even the letterhead of *India* made the proud claim: 'A Weekly Tamil magazine on modern lines. Published every week with cartoons.'[5]

Image 10.1: The English suck Rs 45 crore from India every year. This was a standard theme in pre-independence cartoons.

Source: *India*, 8 September 1906.

However, the immediate inspiration behind this innovation is not clear. Given Bharati's wide exposure to journalism across the English-speaking world, foreign inspiration cannot be discounted. For instance, reviewing the *'Hindi' Punch*, Bharati expressed the hope that it would aspire to emulate the *Punch* of London (*India*,

20 October 1906). Bharati also reproduced cartoons from foreign periodicals, such as the then well-known *Review of Reviews* and the French *Pasquino*.

Image 10.2: Lord Morley milks the cow (India) dry, while the calves (Indians) starve. Another classic depiction of the drain of wealth from India.

Source: *India*, 29 September 1906.

From 8 September 1906 until it closed shop in March 1910, *India* published cartoons almost every week, especially on its title page. There were a few recurring themes in the cartoons. One standard theme was the exploitation of India by the English. Invariably, England is personified as John Bull, a plump Englishman in a bowler hat. John Bull is either milking a cow (Mother India) dry while children (Indians) starve, or he is exporting grains to England while skinny, emaciated Indians look at the ships carrying grain longingly. Taking the nationalist argument of 'drain of wealth' quite literally, in one cartoon we see an Englishman sucking up India's wealth through a straw. An even better target of Bharati's vicious cartoons was the Moderate faction of the Indian National Congress (INC), who believed in constitutional agitation and was termed the 'honest swadeshi'. As a champion of Bal Gangadhar Tilak's camp, he targeted the

Moderates for their complicity and hypocrisy in their support of the British against the Extremist faction.

Image 10.3: The owls (the Moderates) seek refuge from sunlight (Swadeshism) by hiding in a tree hole (the Madras Congress Convention). The use of animals and birds to stand in for people was a part of the folk symbolism in pre-independence cartoons.

Source: *India*, 17 October 1908.

A very interesting aspect of Bharati's cartooning was his employment of traditional lore, especially proverbs and Hindu mythology. Often, a proverb was visually translated into a cartoon. For instance, when Lord Morley, the British Viceroy, set out to dig a well, out of it emerges a ghost (symbolising the Hindu–Muslim question)—this was a critique of the Minto–Morley constitutional reforms of 1909, which provided very limited franchise to Indians but offered safeguards for Muslim minorities

In the 1920s, as the cartoon slowly began to come into its own in Tamil journalism, the English press in Tamilnadu was lagging far behind. As late as 1935, the great *The Hindu* did not publish cartoons; and when it did, it preferred to reproduce David Low's syndicated cartoons rather than employ its own cartoonist (Parthasarathy 1977, 368). In the late 1920s, *Justice*, the organ of the non-Brahmin movement, published sharp cartoons on the machinations of the Swaraj Party, the faction within the Congress that advocated entry into the legislature.[15] *The Indian Express*, founded by Varadarajulu Naidu before being taken over by Ramnath Goenka, also appears to have published a few cartoons by Mali in the early 1930s.[16]

The years following the Civil Disobedience Movement were the heydays of Tamil cartooning. This period saw the rise of the '*kalana pathirikai*' ('the quarter-anna magazine', named after its price). T. S. Chockalingam's *Gandhi* was the first, followed by *Suthanthira Sangu* (see Venkatraman 2001 for reproductions of cartoons from the latter). Published sometimes as frequently as thrice a week, of no more than eight Crown Quarto-sized pages, these magazines routinely published a cartoon on their front pages. They sold tens of thousands of copies, earning the wrath of the government.

Ananda Vikatan, a tottering humour magazine taken over by S. S. Vasan (the movie mogul who later became an all-India figure as the proprietor of Gemini Studio) in 1928, further secured the cartoon's place in Tamil journalism. Until the end of the twentieth century, the cartoon was most closely associated with *Ananda Vikatan* in the popular Tamil imagination, and with a series of cartoonists such as Mali, Oomen, T. S. Sridhar, and Madhan. With the institutionalisation of Carnatic music and the consequent popularity of musicians, caricatures made a strong entry as well. Nationalist politicians, too, soon became the subject of caricature. Gandhi, with his large ears and broad smile, was of course a particular favourite, as was C. Rajagopalachari with his hanging lower lip, sharp nose, dark glasses, and shrewd demeanour.

By the early 1930s, cartooning was such an accomplished art in Tamil journalism that even the famed *Review of Reviews*, published from London, made appreciative mention of these cartoons (Ramaiah 1934).

It was at this time that the cartoon came to be known by various names in Tamil. If Bharati used the term '*chithiram*' (depiction, drawing) to refer to cartoons, the newspaper *Taminadu* preferred the term '*vinoda padangal*' (bizarre or strange pictures) in the 1920s. In the 1930s, B. S. Ramaiah employed the term '*goodartha padangal*', suggesting that cartoons conveyed a hidden meaning than the one expressly depicted. It was only in the 1940s, with the arrival of S. B. Adityan and his *Dina Thanthi*, that the now current term, '*karutthu padam*', came to be used and became entrenched. The term suggests that the cartoon conveys a view, or idea, or concept. While the other terms drew from Sanskrit, '*karutthu padam*' possessed the merit of being a pure Tamil word, and was easily adopted.

Another aspect of the cartoon's coming of age was attribution. While the cartoonists of Bharati's times remained anonymous, their counterparts in the 1930s were not only mentioned by name, but were also celebrated. Although B. S. Ramaiah, a contemporary writer and journalist, observed in 1938 that 'The art of cartooning is still in its infancy in our country. Our cartoonists could be counted on one's fingers', (Ramaiah 1938), the point is that cartoonists were believed worthy of enumeration. Apart from Mali, K. R. Sarma too won much praise (ibid.).

However, cartoonists were not independent and worked as per the dictates of editors/proprietors. It is evident from the book of cartoons published by *Tamilnadu* that the cartoonist was a craftsman who executed the ideas of the editor. 'Most of the cartoonists do not express their own opinion on day-to-day happenings. The editorial department asks them to draw such and such an incident in such and such a manner and express such and such an opinion' (Ramaiah 1934). Even Mali, it seems, was no exception. This is a tradition that seems not to have changed even now. It is arguable if, even today, Tamil journalism can boast of independent cartoonists such as O. V. Vijayan, R. K. Laxman, or Ravishankar, who can stand on their own.

Another aspect that needs to be pointed out is the predominance of the political in pre-independence Tamil cartooning. When Partha Mitter states that 'The most popular Bengali cartoons were social', it does sound exceptional to the Tamil reader (Mitter 1994, 166). The hypocritical zamindar, henpecked husband, pompous professor, obsequious clerk, illiterate Brahmin—such caricatured identities are strikingly absent in Tamil cartoons. Tamil cartoonists seemed to have confined themselves to indicting the English.

Perhaps following the pioneering cartoons of Bharati, Tamil cartoonists seem to have drawn extensively from Tamil proverbs, sayings, and Hindu mythology—what O. V. Vijayan calls 'folk symbolism' (Vijayan 2002, 57). Most of the cartoons use such motifs to represent contemporary events. This representational strategy deserves a separate study. Whether this was unique to Tamil cartooning or whether other regional counterparts also used similar strategies is worth exploring.

The year 1947 probably marks a break in the cartooning tradition. As Vijayan remarks,

> The pre-Independence cartoonist had simpler challenges to take on. The reality he was called to comment on could be separated into neat sets of black and whites. His characters were not so much precise political personae as they were folk totems. And he himself was not so much communicating as participating in the struggle along with the vast majority of his readers.... The nationalist consensus, which made these primal totems viable, collapsed with the post-independence polarization.... The cartoonist from now on would have to abandon his folk symbolism, and settle for the less apparent but more demanding job of analysis. (Vijayan 2002, 56–57)

The cartoon in Tamil journalism after 1947 calls for another history.[17]

NOTES

1. There is an all too brief obituary of Mali in *The Indian Review*, January 1947. Interestingly, while stating that he 'endeavoured to give pictorial representation to every feature of South Indian life and scenery', it makes no mention of his cartooning and caricaturing.

2. This chapter originated in Tamil as the introduction to a compilation of cartoons in Bharati's *India* (Venkatachalapathy 1994). English versions have variously appeared over the years (see Venkatachalapathy 1996a, 1996b, 2003). This version incorporates further new material.

3. In 2012, a controversy erupted over the reproduction of a cartoon in an NCERT textbook. Shankar's 1949 cartoon, a comment on the perceived slow pace of the drafting of the Indian Constitution, depicted Ambedkar sitting on a snail while Nehru stood with a whip in hand. In some quarters, the cartoon was deemed to be an insult to Ambedkar. The controversy, in turn, inspired a detailed study of Ambedkar in cartoons. See Shyama Sundar (2019).

4. T. S. Chockalingam, the doyen of Tamil journalism, while surveying the history of Tamil cartoons as early as in 1933 under his pen-name Devidasan, was emphatic in giving credit to Bharati for being the pioneer of Tamil cartooning. See Chockalingam (1933).

5. See Exhibit K in G.O. No. 1103, Judicial, 11 August 1908, and G.O. No. 1542, Judicial & Confidential, 3 October 1911, Government of Madras.

6. For cartoons from Bharati's *India* with commentary and English summary, see Venkatachalapathy (1994).

7. *Swadesamitran*'s assessment was reproduced in *India*, 6 October 1906.

8. Bharatidasan's memoir was first published in the Bharati memorial issue of the Tamil weekly *Hindustan*, 1939. Reproduced in Ilango (1992, 14).

9. G.O. No. 1143, Judicial & Confidential, 31 August 1909.

10. See the copy of the judgment in G.O. No. 1542, Judicial & Confidential, 3 October 1911.

11. *Gandhi*, April–May and June 1933.

12. K. R. Sarma had a long innings drawing for *Tamilnadu*, *Manikodi*, *Suthanthira Sangu*, and *Ananda Vikatan*. As early as in 1916, he published *Sarma's Portfolio of Drawings*, which described itself as 'A Monthly Depicting Current Topics, Art, Education, Mythology, Religion, Humor,

Etc.' I found one issue of this journal in the Tamilnadu Archives as part of G.O. No. 671, Home (Education), 21 May 1917. Another issue is available in the Adyar Library of the Theosophical Society, Chennai. I am given to understand that more issues are available in the National Library, Kolkata.

13. *'Tamil Nadu' Vinoda Padangal*, Vol. 1. Chennai: Tamilnadu Puthagasalai, 1928.

14. Samy claims that S. T. Adityan drew cartoons for *Swadesamitran*, *The Hindu*, *The Mail*, and *The Statesman*.

15. For the cartoons from *Justice*, see *Mirror of the Year*, Madras, 1928.

16. *Gandhi*, April–May 1933.

17. Such a history would have to perforce take account of a brilliant essay, 'Cartoonayanam', by C. N. Annadurai, where he writes at length on the cartoons that appeared in the mid-1960s, criticising Congress rule. See *Kanchi* (Pongal Souvenir), January 1967.

REFERENCES

Chockalingam, T. S. 1933. '*Cartoon Varalaru*' ('History of Cartoons'). *Gandhi (Malar)* April–May.

Das, Durga (ed.). 1970. *Gandhi in Cartoons*. Ahmedabad: Navjivan Publishing House.

Hasan, M. 2007. *Wit and Humour in Colonial North India*. New Delhi. Niyogi Books.

Hung. C. 1994. 'The Fuming Image: Cartoons and Public Opinion in Late Republican China, 1945 to 1949'. *Comparative Studies in Society and History* 36 (1), 122–145.

Ilango, S. S. (ed.), 1992. *Bharatiyarodu Pathandugal*. Chennai: Pari Nilayam.

Khanduri, R. G. 2009. 'Vernacular Punches: Cartoons and Politics in Colonial India'. *History and Anthropology* 20 (4), 459–486.

_____. 2014. *Caricaturing Culture in India: Cartoons and History in the Modern World*. Cambridge: Cambridge University Press

Mitter, P. 1994. *Art and Nationalism in Colonial India, 1850–1922: Occidental Orientations*. Cambridge: Cambridge University Press.

Naidu, S. G. Ramanujalu. 1928. *Chenrupona Natkal*. Amirta Guna Bodhini. Reprinted in A. R. Venkatachalapathy (ed.), S. G. Ramanujalu Naidu, '*Chenrupona Natkal*'. Nagercoil: Kalachuvadu Pathippagam, 2015.

Parthasarathy, R. 1977. *A Hundred Years of the 'Hindu': The Epic Story of Indian Nationalism*. Madras: Kasturi.

Ramaiah, B. S. 1934. 'Piranattil Mathippu Pettra Tamilarin Goodartha Padangal' ('The Cartoons of Tamils That Have Won Respect in Other Countries'). *Manikodi*, 10 June.

——. 1938. 'Chithiramum Chithirakkarargalum' ('Drawings and Artists'). *Hanuman*, Annual Number.

Samy, A. M. 1990. *Ithalalar Adithanar*. Chennai: International Institute of Tamil Studies.

Sarkar, K. 1971. *Cartoons*. Calcutta.

Shankar. 2009. *Don't Spare me Shankar*. New Delhi: Children's Book Trust.

Shyama Sundar, U. 2019. *No Laughing Matter: The Ambedkar Cartoons, 1932–1956*. New Delhi: Navayana.

Thi.Ja.Ra. 1952. *Yosikkum Velaiyile*. Chennai: Kalaimagal Kariyalayam.

Thomas, B. 1994. 'Birth of the Malayalam Cartoon: Scabbard for Satire'. *The Economic Times*, Madras, 24 May.

Venkatachalapathy, A. R. 1994. *Bharatiyin Karuthuppadangal: 'India', 1906–1910*. Madras: Narmadha Padhippagam.

——. 1996a. 'Lampooning the Raj: Subramania Bharati and the Cartoon in Tamil Journalism, 1906–1910'. *ICCTR Journal* V (1–2)

——. 1996b. 'Resisting Oppressive Laws with Impressive Cartoons'. *The Economic Times*, 14 July.

——. 2003. 'Caricaturing the Political: A Brief History of the Cartoon in Tamil Journalism'. *Art India* 8 (4).

——. 2015. S. G. Ramanujalu Naidu, '*Chenrupona Natkal*'. Nagercoil: Kalachuvadu Pathippagam.

Venkataraman, V. (ed.). 2001. *Suthanthira Sangu: Karuthuppadangal, 1930–1933*. Rajapalayam.

Vijayan, O. V. 2002. *A Cartoonist Remembers*. New Delhi: Rupa & Co.

11

The Machine in the Colony

Technology, Politics, and the Typography of Devanagari in the Early Years of Mechanisation*

Vaibhav Singh

On 18 June 1933, the *New York Herald Tribune* carried a feature story under the title 'Teaching a Sixth of the World to Read', with only a slightly more modest subheading: 'Now a Machine is to Carry Literacy to India'[1] (Hambdige 1933). This was effectively the first public announcement for not one but two products of the Brooklyn-based Mergenthaler Linotype Company (henceforth, Mergenthaler). The first of these products was 'Devanagari Linotype', the hot-metal Linotype machine, as adapted to compose Devanagari text. The second was 'Linotype Devanagari', a rendition—and simplification—of the Devanagari script in the form of the typeface carried on the Linotype machine. The *Herald Tribune* article, broadly situating this new development within the perceived educational and literary contexts of India, highlighted two questions of fundamental interest and significance to any historical enquiry—that the impetus for this development should have come from America, and that this seemingly altruistic foray should have come from what was primarily a commercial enterprise. To these may be added the equally critical question of

*Originally published as 'The Machine in the Colony: Technology, Politics, and the Typography of Devanagari in the Early Years of Mechanization', in *Philological Encounters* 3 (4), 2018, 469–495.

why this development should have come about in 1933, and not any earlier or later. It was indeed the first time that mechanical composition of the linecasting variety in any Indian script had been realised, a good three decades after the technology had been developed and established in the provinces of print in the Western world.[2]

It can be argued that, for the most part, technologically deterministic views of typographic change have formed the basis of historical narratives of Indian scripts and their material representation[3] (Kesavan 1997; Naik 1971; Southall 2005). Persisting with the common but reductive explanation that all typographic limitations have been those of technology, however, sidesteps a significant range of questions—not only those about the place and role of typographic networks within larger social and political realms, but also of power relations within the processes of design and technology involved in enabling text-based communication. Unsurprisingly, histories recounted from the point of view of the makers and manufacturers often revolve around origin and dissemination: narratives of invention and innovation in a specific time and place and their subsequent transmission elsewhere, positing the latter process and geographies as largely inconsequential (see, for instance, Boag and Burke 2014; Romano 2014)

Technology and its manifestations—the most famous of which is perhaps the printing press—have been cast as the agents, or the historical actors, in the process of change (Eisenstein 1979). But it is useful to acknowledge that technology also comes within the purview of other forms of agency, particularly that of its adopters and eventual users in a given social context. It is in turn 'acted upon' by forces and entities that have usually not been accorded significant positions in narratives that insist on portraying technological progress as the most significant force, or as an autonomous phenomenon existing outside of social, cultural, and political settings. A machine could indeed be the agent of change, but time and location matter beyond its point of origin, and, as this chapter will argue, beyond the notions of departure and arrival that are lodged firmly in expressions like 'the coming of print' and 'technology transfer'. In the case of Linotype in India, the argument can be extended precisely by subverting the longstanding association of the machine with movement and examining the machine at rest: not only grounded in specific cultural circumstances but also *sans* the universality of its assumed function. The same machine that represented an innovation in twentieth-century New York, an object of interest, and an exhibit in imperial London, could serve as an instrument of power, or a site for social struggle, in colonial Bombay and Calcutta. This chapter will concern itself with some of the less examined aspects of the acculturation of the Linotype in the context of its adaptation to compose Devanagari.

THE MACHINE IN THE MAKING: CONFLICT, COLLUSION, AND THE MECHANICS OF EMPIRE

The Indian subcontinent is home to a rich diversity of languages and scripts: well over 1,500 languages are spoken within its wide expanse, with more than twenty of these possessing upwards of a million speakers each. There have been twenty-two officially recognised languages in the country, written mainly in ten scripts (that is, many languages share the same script)[4] (Census of India 2001). These scripts can be broadly divided into two geographical groups: northern and southern. The northern Indian scripts are Devanagari, Gurmukhi, Gujarati, Bengali/Assamese, and Oriya. Southern Indian scripts comprise Tamil, Telugu, Kannada, and Malayalam. Perso-Arabic has been used extensively in many parts in India, and across the subcontinent in Pakistan and Bangladesh. What is of greater significance in this context, however, is that regions are not exclusive in their use of language and script—it is certainly not unusual to find more than two in use at the same time.

This diversity has had a long and varied history—on some occasions being celebrated as a desirable and enviable quality, and on others, disapproved of as a source of confusion and unnecessary complication, especially in the context of having to print in more than one language and script within a 'national' or 'regional' framework. The relationship of language and script with printing in the subcontinent constitutes a complex history, having been driven by the interests and involvement of diverse bodies: missionaries, merchants, colonisers, local elites, administrators, and colonial subjects. Their respective, often intertwining, approaches to textual traditions, scholarship, access to information, and its circulation have historically prompted a variety of responses and transformations. Various languages like Tamil, Bengali, Persian, and Urdu/Hindi gained prominence in print in different regions, at different junctures, alongside projects of codification and formalisation that extended debates over language and script, particularly in relation to the definition of culture, tradition, and identity.[5] The most interesting manifestations of this phenomenon are to be found in eighteenth and nineteenth-century printing in Indian scripts, especially as a British enterprise.[6]

The debate over language and script has been a long and continuing one, leading Orientalist and linguistic scholars in the nineteenth century to ponder not only a hierarchy of the most prominent or 'appropriate' scripts for a language and a region, but also to make a case for the substitution of one script with another—or, at times, simply to abolish the use of the numerous scripts of India and replace them with the Latin alphabet (see, for instance, Trevelyan 1834; Monier Williams 1859). Sporadic instances of this debate continued to appear throughout the colonial period, and with the gradual strengthening of nationalist sensibilities from the latter half of the nineteenth century, the issue regained prominence by transforming the hierarchical colonial frameworks into an indigenised quest for a 'national' language and script (Dalmia 1997, 146–180). The nature of this debate tended to remain limited to political assertions or nationalistic arguments, without necessarily leading to a greater interest in the scholarly and practical aspects of the scripts and their historical development. Unsurprisingly, across this period the most prominent typographic developments in the subcontinent were initiated and carried out by missionaries of various denominations, or colonial administrators and institutions, using Indian labour and a local workforce that they subsequently trained.[7]

However, for the project of mechanical typesetting in colonial India, there are strong reasons for a reversal of the customary formulation of technological enterprise—the idea that initiative from the metropoles drove improvements in an otherwise stagnant or retrogressive colony. It is known that in the early decades of the twentieth century, mechanical composition for Indian scripts was under consideration by manufacturers of typesetting machinery—invariably situated outside India, but with representatives in the country (Ross 1999; Shaw 1980). What has not been examined, however, is the motivation behind these considerations, and the ample evidence showing that such developments had long been in demand by Indian printers and publishers by the time it was finally acknowledged by manufacturing companies in the 1920s and 1930s.[8] Social and economic imperatives encouraging faster composition and larger circulation of printed matter across the region had come to the fore with the rise of nationalism, the independence movement, and the politics of language and script that emerged alongside. With limited recourse to technical know-how, particularly in an age of proprietary technologies, colonial printing establishments had responded with various schemes to make hand composition in Indian scripts faster and easier to the extent that it was possible, and by approaching manufacturers who could undertake the requisite technical experimentation for mechanical composition.[9]

It was hardly incidental that in the multilingual landscape of the subcontinent, the mechanisation of Indian scripts began with a distinct focus on one script: Devanagari. In a linguistically diverse region, the rise of Hindi as the putative 'national' language, and Devanagari as the related script, was a phenomenon deeply entrenched in political and communal battles that had been waged since the mid-nineteenth century. A manifest outcome of this ongoing strife was the establishment in 1893 of the 'Nagari Pracharini Sabha', one of several partisan bodies emanating from the religious centre of Banaras (Varanasi), promoting and advocating the use of Hindi and Devanagari. Intensifying the linguistic and communal divisions already present, in 1900 the status of both language and script had been ensconced in the 'MacDonnell moment' when, under the colonial regime, Hindi, written in Devanagari characters, was recognised as an official language distinct from Urdu, written in Perso-Arabic characters (Mukul 2015, 4–8; Rai 2001, 17–49).

It was also no coincidence that projects at the two major companies in the field of mechanical typesetting, Linotype and Monotype, were in fact initiated by colonial subjects—individuals, supported by local funds as well as local agendas, who made their way to London and New York to represent and pursue the demand in the colony. Debates on language and script, often along divisive lines, had been instigated by prominent figures of the period in the spheres of literature, publishing, politics, and religion in India. However, in the earliest stages of what became the Devanagari Linotype project, leading to the development of a machine for mechanically typesetting the script, four very different personalities were involved—Hari G. Govil, the 'inventor' of Devanagari Linotype;[10] Chauncey H. Griffith, assistant to the President, and later Vice-President, with the responsibility for typographic development at Mergenthaler; Harold H. Bender, Professor of Indo-Germanic Philology at Princeton University and chief consultant to Mergenthaler on foreign scripts; and William Norman Brown, the first Professor of Sanskrit at the University of Pennsylvania and consultant to Mergenthaler on its various Indian and South Asian projects from the 1930s to 1959.

Hari Govil, the flag-bearer for Devanagari in New York, had been educated at Banaras Hindu University, an institution then newly founded by the prominent political and Hindu nationalist figure Madan Mohan Malaviya, who was also the founder of the Hindu Mahasabha.[11] Govil himself founded the India Society of America and the India Center in New York in the 1920s, promoting 'a more accurate knowledge of the Hindu people, their life and ideals' (*The Brooklyn Daily Eagle* 1930).[12] He had made his way to New York, and Mergenthaler Linotype via London, where his proposal for a Devanagari machine appears not to have been entertained—a portent of the apathy from the London offices of Linotype that would persist even after the project's eventual completion in New York.

Mechanical composition had already made inroads in other regions of the world, and in other scripts besides the Latin alphabet, by the time serious consideration was given to the Indian market by the companies developing the machines. It was, again, not incidental that starting in the early decades of the twentieth century, across an extended period of proprietary technology and corporate hegemony in type-making, the companies involved in the mechanisation of Indian scripts functioned within the ideological framework of Empire—rarely accommodating colonial subjects as historical actors, but instead as temporarily useful informants, echoing the '*sahibs* and *munshis*' mode of engagement of a different era (Das 1978). To the extent that typographic projects for Indian scripts featured in their own accounts and publicity literature, official company narratives often co-opted the initiative for these developments—not unlike the *Herald Tribune* headline—presenting them as their own altruistic ventures for the benefit of the colony. In the development of a 'Devanagari machine', though, both nationalist and Orientalist points of view would appear to have found common cause.[13] The typographic network that enabled the mechanical typesetting of Devanagari contributed to the maintenance of established hierarchies—both within India along communal lines, and internationally in a colonial framework.

THE MACHINE IN TRANSIT: THE LAUNCH OF DEVANAGARI LINOTYPE IN INDIA

Little is known about Hari Govil's activities before the 1920s, the time of his arrival in America—only a biographical newspaper report from 1930 provides an embellished account of his life up to that point (*The Brooklyn Daily Eagle* 1930). On 5 April 1932, Govil was officially retained under contract from Mergenthaler to provide his services in adapting Devanagari to the Linotype according to his proposed scheme (Figure 11.1).[14] The necessary

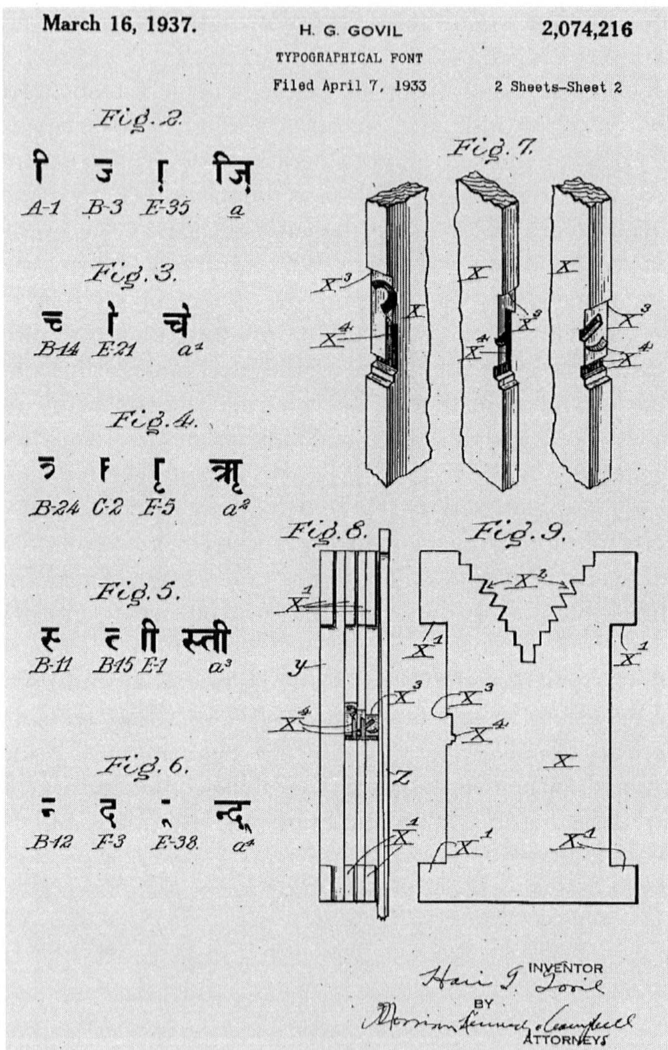

Figure 11.1: A page from the patent application showing Govil's scheme for the formation of Devanagari characters by the combination of separate components. The patent does not include the keyboard layout according to which this division was formulated.

Source: Hari G. Govil, US patent for 'typographical font' (filed 1933, granted 1937).

push and backing for this development may have been provided by the large-scale typesetting requirements of a project initiated at Princeton University. *The Princeton Alumni Weekly* of 5 April 1929 carried a report on a project to catalogue, edit, and publish the manuscripts in the Garrett Collection. The report went on to specify that the Princeton University Press, who were to handle the publishing, would employ the machines and typefaces produced by Mergenthaler, equipped with various scripts. The plausibility of this project serving as the additional impetus is strengthened by the fact that Harold Bender, the chief consultant to Mergenthaler on the Devanagari project, was himself part of the editorial committee for the publication of the Garrett manuscripts.[15] On the other hand, the Monotype Corporation in London had initiated its own Devanagari programme—as early as 1921, but not successfully implemented till 1930.[16] Linotype's interest may also have been occasioned as a competitive response to this development. It is also likely that in the general economic slump of the period, Mergenthaler saw investments in a new market less as a risky proposition and more as a diversification of its interests. Added to that was a certain assurance of academic utility for the machines—highlighted by the potentiality of a healthy clientele in the universities of America and abroad.[17]

The entire process of design and manufacture took place in New York. The process of development as planned and executed by Mergenthaler was remarkably smooth. Studies and reports had been made, drawings prepared by Mergenthaler's staff under Govil's supervision, proofs checked, and corrections incorporated to the extent of general approval from all involved. In addition, publicity matter had been given due consideration and the Devanagari Linotype machine was officially ready for launch in April 1933—almost exactly a year from Govil's official engagement in the project. It is from this point on that the process became more involved, encountering first the issues of positioning this development within the dynamics of international relations, and subsequently landing in the complications of reception and response that it had till then contrived to disregard.

Govil's contract with Mergenthaler required not only that he should demonstrate the machine as and when required, but also that he should sell two Linotype machines to customers in India, at prices and on terms acceptable to Mergenthaler.[18] Within this arrangement, Govil was to leave for Calcutta, where it was hoped the local offices of Linotype would provide him 'a native mechanic skilled in the care and operation of the machine'.[19] Mergenthaler also suggested that Govil should stop at London on his way to India, installing a machine at Linotype & Machinery (henceforth referred to as L&M), the London branch that managed the company's Indian operation, so that its workings could be demonstrated to possible Indian visitors. Remarkably, though, with regard to publicity for the new development, Govil was advised not to associate the machine with the British company directly. It is significant that the question of bilateral relations and contemporary political circumstances had been a secondary one throughout the period of the Devanagari development in America, and the question of acceptability revolved largely around technical and aesthetic dimensions.[20] Against the backdrop of the rising nationalist movement in India, it soon became clear that the British company was in no position to adopt more than a tentative approach to commercially pushing the new project, especially when faced with factors outside the province of technological innovation and practical utility. Professional relationships and work practices in this scenario were also serious obstacles, as early communication between London and Calcutta immediately revealed. A. J. May, the manager of Linotype's Calcutta office, on being informed that he would have to work with Govil, who had not yet sailed for India, wrote:

> It will be a rather difficult position, as I have had a little experience before of Indians who have a certain amount of foreign education grafted on. It will also be a difficult position for anyone of our staff if they have to go out and erect the machine [....] If I send our best Indian mechanic, I can visualise the time he will have, and if a European goes, he cannot be expected to work under instructions of an

> Indian in this country. Even our customers would consider this 'losing of face'.[21]

Govil reached Calcutta on 11 August, and the first Devanagari Linotype arrived there on 13 September and was erected on 15 September 1933, observing social protocol and acceptable arrangements. In the period before the arrival of the machine, Govil began training two operators with the aid of dummy keyboards. The machine was exhibited and a demonstration made to representatives from leading newspapers in Calcutta and a few others from the publishing industry. The second machine arrived in Bombay on 8 November 1933, and a demonstration was held at the showroom of L&M's Bombay office on 14 December. Govil travelled extensively in India—not necessarily in accordance with plans envisaged by Mergenthaler Linotype and L&M—ostensibly in connection with the publicity of the Devanagari machine, but also lecturing and addressing meetings on the adoption of Devanagari as 'an all-India script'.[22] This was a trajectory of Govil's own making and went against the general approach of Mergenthaler, who stood to gain nothing from offering partisan support to any one script over another. However, renewed negotiations over language and script priorities were instantly set in motion by the introduction of the Devanagari Linotype.

By February 1934, one Devanagari Linotype had been sold—to the Prabasi Press, Calcutta, run by Kedarnath Chatterjee, who, having acquired the machine, set about completely revising the keyboard layout, composition scheme, and the design of the typeface that it carried. This revision, which soon officially replaced Mergenthaler's original offering, achieved results that were not vastly different from the original, and were in many instances even inferior to it, but was found 'acceptable'.[23] Govil managed to secure the sale of the second machine, fulfilling his contractual obligation, to Krishna Prasad Dar of the Allahabad Law Journal Press before returning to America.[24] Once he had departed, it appears that the Calcutta office again found itself at the centre of criticism and activity that it was not equipped to handle, but was also not in a position to disregard. In his report submitted to Mergenthaler, Govil bemoaned the lack of trained operators for Linotype composition in Calcutta and reported that the Indian offices of L&M were reluctant to spend money to secure them. Additionally, he noted:

> I found that the present staff of the Linotype Company is in no position to help the sales of the Devanagari Linotype. There is no one on the staff who knows Devanagari or understands anything about it. I am uneasy as to the fate of future sales during my absence. There is nothing I know that is being done by the India office to promote or stimulate sales of Devanagari Linotype while I am away. I must however say that Mr May assisted me in every possible way.[25]

This seems to have compounded a series of conflicting impressions and predictions as to the immediate and future prospects of the development. From London, V. E. Walker, the deputy chairman and managing director of L&M, echoed A. J. May's assessment that 'it is generally thought that the prospect of the sale of a substantial number of machines is rather remote'.[26] Bender retaliated by pointing out Walker's continuing scepticism toward the project, and questioned Walker's understanding of the situation: 'After all, Mr Walker bases his comments on reports from Calcutta, a region where Devanagari is not prevalent. The Devanagari machine should be pushed in regions where Devanagari is used.'[27]

It is useful to reiterate here that Mergenthaler had developed the machine specifically for Devanagari with an understanding that it was the most widely used script in the country, and then despatched the machine to their Calcutta office which functioned as their centre of operations in India. However, given that the office was located squarely in a region where the predominant language and script were Bengali, the employees of the company as well as the prospective users of Mergenthaler's new offering could thus look askance at its immediate relevance and the apparent linguistic dissonance. The gradual shift in consideration, from the limitations of the machine to the geography and affiliation of its users, was only the beginning of a struggle that would soon turn into an elaborate project involving multiple individual and institutional actors—a project to sidestep questions of local technical capability and regain control of the script itself by 'reforming' it.

In the immediate aftermath of Govil's visit, as the Calcutta office went about seeking possibilities for the Devanagari machine's sale in India, it ended up relaying statements of opinion and opposition from its primary and potential client base: newspaper proprietors, textbook publishers, and various government printing offices.[28] These were unfavourable criticisms—in most cases justifiably so—of the peculiarities of the Linotype Devanagari design. Coming from local individuals, presses, and other printing establishments, these responses were generally without critical or constructive commentary. The Calcutta office, unable to address the concerns directly, awaited solutions from London, and London merely transmitted their reports verbatim to New York, which led Griffith to declaim:

> On the whole, the reports from Calcutta [...] clearly indicate complete lack of sympathy with or perhaps a complete misunderstanding of this entire development. I am inclined to feel that the latter is the case, and if we cannot obtain a closer and more sympathetic cooperation I do not think it would be good policy for us to carry on further.[29]

For Mergenthaler, the lack of constructive detail in the criticisms coming from India made it difficult to determine 'accurately what is required'—information was either withheld by parties bargaining in their own interests, or not forthcoming from establishments seeking a more prominent role in the process than Mergenthaler was willing to concede.[30] The determination of specific and usable information was also compounded by the political climate, where the likelihood of the machine's unacceptability due to it being a 'British product' featured prominently in the launch and throughout the publicity campaign. With national sentiment in India 'not very cordial to British business', Govil reported that he had made it a point to 'emphasize the fact that the Devanagari Linotype was an American product', and that he believed the reason why the Indian press welcomed the machine with any enthusiasm and gave it wide coverage was 'precisely because it was not British, but American' and developed in collaboration with one of their own countrymen.[31] In response to the criticisms and reports of diminishing sales possibilities, Harold Bender went so far as to suggest an outright two-pronged approach—he recommended reminding those customers who were part of the British administration, like the various offices and colonial institutions in India, that 'the company producing the machine is British'; and for those customers who were 'primarily Indian and anti-British', like various vernacular newspapers, the fact that the machine to be promoted had been invented and developed in America.[32] However, the bone of contention was not merely the political affiliations of the machine's development, but also the autonomous way in which it had been developed. In the wake of Govil's visit and publicising activities, some prominent newspaper publishers

> [...] thought that L&M Ltd [London] and not mlc [that is, Mergenthaler, New York], had been responsible for Mr Govil's visit and they could not understand [...] why such an experiment was made in this country without previously referring the all-important matter of the type face to printing experts in the territory into which it was proposed to introduce the machine.[33]

It is interesting to recall in this context Bender's rationale, outlined in his report, for going through with the development first and seeking approval from the machine's potential users at a later stage.[34] The primary concern had been to demonstrate the new system as a practicable alternative, offering ease and speed of composition that was, at least in theory, far greater than what could be achieved by hand-setting Devanagari type.[35] The development had been carried out in the belief that its 'obvious' advantages would incentivise progressive establishments to make the investment required. Contrary to these expectations, Mergenthaler would soon find out that printing establishments in India were more willing to accept a slower method or a limitation-ridden development that acknowledged local agency rather than one that appeared to have been transported and imposed.

THE MACHINE AT REST: DEVANAGARI LINOTYPE AND THE SCRIPT REFORM MOVEMENT

Towards the end of October 1934, the Indian National Congress—the largest and most influential political body in India's independence movement—was scheduled to hold a meeting in Bombay. Seeing in this an excellent opportunity for a trial run, the local offices of L&M sought permission from the meeting's arrangements committee to exhibit the Devanagari Linotype machine at the venue, and also probe the possibility of a book by Mahatma Gandhi to be composed mechanically.[36] Linotype's Calcutta office had been given to understand by the prospective publisher that Gandhi had 'specified that the book shall beset by linotype' [*sic*].[37] Even earlier, William Norman Brown—in his capacity as a 'disinterested scholar' and a consultant to Mergenthaler—had asked Richard Gregg, a close friend of Gandhi's, to broach the subject of Linotype's Devanagari development, with which Gregg himself had been much impressed.[38] Given the sceptical reception of the Devanagari Linotype over the first year of its existence, any favourable consideration by a national body held great significance for the machine's prospects in India.

As it turned out, the Indian National Congress committee refused permission for the exhibition of the Devanagari machine at its meeting in Bombay, on the grounds that the machine was a 'foreign invention'. However, as Brown put it, with 'an admirable carelessness for logic', the committee permitted its printing manager to have the machine installed otherwise for the printing of Congress material officially required for the meeting, in both English and Hindi.[39]

The text to be printed thus was the presidential address, bearing an imprint of Linotype—a veritable endorsement of the machine, underscoring the incongruities of policy and utility. Set to be printed and circulated on a large scale, it is difficult to underestimate the influence this opportunity may have wielded in the acceptance of Mergenthaler's Devanagari. In an anticlimactic turn of events, however, after all the arrangements had been made, the sole Devanagari keyboard operator in the employ of Linotype—sent from Calcutta to Bombay for this purpose—could not compose the text in time owing to his lack of experience and slow composing speed.[40] The work was eventually carried out at a local press by hand-setting, using 'about 50 compositors'.

This incident may only be a minor footnote in the early history of mechanical composition in Devanagari, but it points to some of the most remarkable issues in the social and political contexts within which this history must necessarily be viewed. As the aspirations of a progressive modern nationhood gathered force, the dilemmas of cultural identity, and questions about the place of modern technology in it, located themselves at the centre of the debate throughout India's pre- and post-independence period (Fraser 2008; Israel 1994; Jeffrey 2000; Orsini 2002). Early in the first half of the century, the association of technology and modern machinery with oppression and State power was widely translated into a nationalistic anti-technology stance, especially against the 'foreign'. But within this broad ideological position, there was ample room to accommodate the utilitarian benefits of—and an active engagement with—technology on a day-to-day basis.[41] As exemplified in the Congress committee's ambivalent attitude towards Devanagari Linotype, the question of technology—even when 'foreign'—was an open-ended, negotiable concern within the rhetoric of nationalism.

In developing the Devanagari machine and the accompanying typeface independently, regardless of whether Mergenthaler expected to demonstrate its supremacy in the market, or to limit intervention from the colony, local printing and publishing establishments, followed by a segment of the literate elite, responded largely by challenging its authority, and by asserting their own agendas in the socio-political context of language and script. Mergenthaler's enterprise enunciated power through technological exclusivity and large-scale production capability—areas that colonial subjects and local institutions were neither equipped to contest nor willing to sanction outright. However, the counter-bid for control could, and would, be made through a discourse of affiliation and ownership: of language, of script, of culture—assets that could be translated into knowledge unavailable to Mergenthaler, especially not in the form of 'usable information'.

The contradictions and dilemmas relating to matters of policy and the extent of political involvement existed on both sides of the development of the Linotype—in India as well as in America. Govil, with whom Mergenthaler started developing the machine towards the end of 1931, had first approached the company in 1924 for the same purpose. C. H. Griffith recalled in an official memorandum:

> At that time [that is, 1924] the printing and publishing industry in India was not in a prosperous condition, and there was little or no incentive for us to go ahead with this proposition. With the advent of the National movement in India during the latter part of 1930, [*sic*] and a series of Round Table Conferences between the British Government and Indian Nationals, held in London and elsewhere, interest in the native vernaculars, and particularly Hindi, was stimulated to a very great extent, and resulted in a widespread movement to improve and extend Indian national journalism.[42]

It is important to note the connection of the nationalist movement with the development of printing in vernacular languages, and its consequent influence on Mergenthaler's decision to undertake the Devanagari development in the 1930s, and not in 1924. Although the Devanagari Linotype came about in part as an acknowledgement of India's political awakening and as a response to its burgeoning propaganda apparatus, Mergenthaler made it a point to guard its commercial interests by adopting a non-partisan approach, ideologically steering clear of the forces behind the local demand in India. However, once the machine was put on the market, it was apparent that, in the prevailing political climate, arguments for speed and utility alone were not sufficient to sell it. The contradictions in Mergenthaler's non-partisan approach were amplified when, operating between ideologically opposite camps, the company resorted to obfuscating the machine's British and American connections.

The 'wide-spread movement' in the 1930s that Griffith had observed in his memorandum was another programme that accommodated contradictions—it not only sought to widen the reach of print communication with improvement in the printing and publishing of the regional vernaculars, but also envisioned countrywide political unification through an evolving consensus on a national language and a common script for India. Devanagari was largely promoted as the 'all-India' script, although not without the necessary modifications required to represent the non-Hindi sounds of the various languages of the country. In this scenario, the phenomenon of Devanagari 'script reform' found a fertile public arena for the playing out of political, technological, and typographic aspirations.

Whether set by hand or mechanically composed, metal type had obvious physical restrictions in representing syllabic scripts like Devanagari, which require a great degree of overlap and overhangs in their formation (see Figure 11.2)—a characteristic not conducive to the linear setup deriving from an alphabetic script system. For the most part, hand-set Devanagari type did not offer the advantages of speed, efficiency, or quality in the script's representation, prompting efforts to 'modernise' the script itself—which generally meant adopting the characteristics of a linear alphabet. However, the introduction of mechanical typesetting for Devanagari in the 1920s and 1930s—precisely with its promise of speed and efficiency—introduced further problems and restrictions in the representation of the script. The large number of characters required for text composition in Devanagari could not be accommodated on standard keyboards, and technological adaptations tended towards a 'simplification' of the script by reducing the number of characters to a bare minimum and approximating the principles of syllabic composition. Starting in the last quarter of the nineteenth century, the interplay of nationalist sentiment and notions of technological progress and modernity, along with longstanding problems of efficiency in typesetting had thus initiated a period of intense 'script reform' activity in India, where several proposals were made by politically and culturally engaged individuals, as well as institutions, to simplify or modify Devanagari characters. No consensus could be achieved on these proposals, which varied from slight modifications of the script to total graphic and systemic overhauls. The 'reform' of Devanagari eventually managed to attain a very small measure of departure from the script's original form and structure, although it did pave the way for a serious appraisal of issues related to its formal aspects and its standardisation.

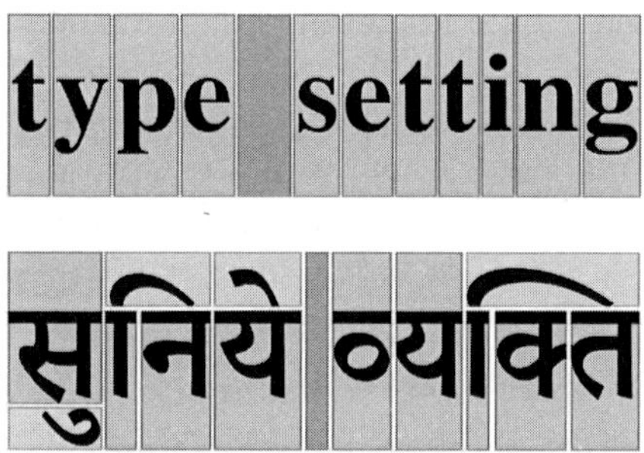

Figure 11.2: A schematic comparison of alphabetic and syllabic script composition in type sorts.

Source: Author.

Note: As the above illustration demonstrates, the construction of alphabetic scripts in hand-set type is comparatively simpler as it required a predominantly linear arrangement of sorts. The syllabic construction in Devanagari, on the other hand, necessitates a number of 'tiers', or divisions above and below the base characters where vowel signs of variable length need to be accommodated (and thus 'overhang').

A number of script reform schemes for Devanagari had indeed been proposed and put to the test prior to the introduction of mechanical typesetting in the early 1930s (Naik 1971, Vol. 2, 471).[43] Among other issues, these had addressed ways to make text-setting faster and easier, but with assurances for the same offered by mechanical composition, a general shift in focus towards a more adaptive approach could be discerned across the schemes in the wake of Devanagari Linotype. On the one hand, this resulted in numerous reform schemes finding their primary function in furthering the agenda of national integration, usually by advocating a new common system of notation. But progressively, it also meant that the reform proposals could be more and more radical, concerned largely with the abstract expression of tradition, modernity, or 'scientific' re-organisation through the modified script, rather than with the devising of practical solutions.

Mergenthaler's Devanagari had met with opposition immediately following the launch of the machine in 1933. Objections had focussed partly on the design of the typeface, which was found to be too light and cramped, and partly on the manner of composition, which gave the text a distinctly unconventional appearance. To accommodate the large number of Devanagari characters (600–800 in foundry type) on a standard Linotype keyboard (with ninety keys), Govil's system of composition employed components of letters, divided vertically, which could then be combined to form complete individual letters. This would have been workable and unremarkable were it not for the Linotype machine's inability to accommodate overhangs in composition—a key requirement for Devanagari. Effectively, Linotype composition, much like some other reform proposals, presented a reduced modification of the script. In this context of the machine's reception, Mergenthaler could not afford to ignore the reform initiatives and activities around the standardisation of Devanagari. Although financial commitment had already been made to develop the machine according to Govil's system, the Company had to acknowledge the evident risks that lay in pursuing its own line of argument too strongly. New developments in the political arena and the vagaries of national opinion in a crucial period of transition could veritably result in the whole development being scrapped.[44] In addition, the authorisation of the reform movement by the appointment of committees at the national level, with numerous conferences across the country, lent the entire enterprise of script reform a sense of urgency and importance—and not the least, transformative power that could dictate what Mergenthaler's 'vernacular' machines were expected to produce.

Mergenthaler found itself in a decidedly precarious position in this milieu—being an interested commercial body, the Company could have no valid say in the matter of script reform. Nor did it want to get involved in the political fray on the grounds that the authority for modification and standardisation lay with the appropriate national committees. However, by the very existence and influence of the system that the Devanagari Linotype machine provided, it was often assumed that Mergenthaler would act as both adjudicator and facilitator of new schemes. The authors of many reform proposals also assumed that the company would oblige and produce test versions of their suggested modifications. Linotype's India offices, managed by British staff not conversant in local languages or scripts, could not provide much help besides forwarding the many proposals and reform schemes they received, from the 1930s well into the 1960s.[45] Remarkably, after Indian independence, the 'script reform' activity of the earlier decades gradually turned into a 'script standardisation' project. This change in rhetoric signalled the consolidation of the numerous disconnected and independent initiatives of the previous era under newly appointed governmental bodies that held a different kind of authority in independent India, compared to what the traditional, reformist, or nationalist arguments for script change had possessed under the colonial administration. For Mergenthaler, this was the beginning of a long engagement with Devanagari and other Indian scripts. The users of the machine, on the other hand, found themselves in a position of active participation, in what was to become a revision continuum. Lasting as long as Linotypes were employed for Devanagari typesetting, this was to be a process fraught with dissatisfaction and incessant modification—and in the technological deadlock of hot-metal, a process driven largely by the constancy of contradictory preferences (see Figure 11.3).

CONCLUSION

The network of individuals and institutions involved in typographic design in India had a crucial role in shaping, and prioritising, the possibilities of printing in the country's many languages. A combination of local and international actors,

देश की आबादी लाखकी वृद्धि

नई दिल्ली, २० अप्रैल। बर्तमा न भारत की जनसंख्या १९४१की ३१करोड़ ९०लाख से गत दस सालोंमें प्रथम मार्च १९५०तक ३४ करोड़ ९० लाख हो गई हैं। इस प्रकार इसमें ३ करोड़ ८० लाखकी बृद्धि हुई हैं। यह तथ्य आगामी आम चुनावोंके लिये जनगणना कमिश्नर द्वारा किये गये हिसाब से ज्ञात हुआ है। हिसाब तरीकोंसे लगाया गया हैं। प्रथम ,१९४१की जनसंख्यामें जन्म मृत्यु ओरभारत बिभाजन से बिस्थापितोंके प्रवाहके आधारपर परिवर्तन । द्वितीय गत पांच दशाब्दियोंकी जनसंख्या रेखाके उतार चढ़ाव के अनुसार जनसंख्याका निर्धारण जनगणना कमिश्नर के अनुसार जनसंख्याके बर्तमान निर्धारित आंकड़े ९५प्रतिशत ठीक हैं। आसाम इसका अपवाद हैं क्योंकि वहां से प्राप्त आंकड़े बहुत निर्भर योग्य नहींहैं। जनसंख्या में सबसे अधिक बृद्धि जो ५ प्रति शत हैं पश्चिमी बंगाल,बिहार राजस्थान, उड़ीसा और पंजाब में हुई हैं और सबसे कम जो कि एक प्रतिशत हैं मद्रास ट्रावनकोर कोचीनमें हुई ।

(हमारे स्टाफ रिपोर्टर द्वारा)

कलकत्ता २० अप्रैल। उपप्रधान मंत्री सरदार पटेल आज नगर में निवास के पांचवें दिन भी अत्यन्त कार्य ब्यस्त रहे। आज सुबह पश्चिमी बंगालके राष्ट्रीय मुसलमान डा० आर० अहमद जनाब जहांगीर कबीरने आप से मुलाकात की ।

उनलोगोंने करीब आध घंटे तक भारत पाकिस्तान समझौते से अल्पसंख्यकोंके ऊपर पड़नेवाले प्रभावके संबंधमें बादबिबाद किया। मालूम हुआ है कि राष्ट्रीय मुसलमानों ने इस बातपरबहुत जोर दिया कि पाकिस्तान को धर्म निरपेक्ष राज्यकी घोषणा शीघ्रकर देनी चाहिये। उनलोगोंने राज्यके मंत्रिमंडल तथा शासनमें राष्ट्रीय मुसलमानोंके प्रतिनिधित्व की जोरदार मांग की। राष्ट्रीय मुसलमानोंकी तरफसे एक लिखित स्मारक पत्र उपप्रधान मंत्री के समक्ष पेश किया गया

आनन्द बाजार पत्रिका तथा युगान्तर के सम्पादकोंने भी सरदार पटेलसे आज प्रातःकाल भेंट की। छात्र संगठनोंके प्रतिनिधियोंने भी उनसे सहायता कार्यके संबंधमें बिचार बिमर्श किया।

स्वल्पाहारके पश्चात सरदार पटेलने आसामके गवर्नर श्री श्री प्रकाश, प्रधान मंत्री गोपीनाथ बारदोलाई तथा आसामके चीफ सेक्रेटरी श्री एस०पी०देशाई से भेंट की। आपलोग आज डेढ़ बजे आसाम से मुलाकात करनेके लिये आये थे।

चुनाव २४ अप्रैल को होगा ।

हिन्दी लाइनोटाइप

(ले॰ श्री कृष्णचन्द्र अगरवाल)

किसी भी भाषा के दैनिकपत्र का उन्नति के लिये यह परमावश्यक है कि उसमें प्रकाशित होनेवाली सामग्री शीघ्रतापूर्वक मुद्रित हो सके। मुद्रण के लिये जहां छपाई के यंत्र में सुधार की आवश्यकता है, उससे अधिक पत्र में दी गयी पाठ्य सामग्री के संयोजन विधि (कम्पोज) में शीघ्रता की ।

हिंदी में दो सौ वर्षों से संयोजन कार्य कारीगरों द्वारा हाथ से किया जाता रहा है। इसविधिमें जहां कार्य में विलम्ब होता है, उत्पादन भी अत्यन्त न्यून ।

अंग्रेजी में पहले मोनोटाइप और इसके बाद लाइनोटाइप का आविष्कार हुआ । हिंदी का कारीगर जहां साधारण रूप से एक दिन में अधिक से अधिक तीन कालम कर पाता है, अंग्रेजी का कारीगर मशीन की सहायता से घंटे में डेढ़ कालम करता है। लाइनोटाइप में अंतर यह है कि जहां मोनोटाइप में एक कारीगर टाइप राइटर सी एक मशीन पर कम्पोज करता है उसके द्वारा प्रस्तुत पाठ्य सामग्री दूसरी मशीन पर शीशे में ढल कर निकलती है एवं तीसरा व्यक्ति उसमें भूल सुधार करता है। लाइनोटाइप में यह तीनों क्रियाएँ एक ही व्यक्ति द्वारा एक ही मशीन पर होती हैं जिसमें कमसे कम पौन घंटा प्रति कालम के समय की बचत होती है ·

हिंदी में मोनोटाइप तो काफी प्रचलित हो गया है किन्तु लाइनोटाइप का प्रयोग हिन्दी वर्णमाला में अधिक संख्याहोने के कारण संभव नहीं हुआ ।

लाइनोटाइप एण्ड मशीनरी कं. के कलकत्ता व्यवस्थापक मि० किंग के अनुरोध पर श्री मूलचन्द्र जी अग्रवाल (विश्वमित्र) श्री बल्देवदास जी अग्रवाल (संसार) श्री मुकुटबिहारी वर्मा (हिन्दुस्तान) और श्री कृष्णचन्द्र अगरवाल ने कई दिनों तक एकसाथ बैठकर आवश्यकीय अक्षरों का एक मानचित्र बनाया जिसके द्वारा लाइनोटाइप मशीन पर हिन्दी संयोजन का पुनः प्रयोग हो रहा है अगर यह पाठकों को पसन्द आया और उत्पादन की दृष्टि से सफल रहा तो हिंदी पत्रकार कला का महान उपकार होगा ।

विश्व शान्ति का प्रयत्न
रूसी प्रचार का सामूहिक विरोध
ट्रूमैनकापत्रोंएवंजनतासेआह्वान

वाशिंगटन, २० अप्रैल। आज राष्ट्रपति ट्रूमैनने अमेरिकन न्यूज प्रेस एडीटर्स सोसाइटीके सम्मेलनमें भाषण देते हुए विश्वके समस्त स्वतंत्र राष्ट्रोंसे रूसी प्रचारके प्रतिवाद और बिरोध स्वरूप सचाई के प्रचार तथा तत्संबंधी आंदोलनमें पूर्ण सहयोगकी जोरदार अपील की। राष्ट्रपति ट्रूमैन ने आगे पत्रोंसे विश्वमें स्वतंत्र पत्र व्यवहारमें रुकावटें दूर करने अथवा कठिनाइयां मिटानेमें सहयोगकी अपील की। क्योंकि जबतक हम दूसरे देशों की जनता तक सच्ची घटनाओं की रिपोर्टें भेजनेमें समर्थ नहीं होंगे,तबतक हम जनताका मस्तिष्क परिवर्तन करने संबंधी संग्राममें विफल होंगे।

मि० ट्रूमैनने एलान किया कि मैंने स्टेट सेक्रेटरी डीन एचसनको शांति के लिये कार्यवाही की दिशामें सचाई के अधिकाधिक प्रयोग और प्रचारके उद्देश्यसे सुसंगठित एवं अधिक प्रभावोत्पादक योजनायें कार्यान्वित करनेका आदेश दिया है। इस कार्यक्रम और उद्देश्यकी पूर्तिमें समस्त व्यक्तिगत एवं सरकारी साधनोंको नियोजित करने संबंधी निर्णय की घोषणा करते हुए प्रस्ताव किया कि मजदूर यूनियनों किसानों तथा व्यापारियोंको अमेरिकाके उद्देश्यकी कहानीकेप्रचारमें सहायक बनना चाहिये ।

11.3: Front page of Hindi newspaper *Vishwamitra*, 21 April 1950.

Note: The image shows three different technologies of production used side by side on the same page. The headlines are in hand-set metal type, the text below it shows Monotype Devanagari, and the extreme right column within borders shows Devanagari text set on the Linotype machine.

Source: Author.

this network enabled not only the realisation of print through technical expertise, but also cultural validation and the pursuit of political aspirations through language and script. The production of printed matter could not be achieved without the mediation of a range of interested bodies that exercised their own rationale and agency in determining what was thus enabled. In pre-independence India, given the nuances of the power struggles inherent in decisions related to language and script, the process of typographical change also afforded a space where colonial ideology could be 'both transmitted and queried, produced and challenged'.[46]

Mergenthaler's Devanagari project had taken place within a framework that had prioritised completing the development first and seeking approval from its potential users as a subsequent step. The reception of the project and the gradual build-up of the 'script reform' movement, on the other hand, had embraced an egalitarian process that called for active mass involvement in the written and printed manifestations of the script to shift the power balance. Whereas Mergenthaler pioneered technical innovation and commercial entrepreneurship, the script reform movement generated a public platform for cultural aspirations, typographic and otherwise, in a politically charged environment. The improvements and changes proposed by various actors in this process were open-ended and incremental in most cases, and often with relatively little material investment in the particulars of the modification itself. Mergenthaler had, conversely, invested a substantial amount of time and money in its Devanagari development, with a view to its commercial feasibility in a potentially profitable market. The processes of script reform in India and Mergenthaler's project had so little in common that their eventual—and prolonged—encounter could not be expected to lead to definite resolutions. It did, however, contribute immensely to a brief florescence of typographic engagement across the country.

ACKNOWLEDGEMENTS

The author would like to acknowledge the following individuals and associated institutions for their help in accessing archives:

Cathy Keen, Joe Hursey, Alison Oswald, Craig Orr, Kay Peterson, and Wendy Shay at the Archives Centre, National Museum of American History, Smithsonian Institution, Washington, D.C. (Mergenthaler Company Records).

Frank Romano at the Museum of Printing, North Andover, MA (Mergenthaler Font Library).

Joseph-James Ahern and Nancy R. Miller at the University of Pennsylvania Archives, Philadelphia, PA (W. Norman Brown Papers).

Rossy Mendez at the Seeley G. Mudd Manuscript Library, Princeton University Archives, Princeton, NJ (Office of Communications Records).

Jan Shearsmith at the Museum of Science and Industry, Manchester (Linotype & Machinery Co. Ltd. Collection).

Fiona Ross at the Department of Typography & Graphic Communication, University of Reading (Non-Latin Type Collection).

NOTES

1. Written by Gove Hambidge, a feature writer at the *Herald Tribune*, and illustrated with photographs from William Norman Brown. 'How Devanagari looks in machine-set characters': a sample of Linotype Devanagari, making its first public appearance anywhere in print, was reproduced on page 21.

2. Line-casting refers to mechanical composition systems (such as Linotype and Intertype) where a line of matrices is assembled to cast a full line, as opposed to individual pieces of type. A few earlier instances of Devanagari mechanical composition did exist prior to the 1930s, in the form of smaller-scale machines like typewriters as well as the Monotype Corporation's hot-metal Devanagari project initiated in 1921. The Mergenthaler Linotype Company followed its Devanagari machine of 1933 with a Gujarati adaptation in 1935 and Bengali in 1936.

3. This is predominantly the case where type and typography are in focus; see, for instance, Kesavan (1997) and Naik (1971). See also Southall (2005). On the other hand, in enquiries related to book history, technology often features as an incidental or unproblematic detail, or as a parallel and autonomous historical strand. See Orsini (2013).

4. Based on the Census of India (2001), which lists twenty-two scheduled languages and 100 non-scheduled languages: a 'scheduled' language refers to the Eighth Schedule of the Indian Constitution, which lists officially recognised languages in the country.

5. For a detailed overview, see Dalmia (1997) and King (1994). For the early history of printing in various Indian languages, see Priolkar (1958).

6. For instance, the projects of linguistic discrimination initiated in the works of British scholars at the College of Fort William in Calcutta at the turn of the nineteenth century (Das 1978, 36–59).

7. For example, the Serampore Mission Press cut and cast the first types for several scripts in the country, or the American Mission Press in Bombay, where new systems of Devanagari type composition were introduced. Individuals in the service of the East India Company, like N. B. Halhed and Charles Wilkins, introduced types for Bengali and Nastaliq (Naik 1971, 268–300); see also Ross (1999).

8. Modern machines had entered the South Asian market in the early 1900s and by 1914, products derived not only from European technical expertise, but also from American enterprise (Arnold 2013, 40–42). Besides inquiries from Indian printing establishments to prominent manufacturers like Linotype and Monotype, and the demand for mechanical typesetting also fuelled experiments like the Bhisotype, and adaptations of the typewriter and the Varityper to compose various Indian scripts.

9. The Kirloskar Press in Pune, for instance, introduced a simplified system of typesetting Devanagari for its eponymous magazine in the 1920s. See Naik (1971, 329–333).

10. Hari G. Govil, US Patent for 'Typographical Font' (filed 1933, granted 1937). As a matter of fact, what Govil patented was not the machine but the 'scheme' for the adaptation of Devanagari by the method of splitting and combining characters.

11. Several Hindu nationalist institutions were indeed founded in the 1920s, including the Rashtriya Swayamsevak Sangh (RSS). See also Freitag (1990).

12. Govil's background and activities in New York are described briefly in Fedirka (2008, 185).

13. A schismatic definition of a pure and original 'Hindu culture', with Sanskrit as the language of its classical antiquity, had been propounded by British and European scholars and Indologists and taken up enthusiastically by the nationalists. See, for instance, King (1994, 23–33). Both Harold Bender and Norman Brown were classical scholars for whom the predominance of Sanskrit, and by implication Devanagari, was not a questionable concern. The emphasis on defining the project as that for a 'Devanagari machine' came from Bender.

14. Personal letter from C. H. Griffith to T. J. Mercer, Vice-President in charge of audits (5 April 1932). Box P3627, File 919-1, NMAH.

15. The Garrett Collection mainly comprised of Arabic, Persian, Ottoman Turkish, and other Islamic manuscripts, and also included Egyptian papyri and Meso-American material. The collection, formally donated only in 1942, derived from Princeton alumnus (and Olympic champion) Robert Garrett, an eminent collector of medieval manuscripts who also underwrote the University's purchases in the 1920s towards enlarging its collections.

16. Monotype Archives, Salfords. 'Index card for Series 155 Devanagari', 31 December 1921. The origins and details of Monotype's Devanagari development are not within the scope of this chapter, and have been covered in Singh (2017).

17. Personal letter from C. H. Griffith to H. H. Bender (14 March 1933). Box P3627, File 919-1, NMAH. Bender had indicated that the Harvard University Press would be a potential purchaser: it had 'published a large number of Sanskrit texts in Devanagari' under the Harvard Oriental Series.

18. Personal letter from C. H. Griffith to Norman Dodge, President, 10 May 1933. Box P3627, File 919-1, NMAH.

19. Ibid. It is not clear why the Company made this assumption, but it is likely that it overestimated labour availability for a new machine. The situation was compounded by the fact that Linotype's Calcutta office was to make the necessary arrangements through instructions from the British company.

20. This does not imply that international politics was completely disregarded in the development. Bender's inquiry into Govil's qualifications had cleared him as not being from the group of 'men of the publicity, and especially propaganda types, representing some particular phases of Indian political or religious sectarian opinion'. H. H. Bender,

'Devanagari on the Linotype', 20–21, 25 January 1932. Box P3627, File 919-1, NMAH.

21. Personal letter from A. J. May to V. E. Walker, 24 May 1933. Box P3627, File 919-1, NMAH.

22. Hari Govil, 'Report on Govil's visit to India for introducing the Devanagari Linotype', 3 April 1934. Govil gave talks at the All India Hindu Conference and Industrial Exhibition, Ajmer; Society for the promotion of Hindi Literature, Indore; and the Indian Oriental Conference, Baroda.

23. This acceptability meant rather less than what Mergenthaler would have wished for. Purchasing the machine gave Chatterjee a licence in matters relating to its improvement, and since his Press was the machine's main user at this stage, he had a greater say in determining acceptability—particularly for his own use—than others who provided criticisms or suggested revisions.

24. Both machines were sold at a substantially discounted price and on a hire purchase contract, spread over three years for one, and fifty-seven months for the other. Letter from V. E. Walker to C. H. Griffith, 14 March 1934, Box P3627, File 919-1, NMAH.

25. 'Report on Govil's visit to India for introducing the Devanagari Linotype', 3 April 1934, 10–11.

26. Personal letter from V. E. Walker to C. H. Griffith, 14 March 1934, Box P3627, File 919-1, NMAH.

27. Personal letter from H. H. Bender to C. H. Griffith, 19 May 1934, 2, Box P3627, File 919-1, NMAH. Bender wrote: 'I have the impression that Mr Walker cherishes a certain prejudice against the Govil scheme; that he really doesn't believe in it; but that he will, of course, do all that your Company desires him to do in furthering it in India.'

28. Among those who were consulted and offered criticisms were proprietors of leading newspapers like *Hindustan Times*, *National Call*, and *The Leader*, and printing establishments like The Job Press, Cawnpore; Radhey Shyam Press, Bareilly; The Indian Press, Allahabad; The Law Journal Press, Allahabad; and the Kadga Vilas Press, Patna.

29. Personal letter from C. H. Griffith to Norman Dodge, 11 June 1934, Box P3627, File 919-1, NMAH.

30. Report by Tom King, 20 April 1934: '[Mr Ghosh of the Indian Press] does not like our face, which he considers much too light.' Report by Tom King, 11 May 1934: 'Our face is not acceptable and must be re-cut to resemble the types of the Gujerati Type Foundry, Bombay, if it is to become popular.'

31. Personal letter from H. G. Govil to C. H. Griffith, 18 June 1934, Box P3627, File 919-1, NMAH.

32. Personal letter from H. H. Bender to C. H. Griffith, 19 May 1934, 9, Box P3627, File 919-1, NMAH.

33. Report by Tom King, 11 May 1934, Box P3627, File 919-1, NMAH.

34. H. H. Bender, 'Devanagari on the Linotype', 25 January 1932, Box P3627, File 919-1, NMAH.

35. This assumption did not take into account other factors involved in text composition besides technology, such as labour. The following section provides a relevant example.

36. W. N. Brown, Report no. 1, September 1934, Box P3627, File 919-2, NMAH. Letter from V. E. Walker to Norman Dodge, 11 September 1934, Box P3627, File 919-2, NMAH.

37. As it turned out, it had been a 'complete misunderstanding', but irrespective of the veracity of the statement, the prospect was too important for Mergenthaler to ignore in view of Gandhi's national standing and potential influence in getting the machine accepted nationwide. This misunderstanding also lent urgency to the development of Mergenthaler's revised Devanagari typeface which, within a year, replaced the original.

38. Brown did not think it wise to go and see Gandhi himself, as he considered there was 'too much danger it would react unfavorably upon the Sch. of Ind. and Iran. Stud. [*sic*]'. Letter from W. N. Brown to H. H. Bender, 8 October 1934, Box P3627, File 919-2, NMAH.

39. W. N. Brown, 'Report no.1', September 1934.

40. W. N. Brown, 'Report no. 5', 3 November 1934, Box P3627, File 919-2, NMAH. The Devanagari operator, identified only as Iqbal, very likely a Bengali speaker not fully conversant with Devanagari, had about two days for the work and managed half of it before the 'Congress authorities' realised that it would not be finished in time.

41. See for instance Arnold (2013, 10):

> By the 1930s political activists, policemen, school teachers, and health workers arrived in villages on bicycles and used magic-lantern slides or cinema shows to entertain, educate, or cajole their audiences. They typed reports on their visits or phoned their superiors. When Gandhi arrived to speak against modern machines he frequently did so by motorcar, his thin voice amplified by the microphone and loud-speakers.

42. C. H. Griffith, 'Memorandum for A. P. Paine', 10 February 1936, Box P3627, File 919-3, NMAH.

43. Naik lists more than fifteen reform schemes and proposals in the period leading up to mechanical composition in the 1930s.

44. The example of the Turkish adoption of the Latin alphabet was evoked frequently in the exchange between people involved in Mergenthaler's Devanagari project, and the possibility of a radical change in policies could not be overruled in the contemporary political climate.

45. See, for instance, proposals by Y. M. Nanal, H. H. Bender to C. H. Griffith, 21 November 1934, Box P3627, File 919-2; proposal by K. N. Misra (Misra scheme), W. N. Brown to C. H. Griffith, 2 December 1945, Box P3618, File 919-A; proposal by Shrinivas of Benaras, W. N. Brown Report, 29 March 1947; proposal by Motilal Gurtu, W. N. Brown to C. H. Griffith, 24 December 1948; and proposal by Satyendra Kumar Gupta, W. N. Brown to C. H. Griffith, 1 January 1949. Also see Letter from Balchandra Shankar Sathe, 19 March 1950, Box P3627, File 919-3, NMAH.

46. As noted in a different context by O'Gormon (1994, 308).

References

Arnold, D. 2013. *Everyday Technology: Machines and the Making of India's Modernity*. Chicago and London: University of Chicago Press.

Boag, A., and C. Burke (eds). 2014. *History of the Monotype Corporation*. London: Printing Historical Society, Woodstock, Vanbrugh Press.

The Brooklyn Daily Eagle. 1930. 'India's Culture', 13 April.

Dalmia, V. 1997. *The Nationalization of Hindu Traditions: Bharatendu Harischandra and Nineteenth-Century Banaras*. New Delhi: Oxford University Press.

Das, S. K. 1978. *Sahibs and Munshis: An Account of the College of Fort William*. New Delhi: Orion Publications.

Edgerton, D. 2006. *The Shock of the Old: Technology and Global History since 1900*. London: Profile Books.

Eisenstein, E. L. 1979. *The Printing Press as an Agent of Change: Communications and Cultural Transformations in Early-Modern Europe*. Cambridge: Cambridge University Press.

Fedirka, S. A. 2008. 'Towards a Locational Modernism: Little Magazines and the Modernist Geographical Imagination'. Ph.D. dissertation, Arizona State University.

Fraser, R. 2008. *Book History through Postcolonial Eyes: Rewriting the Script*. New York: Routledge.

Freitag, S. B. 1990. *Collective Action and Community: Public Arenas and the Emergence of Communalism in North India*. New Delhi: Oxford University Press.

Govil, Hari G. 'Typographical Font', US Patent (filed 1933, granted 1937).

Hambdige, Gove. 1933. 'Teaching a Sixth of the World to Read: Now a Machine is to Carry Literacy to India'. *New York Herald Tribune*, 18 June.

Hobsbawm, E. 1994. *Age of Extremes: The Short Twentieth Century 1914–1991*. London: Michael Joseph.

Israel, M. 1994. *Communication and Power: Propaganda and the Press in the Indian National Struggle, 1920–1947*. Cambridge: Cambridge University Press.

Jeffrey, R. 2000. *India's Newspaper Revolution: Capitalism, Politics and the Indian Language Press 1977–1999*. London: Hurst & Company.

Kesavan, B. S. 1997. *History of Printing and Publishing in India: A Story of Cultural Reawakening*, 3 vols. New Delhi: National Book Trust.

King, C. R. 1994. *One Language, Two Scripts: The Hindi Movement in Nineteenth Century North India*. Bombay: Oxford University Press.

Masten, J., P. Stallybrass, and N. Vickers (eds). 1997. *Language Machines: Technologies of Literary and Cultural Production*. New York: Routledge.

Monier Williams, M. 1859. *Original Papers Illustrating the History of the Application of the Roman Alphabet to the Languages of India*. London: Longmans, Brown, Green, Longmans, and Roberts.

Mukul, A. 2015. *Gita Press and the Making of Hindu India*. Noida: HarperCollins.

Naik, B. S. 1971. *Typography of Devanagari*, 3 vols. Bombay: Directorate of Languages.

O'Gormon, F. 1994. *The Victorian Novel*. London: Michael Joseph.

Orsini, F. 2002. *The Hindi Public Sphere 1920–1940: Language and literature in the Age of Nationalism*. New Delhi: Oxford University Press.

____ (ed.). 2013. *The History of the Book in South Asia*. Surrey: Ashgate.

The Princeton Alumni Weekly. 1929. 'Project to Further Human Knowledge: Garrett Collection of Manuscripts to be Edited—University Press to Publish Results with New Equipment', 5 April.

Priolkar, A. K. 1958. *The Printing Press in India: Its Beginnings and Early Development*. Bombay: Marathi Samshodhana Mandala.

Rai, A. 2001. *Hindi Nationalism*. New Delhi: Orient Longman.

Romano, F. 2014. *History of the Linotype Company*. Rochester: RIT Press.

Ross, F. G. E. 1999. *The Printed Bengali Character and its Evolution*. Surrey: Curzon Press.

Shaw, G. 1980. 'Printing in Devanagari: The Evolution of Types in Devanagari Script'. *Monotype Recorder*, new series 2, 28–32.

Singh, V. 2017. 'Devanagari Type in the Twentieth Century: Motivations, Imperatives, Technology, and the Design Process'. Ph.D. dissertation, University of Reading.

Southall, R. 2005. *Printer's Type in the Twentieth Century: Manufacturing and Design Methods*. New Castle and London: The British Library and Oak Knoll Press.

Stark, U. 2007. *An Empire of Books: The Naval Kishore Press and the Diffusion of the Printed Word in Colonial India*. New Delhi: Permanent Black.

Trevelyan, C. 1834. *The Application of the Roman Alphabet to All the Oriental Languages*. Serampore: Serampore Press.

12

Politics of Script Selection and Meetei Identity, 1978–1979

Thongam Bipin

Introduction

Bangla script was used for more than a century to write Meeteilon[1] (also officially known as Manipuri), the language spoken by the Meetei community of Manipur. A link and an official language of the state, Meeteilon is spoken in the Imphal valley with certain variations in some pockets. Over the centuries, the language has undergone significant changes, particularly due to the influence exerted by Hinduism and its literatures. In the second half of the twentieth century, concerted efforts were made to revive the 'original' Meetei *Mayek*[2] (script), which had become obsolete under the effects of both colonial education policies and Hinduism. John Parrat (2005, 26) observes that the colonial recruitment policy, which favoured the Bengalis and Bangla-speaking Meeteis from Assam, brought the Meetei script to an end. Chongamtham Manihar Singh (1996) underscores the Meetei resistance to the imposition of the Bangla script, stating that the people of Thoubal village, as a form of rebellion, refused to learn the new Bangla language and script in the late nineteenth century.

Nineteenth-century north India experienced a deliberate attempt to bifurcate a spoken language into two on the basis of the script used to write it: Urdu and Hindi (King 1994). This can be seen as a plot to bring about a divide between the Muslim and the Hindu. However, the case of the Meetei, with their two scripts, is different. It does divide Meetei into camps, but not along communal lines like in nineteenth-century north India. There is a visible movement away in the Meetei language and script, from a Hindu/India to a de-Hinduisation by reclaiming an indigenous past. In the southern states of India, particularly in Tamilnadu and then Andhra Pradesh, language became a violent source of contention between these states and New Delhi (Mitchell 2009; Ramaswamy 1997). We witnessed a contradictory political performance in the northern states, which Jha (2017) termed the 'Hindi belt'. His study on Maithili presents a different approach to language, given Maithili's ambiguous relationship with the 'national language', Hindi. It did not exhibit a complete opposition to Hindi's appropriation, but was accommodative of Hindi's status as a 'national' language. While it did not break away from Hindi, there was a co-existence of both languages. However, the Maithili language movement resisted attempts to describe it as a dialect of Hindi. Hindi thwarted all attempts on the part of linguistic communities to demand their specific identities, viewing such demands as parochial, and hence as a challenge to itself. Jha argues that such discourses were the reason why the Maithili movement offered a milder resistance than that presented by the southern states.

The Meetei language and script movement was violent in its history. Although Manipur is a small state, this ability to be violent, unlike in the case of Maithili, can be attributed to its strong anti-Hindi/Hindu past (especially in the last century). The presence of an armed resistance movement can also be a useful point of reference in understanding this phenomenon. The arrival of an 'original' Meetei script can be read as an assertion of Meetei identity and nationhood against the dominant presence of Hinduism. The Meetei movement[3] (Nilbir 1991; Singh 2016; Singh 2012) embraces the pre-Hindu Meetei religion, *Sanamahi laining*, bringing it into public spaces where it exhibits a potential to unsettle the sacred Hindu public sphere.

This chapter will attempt to understand the nature of identity formation and claim for nationhood put forward by various groups. It sets out to make sense of Meetei claims to identity and nation in the twentieth century. The first section provides a brief account of Meetei history and revivalism. The second section offers a detailed study of the minutes of the expert committee meeting, its varied and contradictory positions, along with an explanation of the debates. In the third section, I attempt to extend revivalist ideals into everyday practices, and study their confrontation with the 'real'. A pursuance of these ideals can sometimes take violent forms, and at other times, lead to negotiation. The claim and assertion of Meetei revivalists for an 'authentic' Meetei nation forms an ongoing struggle against the real, dominant Hindu mind of the Meetei public.

MEETEI REVIVALISM AND THE RESURGENCE OF MEETEI TRADITIONS

Hinduism was made the state religion of Manipur under the Meetei king Pamheiba (1709–1748) in the early eighteenth century. In this encounter between the new religion of Hindusim and Meetei belief, Hinduism, with the support of the king, was able to tame and subdue Meetei to a considerable degree. Apart from religious conversions, the state apparatus unleashed violent practices such as the renaming of places, deities, and personal names, the destruction of religious structures, cremation of buried Meetei bodies, and a Hinduised rewriting/retelling of the history of Manipur and Meetei (Kabui 1991). The translation of Hindu texts[4] and burning of Meetei manuscripts were direct and coordinated acts, intended to replace the Meetei faith with Hinduism.

The revival of a pre-Hindu Meetei social and political world began in the first half of the twentieth century. The formation of independent religious groups, such as Apokpa Marup in Cachar (present-day Silchar district of Assam), begun by Naoria Phulo (1888–1941), and Meetei Marup in Manipur in 1945, transformed the revival into a movement. It was meant as a deliberate socio-political engineering of the Meetei community. Naoria Phulo played a crucial role in reviving Meetei consciousness with the formation of Apokpa Marup. Frustrated with the Meetei of his time for their imitation of *mayang*[5] ways of life (which they saw as a mark of modernity), he believed that the Meetei laboured under self-hate, which led to their disowning their own religion, history, language, and god, accepting the *mayang* religion and language in their place. When Phulo and his followers were ostracised in 1931 for working against the interests of Hinduism, he seized that moment, subverted its meaning, and turned it into an advantage. Viewing that moment as emancipatory, he proclaimed that the Meetei no longer had to hide their real identity (Phulo 2010). In Phulo's eyes, they would cease to be the slaves of Hinduism. His activities and major writings emphasised the need to embrace Meetei history, language, religion, and, importantly, modern science, to emancipate Meeteis from the hold of Hinduism. Crucial to Meetei revivalism in general and Phulo in particular was an acceptance of the 'poor' Meetei religion and language as their own in order to revive the pre-Hindu Meetei past. In the second half of the twentieth century, Meetei revivalism inspired the armed struggle and confronted a new challenge—the struggle to turn its ideals into everyday practice/performance.

As a term, 'revivalism' needs to be located within politics, as it is often entangled with the nation. It demands and reconstitutes a new form of the nation where the original native elements seek to replace the present form. The nature of the nation form/ation in South Asia and in most non-Western countries is deeply intermeshed with aspirations and issues around nation/alism. In most non-Western postcolonial countries, revivalism as a socio-political movement aims to realise an authentic nationhood, a move that reveals a desire to replace the 'present' with what is dubbed an 'authentic' tradition. Such a desire is often animated by 'our attachment to the past', and a 'feeling that the present needs to be changed, that it is our task to change it' (Chatterjee 2012, 151). Phulo asserted that they were simply *lambi amanba samba* (amending old roads), and that if there was something missing in his community, it 'should be invented'. For Phulo and other revivalists, the resurgence of culture was their primary goal. The normative presupposition in the East thus seems to be based on a modern political imagination that presumes the nation form to have been secured and accomplished in the past, giving rise to the prevalent belief that the past should legitimately guide our present politics.

The invention of tradition (Hobsbawm and Ranger 1983) becomes a political exigency and a means through which a community maintains continuity with its 'historic past'. They illustrate how the invention of tradition (revivalism) in the present becomes unfeasible because society and community have undergone change which are often unrecognisable when compared with the past. According to them, revivalism is the '... contrast between the constant change and innovation of the modern world and the attempt to structure at least some part of social life within it as unchanging and invariant...' (ibid., 2). Revivalism as a political movement in Manipur reflects such a continuity with a historic Meetei past, and attempts to realign the present with the nation that past had secured. This realignment became a necessary political task as a result of the discontinuity or incoherence that Hinduism had brought about in Meetei history. The revivalists see a crisis in the present, established in relation to the past; here, the present is viewed as an unrecognisable version of an 'authentic' historic past. The fall from a glorious and authentic past tradition to this unrecognisable present produces a sense of discontinuity. It instils a sense of incompleteness[6] and fear of a loss of history and identity. And this fear and loss become the political reason for the revival of a specific cultural past.

THE SCRIPT DEBATE

The question of script is an important element of revivalism that haunted the Meetei revivalists, beginning with Naoria Phulo. In 1978, the Yangmasho Seiza-led Manipur government issued an extraordinary notice in the *Manipur Gazette*: they intended to constitute an expert committee that would select a 'correct' and 'accepted' Meetei *Mayek*.[7] This expert committee held twenty-four meetings from 1 December 1978 to 31 July 1979.[8]

They recommended the Meetei script, which was accepted by the Government of Manipur in April 1980 (Ningthouja 2011). However, it took more than three decades and violent movements before this could be officially reintroduced in schools in Imphal valley in 2006. In the hill districts of Manipur where the tribal populations reside, the language is written in Roman script, after an agreement was reached with the Government of Manipur and the script revivalists. This arrangement was made so as to not antagonise the tribal population, and signifies the longstanding conflict between the valley Meetei and the hill tribes.[9]

The script is not a mere visual representation of sounds and language[10] for Meetei revivalists. Of the government-approved twenty-seven letter Meetei script, the first eighteen are considered foundational/original Mayek, also known as *eepi Mayek*. The remaining nine are referred to as *lom* or additional letters. The *eepi Mayek* have been created from the image of different body parts, and are pronounced after the name of each body part in Meeteilon (Meetei 2016; Ray 2009; Tamphajao 1992). Meetei numerals are also claimed to be based on the image of a foetus, with each numeral representing the nine-month journey of the foetus inside a mother's womb. This is an attempt to re-establish an ontological and epistemological connection between Meetei *Mayek* and the Meetei community. The proponents of the movement considered Bangla an imposition, as foreign, and as meddling with the 'authentic' Manipuri (read Meetei) identity. The assertion for a distinct representation and revival of their script represents a resistance to homogenisation and assimilation under a Hindu tradition. However, there was an equally strong attempt to freeze Meeteilon within the folds of an Indo-Aryan tradition (Singh 1975).

In the minutes of the meeting of the script expert committee, members are seen to be divided along varied ideological lines. Their ideologies are informed by their attachment to a particular past and present, and these are in turn informed by what Partha Chatterjee (2015, Introduction) understands as an allegiance and desire to be part of specific histories and ideologies. The 1978–1979 meeting was preceded by several script conferences held at the *leipakki* (land) level to decide on the correct script (Meetei 2016). According to Mangangcha Ibomcha (2002), as many as four *leipakki* conferences were held from 1958 to 1972. An emphasis on *leipak* helps to reclaims the authenticity and legitimacy of the Meetei community and nation. These conferences were held for the land, a land linked to the idea of a nation located in the past. It invokes an ownership of and loyalty to a certain Meetei past, thereby challenging the meaning attributed to the same land in the present.

Several expert committee members submitted various *Mayek* to the committee. The report states that Kangjia Gopal and Yumnam Tamphajao proposed the eighteen letters that Meetei *Mayek* derived from *Wakoklol Thilel Salai Amailol Pukok* and *Wakoklon Hilel Thilel Salai Amailol Pukok puyas*,[11] respectively. Both Gopal and Tamphajao spoke of the centrality of the eighteen letters in the Meetei community, barring the difference in the representation of *lom* (the additional nine letters). Laishram Kulachandra supported these eighteen letters with the *lom*. L. Mohendra spoke in support of *Yelhou Mayek* of Naoria Phulo, while Professor W. Tomchou supported the twenty-seven letters proposed by Kulachandra, with the omission of two vowel sounds: *ee* and *oo*. After deliberating on the submitted scripts, at the eleventh meeting on 9 February 1979, the committee concluded that there were two schools of Meetei script: *Yelhou Mayek* and the alphabet of twenty-seven letters (Report 6). Discussion on *Yelhou Mayek* was minimal, as the general consensus of the committee was that the proposed script should have a source *puya*. The Yelhou script could not produce a source *puya*, which went against the grain of revivalism. Revivalism in general, and script revivalism in particular, rest on the notion that the past should act as the source for the present. Since *Yelhou Mayek* could not place its source *puya*, it was deemed an invented script. The major discussion took place in the second school of script, often with fierce disagreements.

Although it was generally agreed that every script should have a source *puya*, the question of what could be considered 'authentic' *puya* further complicated and delayed the script debate. In his book published just a few days before the committee meeting, N. G. Kangjia argued that *Yumsalon*, a *puya*, could not be considered authentic as it contains 305 Bangla letters, and the numerals, too, are written in Bangla. The *puya* also contains Hindu mythological characters like Sita and Hanuman (Kangjia 1978, 31-32). He believed the *puya* was probably written after the arrival of Hinduism in Manipur, and could only be reinstated as an authentic *puya* after being purged of all foreign characters: 'If the *puya* is not rewritten in the eighteen letters; if the *puya* does not remove all the foreign letters and elements for the satisfaction of the people [of Manipur], no one will accept it as *puya* of Kangleipak [Manipur]' (ibid., 32; insertions and translation mine). His idea of an authentic *puya* was declared once again in the meeting, and would go on to play a critical role. His definition of *puya* was challenged by other members, indicating the untranslatability of an authentic past into a very changed present. For example, in the meeting, Tomchou advocated that the selection of Meetei *Mayek* should base its resources on different *puyas*, and not just a single *puya*. His emphasis on multiple *puyas* was significant, considering his disagreement with the eighteen-letter *Mayek* proposed by Kangjia and Iboyaima, which claims a single *puya* as a source.

After a long discussion, the expert committee members came to the agreement that *eepi Mayek*, the first eighteen letters, form the core letters of the Mayek. Although there was no contention vis-à-vis the *eepi* letters, the *lom* generated arguments, which informed the varied, often incompatible, strands of Meetei nationalism. Kangjia and Tamphajao insisted that the eighteen letters were sufficient for writing the Meetei script, submitting that the *lom* represent sounds that had become part of the Meetei language after the arrival of Hinduism. They argued that *lom* simply replaced the *eepi* sounds; for example, the /p/ sounds were replaced by the aspirated /b/ due to the Indo-Aryan influence (or Hinduism). In Meetei language, *leipak* and *leibak* are equivalent words for the English land/country/nation. According to Kangjia and Tamphajao, *leipak* is the original Meetei word, and *leibak* is a post-Hindu contamination. A majority of members, however, demanded that the *lom* be included in the new Meetei script.

After acceding to the demand of the other members, Kangjia and Tamphajao suggested that if these sounds were to be included, they could be represented by either placing a dot or underlining the *eepi* letters from which the *loms* have been derived. However, once again most members preferred distinct symbols for each *lom*.

The idea that *puya* should function as the only legitimate source for script revival appeared once again in the argument of Tomchou, who seemed to be pushing to 'contaminate' an authentic Meetei identity. Tomchou asserted that the *loms*, with their distinct letters, were not alien to the Meetei script, but were in vogue in some *puyas* such as *Nongshaba puya*, *Yumdaba puya*, and *Nongchup Haram puya*. He promised to submit the *puyas* in the next meeting of the committee, but failed to do so. Similarly, another member, Kulabidhu, could not submit his *puya* in support of his claim for distinct *lom* letters. However, both members submitted the *Laxmi Charit*, *Hakchangi Laifamne*, and *Hidak Lanthakki Maram* to prove that the *loms* endorsed by them were indeed in vogue (Report, 22). Predictably, Kangjia provided proof from various *puyas* showing that the original *eepi* letters had been used in place of *loms*. He submitted a Meetei script primer which he believed was used during the reign of King Bheigyachandra (1748–1799). In this primer, new letters were encircled to establish that they were new entries (ibid., 23). He arguesd that the *Wakoklon puya*, the source of his script, demonstrates the use of *loms*. Reiterating his notion of an authentic *puya* as a means to refute Tomchou's argument, Kangjia stated that *puyas* written after the arrival of Hinduism could not be termed as *puya* at all. In defence of the distinct letters of each *lom*, Tomchou argued that the *lom* was based on a scientific approach. Other members supported Tomchou, saying that it would be convenient for writing and was thus the correct representation.

For Kangjia and other revivalists, revivalism was a process of purification, of de-Hinduisation while reclaiming their Meetei identity. However, even in such a moment, they negotiated with other members. This negotiation signifies an agreement with the inevitability of contamination as a process of identity formation. A steadfast insistence on the authentic past of the script created a stalemate in the committee meeting, and served as a deterrent in the script being approved and used as a replacement for the Bangla script.

In the meeting held on 8 March 1979, the committee placed the following three points: (*i*) that before King Bheigyachandra, *loms* were not used in the books written in Meetei *Mayek*; (*ii*) that the eighteen letters are the original ones; and that (*iii*) nine additional letters were added to represent the new sounds (Report, 24). Kulachandra objected to these points, making a strong case for the distinct *loms* and alleging that Kangjia and Tamphajao had influenced the committee members. He said that just because some letters (read *loms*) used in the *puyas* (again, not all *puyas*, but those that Kangjia had in his possession) are similar to other letters (read Bengali), it cannot be logical for Kangjia to claim that the former were merely alterations of the latter. This became an interesting argument in the debate on the authentic *puya*, and its concomitant language, script, and identity.

It is imperative to see how these two groups within the same script use *puyas* from different periods. Kangjia and Tamphajao claimed to use *puyas* written before the arrival of Hinduism, while the others used *puyas* written after the entry of Hinduism. Such classifications, and the use of certain *puyas* from different time periods, revealed their ideological positions and affiliation with a specific nation-form. Kangjia and Tamphajao's idea of and criteria for reimagining a Meetei identity is an untainted version, fixed in the past. Their notion of community is animated by their sharp assertion that the 'present needs to be changed, that it is our task to change it' (Chatterjee 2012, 151). The second group also believed that the script should be derived from *puyas* and that Meetei identity needs to be revived, but, as stated earlier, the source *puyas* they used were written/rewritten after the arrival of Hinduism. Interestingly, neither group refutes the charges levelled by Kangjia and Tamphajao regarding the authenticity of *puyas*. Once the familial relation between *puya* and *Mayek* had been established, they merely attempted to broaden the definition of *puya* instead of seeking a single authentic and antique *puya*. In fact, Tomchou alleged in his turn that *Wakoklon* was not an authentic *puya*. This counter-allegation, and Kangjia's insistence on the same *puya*, are part of their larger claim to history and nationhood. Kangjia's historical claim was thwarted by Tomchou's insistence on a Hindu lineage, under the garb of a scientific approach to the *Mayek* debate. In the meeting, Tomchou and Kangjia represented two streams of Meetei consciousness: the normative Meetei and the *angaoba* (Meetei word for 'mad'). It is worth mentioning here that the revivalists are pejoratively called *angaoba* by dominant Meetei Hindus. The normative Meetei represented by Tomchou is open, inclusive, scientific, and not ranged against Hinduism. On the other hand, Kangjia is rigid, anti-Hindu, and 'non-scientific' in his approach to *Mayek* revivalism.

The 'scientific' reasoning offered by Tomchou and others in their defence of the distinct *lom* can be read as an attempt to hold on to the religion that the Meetei revivalists were seeking to annihilate. It is this politics that undergirds the debate on the Meetei *Mayek*, *lom*, and the Meetei numeral. The so-called 'scientific' approach to script selection forecloses the revivalist argument and its negotiation with modernity. Such a foreclosing is a discursive exercise derived from the modernity of current times (Chatterjee 2012, 2015), where ideas set against it are dubbed as 'pre-modern'. In the meeting, Tomchou's arguments fell within the grey area between science (rationality) and Hinduism. Kangjia's assertion that *loms* could be symbolically represented by their original *eepi* letters was contested, and he was accused of being orthodox and pre-modern. However, in Kangjia, one sees a refusal to participate in a debate where rationality served as the pre-condition for arguments. He was aware of the discursive production of the rational domain, where his assertion of a Meetei script would only be subsumed to Hinduism.[12] His consistent rejection of Tomchou's rational argument through the invocation of *puya* is an indication of the Meetei revivalists' attempt to free themselves from the hegemony of the Hindu mind and establish an independent Meetei. This refusal to participate in a reaffirmation of the Hindu mind and public was the reason behind their being termed *angaoba*. Such a discursive production of the category of *angaoba* Meetei has its roots in early twentieth-century literature.

Logic dictates that an *angaoba* cannot contribute to their society or community.

In a meeting held on 10 April 1979, the committee voted to include the nine additional *loms*. The report states, 'The committee has decided to include the nine letters [*loms* or additional] as the *majority* of the members have agreed to it' (Report, 29; translation and emphasis mine). After a brief deliberation, the committee further decided that the nine additional letters would be read after the original letters. Tomchou, however, preferred to read the *loms* according to their sounds in Devanagari. The meeting also discussed issues of punctuation and numerals. The last meeting of the committee was held on 31 July 1979, and the report was submitted to the chief minister on 6 August 1979.

CONCLUSION

More than four decades after its approval by the government and nearly two decades after it was officially introduced in schools in the Imphal valley, the Meetei script continues to struggle to occupy Meetei public spaces. The script was introduced in schools after the script revivalist groups set fire to the central library in 2005. MEELAL (Meetei Eyek Erol Loinasillon Apunba Lup), a group that led the later script revival movement, has often been violent in its approach. In its early years, MEELAL insisted that every billboard, signboard, vehicle number plate, etc., should compulsorily carry Meetei *Mayek* characters. There have been reports that certain books were banned because they contained foreign words. Even in Manipuri films in recent times, there is an undeclared agreement that foreign words should be avoided. Such words are bleeped out in films made before this consensus took place. More often than not, 'foreign' words are restricted to Hindi/Sanskrit/Bangla. However, English words are accepted. These movements have often been met with apprehension by the general public.

While the script has been (relatively) successfully used in school textbooks, it continues to find little or no space in Manipuri dailies. The transition to a Meetei script from Bangla is slow, and the reason is often attributed to the readership. The older generation of Meetei, who are literate in the Bangla script, shows little willingness to learn the Meetei script. This may result from a resistance to the growing realisation that Meetei revivalists, that is, the *angaoba* Meetei, have arrived in the Meetei public sphere, and can also be inferred as a resistance to a new imagination of the Meetei community/nation. There was a similar resistance to the demand for the reintroduction of the script in schools in Manipur. Script revivalists attribute the delay in introducing the script in schools to the Meetei mind, which remains rigidly 'Hindu'.

In a public meeting held on 27 January 2021, MEELAL took a decisive decision: that the transition of Manipuri dailies (of Imphal) to the Meetei script from Bangla should be completed by 5 February 2022[13] (the reason for this particular deadline, however, is not clear). In the meeting, it was lamented that even fifteen years after the script was introduced in schools, the general script literacy rate was unsatisfactory. Despite accepting that this would not be an easy transition, the script literacy rate was an indication of the general disinterest among the older generation in learning it (*Sangai Express*, 2021). For MEELAL, printing Manipuri dailies in the Meetei script was important not only as a matter of pride, but also because this would help to initiate the general population into learning the script. In a local cable TV discussion[14] on the issue of Manipuri dailies using the Meetei script, the MEELAL representative was repeatedly asked whether this transition could possibly be effected in a period of one year. The representative recalled the nearly fifty years of the script movement, reminding the others that the script had already been reintroduced in schools. If the general population showed a willingness to learn the script, it was indeed possible. He also mentioned that the group would provide all possible help to the dailies, and stated that while the deadline was tentative, they were pushing for it. The manner in which the questions were asked, often similar in both intent and content, made it seem as though the anchor wanted the representative to admit the infeasibility of the deadline, thus highlighting the irrational 'madness' of the revivalists. Senior journalist and author Pradip Phanjoubam, on the other hand, was asked to provide a rational critique of the matter.

Such a debate was not formed out of thin air. The script debate in schools, and now in the media, is part of a temporal transition of the Meetei community. The movement is open-ended, and continues without any sign of closure. It seems to move towards an unachievable destination, a final community which will never arrive.

Notes

1. Manipuri is also known as Meeteilon, meaning simply the language of the Meetei. Despite the change in script, Bangla script continues to hold an important place in literary and media spaces. All the major Manipuri dailies are printed in the script, with little to no space given to the old Meetei script.

2. The script is officially identified as Meetei Mayek, where 'mayek' is the English equivalent of the word 'script'. In this chapter, I use 'mayek' and 'script' to mean the same thing.

3. The movement is known by different names, such as Meetei revivalism, Sanamahi revivalism, etc. However, I use 'Meetei movement' to encapsulate other facets of the revival, and understand Meetei as a political category that can critique the dominant Hindu public.

4. See Naorem (2018) to understand the process and politics of translation of Hindu texts into Manipuri. These helped in myth-making to give Manipur and Meetei a Hindu lineage after the arrival of Hinduism in Manipur.

5. *Mayang* is a Meetei word, commonly used to identify people from other parts of India.

6. See Arjun Appadurai's exploration of the nation form and the sense of incompleteness in the making of the former in his *Fear of Small Numbers* (2006).

7. However, Professor Kangjia, one of the members of the Meetei Mayek Expert Comittee (1978), asserted that instead of calling the script Meetei *Mayek*, it should have been named Kanglei *eyek*. He believed that nomenclatures like Meetei *Mayek* are an injustice to the hill tribes, particularly those who participated in the script movement.

Kanglei *eyek*, on the other hand, is a generic term that does not privilege one community over another, and has the potential to unify the valley and the hill.

8. It is interesting to note that the Manipuri Language Act, 1979, recognised Manipuri as the official language of the state. It further adds that the official Manipuri is Meeteilon, written in the Bengali script and spoken by a majority of the Manipur population (Ningthouja 2011, 217). This is interesting because the same Government of Manipur that set up an expert committee to select an acceptable script went ahead to pass a language act that recognised the Bangla script.

9. See Shimray (2007) on the issue of Meetei Mayek in the hills district of Manipur.

10. See T. T. Haokip (2013) for an alternative perspective. He propagates that script and language have no relationship apart from a mere representation of acoustic by visual representation. Therefore, as a corrective measure for the present political stalemate in Manipur, he suggests that Meetei should use the Roman script instead of demanding a Meetei script at the moment. The tribals of the hills should also not oppose the Meetei language written in Roman script, as the language has assumed the role of *lingua franca* even amongst the tribals.

11. There are marginal differences in these two *puyas*, which can be ignored. The only difference in the title of the *puyas* is the inclusion of the word *Hilel* in the second.

Puya is a sacred text of the Meeteis. They are written in Meetei *Mayek* on Meetei religion, belief, customs, and law. After the arrival of Hinduism, they were rewritten in the Bangla script, and as many as 124 different *puyas* were burnt by the king under the instruction of his guru, Shanti Das, in the eighteenth century. Meetei *maichous* (scholars) kept several *puyas* in their personal possession, notwithstanding the king's order to submit them to the palace to be destroyed.

12. For more on this, see Bipin (2020).

13. The transition from Bangla to Meetei Mayek in Manipuri dailies is still incomplete, with the former continuing to occupy a bigger space.

14. ISTV, Discussion Hour, 27 January 2021.

REFERENCES

Appadurai, Arjun. 2006. *Fear of Small Numbers: An Essay on the Geography of Anger*. Durham and London: Duke University Press.

Bipin, T. 2020. 'Khwairakpam Chaoba's "Basanti Debating Club" and Birth of a Mid-20th Century Meetei Literary Renaissance Triggered by a Resistance to Identity Hegemony'. *Imphal Review of Arts and Politics*, 25 July. Available at https://imphalreviews.in/khwairakpam-chaobas-basanti-debating-club-and-birth-of-a-mid-20th-century-meetei-literally-renaissance-triggered-by-a-resistance-to-identity-hegemony/ (accessed January 2025).

Chatterjee, P. 2012. *Empire and Nation: Essentials Writings, 1985–2005*. Ranikhet: Permanent Black.

_____. 2015. 'Introduction'. In Raziuddin Aquil and Partha Chatterjee (eds), *History in the Vernacular*. Ranikhet: Permanent Black, 3rd edn.

Haokip, T. T. 2013. 'The Politcs of Meitei Mayek'. *NNEIS*, 22–32.

Hobsbawm, E., and T. Ranger (eds). 1983. *Invention of Tradition*. Cambridge: Cambridge University Press

Ibomcha, M. K. 2002. *Meetei Mayekki Waari Leekhun* (*The Origin of Meitei Mayek*). Imphal: Self-published.

Jha, M. K. 2017. *Language Politics and the Public Sphere in North India: Making of the Maithili Movement*. New Delhi: Oxford University Press.

Kabui, G. 1991. *History of Manipur: Pre-colonial Period*, Volume One. New Delhi: National Publishing House.

Kangjia, N. G. 1978. *Kanglei Eyekki Waari* (*History of Kanglei Eeyeks*). Imphal: Puyamcha Iboton, on Behalf of Protection of Kanglei Eyek.

King, C. R. 1994. *One Language, Two Scripts: The Hindi Movement in Nineteenth Century North India*. Bombay: Oxford University Press.

Manipur Gazette, Extraordinary, No. 387, Imphal, 18 November 1978.

Meetei, N. M. 2016. 'Centrality of Body Politics in Thokachanba's Script and Cultural Revivalism in Manipur'. In Arambam Noni, and Kangujam Sanatomba (eds), *Colonialism and Resistance: Society and State in Manipur*, 218–237. New York: Routledge (South Asia edition).

Mitchell, L. 2009. *Language, Emotion, and Politics in South India: The Making of a Mother Tongue*, Ranikhet: Permanent Black.

Naorem, D. 2018. 'Myth Making and Imagining a Brahmanical Manipur since 18th Century ce'. *RAIOT: Challenging the Consensus*, 2 April. Available at https://raiot.in/myth-making-and-imagining-a-brahmanical-manipur-since-18th-century-ce/ (accessed January 2025).

Nilbir, S. 1991. 'The Revivalist Movement of Sanamahi'. In Naorem Sanajaoba (ed.), *Manipur: Past and Present (The Heritage and Ordeals of a Civilisation)*, Vol. II, History, Polity, and Law. New Delhi: Mittal Publications.

Ningthouja, M. 2011. *Freedom from India: A History of Manipur Nationalism (1947–2000 A.D.)*. New Delhi: Spectrum Publications.

Parrat, J. 2005. *Wounded Land: Politics and Identity in Modern Manipur*. New Delhi: Mittal Publication.

Phulo, N. 2010. *Laininghan Naoria Phulogi Wareng Apunba* (*Complete Works of Laininghan Naoria Phulo*). Imphal: Ibungo Laishramcha Minabanta, M. S. Tampha Publications.

Ray, S. 2009. 'Writing the Body: Cosmology, and Fragments of Modernity in Northeastern India'. *Anthropological Quaterley* 82 (1), 129–154.

Ramaswamy, S. 1997. *Passions of the Tongue: Language Devotion in Tamil India, 1891–1970*. Berkeley: University of California Press.

Report, Meetei Mayek Expert Committee Meeting, 1978–1979.

Sangai Express. 2021. 'Change to Meetei Mayek by Feb 5: MEELAL to Manipuri Newspaper', 28 January. Available at https://e-pao.net/GP.asp?src=9..290121.jan21 (accessed January 2025).

Shimray, U. A. 2007. 'Meitei-Mayek: Uneasy Script'. *E-Pao*, 3 October. Available at http://e-pao.net/epSubPageExtractor.asp?src=news_section.opinions.Opinion_on_Manipur_Integrity_Issue.Meitei-Mayek_Uneasy_script (accessed January 2025).

Singh, K. B. 2016. 'Religious Revivalism and Colonial Rule: Origin of the Sanamahi Movement'. In Arambam Noni and Kangujam Sanatomba (eds), *Colonialism and Resistance: Society and State in Manipur*, 75–90. New York: Routledge (South Asia edition).

Singh, M. C. 1996. *A History of Manipuri Literature*. New Delhi: Sahitya Akademi.

Singh, N. J. 2002. *Colonialism to Democracy: A History of Manipur, 1819–1972*. Guwahati: Spectrum Publications.

_____. 2012. *Religious Revitalisation Movements in Manipur*. New Delhi: Akansha Publishing House.

Singh. N. K. 1975. *Manipuri Language: Status and Importance*. Imphal: N. Tombi Raj Singh, Uripok Ningthoujam Leikai.

Tamphajao, Y. 1992. *Meetei 18 gi Kanglon amasung Wang-oo-lon* (*Philosophy and Science of Meetei Alphabets*). Imphal: Mangangcha Keisham Ibomcha.

13

The Late Colonial Telugu Textbook
A Material Embodiment of Dissent, Debate, and Knowledge

Sasi Kiran R. Mallam

A book is a material embodiment of, if not a consensus, then at least a collective consent.
Johns (1998, 3)

The domination of a people's language by the languages of the colonizing nations was crucial to the domination of the mental universe of the colonized.
Ngũgĩ wa Thiong'o (1986, 16)

Introduction

The role of language in the colonial project can be aptly summarised in the lines quoted above from Kenyan academic and writer Ngũgĩ wa Thiong'o's work, *Decolonizing the Mind* (1986). In *Colonialism and Forms of Knowledge*, Bernard Cohn (1996, 4) observes that the British did not merely conquer a territory when they colonised India, but invaded an epistemological space. All that they encountered here was not comprehensible to them. The textbook was to become an instrument in the process of this invasion, enabling comprehension and bringing an order and fixity to what the colonisers perceived as a chaotic education and an absurd and incoherent language. At the same time, the vernacular textbook also became a space where debates occurred and dissent was expressed by an elite who was subject to the forces of colonial modernity and divided on the question of language.

The Telugu textbook had a turbulent history during the late colonial period, marked by caustic debates, faint hints of fanaticism, and expressions of dissent. This textbook was the mark of Ngũgĩ wa Thiong'o's 'mental universe' and Cohn's 'epistemological space'. From its conception, the textbook involved a range of diverse actors, but more importantly, it was a rare instrument that included both the colonial subject and the colonial State. The textbook, in the context of colonial rule, can be read as an embedded media object in an assemblage of overlapping networks of vernacular cultural production, public sphere, and educational bureaucracy of the State. Telugu textbooks had eventful journeys as they were caught between disparate worlds—the high literary verse and simple prose styles of Telugu, the colonial government, and the Telugu public sphere. For instance, textbooks were drawn from literary texts which were written in a highly codified style, and they had to be made simpler for students to understand. A frequent criticism[1] levelled was that often, even the teacher could not fathom the complex Telugu text.

The following scholarly works deal with various themes in the history of the book and print cultures of India: A. R. Venkatachalapathy (2015) on Tamil print cultures; Ulrike Stark (2009) on the Naval Kishore Press; Anindita Ghosh (2006) on popular Bengali print cultures;, and Rochelle Pinto (2007) on print in nineteenth-century Goa. T. V. Venkateswaran's (2007) work on science books documents some crucial moments in the history of Tamil textbooks. J. Mangamma's book (1975) on Telugu print cultures of the late eighteenth and early nineteenth century is one of the first in India to focus exclusively on colonial print history, and dealt also with vernacular textbooks. Lisa Mitchell's work (2009) focuses on how pundits were replaced by printed textbooks, which provided the foundation for curricular agendas. While textbooks feature sporadically in some of the works listed above, in the context of Telugu there has not been a lot of work, especially from the late colonial period. This chapter attempts to document and connect a few facets of the history of the Telugu textbook and studies Telugu textbooks of the early twentieth century, and their role in shaping the linguistic and epistemological discourse of the time. The chapter will not document a chronological history of textbooks, but will rather engage with the embeddedness of the textbook in the cultural milieu of the late colonial period. The few intricate processes that the chapter engages with are the authorship of the book itself, the selection process of textbook committees, the prejudices of influential members of these societies, and the back and forth between the government and the larger public sphere vis-à-vis the rolling back of certain decisions.

Hohne, as cited by Annekatrin Bock (2018, 60), refers to textbooks as 'informatorium', 'pedagogicum', 'politicum', and a 'constructorium'. Textbooks are sources of information, instruments of pedagogical instruction, objects of social and political debate, as well as constructed media. This constructed nature, according to Hohne, ties the ways in which knowledge is produced to the heterogenous actors or arenas functioning within their own milieus. The late-colonial Telugu textbook certainly fits the above definition, as the chapter will demonstrate in later sections. The 'constructorium' of the Telugu textbooks was a result of multiple negotiations by human and institutional actors, who were influenced by the larger socio-political-cultural climate of their time.

The first problem before the colonial educational machinery was the selection of texts from what they perceived as a vacuum. After the initial textbooks had been selected and necessary processes put in place, the second problem was deciding on the style of language which seems to come up organically. As these deliberations were going on, the question of knowledge in the vernacular was also being addressed through the textbook.

Vernacular Textbooks and Early Print Capitalism

Vernacular publishing efforts in the early twentieth century were not very lucrative, except in the genre of textbooks. Textbooks could arguably be called the first successful venture in the Telugu print space, as their print runs were significantly larger than other genres. Textbook print runs were in the range of 2,500 to 5,000 copies, while the average print run would be close to 1,000 copies.[2] A few textbooks[3] had print runs of even 50,000 copies.

> What book-reading enterprise there is, due entirely to the exertions of that venerable body, The Board of Studies and upon their command—'Thou Shalt Read!' and straight thousands of unfortunate young men read books that no mortal can read without profit or pleasure. (Gurajada 1909, iii)

In this quote from the Preface of the second edition of his path-breaking play, *Kanyāśulkam*, Gurajada reveals the nature of the Telugu publishing industry. As stated earlier, school textbooks in Telugu were a lucrative and influential publishing genre. Gurajada (2012, 827) notes that unlike in India, authorship is a paying profession in England; authors in India, however, cannot afford to just depend on literature, but instead must rely on a teacher's post in a school or some other appointment.[4]

Kandukuri Viresalingam ran the periodical *Vivekavardhini*. He notes in his autobiography (Kandukuri 1911, 83) that he never expected it to be a source of livelihood. But since his books were lauded in the press and several schools prescribed them as textbooks, he earned royalties from them. He mentions that the Rs 200 royalty that he earned in three months from his grammar book and the Rs 1,000 that he earned from *Nīti-candrika* gave him the confidence to pursue a career as an independent author.

Some of the questions that this chapter will address are: What were the processes through which texts were transformed into textbooks? What role did textbooks play in the standardisation of the vernacular in terms of form and content? How did the textbook become an epistemological instrument in disparate knowledge systems?

EDUCATION POLICY AND EARLY TELUGU TEXTBOOKS

J. Mangamma (1975, 199), while documenting the early books used in schools in the Madras Presidency, observes that since there was no official system of education in the first half of the nineteenth century, each school selected its own books, most of which were either reproduced from the teacher's memory or read out from manuscripts.

In the first half of the nineteenth century, many of these books were in manuscript form and only the efforts of Collectors from the Civil Service of the East India Company, like A. D. Campbell, ensured that they were printed. The most common books used in schools were the *Rāmāyaṇa*, *Mahābhārata*, and *Bhāgavatamu*, stories read for their morals like *Pañcatantra* and *Bethāla Pañca Vimsate*, and grammars and dictionaries like *Āndhra Dipica* and *Śabdamanjari*. Most books were written in verse, using a high literary dialect. Another important book was the *Pĕdda Bāla Śikṣa*, a compendium of lessons in literary composition, prosody, spelling, Sanskrit hymns, geography, history, stories of morals, and arithmetic, prepared by Puduri Sita Rama Sastri, which was used in many schools across the Telugu-speaking regions of the Madras Presidency. Colonial educators and missionaries like John Murdoch advocated vernacular education, and in a few instances even used the vernacular to teach English.[5]

Text to Textbook

In the nineteenth century, many existing texts from Telugu literature were prescribed as textbooks. For instance, excerpts from works like *Sumati Śatakamu* and *Nīti-candrika* were prescribed to teach morals. *Sumati Śatakamu* belonged to the *Śataka* genre of Telugu literature, which typically contains close to 100 verses. This work of literature found its way into a 1930 Telugu textbook, *Ānanda Vācakamu* (Velcheru 2016, 178). The process of transforming a book into a textbook involved textbook committees, which usually comprised of prominent members of the Telugu intelligentsia. The book in itself, however unorthodox, never seemed to cause any major trouble, although there was sporadic critique from a few quarters or an occasional ban from the colonial government. But when the same book transformed into a textbook, it triggered movements and angered the aristocratic and Brahmin elite, prompting them to mobilise support and start literary associations. What was it about the textbook that roused such extreme reactions? *First*, the textbook was not only a mass-produced commodity, it was also a potent ideological instrument that could shape an entire generation. *Second*, the textbook was perceived as a permanent entity that would eventually lead to the standardisation of its form and content. The processes involved in this transformation also reveal the limited agency that the colonial government allowed the local intelligentsia in these matters.

There was an indigenous system of education in place in pre-colonial times, where villages had teachers who would teach the children literature, epics, grammar, and basic arithmetic. For several decades during the East India Company rule, interference in education was not considered a priority. Before the formation of an educational department, there was no concerted effort from the government vis-à-vis school education. One of the first colonial officials to take a step in this direction was Sir Thomas Munro, who gathered information through the Collectors about indigenous schools and the education they imparted. The reports drawn indicated that indigenous schools imparted an education that was of little practical value, and involved memorising verses without understanding them, primarily because of the unintelligible literary style. They observed that the purpose of this education seemed to be the cultivation of memory, and the teachers were Brahmins who possessed no qualifications (Satthianadhan 1894). The early textbooks had the responsibility of structuring the teaching process and canonising knowledge. In the absence of a formal system of examinations and degrees, what counted as education in indigenous schools seemed absurd to colonial officials like Munro and Campbell.

The reason for this perception of difference could be further understood by looking at the way in which colonial officials dealt with vernacular grammar. Bernard Cohn's work (1996, 55) directs us towards a nuanced understanding of the epistemological differences between the British and the local intelligentsia when it came to making sense of Indian languages. While mentioning the colonial officials' indignation with the pedantry and the demands of memorisation, Cohn alludes to the differences in the way each party approached the language—the Western official's approach was practical, as he sought to codify and standardise, while the Indian approach was the opposite. For instance, Rama Sundari Mantena (2012, 169) notes that medieval Telugu grammars were never meant to initiate speakers into the language by simplifying it; rather, they were meant to sanctify the language.[6] The textbook was another vehicle to formalise what colonial officials perceived as an informal and unusual education. The Telugu textbook stands at loggerheads with the Western approach, and tries to preserve the vernacular past.

The Textbook Committee

One of the early textbook committees—before the colonial government formalised them—was the Madras School Book Society, established in 1820 with encouragement from Thomas Munro. It comprised a mix of locals and colonial officials. '… [T]he general diffusion of useful knowledge by the supply of approved schoolbooks at the cheapest possible rates and for furnishing other elementary works, both in English and the Vernacular language' (Venkateswaran 2007, 93).

While T. B. Macaulay's *Minute on Education* (1835) sealed the fate of vernacular languages, Wood's *Despatch of 1854* (sent by Sir Charles Wood to Lord Dalhousie, the Governor-General of India) reinvigorated vernacular languages by recommending their use in teaching at the school level. This led to a need for more textbooks and the incorporation of processes for their selection, which included a proposition for textbook committees comprising the local intelligentsia, who were suddenly given the authority to decide which books could be recommended as textbooks.

> That the Text-book Committees in the several Provinces include qualified persons of different sections of the community not connected with the Department, and that

> to these Committees should be submitted all textbooks, both English and vernacular, that it is proposed to introduce into schools, and all textbooks now in use that may seem to need revision. (Satthianadhan 1894, lxxix)

This clause made the inclusion of qualified persons from different sections of the community,[7] who were not connected with the educational department, mandatory. This paved the way for the local intelligentsia to take control of this crucial aspect of classroom education, and they eventually became the gatekeepers of language and knowledge. Although the final decisions were to be taken by the colonial officials, they largely agreed with the opinion of the more powerful group. Recommendations to textbook committees also included the suggestion that care be taken to avoid textbooks that are aggressive in tone, or known to give unnecessary offence to any community. This was the official policy even before the formation of formal committees. The textbook committee represented a consolation to the exploitative colonial rule, although it must be noted that the powers that the committee enjoyed were more of an exception than the rule.

RELIGIOUS MATTERS AND TEXTBOOKS

The nineteenth-century textbook witnessed several minor scuffles related to their religious content. Discussing the textbook discourse in the mid-nineteenth century, Gupta (2007, 1117) notes the influence of missionaries and Brahmins in shaping it. For instance, *Selections from Vemana* was used in the Madras Presidency as a Telugu poetical textbook for third-form students. Vemana's verses had reserved the staunchest of criticism for Brahmanical scriptures and beliefs, which aroused the disapproval of many Hindu teachers, four-fifths of whom were Brahmins. With their official support, *Selections from Vemana* was excluded by the textbook committee.

The reason cited was the equal right of orthodox Hindus to complain as the clergy in England would, if such dissent had been expressed in their textbooks. There were similar instances where textbooks prepared for missionary schools carried objectionable theological ideas against Islam. Textbooks were also indicative of religious influences, as well as the largely neutral stance taken by the colonial government in such matters.

Negotiating Literature, Language, and the Notion of Fixity

Velcheru (2004, 160) suggests that printing, and the opportunities it created for Telugu prose, were held hostage by the pundits, given that most managers of the printing presses were pundits. Quoting the example of the Vavilla Press, Velcheru observes how hundreds of classical Telugu texts, taken from manuscripts, were edited following Cinnaya Suri's[8] grammar. Cinnaya Suri's popularity was in large part due to his influential position in the education spaces of the time, and the success of his textbooks. There are other instances that demonstrate the changes that print brought into the literary sphere. The pundit at the government library, Veturi Prabhakara Sastri, wrote the following in the context of the language debates in a letter to Gidugu Ramamurti:[9]

> There were hundreds of books in spoken/colloquial language. Print brought in this unfairness (of using granthika language in every book).... All the commentaries even in the poetry books are also written in the colloquial.... Most of the prose books which were written before Cinnaya Suri are in the colloquial. (Gidugu 1933, 14)

Several textbooks were also edited along similar lines with the purpose of 'fixing' the language. Another perspective is that print privileged the *granthika* style (the high literary prose form followed by most authors of the time) because it had the grammar to back it up, and the colonial education machinery decided to standardise *granthika* by prescribing books like *Nīti-candrika*[10] written by Cinnaya Suri. The colloquial style, on the other hand, did not carry grammar authored by the pundits, and the grammar books of Brown, Campbell, and Arden could not be accepted as they fell outside the sphere of punditry. At the same time, print also provided opportunities for producing texts outside the *granthika* style, irrespective of whether they were approved or not, enabling the likes of Gurajada to publish works in the colloquial. Gurajada's play *Kanyāśulkam* was one of the first attempts to use colloquial language in a prose work. He took up the cause of Telugu language reform along with likeminded people like Gidugu Venkata Ramamurti.

FIXITY AND THE PRINTED TEXTBOOK: THE CASE OF *NĪTI-CANDRIKA*[11]

Nīti-candrika was a compilation of two Sanskrit texts—*Hitopadesa*, authored by Narayana Pandita, and *Pañcatantra*,[12] authored by Vishnu Sharma. While *Hitopadesa* primarily had stories that alluded to morals, *Pañcatantra* also had stories on statecraft. Cinnaya Suri adapted stories from both texts in *Nīti-candrika* and divided it into four parts: *Mitra Labhamu*, *Mitra Bedhamu*, *Sandhi*, and *Vigrahamu*.

Nīti-candrika remained a prescribed textbook for many years. *Mitra Bedham*, a fable from *Nīti-candrika*, was one of the prescribed textbooks for matriculation students. In 1932, Gidugu (2014, 62) picked up a phrase from this textbook and sought to clarify a few observations regarding it. As he returned to earlier print editions of the same book edited by different Telugu pundits, he realised that none of them could clearly express the meaning of this phrase. Finally procuring the first two editions of the book (dating back to 1853 and 1856), he noticed quite a few departures from Cinnaya Suri's version in the present-day versions. He observed that this book was a prescribed textbook for eighty years and such inconsistencies in language use warrant separate commentaries written by experts (ibid., 69).

After the death of Cinnaya Suri, the book went through several editions. In the process, while the authorship was attributed to Cinnaya Suri, the editions were edited unofficially by several pundits who introduced their own notions of grammatical and lexical authenticity. These instances again demonstrate that print technology alone cannot guarantee consistency, which is left to the human actors involved in the process. It is ironic that these texts of Cinnaya Suri went on to become the benchmark and an obstacle in the way of language reform.

A few years later, *Nīti-candrika*,[13] this time authored by Kandukuri Viresalingam, was prescribed as a textbook for the SSLC examination. To draw a parallel with astronomer Tycho Brahe,[14] who had his own printing press, Cinnaya Suri, too, printed *Nīti-candrika* in his own printing press, Vani Darpana Mudraksharashaala, to bring about changes in the way certain letters were printed in Telugu. But once the text moved outside his purview, the fixity of the book was lost.

Taking the example of another book, *Seshayya Vyākaranamu* (grammar), published by the education department, Gidugu (2014, 569) points out differences in the 1857 and 1875 editions. The 1875 edition was converted into the *granthika* dialect, while the 1857 edition was written in the colloquial. Using manuscripts and going back to earlier editions of books, Gidugu documents instances across different genres where the colloquial language is used. The treatise *Gadya Cintamani* (Gidugu 1933) also illustrates with examples the manner in which several manuscripts written in the colloquial style were converted into the literary style when printed versions were created.

Adrian Johns (1998, 10) notes that fixity, according to Eisenstein, is the mass reproduction of the same text, irrespective of location and occasion, and this becomes the most important attribute of his conception of print culture. Eisenstein noted that print also circumvents the corruption that seems to be part of a 'script culture', but Johns disputes these notions, drawing on instances from the works of Tycho Brahe and the risks posed by piracy. When applied to the Telugu context, the notion of fixity of a text comes into question, as later editions were edited by different pundits after the demise of Cinnaya Suri (Gidugu 2014, 62).

FIXING A STYLE FOR THE VERNACULAR

In 1869, the Registrar of Books wrote in the remarks section of the catalogue entry of a school primer titled *Bala Viveka Cintamani*: 'A School Primer in Telugu, with a chapter on the art of Telugu versification, *altogether beyond the comprehension of children*' (Registrar of Books 1869; emphasis mine). This comment reveals an important question that the Telugu public sphere had to deal with in the early twentieth century. As more and more texts from the Telugu literary canon were prescribed as textbooks, the problem of unintelligibility—owing to the high literary style of these texts—came to the forefront. It should also be noted here that there was a paucity of comprehensible Telugu literature, and attempts to create a new prose literature for students were made after the colonial government's establishment of the Public Instruction System (Gidugu 2012, 3).

Francesca Orsini (2010, 92) notes, in the context of Hindi, that textbooks played an important role in shaping the public language. She also observes how the centralised education system and the publication of statistics around the print industry and education enhanced the importance of these spaces. The Telugu school textbook became the site of contestation for the assertion of power in academia and the subsequent language debates. These debates, centred round textbooks, and the resulting deliberations use textbooks and their language to demonstrate the lack of consistency of a certain style of language.

When a few books by the Vijnana Chandrika Mandali[15] were prescribed as textbooks, Gurajada objected, because there was a good likelihood that the language used in these books would be standardised for decades to come, as had happened in the decades after Cinnaya Suri's grammar and style of language were standardised. It had taken almost 100 years for the process to be reversed.

The question of canon also comes up many times in the language debates. Post Cinnaya Suri, the pundits considered his works canonical. While the language reform debate was going on, the modern standard Telugu prose was discredited by classicists for its lack of a canon. When textbook committees were formed, the reformists had very few books to offer as being standard. Gidugu, in his *A Memorandum on Modern Telugu* (2012), tried to discredit the *granthika* school by unearthing the canon, and proving repeatedly that there was never a set canon and that the *granthika* style was the result of different mistakes committed by various authors.

Gurajada (1914, 46), in his minute of dissent, noted that the breach of *sandhi*[16] became a convention and an end in itself after the Upayukta Grandakarana Sabha (textbook committee) discarded difficult composite words with *sandhi* in a textbook titled *Outlines of Geography* in 1856. It is also important to note that Cinnaya Suri was an honorary president of the Sabha. Velcheru (2004, 154) observes that Cinnaya Suri's grammar, *Bala Vyākaranamu*, was widely used in all the schools, and this was the first time that such a standardisation was taking place in Telugu (the system of a school-leaving exam with a corresponding certificate was non-existent earlier).

After Cinnaya Suri, Kandukuri Viresalingam filled the space of the successful textbook author. Viresalingam co-authored practically every standard Reader printed by the SPCK (Society for Promoting Christian Knowledge) press, in the range of 5,000 to 50,000 copies (Registrar of Books 1909). He was very influential in textbook printing, and his style slowly became a standard and was emulated by publishing houses like Vijnana Chandrika Mandali, who were also venturing into publishing textbooks.

Viresalingam's style was appreciated in *The Hindu* (Kandukuri 1915, 142) in 1878. The newspaper lamented the lack of good books in the vernacular and the unintelligibility of the few available books. It suggested that the golden mean for the language could be between the high dialect and the bland prose of translations by the Christian Vernacular Society, asserting that Viresalingam had achieved that 'happy mean'.

With the introduction of a 'Vernacular Composition and Translation' paper for the Secondary School Leaving Certificate (SSLC), the need to select textbooks for this paper arose. Textbooks played a major role in the language standardisation process, and it is thus not surprising that the trigger for the bitter language debates was an issued order recommending the use of *Greeku Mytthulu*, which was written in the colloquial,[17] as a non-detailed textbook for the SSLC final examination. The education department issued another directive to list the following books, which could be referred to as 'Modern Telugu' books.[18]

1. Brown's Reader
2. The first part of Arden's Telugu Grammar
3. Enugula Veeraswami's *Kasiyatra Caritra*

These decisions were the result of deliberations between J. A. Yates, Gurajada, Gidugu, and P. T. Srinivasa Iyengar,[19] and the university. It is this controversial space that the textbooks of the time inhabited. The language style used in most of the books published by the likes of Vijnana Chandrika Mandali was '*sarala granthika*', a slightly simplified version of the high literary style or '*Granthika*', and the classicists tried, and eventually succeeded, in standardising this style of language by ensuring their prescription as school textbooks.[20] The classicists considered this a safer compromise than going for the colloquial style, which they termed a 'vulgar' style (*gramya*, or a colloquial style).

In view of the difference of opinion regarding the choice of language to be used in Telugu composition, the University of Madras Syndicate appointed a Composition Committee to sort out issues related to the style of language to be used, and also chalk out a list of prescriptions and proscriptions for the students. The Committee continued its deliberations from 1911 to 1914[21] on several finer details, like making lists of loan words and archaic forms from several books. Textbooks featured significantly in these discussions. The colonial government issued a G.O. No. 196. Educational, dated 22 February 1915, and observed that it was not in a position to recognise 'modern' Telugu based on the Committee's report (Jayanthi 1936, 45).

K. Purushotham (2014) outlined the limits of these language reform debates. He observed that even the modernists privileged the dialect of the Delta region of Andhra, while ignoring the Rayalaseema and Telangana dialects. The other point that emerged from Purushotham's critique is that the entire language reform movement needed to be contextualised as a non-Shudra, non-Dalit reform.

ŚṚṄGĀRARASA[22] AND TEXTBOOKS

During the same deliberations, the selection of certain classic Telugu texts as textbooks revealed the effect of the Victorian sensibilities that were a part of colonial modernity. The colonial government banned certain Telugu classics and initiated legal proceedings against the publishers, Vavilla Press, in 1910. This ban instilled a fear among the classicists that all Telugu literature with objectionable content would be banned, as *Śṛṅgārarasa* dominated the genre of *Prabandha*.[23] The consequences of these texts being prescribed as textbooks were debated. The pundits supported the inclusion of erotic literature as it was a part of literary traditions, noting that any deviation would cause great damage to the language and its literary corpus, while the reformers considered it immoral to let schoolchildren study passages with erotic descriptions. The pundits also noted that older poets had based their rules of art on texts dominated by *Śṛṅgārarasa*, and hence excluding these books would mean that a principal means of judging the grammatical forms of Telugu works would be lost. They argued that merely reading erotic poems would not tempt students into evil ways, but the reformists believed that these books should be kept out of the reach of children. 'The modern Indian teacher following the traditions of the west, protests that such literature is poison, and its teaching militates against the influence of all of the moral factors of modern education' (Gidugu 2012, 58).

Even in this instance, the textbook brought out contradictions and complexities resulting from colonial modernity. While the pundits' primary interest in resisting the expurgation of these texts was the preservation of tradition, it is also interesting to note that reformists like Viresalingam[24] and Gidugu adopted a conservative stand in this matter.

TEXTBOOK AS AN INSTRUMENT OF KNOWLEDGE

Of all the media of modern scientific knowledge, textbooks were the most crucial as they canonised knowledge and were the most accessible vehicles of modernity. By the early twentieth century, several attempts had been made to translate English textbooks into the vernacular, in some instances by the government, but mostly through vernacular publishing efforts of the local intelligentsia. One criticism levelled at most prescribed textbooks of the time was that they were literary in nature and provided no 'useful knowledge'. The Telugu science textbooks were meant to address this criticism. Komarraju Venkata Lakshmana Rao and other members of the Telugu intelligentsia who had received a colonial education realised the 'usefulness' of modern Western knowledge in the economic growth of the country. The main obstacle in the diffusion of this knowledge was the English language. All these books were in English, and although large-scale translation projects had been taken up officially in languages like Marathi by the government and some private institutions, there was no similar effort in the Telugu language.

Deepak Kumar (1995, 144) notes that the job of writing books in the vernacular or translating the standard English ones into local languages fell largely on individuals or societies like the Aligarh Scientific Society and those dealing with schoolbooks at Agra and the Presidency towns. The early twentieth century saw the emergence of vernacular publishing houses and literary societies like the Vijnana Chandrika Mandali and Sugnana Grantha Ratnavali, which published science books. The editor of Vijnana Chandrika Mandali, Komarraju (1923, 160), noted in an essay that vernacular textbooks were essential, primarily because they made the process of learning easier for students. Most of the science textbooks were available in English, which was an alien language for students, thus triggering the need for translations into the vernacular.

The Locked Room of Knowledge

The Telugu intelligentsia identified two broad problems with the state of education in the Telugu-speaking regions of Madras Presidency. The *first* was the medium of instruction (English), and the *second* was the problem of translating Western knowledge into the vernacular. Komarraju (1910, 59) uses the metaphor of a locked room to explain the predicament caused by English as the medium of instruction. He wrote that all scientific knowledge was locked in a room called 'English language', and the key was 'ABCD'. This led students to waste seven to eight years of their education in just becoming fluent in the '*pāra bhāṣā*' (foreign language) of English. The vernacular textbook was the way to opening this room for the large section of population unfamiliar with English and Sanskrit. Komarraju cites the following example to illustrate the problems arising from a lack of scientific vernacular literature.

The Ayurveda college in Chennai taught its students an introductory course in 'Physiology and Anatomy', but this was tough for the teachers to teach as there was no equivalent book in Telugu and the students did not understand the English textbook. He also discussed how, in some cases, subjects were dropped entirely from the curriculum as there were no relevant textbooks. He finally noted that 'knowledge cannot be held hostage to a particular language', and stressed the need for a vernacularisation of the science. He also discussed the mismatch between the standard of English used in the science and mathematics textbooks and the student's fluency in the language, because of which students end up learning everything by rote. Here, he also mentioned the other problem—'Sanskrit'. Most books in Ayurveda were written in Sanskrit. But in this case, a vernacular publishing house, Ayurveda Grantamala, had taken up the production of Ayurveda books in Telugu. Similar issues were faced by the National College in Machilipatnam with respect to the selection of books.

In the Preface to a physical science primer (Sitaramaiah 1910), the author praises the colonial educational department for encouraging lessons on natural objects in elementary schools. This was meant to develop the children's observation and reasoning powers and provide a corrective to the speculative aspect of the Indian mind. The textbook, in this case, is seen as a vehicle of modernity, with the responsibility of steering the Indian mind out of a speculative state and onto a more observational and reasoning state.

ACCOMMODATING INDIGENOUS FORMS OF KNOWLEDGE IN TEXTBOOKS

An alternative school of thought was shaping up under the influence of the nationalist movement, which wanted to give space to indigenous forms of knowledge in textbooks. The Telugu science textbook became the site for these epistemological negotiations. The book on cholera (1914), when examined in terms of its structure, reveals a lot about the way knowledge was negotiated in these books. This book was quite successful in terms of its print run—three editions and upwards of 10,000 copies. It was also prescribed as a textbook in some schools. In its initial pages, the author lists the local names of the disease and addresses the superstitions surrounding it. He then describes the ways in which the disease spreads, and notes that learning about the disease will make people break free of superstitious thinking and save lives. The first part describes the treatment suggested by Western medicine and the second section describes the treatment suggested by Ayurveda exponent Pandita D. Gopalacharyulu. Both remedies are given equal importance in the book. This juxtaposition of the indigenous with the Western can be seen in other Telugu science textbooks as well.

The process of writing science textbooks in Telugu also encouraged authors to reflect on their own knowledge systems, and even though they were engaged in the translation of Western knowledge, they included indigenous knowledge wherever they saw an opportunity. While some authors like Viresalingam discovered Indian astronomy in the process, some others like Komarraju were of the opinion that there was no tradition of natural sciences in India, since the focus was mostly on metaphysical knowledge.

In 1888 and 1895, Viresalingam (1915, 192) published *śareera śāstramu* (physiology) and *Jotiśya śāstramu*[25] (astronomy) books in Telugu. In his autobiography, Viresalingam delves into the details of the authorship of these books and notes that while he referred to English books, he also tried to study Indian texts on these subjects. When he could not find any published books, he tried to access the unpublished palm leaf manuscripts of ancient authors, like the *Susruta* from Calcutta. To research the second book, he referred to Sanskrit works like *Surya Sidāntamu*, *Pañcasidānthika*, and *Sidānta Siromani*.

Words and Knowledge

Textbooks were also sites where Western concepts found expression in the vernacular. Coining technical terms was a prerogative of the authorship of vernacular books, which situated the vernaculars in the linguistic and epistemological space dominated by English and Sanskrit. This coining of technical terms was less of an exercise in modernity and more of an assertion of linguistic identity. Komarraju, who was at the forefront of the vernacular textbook project in Telugu, advised the following method for coining technical terms.

- Use Telugu words as far as possible and retain the same nomenclature used in earlier Telugu books so that there is no scope for confusion. This is for words already in existence.
- If there are no Telugu words, then authors could follow the nomenclature suggested by the Nagari Pracharini Sabha. (These words were in Sanskrit).

- If there are no earlier books on the subject and no suggestion from the Sabha, either, then the author is free to coin a new word.
- If coining a term is impossible, then use a transliteration of the English word as it is. This should be a last resort; he also spoke against authors who recommend using only an English transliteration for all scientific terms. He quotes the example of German, where authors did not import nomenclature from Greek or Latin, but developed their own (Komarraju 1923, 167)

Komarraju (ibid., 166) requested teachers to adapt these science textbooks, even if the Committee had not approved them. The publishers, in an attempt to expand the readership of textbooks, also tried to encourage readers other than students. For instance, the copy of advertisements for the Natural Science Primers (Manager 1910, 17) had two different sales propositions. The *first* mentioned the simple style of the books; anyone who could read Telugu would be able to both understand and explain it to others. Women's education was one of the issues highlighted by a few publishing houses of the time. This advertisement specifically mentions that a woman can educate her children and satisfy their curiosity through these books. The *second* proposition was aimed at teachers: the advertisement claimed that the chapters were designed as per the latest rules and could be used by elementary school teachers as well. Komarraju (ibid.) encouraged publishers to venture into science publishing by referring to the growth in publication numbers: while earlier, a book used to sell 500 copies in three years, a book's print run now was in the range of 2,000–3,000 copies per edition, with some successful books running into multiple editions.

When books were recommended as textbooks, they occasionally revealed the contradictory intentions of colonial officials and the native intelligentsia. For instance, the Vijnana Chandrika Mandali published a book on physics, authored by Mantripragada Sambasiva Rao, in 1909. The same book was republished in 1914 after being approved by the government textbook committee. The differences in the para-texts of these two editions serve as a premonition of the postcolonial future awaiting the vernacular. The Preface written by the editor of the 1909 edition describes why the book was titled *Padardha Vijnana Sastramu*, despite opposition from various quarters. The author details a brief history of the Telugu science book, and delves into the importance of vernacular science books for the development of the nation.

The Foreword to the 1914 edition was written by William J. C. Penn, Principal of Noble College in Machilipatnam. His main concern seems to be whether the author has used 'universally recognized terms', because students in the higher forms have to know these terms (which, naturally, were English terms). Penn's concern with 'universal' terms and the earnest and idealistic 'vernacular' efforts of the Telugu intelligentsia (including Komarraju) follow starkly different directions. Vernacular languages were playing second fiddle to English, for all practical purposes. The differences in the nature of the para-texts of these two editions exemplify the lack of institutional support for the creation of a truly vernacular medium of education, which was considered a temporary arrangement till the students started learning sciences in English. While members of the Telugu intelligentsia were seeking ways to bridge the linguistic and epistemological gap between the coloniser's English and the subject's vernacular through the medium of the textbook, the larger educational policy of the time did not favour such attempts.

CONCLUSION

In many ways, textbooks are also archives, in the sense that they were sites for the canonisation of knowledge and literary practices. The important aspect of their archival nature is that they were created in large part by colonial subjects, unlike most other archives, which were created by the State. This makes them even more important as they enable us to understand the perspectives, aspirations, and insecurities of the subjects.

The vernacular textbook was also representative of the limited liberties that subjects were granted by the colonial regime. Some of the evolutionary moments in the history of the Telugu textbook discussed here also allude to a mind in transition, from tradition to modernity, with caution and trepidation. From delivering an exclusively moral, liturgical, and literary education in the nineteenth century, the Telugu textbook in the early twentieth century moved towards becoming a vehicle for translated Western knowledge. In this process, the textbook also transcended its designated position as a medium of education, with teachers and students as the actors, and took on a larger and more central role by triggering linguistic and epistemological debates.

One recurring motif in the creation of the Telugu textbook was dissent, for religious, moral, linguistic, or epistemological reasons. It is apparent that dissent, more than consent, shaped the Telugu textbook. To modify Johns' definition: the Telugu textbook is the material embodiment of dissent, expressed mostly by elite colonial subjects. This dissent was more pronounced as all other avenues of their vernacular past seemed to have been seized by a colonial modernity that was threatening the future of the literary corpus that was an important source of elite Brahmin privilege. The textbook was one space where they enjoyed a sense of control, and they were reluctant to give this up.

Notes

1. Both Gurajada Appa Rao and Gidugu Ramamurti, proponents of language reform in Telugu, were staunch critics of the high literary style of the language. In their articulation of language reform, they pointed out that teachers often found it tough to understand the language used in the books they used to teach students.

2. This average is based on publishing numbers from the Catalogue of Books (Registrar of Books 1909).

3. Viresalingam's revised versions of primers, authored by Marsden (Registrar of Books 1909).

4. In terms of authorship, Gurajada observes that the conditions of production and circulation of books in India differ materially from those in European countries.

5. John Murdoch also brought in novel ways of teaching English using bi-lingual materials and encouraged using vernaculars to teach even English. The English-Telugu bilingual textbook was born out of his criticism of applying British models and Materials to Indian Schools. (R.Vennela and Smith 2019: 104)

6. Mantena quotes Velcheru Narayana Rao's observations on medieval grammar in her work on colonial philology.

7. In the case of committees formed for the selection of textbooks and deciding on other matters of importance in the Board of Studies, there was no representation from different committees; these committees, almost exclusively, were the preserve of Brahmins.

8. Cinnaya Suri was an influential Telugu grammarian and author, and the first Telugu headmaster of Madras University who dedicated his work, *Niti Chandrika*, to A. J. Arbuthnot, Secretary to the Madras University and College of Fort Saint George, indicating the patronage he received from the colonial government.

9. Gidugu Ramamurti embarked on this project of revisiting Telugu literature and going back into earlier editions of the work in a bid to prove the existence of the colloquial style in literature before Cinnaya Suri's standardisation efforts. He procured several manuscripts and books from different libraries. In one instance, in a rejoinder to Jayanthi Ramayya Panthulu, Gidugu observed, '[M]y standard is manuscripts, your standard is printed material' (Gidugu 2014, 761)

10. A more detailed account of the reasons for the standardisation of the granthika style is provided in Velcheru Narayana Rao's essay 'Print and Prose' (Velcheru 2004). A choice had to be made between karanam prose and pundit prose, and the colonial officials choose the pundit prose as pundits had greater scholarly credentials than the karanams.

11. The cover page of the books reads 'Neeti Chandrika or 'Moral Stories'.

12. Ravipati Gurumurti Sastri had authored the earlier adaptations of *Pañcatantra* in 1834 and 1848 as a textbook for those learning the Telugu language.

13. This book was first mentioned in the Registrar of Books (1875, 7) catalogue, and is described as 'A new prose book of fiction based on the story of the Third Book of the Pañcatantra intended for advanced Telugu students', and had a print run of 1,000 copies.

14. Tycho Brahe controlled his own printing operation (Johns 1998,15).

15. Vijnana Chandrika Mandali was one of the first literary societies and publishing houses from the Madras Presidency that published books in the genres of biography, the sciences, history, historical novels, and encyclopaedias in Telugu from 1907–1933.

16. Telugu grammatical rules related to conjunction.

17. It was a controversial book, primarily because it avoided the use of *sandhi.*

18. The details of the deliberations have been drawn from the biography of Gidugu by Dasarathula (2009).

19. Gurajada Appa Rao was the epigraphist to the Maharaja of Vizianagaram and the Gidugu Ramamurti was Professor of History in Raja's College, Parlakamidi, Iyengar was the Principal of AVN College. The four were together referred to as *Dustachathushtayamu*—The Evil Four—by the classicists

20. In one of its Annual Reports, the Mandali thanks the Madras School Book Society for their patronage (Vijnana Chandrika Mandali 1913).

21. Convener: Venkata Ranga Rao, Members: K. V. Lakshamana Rao, Jayanti Ramayya Panthulu,Vedam Venkataraya Sastri, P. T. Srinivasa Iyengar, Gurajada Appa Rao, Gidugu Ramamurti, and B. Sheshagiri Rao.

22. Erotic genre.

23. *Prabandha* is described as a genre with ornate, descriptive, and elaborately stylised form of poetry. Most works in this genre are excessively erotic, as described by Velcheru (2016, 369).

24. Viresalingam minced no words in his stance on the erotic nature of the Prabhandhas:'The poetical works, called the Prabandhas are like public prostitutes, by a display of their ornaments and superficial charms and by their fascinating words they beguile people and lead them away from the path of virtue' (Gidugu 2012, 61).

25. Viresalingam's book is not on astrology but on astronomy, which can be concluded from the description of topics provided in his autobiography.

REFERENCES

Achanta, L. P. 1914. *Cholera*. Madras: The Vijnana Chandrika Mandali.

Bock, A. 2018. 'Theories and Methods of Textbook Studies'. In Eckhardt Fuchs (ed.), *The Palgrave Handbook of Textbook Studies*, 57–70. New York: Palgrave Macmillan.

Cohn, B. S. 1996. *Colonialism and its Forms of Knowledge*. Princeton, NJ: Princeton University Press.

Dasarathula, N. 2009. *Gidugu Ramamurthy Jeevitham—Rachanalu*. Hyderabad: Naimisha Publishers.

Ghosh, A. 2006. *Power in Print: Popular Publishing and the Politics of Language and Culture in a Colonial Society, 1778–1905*. New Delhi: Oxford University Press.

Gidugu, R. V. 1933. *Gadhya Chintamani*. Madras: Vavilla Press.

_____. 2012. *A Memorandum on Modern Telugu*. Hyderabad: Vedagiri Communications.

_____. 2014. *Rachanasarvasvamu*. Hyderabad: Telugu Akademi.

Gupta, V. 2007. 'Social Agenda of Colonial Education: Textbook Discourse in the Mid-Nineteenth Century'. *Proceedings of Indian History Congress*, 1112–1123.

Gurajada, A. R. 1909. 'Preface to the Second Edition'. In Sri Sri and Appa Rao Gurajada, *Kanyasulkam*, 25–29. Jayanthi: Vijayawada.

_____. 1914. *The Telugu Composition Controversy: Minute of Dissent*. Hyderabad: Vedagiri.

_____. 1986. 'Preface to the Second Edition'. In Eswara Rao Cetti, *Gurajada Rachanalu: Kanyasulkam*, iii–v. Hyderabad: Visalandhra Book House.

_____. 2012. 'Authorship in India'. In Gopalakrishna Pennepalli (ed.), *Gurajadalu*, 827–828. Hyderabad: Emesco Books.

Jayanthi, R. P. 1936. *Andhra Sahithya Parishta Vruthaanthamu*, Silver Jubilee Year. Kakinada: Andhra Sahithya Parishat.

Johns, A. 1998. *The Nature of the Book: Print and Knowledge in the Making*. Chicago: The University of Chicago Press.

Kandukuri, V. P. 1911. *Sweeya Charitramu: Prathama Bhaagamu*. Madras: Vijnana Chandrika Mandali.

_____. 1915. *Sweeya Charitamu: Rendava Bhagamu*. Chennai: Vijnana Chandrika Mandali.

Kesavan, B. S. 1997. *History of Printing and Publishing in India*. New Delhi: National Book Trust of India.

Komarraju, V. L. R. 1910. 'Aurangajebu Thana Guruvunaku Raasina Utharamu'. *Andhra Patrika Annual Number*, 57–59.

_____. 1923. *Lakshmanaraya Vyasavali*. Chennai: Vijnana Chandrika Mandali.

Kumar, D. 1995. *Science and the Raj: A Study of British India*. New Delhi: Oxford University Press.

Manager, V. C. M. 1910. 'Advertisements'. In Sitaramaiah K. (ed.), *Prakruthi Sastramula Prathama Patamulu*, 1–17. Madras: Vijnana Chandrika Mandali.

Mangamma, J. 1975. *Book Printing in India, with Special Reference to the Contribution of European Scholars to Telugu (1746–1857)*. Nellore: Bangorey Books.

Mantena, R. S. 2012. *The Origins of Modern Hisoriography in India*. New York: Palgrave Macmillan.

Mantripragada, S. R. 1914 [1909]. *Padhartha Vijnana Sastramu*. Madras: Vijnana Chandrika Mandali.

Mitchell, L. 2009. *Language, Emotion, and Politics in South India: The Making of a Mother Tongue*. Bloomington: Indiana University Press.

Ngũgĩ wa Thiong'o. 1986. *Decolonizing the Mind: The Politics of Language in African Literature*. Harare: Zimbabwe Publishing House.

Nidudhavolu, V. R. 1962. *Chinnayasuri Jeevithamu*. Madras: Nidudhavolu Venkata Rao.

Orsini, F. 2010. *The Hindi Public Sphere 1920–1940*. New Delhi: Oxford University Press.

Pinto, R. 2007. *Between Empires: Print and Politics in Goa*. New Delhi: Oxford University Press.

Purushotham, K. 2014. 'Prosifying the Poesy: A Dalit Critique of Modernisation of Telugu'. *Economic and Political Weekly* 49 (6), 39–43.

Registrar of Books. 1869. *Catalogue of Books Printed in the Madras Presidency: 2nd Quarter of 1868*. Madras: Educational Department Fort St.George.

_____. 1875. *A Catalogue of Books Printed in the Madras Presidency during the Months of January, February and March of 1875*. Madras: Fort St. George Gazette Press.

_____. 1909. *Catalogue of Books*. Madras: Fort St.George Gazette.

Satthianadhan, S. 1894. *History of Education in the Madras Presidency*. Madras: Srinivasa Varadachari & Co.

Sitaramaiah, K. 1910. *Physical Science Primer*. Madras: Vijnana Chandrika Mandali.

Stark, U. 2009. *An Empire of Books: The Naval Kishore Press and the Diffusion of the Printed Word in Colonial India*. Ranikhet: Permanent Black.

Stone, J. H. 1918. *Report on Public Instruction Madras for 1916–17 and for the Quinquennium 1911–12 to 1916–17*. Madras: Office of the Director of Public Instruction.

Venkateswaran, T. V. 2007. 'Science and Colonialism: Content and Character of Natural Sciences in the Vernacular School Education in the Madras Presidency (1820–1900)'. *Science & Education* 16 (January), 87–114.

Velaga, V. 2012. *Telugu Mudrana: Prachurana Vikasam*. Tenali: Velaga Venkatappayya.

Velcheru, N. R. 2004. 'Print and Prose'. In Stuart Blackburn and Vasudha Dalmia (eds), *India's Literary History: Essays on the Nineteenth Century*, 146–167. New Delhi: Permanant Black.

_____. 2016. *Text and Tradition in South India*. Ranikhet: Permanent Black.

Venkatachalapathy, A. R. 2015. *The Province of the Book: Scholars, Scribes, and Scribblers in Colonial Tamilnadu*. Ranikhet: Permanent Black.

Vennela, R., and R. Smith. 2019. 'Bilingual English Teaching on Colonial India: The Case of John Murdoch's Work in Madras Presidency, 1855–1875'. *Language & History* 62 (2), 96–118.

Vijnana Chandrika Mandali. 1913. *Karyanivedanamu*. Chennai: Vijnana Chandrika Mandali.

Notes on the Contributors

Thongam Bipin is an independent research scholar based in Imphal. His research interests include Northeast India, the nation-state, language debates, B. R. Ambedkar, and Phulo.

Amelia Bonea, a Lecturer in Global History of Science, Technology, and Medicine at the University of Manchester, is a historian of science, technology, and media, specialising in colonial South Asia, the British Empire, and Japan. Her book, *The News of Empire: Telegraphy, Journalism, and the Politics of Reporting in Colonial India* (2016), won the American Historical Association's Eugenia M. Palmegiano Prize for the best book on journalism history.

Carmel Christy K. J. is Assistant Professor of Journalism at Kamala Nehru College, University of Delhi, and a postdoctoral research associate at the Gladstein Family Human Rights Institute, University of Connecticut. Her research explores the intersections of caste, gender, environment, and urban space in India, with a particular focus on spatial justice and protest movements. She is the author of *Sexuality and Public Space in India: Reading the Visible* (2019).

Sai Amulya Komarraju is Assistant Professor in the area of Communications at the Indian Institute of Management, Ahmedabad. Her research focuses on feminist communication studies, digital cultures, and the future of work(ers). She has co-authored *Digital Expressions of the Self(ie): The Social Life of Selfies* (2024).

Brian Larkin is Professor of Anthropology and Director of Graduate Studies at Barnard College, Columbia University. His research explores the impact that media technologies in Nigeria have on politics, religion, and urban culture. He is the author of *Signal and Noise: Media Infrastructure and Urban Culture in Nigeria* (2008) and co-editor of *Media Worlds: Anthropology on New Terrain* (2002).

Dickens Leonard is Assistant Professor of Literature, Department of Humanities and Social Sciences, IIT, Delhi. He was formerly a DAAD-visiting Ph.D. Fellow (2016) at the Centre for Modern Indian Studies, Göttingen, Germany. He has published journal articles on anti-caste thought and Tamil films. He is presently writing a monograph on Iyothee Thass's Tamil Buddhism as a visiting fellow (2025) in South Asian Studies at Brandeis University, Boston.

William Mazzarella is Professor of Anthropology and Social Sciences, University of Chicago, and Faculty Fellow at the Chicago Centre for Contemporary Theory. His interdisciplinary work spans anthropology, media studies, critical theory, psychoanalysis, and South Asian studies. His research explores the interplay between social energy and its containment, with a particular interest in charisma, mass publicity, and crowd affect.

K. A. Nuaiman is Assistant Professor of media studies at the Department of Journalism and Mass Communication, University of Calicut. His research explores the intersections of media, religion, and popular culture in South Asia. His current research projects investigates reading and writing cultures along the Malabar coast of the Indian Ocean littoral.

Sasi Kiran R. M. is Assistant Professor of Communication at FLAME University, Pune. His research focuses on print cultures, media history, and cultural studies. His current research projects explore vernacular modernities in South Asia.

Vaibhav Singh is an independent typographer and type designer. Chairman of the Printing Historical Society, he is also the editor and publisher of *Contextual Alternate*, an interdisciplinary journal of typography, design, and history. Vaibhav's research interests revolve broadly around typographic history, printing, publishing, and textual communication, and in particular, aspects of design and technology for Indian languages and scripts.

Ashley Tellis is a freelance academic, arts and cultural journalist, editor, and poet based in New Delhi. His research focuses on gender, literature, and minority identities. He is the co-editor of *The Global Trajectories of Queerness: Re-Thinking Same-Sex Politics in the Global South* (2015) and author of *Modernism: Texts and Contexts* (2022).

P. Thirumal is Dean, Sarojini Naidu School of Arts and Communication, and Professor of Communication Studies, University of Hyderabad. His research spans cultural histories of Northeast India, technology studies, caste embodiment, and discrimination in higher education. He is the co-author of *Modern Mizoram: History, Culture, Poetics* (2019).

A. R. Venkatachalapathy, a professor at the Madras Institute of Development Studies, Chennai, has taught at universities in Tirunelveli, Madras, Singapore, and Chicago. He has published widely on the social, cultural, and intellectual history of colonial Tamilnadu in Tamil and English. His recent book is *Swadeshi Steam: V.O. Chidambaram Pillai and the Battle Against the British Maritime Empire* (2023).

Index

Adi Dravida Maha Vigada Thoodhan 184
Adi-Dravida Mitran 184
Adi-Dravida(s) 183–184, 186–187
  intellectuals 184, 186
Adivasi(s) 135, 143, 148, 175
Advertising 32, 222, 225, 227–228, 230
Aesop's Fables 279
Aesthetic(s) 2, 5, 14, 33, 52, 102, 113, 115–117, 119–120, 137, 140–141, 167, 298
  expectations 119–20
  investment 115, 116
Africa 46, 51, 53, 85–87, 176, 180
African audience 51, 86
Agency 8, 19–20, 30–31, 35, 39–40, 96, 145–146, 222, 290, 302, 311, 342
Ahmad, Ado 68, 73, 82–84, 86
  da so da K'auna I, II 68
  Inda so da K'auna I, II 73
Aligarh Muslim University (AMU) 20, 163–166
Aligarh Scientific Society 352
Allahabad High Court 163, 165
Allahabad Law Journal Press 299
All-Indira Radio (AIR) 212, 220
Alphabet 292, 295, 306, 326
Al-Shafi'i, Imam 112
  Kitab al Umm 112
Alterity 193, 196
Ambedkar, Babasaheb B. R. 6, 132–133, 177, 179–180, 275
American Motion Picture Exporters and Cinema Association (AMPECA) 54
Amrita Bazar Patrika 274
Ananda Vikatan 273, 283
Andhra Pradesh 231, 321
Anglo-Indians 258, 262
Anti-caste
  imaginary 20, 176
  matter 19, 133, 136
  thought 151, 176
Apokpa Marup 322–323
Appraisal 15, 307
  visceral modes of 15
Arabian Sea 4, 95, 258, 264
Arabic typographic printing press 119
Armed resistance movement 321
Armed struggle 323
Artefacts 3–4, 33, 142
Arts 2, 17, 21, 51, 86, 105, 108, 113, 115–116, 120, 138, 142, 148–149, 187, 190, 230, 251, 263, 273, 284, 348, 351
  calligraphic 105
  expressive 2, 148
  fine 2
  forms 21, 251, 273
  History 2
  institutions 2
  performative 138, 148

spatial 148
theatre 2
visual 105
Asceticism 184, 195
Asian College of Journalism (ACJ) Conference 160
Assam 232, 320, 322
Associational networks 133
Association of Nigerian Authors Review 83
Astrology 194
Astronomy 194, 355
Audience(s) 17, 51, 53, 55–56, 58, 78, 80, 85–86, 113, 162, 212–213, 218, 220, 222, 228–230, 232–234, 237–238, 240
Austro-Prussian War 37–39
Authority 2, 54, 62, 76, 78–79, 84, 95, 105, 110, 120, 140, 146, 192, 196, 218, 237, 240–242, 304, 309, 343
parental 76, 79, 84
religious 95, 110, 120
Autonomy 76, 213
Awakening 184, 195, 305
religio-cultural 184, 195
socio-political 195
Ayurveda 353–354
Ayurveda Grantamala 353

Bahujan 133, 135–136, 138–141, 143–144, 148, 152
Bala Viveka Cintamani 348
Banaras Hindu University 294
Banaras (Varanasi) 293–294
Bangladesh 142, 291
Bangla script 320, 329, 332
imposition of the 320
Basel Missionaries 100
Basel Mission Press, Tellicherry 100
Battala press 142
Battutah, Ibn 109–110, 114
Rihla 109
Bhadralok 142
Bhagavad Gita 6
Bharati, C. Subramania 273, 275–282, 284–285
cartooning 278
cartoons 275, 277–282, 284–285
commentaries 280–281
exposure to journalism 276
Bias 20, 34, 37, 177, 230
Bible, the 103, 114
Bibliographies 99
Bihar 231, 233
Binarism 50
Body 16, 146, 150
biological 146
female 150
Indian (male) 16
recalcitrant 16
transformative capacity of 146
Bollywood 18–19, 251
Bombay Samachar 39
Books and pamphlets 1–3, 10, 13, 16, 18, 22, 29, 36–37, 47–48, 54, 59–62, 65–76, 78–84, 86, 95–100, 102–120, 132, 159–160, 167, 177–179, 184, 187, 195, 274–275, 284, 303, 327, 329, 331, 337–341, 343, 345–357
Arabic 117, 119
collections 110, 115
fiction 159
first Malayalam 115
history of the 36, 338
Islamic 97, 112, 117
lithographed 99, 105
Malayalam 97–99, 115
Muslim 98–100, 112–113
printed 67, 97–100, 106–107, 115, 117, 119–120, 178

production 108, 113–115, 117, 120
reading 69, 81, 84, 195, 340
typographically printed 106, 117, 119
typographically produced 106
Brahmanism 20
Brahminism 17, 183, 185–188, 192, 197
war against 185
Brahmin(s) 4, 11–14, 138, 157, 178, 180, 184, 189, 191–192, 195, 283, 285, 342, 344, 358
Britain 37–38, 117
British
Empire 29–31
imperial domination 29
India 5–6, 97–99
Museum 97–99
British Broadcasting Corporation (BBC) 213
Broadcasting 211–213, 215, 218–219, 221, 225, 228, 230, 234
policy 215, 219, 221
revolution 213
Brown, William Norman 294, 303, 345, 350
Buddhism 5, 20, 179–183, 185, 189–190, 194
as an anti-caste religion 179, 189
Buddhist movement 180–181, 195
Budurwar Zuciya 67
Bureaucracy 338

Calligraphy 4, 113, 115–117
Arab/Arabic 115–117
Islamic 116
medieval 4
Capitalism 15, 61, 177, 194, 339
print 177, 194, 339
Carnatic music, institutionalisation of 283
Cartesian methodology, notions of 9
Cartoon and caricature 9, 17, 21, 63, 273–285
Cartoonist(s) 273, 280, 283–285
Casteism, secular criticism of 151
Casteless 136, 138, 140, 149, 189, 192–195, 197
Caste(s) 2, 7, 9, 11–12, 17, 19–20, 22, 133, 135–138, 141–152, 157, 161–162, 166, 169, 175–197, 234–235, 263, 265
dominant 194, 234
embodiment of 137, 144, 148
experience 136, 193
history(ies) of 17, 169, 176
low/lower/lower- 7, 12, 142, 146, 186, 235, 263, 265
society 181, 188, 197
system 141, 145
upper 2, 7, 19, 142, 146, 149–150, 166, 175, 178, 181, 197
Catalogue of Malayalam Books in the British Museum 97
Censorship 29, 35, 54
Chanda Committee 219
Characters 100, 105, 294, 296, 307–308, 331
Arabic 100, 294
Devanagari 294, 296, 307–308
Meetei Mayek 331
movable type 105
Perso-Arabic 294
Chatterati 138
Chatterjee, Partha 1, 325
Chicago Defender, The 180
Children 70, 76, 83–84, 132, 149, 220, 227, 233, 277, 342, 348, 351, 354, 356

African-American 132
China 211
Chitravali 282
Chotta Mumbai 255, 263–265
Chronology 17
Cinema Distribution Circuit 54
Cinema/Film 3, 8–9, 17–21, 46–61, 64–66, 69–73, 78–82, 85–87, 142, 144, 156, 158, 217, 220–223, 228, 231, 251–266, 331
America America America 255
American 52, 54–55, 57–58
Arab 55
Arabic 54
Bombay 55
Chinese 47
commercial 57, 142
Deshadanakkili Karayarilla 255, 258–259
editing 256, 258, 263–264
Egyptian 87
English 54
Gandhinagar 2nd Street 255
Hindi 55, 59–60, 231
Hollywood 19, 47, 50–51, 57, 59, 65, 79, 251
imitations of 55
imported 51
Indian 18, 46–61, 64–66, 69–73, 78–82, 85–87, 142, 251
industry 21, 142, 252
Irupatham Noottandu 255
Lebanese 54
Malayalam 21, 142, 251–261, 263–266
Manipuri 331
masala 55, 228
narrative style of the 56
New Delhi 255
production 17, 21, 255
studios 20–21, 251, 255–256
Western 57–59
women's 72
Cinematic
climax 263
imagination 265
presentations 265
visuals 258, 262
Cinematography 264
Citizenship 8, 15, 18, 252
Citizenship Amendment Act (CAA) 15
City Television Kano (CTV) 47
Civil Disobedience Movement 283
Civilisation 7, 137, 186, 189, 195
Civil & Military Gazette, The 28
Civil rights 132, 158
movement 132
organisations 158
Civil society 1, 186
Class 36, 57, 61, 66, 120, 147, 157, 161, 166, 169, 184, 191, 215, 220–222, 227–228, 231, 235, 237, 260–265
higher 191
lower 261, 263–265
upper 57, 166, 261
Close television 230–231
CMS Press, Kottayam 115
Cohn, Bernard 337–338, 342–343
Colonialism and Forms of Knowledge 337
Colonial
administration 30, 37, 39, 309
government 29, 33, 35, 281, 338, 341–343, 345, 348, 350–351
period 12, 32–33, 176, 182, 184, 187, 292, 338–339
rule 22, 33, 36, 50, 263, 338, 344
State 30, 39, 178, 338
Colonial India 27, 29, 32–33, 35, 41, 143, 274–275, 293

newspapers in 35, 41
Colonialism 2, 13, 16, 32, 35, 50, 137, 178, 195, 337
Coloniser(s) 16, 48–50, 264, 292, 337, 357
Comedy 55, 85
Commentary(ies) 6, 98, 111–113, 116, 118, 181–182, 187–188, 193, 234, 275, 280–281, 301, 345–346
Commercialism 227
Commercial revolution 215, 220, 225, 227, 241
Commodification 69, 76
Communal
battles 293
divisions 294
lines 295, 321
relations 2
strife 279
Communication(s) 1, 3, 9–10, 14, 27–32, 35, 38–40, 47, 108, 120, 140, 196, 210, 215, 219, 221, 224, 226–227, 231–232, 235, 238, 240, 281, 290, 298, 306
forms of 108, 120
technology(ies) of 10, 27, 29, 31, 35, 39, 235
telegraphic 29–30
Community(ies) 1, 4, 9, 12, 15, 17, 19, 22, 28, 34, 37, 57, 95–97, 99–101, 103, 105–108, 111, 113–115, 120, 132–133, 139, 143–144, 147–148, 152, 157, 176–178, 180–182, 186, 189–190, 193–197, 218–220, 234, 238–239, 258, 262, 264–265, 320–326, 329, 331–333, 343–344
casteless 176, 189, 197
imagined 34, 106
Compassion, universal 191, 193
Conflict(s) 18, 60–61, 64, 68, 76, 79–80, 86, 143, 227, 291, 325
tradition and modernity 18
Connectivity 253, 255
Consciousness 15, 61, 156, 162, 194, 217, 241–42, 322, 330
Conservatism 120
Constitutional rights 149
Consumerism 227, 230
Content 8, 13, 33–35, 40, 96–98, 102, 112–113, 138, 140–144, 169, 180, 195, 213, 220–221, 223–224, 227, 229–230, 234, 240, 332, 340, 342, 344, 351
moderation of 143
nature of 113
presentation of the 102
radical 180
television 230
Controversy 48, 61, 80, 84, 275
Copyright 97–99, 210
Copyright and Deposit Act 98
Coronation Memorial Press (CMP) 119
Corporeality 148, 169
Corruption 58, 76, 164, 214, 347
Cosmology 60, 189
Cosmopolitanism 52, 265
Countercurrents 144
Courtship 61, 64
COVID-19 15
lockdowns 254
Creativity 49, 232
Crime 63, 68, 141
Criminal activities 265
Crises 3, 84, 145, 324
Cultural
artefacts 3, 142
community 12, 194
flows 19, 48, 50, 52, 86–87
forms 16–17, 21, 51, 53, 61
histories 4–5, 7, 13, 22
imperialism 19, 47, 50, 85, 213
institutions 1, 4, 21–22

media 51, 156
practices 62
production 22, 50–51, 134–135, 338
space 85, 191
transition 18, 29
transnational flows 19, 48, 86–87
values 17, 53, 55, 70, 218
Culture(s) 2–4, 6–7, 10, 15, 19, 46–49, 51–54, 56–60, 63, 65–67, 70–72, 79–80, 82–86, 95–96, 101, 105–106, 108–109, 113, 115, 118, 120, 138, 141–143, 147, 158, 180, 182, 184, 189–190, 192–193, 195, 222, 224, 228, 231–232, 235, 292, 305, 323, 338, 347
literary 2, 4, 67, 101
performative 6, 138
popular 46–47, 58, 65, 72, 80, 85–86
writerly 19, 108, 113
Cybercrime 141
Cyberspace 144

Dalit-Bahujan
community 133, 152
intellectuals 133
online portal 144
Dalit-Bahujan-Adivasi 135, 148
Dalit-Bahujan(s) 133, 135–141, 144, 148, 152
Dalit Camera 19, 133, 144
Dalit(s) 8, 20, 132–133, 143, 146, 157, 175–177, 180–81, 184, 189, 193–197, 236–237, 258
activism 19, 133
ambition of 143
articulations 176
class-privileged 157
communities 19, 196
educated 146
forums online 149
intellectuals 176, 183, 187, 197
literary works 135
literature and poetry 144
migration 176
mobilisation 133
movement 133, 138
networks of 133
subaltern intellectuals 194
threats against the 237
woman/women 143, 149–150, 152
writing 157
Dan'Azumi Baba 68
Rikicin Duniya I, II, III 68
Dance 2–3, 139, 220
Da'wa activities 108
Decentralisation 224, 229–230
De-Hinduisation 321, 328
Delhi Sketch Book 274
Democracy(ies) 14, 22, 164, 216, 220
deliberative 14
social 22
Design and manufacture 297
Desire(s) 2, 7, 20, 59–60, 64, 76, 78–79, 86, 137, 161, 167–169, 193, 220–222, 226–227, 229, 231–232, 240, 242, 263, 323, 325
formlessness of 169
individual 64, 76, 78–79
mutually exclusive 232
Deterritorialisation 49
Devanagari development 298, 303, 305, 311
Devanagari Linotype 289, 294–295, 297, 299–301, 303–305, 307, 309
launch of 295
Devanagari machine 294–295, 299–301, 303–304
exhibition of the 303

Devanagari script 21, 289, 291, 293–311, 331
as an all-India script 299
mechanical typesetting for 295, 306
reform schemes for 307
standardisation of 308
Devanagari 'script reform' 306
Development(s) 1, 3, 12, 20, 29–31, 36, 58, 77, 79, 108, 110, 115–116, 144, 210, 212, 214–231, 234, 237, 239–242, 252, 254, 257, 259–260, 263, 276, 289–290, 292–295, 297–298, 300–303, 305, 308, 311, 357
discourse of 229
historical 292
information 219
limitation-ridden 302
paradigm 216
postcolonial 259, 263
schemes 212, 259
socioeconomic 216
television (TV) 20, 210, 218, 221–224, 226–230, 237, 239–242
village-based 260
Dhamma doctrine 188
Diacritical marks 117–118
Dialogues 20, 47, 55, 85, 238, 263, 265
Dictionaries 103, 341
Digital
archive(s) 133, 136, 141–144, 152
archiving 19, 132–133, 135
culture 141
humanities 16
media 135, 143, 146
Digitality 135
Dignity 20, 132, 242
Dimendberg, Edward 251
Film Noir and the Spaces of Modernity 251
Dinar, Malik b. 107–109, 116
Discourse(s) 35, 62, 69, 80–81, 134, 137, 147, 150, 175, 180–181, 189, 191, 197, 216, 218, 226, 229, 240, 252, 304, 321, 339, 344
anti-Brahmin 180
architectural 252
Dalit 180
epistemological 339
national 180
nationalist 137, 191
philosophical 216
political 216
religio-cultural 181
telegraphy-in-(colonial) 35
Discrimination 191, 193, 234, 237
Dispositif 9
Disposition 6, 15–16, 139–141, 144
affective 139–140
anti-caste 144
dominant 141
Dissent 337–338, 344, 349, 358
Diversity 41, 175, 222, 225, 241, 253, 256, 291
lack of 175
Dominant order 141
Domination 4, 29, 49–50, 85, 181, 337
Western 50
Don't Spare Me Shankar 275
Doordarshan (DD) 211–215, 221–223, 225, 227–228, 230–232, 234, 238–239, 241
expansion of 215
monopoly 211, 214
National Programme 221, 225, 230
production style 222
Doxography 5

Drama(s) 47, 55, 67, 223, 236, 238
  clubs 67
  Nigerian 47
Dravidian movement 184, 281
Dualism 33, 150
Dutch 253, 257–258, 263

Early modern period 14
East Asia 36, 40
East India Company 32, 341–342
Economic
  arrangements 8
  crash 61
  development 254
  flows 48
  hegemony 50
  needs 180
  problem 63
  restructuring 253
  standing 39
Economy 3, 17, 54, 61–62, 135, 139, 148, 178, 253–254, 260
  agricultural 254
  agriculture-based 260
  capitalist 139
  colonial 178
  developing 148
  global 253
  neoliberal 3
  political 17, 54, 148
  Savarna 139
Education 6, 62, 66–67, 81, 109–110, 132, 183, 186, 218, 221, 223–224, 231, 298, 320, 337, 340–345, 347–348, 350–353, 356–358
  centralised system 348
  classroom 344
  colonial 320, 345, 352
  compulsory primary-school 62
  foreign 298
  indigenous system of 342
  Islamic 62
  literary 358
  liturgical 358
  medium of instruction 353
  modern 351
  moral 6, 358
  policies 320, 340
  religious 109–110
  school 62, 342
  spiritual 6
  vernacular 341
  Western 67
Educational
  institutions 133, 135, 259
  system 113, 118
Eepi Mayek 325, 327
Efficacy 6, 225, 240
  cultural and ethical 6
Emancipation 148, 180, 216
  Subaltern 180
Embodiment 135, 137, 141, 144–146, 148, 185, 337, 358
  material 337, 358
  transformative capacity of 144, 146
England 54, 277, 340, 344
Englishman, The 39–40
Enlightenment 10, 14, 116, 216–217
Entertainment(s) 51, 55, 86, 212–215, 220–221, 223, 225, 228, 231, 234, 239–240
  commercial 51, 215, 240
  film-based 220
  imported commercial 51
  urban 223, 225
Epics 56, 181–182, 342
  religious 56
Epistemology 103
Equipmentality 9
Ethical
  action 186–187

dissonance 78
foundation 166
imaginary 180
order 13
principles 193
rationality 141
Ethnicity 15
Europe 10, 34, 77, 114, 116–117, 159, 216
European
Enlightenment 10, 116
expansion 49
narcissism 50
Exclusion 135, 152, 190
mass 190
Expenditure 135
Exploitation 234, 237, 277
Ex-Untouchables 179

Fact-finding 164–166
mission 165–166
report 166
Fakhr al-Din, Muhammad ibn Ibrahim 98
Kasd ul Sabil 98
Falsehood 187–188, 191
Family planning 221
Fanaticism 338
Fan culture 85
Fantasy 16, 52, 59–60, 64, 69, 87, 230
collective 16, 60
concept of 69
Fashion(s) 7, 17, 47, 53
Indian 53
Fatwas 111, 113, 115
Female 62–63, 72, 150, 183, 226
foeticide 183
seclusion 72
Festivals 180, 262
Fiction 55, 65, 80–81, 159
Finance 15
Financial flows 52
Fiqh (jurisprudential) literature 111–112
First Indian Press Commission 32
Fixity 14, 105–106, 337, 345–347
Folk 55, 61, 78, 157, 223, 230, 232, 238, 278, 285
art 230
drama 55
lore 3, 6, 179
tales 61, 78
Ford Foundation 219
Fort Kochi 257, 261, 263–265
Foucault, Michel 144–145, 159, 169, 216
Political Anatomy 145
Volonte de Savoir 159
Freedom of choice 83–84
Freedom struggle 241–242
Free Press Journal 273
Freudian dreamwork 167
Friend of India 36

Gadya Cintamani 347
Gandhi 283
Gandhi in Cartoons 275
Gandhi, Indira, Indian Prime Minister 212, 215, 219–220, 235
as Minister of Information and Broadcasting 219
Emergency 212, 215, 223, 234
experiment with dictatorship 212, 235
Gandhi, Mahatma 6, 254, 303
vision of villages 254
Gandhi, Rajiv 212
Gandhi, Sanjay 212
Garibi hatao 220
Gay 20, 159–160, 163–165
lovers 159
sex 160, 164

Gender 2, 9, 64, 66, 72, 144, 161, 169
  interaction 64
Genealogy (nasaba) 21, 109–110
  familial 109, 110
Generosity 188
Genres 17–18, 21, 55, 58, 60, 65, 78–79, 87, 111–112, 142–143, 169, 251, 265, 339–341, 347, 351
  historical and political reading of 21
  history of 17
  Western 79
  Western film 58
Geographic peripheries 30
Geography(ies) 3, 14, 16, 107, 231, 251–252, 256–257, 259, 262–266, 290, 300, 341, 349
  cinematic 251–252, 257, 263, 265–266
  disembodied 259
  embodied 252, 257, 262
  political 14
  sacral 14
Germany 219
Ghalib, Mirza 162
Ghazal(s) 160–163, 169
Ghose, Aurobindo 279
Ghosh, Anindita 36, 142, 338
Gidugu 345–351
  Memorandum on Modern Telugu, A 349
Girl(s) 62, 64, 68–69, 73, 75–77, 81, 84, 109, 259
  teaching 77
Globalisation 15, 17, 22, 30–31, 48, 211, 213
  processes of 30
Global Now 15
Goa 11–13, 338
Goods 65, 77
  electronic consumer 77
  imported 65
Governance 182
Government of India/Indian government 29, 39, 213, 218, 220, 222–224, 227, 230, 232, 241
  First Five-Year Plan 29, 219
Government of Manipur/Manipur government 324–325
Govil, Hari G. 294–302, 305, 308
Grammar 103, 166, 194, 340, 342, 345, 347–350
  vernacular 342
Gujarat 231
Gurajada 340, 346, 348–350
  minute of dissent 349

Habitus, concept of 145
Handwriting 105, 113, 115
Harihar Nagar 255, 260
Harijans 236
Hausa
  audiences 56, 80, 85
  behaviour 77
  cinemas 56
  cultural practices 62
  dogon riga 57
  female marriage 63
  folk tales 61
  ideals 75
  littatafan soyayya 47, 65
  lives 69
  palmaran 57
  precedent 65
  social life 47, 59, 85
  tradition 80
  values 77–78
  video(s) 65, 73
  viewers 47–48, 53, 56–59, 64, 85–86
  women 62
Hausa culture 47, 54, 56–57, 65, 70, 82, 86

dialogic construction of 47
influence on 70
significance of Indian films in 47
Hausa-language magazines 80, 83
Hausa-language newspaper 80
Hausa literature 65, 82
publishing of 65
style of 82
Hausa society 59–62, 64, 68, 71, 79, 82, 87
contemporary 61, 64
women in 64, 71
Hausa youth 48, 52–53, 62, 64, 75
attitudes and behaviour of 62
Havas 30
Hegemonic order 135
Hegemony 50–51, 147, 295, 330
corporate 295
Hermeneutics 6, 182, 190
Heterofascism 160
Heterogeneity 8, 50, 86–87
Hicky's Bengal Gazette or the Original Calcutta General Advertiser 32
Hijras 157
Hindu 5–7, 20, 35, 55–56, 179, 181, 183, 185, 192, 274, 278–279, 282–283, 285, 294, 320–323, 325, 327, 330, 332, 344
Hindu Indian culture 56
Hinduism 5, 185, 192, 320–324, 327–330
Hindu Mahasabha 294
Hindu marital code 183
Hindu–Muslim question 278
Hindusim 322
Hindu, The 349
Historicisation 190
Historiography(ies) 4, 20, 27–29, 32–33, 37, 49, 95, 105, 107, 161, 182, 187, 196
African 49
creative 182
European 105
literary 187, 196
nationalist 32–33
queer 20, 161
History(ies) 1–11, 13–18, 20, 22, 27, 29, 31–37, 50, 96–97, 101–102, 105, 107, 116, 136–137, 140, 143–144, 147–148, 150, 156–163, 165, 168–170, 176–178, 180–181, 183, 185, 187–190, 192–194, 211, 214, 216, 218, 251, 256, 274–275, 285, 290–292, 304, 321–325, 330, 338–339, 341, 357–358
alternative 147
aspirational 20
cultural 3–4, 7, 13, 22
intellectual 5, 137
literary 13
material 13
national 17
print and book 2
proto- 7
South Asian 156
technological 7
unexamined 2
History-writing 189
Hitopadesa 346
HIV/AIDS 156
Ho 4, 112
Hollywood 19, 47, 50–51, 57, 59, 65, 79, 251
Homogenisation 213, 241, 325
Homophobia 159–160
Homosexual 160, 162, 165–166
Homosexuality 159, 162, 164–165
importance of 162
Hong Kong 40, 50, 52
Honour 60, 79
Hooch tragedy 258
Human
capacity 216–217

conception 239
unity 191
Human rights organisations 158
Hume, A. O. 185
Hyderabad 1, 10, 230, 256
Hydropolitics 8
Hymns 341
Hypervisibility 156–157

Iconicity 165
Iconography 57–58
visual 58
Idealism 180
Identity(ies) 8, 20–22, 31, 33–34, 136, 147, 157, 161, 166–168, 180, 193, 252, 261, 285, 292, 304, 320–321, 323–325, 328–329, 355
caricatured 285
cultural 161, 304
formation 22, 321, 328
globalised 157
inclusive 193
linguistic 22, 355
Meetei 320–321, 328–329
Muslim 261
national 31, 33
queer 20
regional 31
religious 136, 180, 261
sexual 22, 161
social 8
'traditional' 161
Identity politics 157, 161, 167
globalised 157
sexual 161
Ideology(ies) 1, 15, 35, 190, 211, 220, 227, 311, 325
Brahminical socio-religious 190
colonial 311
Imagination 15, 52–53, 59–60, 69, 115, 167, 260, 265, 283, 324, 332
concept of 53
Gandhian 260
political 324
Imams 109, 112
Imitation 192, 323
Immorality 58, 63, 73
Immunisation 185–186
Immunitas 185–186
Imperialism 17, 19, 29–31, 47, 50, 85, 213
British 29
cultural 19, 47, 50, 85, 213
Income 62, 116, 222, 240
source of 116
Inda 73–77, 84
Independence movement 293, 303
Indeterminacy 138, 254
India
ancient 2
book history of 13
cartoons in 274
cinematic dominance of 87
colonial 2, 29, 32–33, 35, 41, 143, 274–275, 293
contemporary 16, 159, 175
fight for independence 33, 35
history of print in 96
history-writing in 189
independent 20, 309
Linotype in 291, 295
media history of 10
media/technologies in 3
modern 139
nationalist movement in 298
national sentiment in 301
nineteenth-century 31, 34–37, 40–41
postcolonial 165
post-independence 2
pre-independence 311
press in 18, 31, 33, 35
sacral geography of 14
script reform in 311

scripts of 292
television in 20, 240
typographic design in 309
India International Centre Quarterly 55
Indian advertising industry 222
Indian audiences 55–56, 213, 228
two-tier model of 228
Indian broadcasting 213, 221
Indian cinema/film 18, 46–61, 64–66, 69–73, 78–82, 85–87, 142, 251
characters in 53, 57
complaints made against 81
culture of 60, 72
dominance of 54
genre of 60, 78
influence of 66, 85
Mother India 85, 277
narratives of 48, 59, 142
narrative structure of 56
pervasiveness of 85
popularity of 48, 50–51, 53
screening of 72
significance of 47, 52
south 251
style and themes of 58
translation of 56
Indian Constitution 148
Indian Copyright Deposit Act (1867) 97
Indian culture 56, 59
Indian development television 239, 242
Indian Express, The 283
Indian historiography 27
Indian history 162
Indian journalism 18, 33
Indian languages 2, 177, 213, 343
Indian LGBTQI movement 163
Indian media 156–157, 160, 164, 169–170, 175
Indian National Congress (INC) 185, 277, 303
Indian nationalist movement 275
Indian nationhood 16
Indian newspapers 33, 39
role of 33
Indian Ocean 110–112
Indian past 4
Indian press 32–33, 301
history of the 32
Indian Press and Deposit Act 98
Indian radio 222
Indian religious epics 56
Indian scripts 290–293, 295, 309
mechanisation of 293, 295
Indian sexual relations 53
Indian society 4, 53, 183, 227
contemporary 53
criticism of 183
Indian Space Research Organisation (ISRO) 220, 234
Indian State 2, 22
formation and conduct of the 2
nascent 2
Indian telegraph 29
Indian television 210–211, 213–216, 219–221, 225, 228
commercialisation of 213, 215
Crash Plan 225
history(ies) of 211, 214, 216
India Office Library 98
India's
agricultural economy 254
independence movement 303
television market 211
India Society of America 294
Indology 4–6, 137
classical 5
colonial 6
critical 5
Industrialisation 251

Industry(ies) 21, 28, 142, 186, 212, 222, 252, 299, 305, 340, 348
advertising 222
Inevitability 211, 215, 225, 328
historical 211
Inflation 62
Information 27, 30, 34–35, 38–40, 54, 95, 99, 102, 144, 148, 181, 184, 219, 223–225, 230, 234, 240–241, 292, 301, 305, 339, 342
access to 292
centres 30
circulation of 27
creation and dissemination of 148
lack of 54
networks 34
technologies 95
transfer 223–224, 240
transmission of 34
Informatorium 339
Infrastructure(s) 8–9, 15, 139, 225, 258
broadcasting 225
-building 8
hydraulic 8
physical 139
Injustice 176
Innovation(s) 5, 120, 275–276, 281, 290–291, 298, 311, 324
aesthetic 5
literary 5
philosophical 5
technical 311
technological 298
Inquiry 3, 7, 27, 36–37, 79, 96, 158
historical 158
social 79
Institutional affiliations 110
Institutionalisation 22, 178, 283
Institution(s) 1–4, 21–22, 120, 133, 135, 146, 178, 240, 259, 293–294, 302, 304, 306, 309, 352
colonial 178, 302
democratic 3
liberal 3
private 352
secular 3
social and cultural 1
Instrumentation 58
Intellectual exercise 111
Intelligence 36–37, 39, 40, 281
official 39
political and commercial 37
reporting 40
shipping 37, 40
Intelligibility 13, 15, 17, 152
limits of 17
Interaction(s) 6–8, 18, 28, 31, 41, 48, 63–64, 75, 95, 102, 145–146, 166, 230
micro-level 145
quality of the 102
sexual 48, 64, 75
social 75
Interactivity 224, 241
Interconnections 22, 52
Internet 27, 133, 135, 147–48, 157, 164, 197
Interpretation 3, 6, 19, 98, 152, 167, 188, 190, 196
Invention 103–104, 113, 225, 290, 303, 324
foreign 303
Invisibility 156, 176
Invisibilisation 175
Iskanci 73
Islam 84, 95, 100–101, 107–109, 111–112, 116, 120, 345

process of writing books in 111
teachings of 84
Islamic
classical text 98
knowledge tradition 110, 115, 118
law 62
learning 109, 116
orthodoxy 62
religious content 97
religious law (*Sharia*) 111
religious literature 114
revitalisation 61
scholarly tradition 118

Jangama mendicants 6
Japan 40
Japan Times, The 40
Subscription Telegrams 40
Joshi Committee's report 227
Journalism 1–3, 18, 27–29, 31–33, 37, 40, 158, 160, 178, 181–183, 189, 196, 273, 275–276, 282–285, 305
Dalit absence in 183
growth of 178
history(ies) of 27, 275
real 158
research and teaching in 3
style of 32–33
yellow 33
Journal of the International African Institute 46
Journal(s) 46, 52, 179, 181–182, 184, 189, 193–196, 273–274, 276, 282, 299
Swadeshi 282
Justice 181, 230
Justice 283

Kabir, Sheikh Zainuddin Makhdoom 111
Hidayat al-Adhkiya' ila tariq al-Awliyya 111
Kachodappattu 98
Kantian distinction between public and private reason 14
Kant, Immanuel 14, 217
Karnataka 231
Kerala 34, 97, 114, 115, 119, 261–262
Keyboard(s) 296, 299, 304, 306, 308
Devanagari 304
dummy 299
layout 296, 299
Linotype 308
standard 306
Kheda Communication Project/ Kheda Project 20, 232–235, 237–240
Kheda television 236
Kim Il Sung 212
Kipling, Rudyard 27–28
Knowability 138
Knowledge
bearing 143
canonisation of 357
democratisation of 120
emancipatory 190
formal production 11
forms of 6, 152, 337, 354
indigenous forms of 354
medicinal 187
metaphysical 355
modern 22
orders of 101
philosophy of 96
practice(s) of 120, 179, 182, 188–190, 197
resources 187
scientific 352–353
systems 340, 354
Western 352–353, 358

Kochi 20–21, 251–266
cinematic geography(ies) of 251–252, 257
geographical peculiarities of 257
growth of 252
urban spaces of 265
Kongu 19, 149–152
Kunhi Moosa, Kuriyadath 95, 99
Alif Laila Va Laila 95

Labour/Labourer 139, 151, 176, 226, 293
indentured 176
Indian 293
kinds of 139
migration 176
Lahore Tribune 34
Lal Media, Kochi 255
Language and script 2, 105, 112, 117–118, 161, 166, 177, 182, 187, 194, 211, 291–294, 299–300, 304–306, 309, 320–321, 337, 343, 352, 357
Arabic 4, 36, 54, 98, 100, 104–105, 108–109, 111–112, 115–120, 291, 294
Arabic-Malayalam 98, 118
Arabic naskhi 117
Assamese 291
Bengali 7, 22, 35, 274, 285, 291–292, 300, 329, 338
characteristics of the 117
Chinese 36, 47, 51
choice of 18, 21–22
cursive 117
debates 324, 333, 345, 348, 350
Devanagari 21, 289, 291, 293–211, 331
diversity of 291
English 65, 352–353
European 105, 117
foreign 86, 294, 353
granthika 345–347, 349–350
Gujarati 39, 234, 274, 291
Gurmukhi 291
Hindi 53–56, 59–60, 175, 225, 231, 234, 274, 276, 292–294, 303, 305–306, 310, 320–321, 331, 348
inconsistencies in 346
Indian 2, 177, 213, 290–291, 292–293, 295, 309, 343
international 156
Japanese 36, 40
Kannada 6–7, 11, 276, 291
local 309, 352
Maithili 321
Malayalam 21, 97–100, 112, 114–115, 118, 142, 251–266, 274, 291
Manipuri 320
Marathi 352
Meetei 22, 320–321, 325–328, 330–332
Meeteilon 320, 325
national 292–293, 306, 321
northern Indian 291
official 294, 320
officially recognised 291
Oriya 291
Pali 182, 187
palm 178–179, 181, 187, 196
Persian 36, 118, 292
Perso-Arabic 4, 291, 294
Ponnani Arabic 117
print inscribed 177
priorities 299
reform 306–309, 311, 346–348, 350–351
reform movement 303, 311, 351
role of 337
Southern Indian 291
spoken/colloquial 320, 345–347
style of 339, 348, 350

Tamil 20–21, 118, 143, 175–185, 187, 189, 191–196, 273–276, 281–285, 291–292, 338
Telugu 22, 276, 291, 337–341, 343–358
Urdu 36, 118, 274, 292, 294, 320
vernacular 305, 343, 357
Vernacular 343
Latin Catholics 258, 262, 265
Laxman, R. K. 285
Learning
book-based 110
Islamic 109, 116
religious 6
secular 6
Legacy(ies) 19, 132, 179–181, 183, 188, 197, 215
Letters 11, 67, 75, 80, 83–84, 104–105, 116–117, 308, 325–331, 347
Arabic 104, 117
eepi 327–328, 330
lom 328
LGBTQI 17, 157–159, 161–163, 165–166
books on 159
characters 158
films on 158
issues 158–159
judgements on 158
media 157, 163
movement 163, 166
representation 161
websites 158
Liberalisation 15, 21, 133, 231, 253, 260
economic 260
policies 21, 253
Liberation 132, 214
neoliberal 214
Liberty 222
Library(ies) 98, 110, 113, 117, 132, 180, 331, 345
accessibility of 113
necessity of 132
Life and knowledge 9, 11, 15
Life/Lives 1, 4, 7–11, 15–16, 18, 21, 28, 47, 49–53, 57–60, 63, 69, 74–75, 78, 82, 84–85, 87, 97, 108, 116, 136, 143, 149–151, 159–160, 162, 164–165, 179, 181, 183, 185, 187–193, 197, 210–211, 213, 217, 223, 226–227, 229–233, 235, 237–238, 254, 258–264, 294–295, 323–324, 354
African 51
associational 1
Brahminical way of 191
cinematic 21
contemporary 87
emotional 63, 75
ethical practice of 185
everyday 84, 87, 210, 254
forms of 15
internal 7
living 18
local 237
middle class 262
Nigerian 50
non-Western 50
physical 63
political 191
poverty-stricken 262
public 57, 136
real 82, 258
social 47, 53, 59–60, 85, 190, 324
traditional 57
transformation of 193
Western 50, 58
Lifestyle 82
Life-worlds 4, 97, 231

Liman, Maryam Sahabi 73
Kishi Kumallon Mata 73
Linguistic
dissonance 300
divisions 294
Linotype 21, 289, 291, 294–295, 297–301, 303–305, 307–310
acculturation of the 291
development of the 305
machine(s) 289, 297–298, 303, 308–310
Linotype Devanagari 289, 301
Linotype & Machinery (L&M) 298–300, 302–303
Lipi 108
Ponnani 108
Literary
activities 97, 99
associations 342
cultures and oral traditions 101
forms 36, 161
works 135
Literature 4, 37, 47, 55, 60, 65, 67, 82, 102, 111–112, 114, 132, 134, 137, 141–142, 144, 148–149, 163, 178–179, 181–185, 187, 195, 229, 294–295, 320, 330, 340–342, 345, 348, 351, 353
erotic 351
non-Western 102
oral 60
Perso-Arabic 4
publicity 295
Punjabi 142
religious 114
scientific vernacular 353
Telugu 341, 348, 351
Lithographic
modality 105
printing 99, 102, 106–107, 119–120
printing press 100, 107, 119
type 100
Lithography 19, 99–101, 103–107, 114–115, 117–120
as a technology 19, 107
invention of 103
self-presentation 101
'Little magazine' movements 176
Livelihood 12, 116, 340
Localisation 229
Lom(s) 325–331
Love 46–48, 53, 56–57, 59–61, 63–65, 68–70, 73–75, 77–79, 81–84, 86, 149, 160, 162, 188, 230–231, 262–263
affairs 78
and romance 47
Bombay melodrama style of 73
commodification of 69
conflict over 68
contemporary 69
declarations of 75
expressions of 83
lack of 69
language and behaviour of 81
modern 86
modes of 48
romantic 60, 63, 77, 79
shift in styles of 75
story(ies) 47–48, 65, 74, 82, 262–263
Loyalty 144, 326

Macaulay, T. B. 343
Minute on Education 343
Machinery 161, 293, 298, 304, 339, 345
colonial educational 339
Madhya Pradesh 233
Madras (Chennai) 21–22, 99–100, 159, 181, 184, 189, 194–195, 219, 239, 251–252, 256, 278, 281, 340–341, 343–344, 350, 353

Madras Presidency 22, 189, 340–341, 344, 353
Madras School Book Society 343
Madurai Prabhandham 184
Magazine(s) 65, 80, 83, 175–176, 179–180, 189, 274, 276, 283
  humour 283
  romance 65
Mahabarata, the 56
Maithili language movement 321
Makhdoom 110–113, 115
  Qurrat al-'ayn 112
Malabar 19, 95–100, 107–114, 116–117
  as a knowledge hub 109
  book before print 107
  introduction of Islam in 108
  mosque-centred educational activities in 109
  mosques in 109, 110
Malabar Coast 95, 107–108, 110–112, 114
  books written in the 112
Malayala Manorama 257–258
Malayalam cinema/film 21, 142, 252–261, 263–266
  cinematic frames of 252
  production 255
Malayalam First Reader, The 100
Malaysia 264
Mandal Commission report 133
Manipur 22, 320–322, 324–325, 327, 332
  history of 322
  political movement in 324
Manipur Gazette 324
Manipur nationalist movement 22
Manuscript(s) 6, 99, 102, 104–106, 109, 111–112, 115, 118–120, 136, 178, 297, 322, 341, 345, 347, 355
  Arabic 109, 111–112
  culture 106, 118, 120
  production 105, 120
  tradition(s) 115, 118–119
Manu Smriti 6
Manu Smriti Dharma 6
Mappila Muslim(s) 96–97, 99–102, 105, 107, 110–111, 113–115, 117, 119
Mappilas 96–97, 99–102, 105, 107, 110–111, 113–115, 117, 119
Marginalisation 149
Marginalised communities 157, 182
Market(s) 47, 54, 65, 67, 81–82, 139, 211–215, 218, 226, 228, 240–241, 253, 295, 297, 304–305, 311
  populism 214, 228
  research 212, 226
Marriage(s) 57, 59–64, 68–71, 74–78, 83, 180, 183, 262
  age and conditions of 61
  arranged 59–60, 69, 74, 83
  choice of 69, 77–78
  first 68, 262
  forced 68–69, 76, 83
  Islamic/Muslim 63–64
  love 59–60
Mass communication 3, 221
Mass media 52, 158, 217, 224, 234, 241
Materialism 58–59, 61–63, 69, 75–76
Materiality 16, 140, 230
Mathematics 194, 353
Mayek revivalism 330
Mazzharul Uloom Press, Thalassery 95
Mecca 109
Mechanical composition 290, 293, 295, 304, 307
Mechanical typesetting 293–295, 306–307

Media 1, 3–4, 7–11, 13–20, 22, 27–29, 31, 35, 37, 41, 46–49, 51–52, 66, 72, 79, 85, 87, 95–96, 101, 107, 133, 135–137, 142–143, 146–147, 151–152, 156–166, 169–170, 175, 177, 197, 210–211, 213–214, 216–218, 221, 224, 231, 234, 236, 241, 255, 266, 333, 338–339, 352
  and literary practices 4
  and modernity 211
  environments 51–52
  forms of 96, 157
  history 3, 10, 17–18, 20, 31, 37, 156–157, 162–163, 169–170
  mainstream 14, 133, 152
  ocular-centric 20, 142
  practices 4, 14, 18, 20, 27
  studies 9, 14, 49, 51, 162, 266
  technology 3–4, 7–9, 11, 14–16
  transnational 48, 72, 79
  understanding of 4, 9, 17, 52
  Western 47
Medicine 179, 184, 194–195, 354
  Western 354
Meetei 22, 320–333
  community 320, 322, 325–326, 332–333
  consciousness 322, 330
  Hindus 330
  history 322–324
  language and script movement 321
  movement 321
  numerals 325, 330
  revivalism 322–323
Meetei Eyek Erol Loinasillon Apunba Lup (MEELAL) 331–332
Meetei Marup 322
Meetei Mayek 320, 324–327, 329–331
Melodrama(s) 51, 55, 73
Merchant(s) 15, 292
Mergenthaler Linotype Company 289, 294–295, 297–305, 308–309, 311
  Devanagari project 297, 311
Metallurgy 7
Metro Manorama 257
Middle class/Middle-class 36, 157, 215, 220–222, 231, 235, 237, 260, 262
  problems 237
Middle East 54, 87
Ministry of External Affairs 212
Ministry of Home Affairs 212
Ministry of Information and Broadcasting 230
Minority(ies) 137, 141, 156–157, 256, 258, 278
  religious 256, 258
Minto–Morley constitutional reforms of 1909 278
Mir Taqi Mir 162
Missionaries 6, 97, 100, 114–115, 119, 292, 341, 344–345
  activities 100, 114
Mitter, Partha 274–275, 285
Mobilisation 31, 33–34, 133, 184, 195
  political 31, 34
Modernisation 21
Modernity and tradition 48, 50, 78
Modesty 64, 71
Mohammed, Adamu 64, 68–69, 82–83
  Garnak'ak'i 64, 68
Monastery 12–13
Monotype 294, 297, 310
Monotype Corporation, London 297
Monotype Devanagari 310
Moral universe 57, 59, 76
Morphogenesis 136

Mosque(s) 59, 108–110, 117
Motivation(s) 57, 114, 293
Movies 51, 215, 236, 260, 283
Munro, Sir Thomas 342–343
Mushaira 162
Music 47, 53, 55, 104, 118, 142, 223, 259, 283
Muslim and Hindu divide 320
Muslim–media interactions 95
Mutts 178
Mutual
  aid 68
  exchange 136
Myanmar (Burma) 142, 176
Mythology 55, 278–279, 285
  Hindu 278–279, 285
  Indian 55

Nagari Pracharini Sabha 293, 355
Narrative(s) 3–4, 7, 10–11, 18, 28–29, 32–33, 41, 48, 53, 55–57, 59–60, 64, 69, 77–79, 85, 132–133, 142, 147, 160, 165, 179, 182, 191, 257–259, 261, 264–266, 290, 295
  anti-caste 179
  colonial 18
  cultural 257
  development 77
  developmental 257
  family 18
  fictional 64
  hegemonic 11, 133
  Indian 69
  Kuranko 60
  nationalist 18
  power of 60
  romance 64
  tensions 53, 57, 59–60, 77
Nasiha 80–83
National
  boundaries 49, 56
  integration 225, 307
National Aeronautics and Space Administration (NASA) 219
Nation/alism/Nationalism 2–3, 20, 34, 55, 181, 196, 225, 293, 304, 323, 327
  cultural 225
  Indian 20, 55
  Meetei 327
  rise of 293
Nationalist
  movement 22, 186, 275, 298, 305, 354
  sensibilities 292
  sentiment 306
Nation-building 139
Nationhood 16, 304, 321, 323, 330
Nation-State(s) 31, 35, 216
Native Newspaper Reports 281
Naval Kishore Press 338
Naved, Shad 20, 160
Nayanar, Valluva 187–188, 194
  Thirikural (*Thirukkural*) 187
NCERT 275
NDTV 165, 166
Negotiations 21, 101, 299, 322, 328, 330, 339, 354
Nehru, Jawaharlal, Indian Prime Minister 29, 139, 241, 275
Neoliberal policies 253
New media 28, 133, 135–136, 146, 152
News 11, 18, 28–31, 35–40, 74, 104, 143–144, 175, 180, 220, 223, 225, 258, 276
  agencies 30–31, 38
  flows of 18, 30
  international 38, 180
  telegraphic 37–39
Newspaper press 30–31, 37
  development of the 30, 31

Newspaper(s) 7, 16, 27–41, 80–81, 83, 133, 143, 158–159, 175, 181, 274, 281–282, 284, 295, 299, 301–302, 310, 349
  Anglo-Indian 39
  Arabic 36
  British 36
  colonial 7, 143
  content of the 34
  English-language 31, 37–39
  Gujarati 39
  Hausa-language 80
  Hindi and English 175
  Indian-language 274
  industry 28
  interactions and connections 41
  modern 29
  Persian 36
  reportage 159
  reporting 28, 37
  role of 31
  subscription 40
  vernacular 30, 33, 302
News production and circulation 35–36
  complexity of 35
  processes of 36
News reporting 28, 35, 37, 40
  English-language 37
  evolution of 35, 37, 40
  patterns 35
  styles of 40
New York Herald Tribune 289
New York University 52
Nigeria 46–48, 50, 53–56, 61–62, 67, 80–81, 85–87
  films imported into 53
  independence in 1960 50, 67
  media and film in 47
  popularity of Indian film(s) in 48, 50
Nigerian
  culture 48
  economy 62
Nigerian Film Distribution Company (NFDC) 54
Nigerian Hausa attachment 18
Nigerian viewers 58
Non-Brahmin movement 283
Non-Muslim lithographic press 100
Non-Muslim printing 99
Non-partisan approach 305
Non-violence 189
Non-Western world 11
North Africa 87
Northeast India 18, 142
Northern India 36, 119
Northern Nigeria 46–47, 50, 54, 56, 62, 67, 86–87
  cultural environment of 87
North India 274, 320–321

Oil boom 58, 61
Online
  portals 19, 144
  spaces 135
Online Dalit activism 19
Online disembodiment thesis 141
Oppression 49, 132, 136, 145, 180, 304
Orality(ies) 101, 105, 120, 142, 177
Orientalism 190
Orsini, Francesca 3, 36, 304, 348
Oru Paisa Tamizhan 181, 194
Ottoman Empire 38
OTT platforms 158
Out-caste/Outcaste 176–177, 193
Oxfam India 175

Paganino's Qur'an 117
Painting(s) 116, 134, 142
Pakistan 119, 291
Palm leaves 12–13

Pamheiba, Meetei king 322
Pañcatantra/Panchatantra 279, 341, 346
Panchamas 194
Paraiyan 184, 194
Parallel modernity 53, 87
Parental authority and individual desire 79
Patriarchy 183
Patronage 6, 39, 119, 178
Peasants 139, 227
Pedagogy 1, 22, 229
Penguin Book of Indian Cartoons, The 275
Periodicals 21, 27, 31, 273–74, 277, 282, 340
Perso-Arabic past 4
Personality(ies) 2, 13, 294
Personal stories 144
Personhood 150
Philological Encounters 289
Phulo, Naoria 322–324, 326
Physiology 353, 355
Pioneer, The 28, 36
Plague relief measures 37
Planning Commission 240
Pleasure(s) 3, 47, 53, 55, 218, 221–222, 224, 227, 240, 340
Poem/Poetry 19, 79, 144, 149–150, 159–160, 162, 167–169, 345
Political
  climate 301, 305
  community 4, 177, 186
  messages 279, 281
  mobilisation 31, 34
  needs 111
  practice 132, 135, 193
Politics 8, 34–35, 68, 85, 134–136, 141, 147, 157, 161, 167, 181, 183, 235, 281, 289, 293–294, 320, 323–324, 330
  archival 136
  communal 35
  factional 35
  liberatory 141
  nationalist 281
  of access to water 8
  sexual minority 157
  televisual 235
Pollock, Sheldon 3, 5, 137
Ponnovium, Anbu 183–186, 188
Poologa Vyasan 184
Portuguese 11, 14, 257, 263–264
Portuguese Goa 11
Postcolonialism 50
Post-coloniality 47
Post-independence period 29, 33, 304
Post-World War II 216
Poverty 82, 220, 226, 262
  problems of 82
Power 2, 8, 12, 17, 49, 59–60, 65, 100, 105, 134, 136, 139, 145–146, 182, 184, 189–190, 192–193, 197, 211, 222, 230–231, 290–291, 304, 308, 311, 348
  struggles 145, 311
Prabasi Press, Calcutta 299
Practice(s) 2, 4–5, 7, 9, 14, 16, 18, 20, 22, 27, 38, 53–55, 62, 67, 72, 98, 101, 107–108, 110–111, 113–114, 116, 120, 132, 135, 145–147, 158, 161, 164, 177–180, 182–185, 188–194, 196–197, 219, 230, 238–239, 241–242, 298, 322–323, 357
  discursive 7
  epistemological 179
  intellectual 183
  interpretative 193
  journalistic 179, 196
  non-discursive 7
  physical 145, 147
  psychological 145, 147

textual 182
Press 7, 18, 20, 27–37, 39–40, 46, 81, 83–84, 95, 98–101, 107, 114–115, 119–120, 142, 166, 181, 222, 273–275, 282–283, 290, 297, 299, 301, 304, 338, 340, 345, 347, 349, 351
as an instrument of propaganda 31
colonial 31, 32
English-language 36, 40, 275
freedom 32
history of the 18, 27, 31–32, 36
Indian-language 274
networks 35–36
telegrams 39
Print 2–5, 8, 13–14, 19, 34, 36, 67, 95–97, 99–102, 105–107, 113–115, 117–118, 133, 135, 143, 148, 152, 156, 176–179, 181–183, 187–190, 193–197, 217, 290–292, 306, 311, 338–340, 345–348, 354, 356
advent of 97, 99
capitalism 177, 194, 339
culture(s) 3–4, 19, 95, 101, 105, 182, 338, 347
journalistic 179, 183, 194, 197
media 19, 133, 135, 156
modern 4, 177
modernity 177, 182, 193
typographic 19, 118
Print (capitalist mainstream) media 133
Printing and publishing 7, 11–12, 19, 27, 31, 38, 65, 67, 95, 97–107, 113–115, 117–120, 177, 181, 282, 290, 292–294, 297, 299, 301–306, 309, 332, 339, 340, 345, 347, 349, 352–353, 356
establishments 293, 301–302, 304
industry 299, 305, 340
machine 11, 12
science 356
Telugu 340
typographic 99, 105, 117–120
vernacular 339, 352–353
Printing press 7, 27, 31, 98–101, 107, 114, 117, 119–120, 290, 345, 347
first 114, 119
lithographic 107, 119
Muslim 98–100
Muslim-owned 98
type for the 7
typographic 119
Printing technology(ies) 7, 19, 95, 97, 99, 101, 113–114, 120
forms of 99, 101
Privatisation 213
Profession(s) 103, 107–108, 113, 116, 340
Propaganda 31, 212, 220–221, 305
Prophet Mohammed 47
Prose 162, 182, 188, 281, 338, 345–346, 348–349
journalistic 188
Proselytisation 14
Prostitute(s) 63, 69
Public
debate 48, 79, 81, 187
memory 133, 189
reason 15, 143, 217
Public Culture 52
Public opinion 33, 175, 281
policy of surveillance of 281
Pulavar, A. P. Periyasamy 194
Pulavar, T. I. Swamykannu 194
Punch 274, 276
Punjab 34, 119, 274
Purification 328
Puya(s) 326–330
authenticity of 329

definition of 327, 329
invocation of 330

Qissat Shakarwati Farmad 109
Queer movement 164, 166
Qur'anic readings 107
Qur'an, the 107–109, 113, 115–117
Muslim rejection of the first printed copy of 117

Radio 16, 65, 212, 217, 219, 222
Rajasthan 231, 233
Rajiv Darshan 212
Ramasamy, Periyar E. V. 177, 179
Ramayana, the 56
Rangoon Pravesa Thirattu 184
Rationality(ies) 12, 141, 183, 188, 330
Readership 34, 332, 356
Reading 14, 20–21, 36, 47, 65, 69, 81, 84, 101, 104, 120, 135–137, 142, 150–151, 156, 158, 162, 166, 169, 176–178, 180, 188–189, 194–195, 218, 252, 340, 351
mode of 158, 178
psychoanalytic 158
Reading and learning practices 178
Reading-writing practices 178
Rebellion 76–77, 320
Red Sea 38
Reform movement 308, 311, 351
Registrar of Books 348–349
Religion 20, 47, 55, 77, 80, 83, 95, 137, 147, 176, 179, 181, 183, 185, 189, 294, 321–323, 330
anti-caste 179, 189
devotion to 83
Hindu 55
Meetei 321, 323
Religious
centres 4, 19, 114
communities 19, 99, 265
conversions 322
education 109–110
faith 141
practice 54–55, 190
texts 6, 12–13
values 56, 59, 77
Reports on Publications 97, 99
Representational regimes 139
Reproduction 101–103, 105, 107, 119, 281, 347
mass 102–103, 107, 347
textual 107, 119
Research and teaching 3
Resistance 6, 33, 49–50, 85–86, 120, 133, 147, 166, 225, 320–321, 325, 332
African 50
concepts of 49
Meetei 320
romance of 49
Resources 1, 30, 97, 176, 179, 182, 185, 187–188, 253, 327
exchange of 253
transnational flow of 253
Responsibility 60, 64, 69, 76, 78, 294, 342, 354
social 69, 76, 78
Reuters 30–31, 38–40
monopoly 30
Reuters Telegrams 39
Revenues 109, 139, 225, 227, 230
Review of Reviews 277, 284
Revivalism 322–324, 326, 328, 330
Rights 62, 83, 132, 149, 151, 158
fight for their 83
of the oppressed 83
to entertainment 228
Rohith Vemula movement 10, 146
Romance 47–49, 55, 63–65, 80, 84, 87
English 65
Indian 48

popular culture of 80
Romantic insistence 60
Romanticism 168
Round Table India 19, 133, 144
Rural
broadcasting system 225
development 210, 215, 219, 222, 225
Rural India 233
Russia 38

Sacrifice 78–79, 239
animal 239
Sagir, Shaikh Zainuddin Makhdoom 111–112
Ajeebathul Ajwiba 111
Fata al-mu'in 111–112
Saivism 5
Same-sex
culture 158
desire 161, 168
sexuality 158
stories 159
subjectivity 157
Same-sex subject 156–158, 162
depiction of the 157
hypervisibility of the 157
South Asian 158
Sanatana dharma 186
Sanskrit language 4–5, 182, 187, 284, 294, 331, 341, 346, 353, 355
death of the 5
Sarabhai, Vikram 221, 223–224, 233
Saraswat Brahmins 11–12, 14
Sarojini Naidu School of Arts and Communication, University of Hyderabad 1, 9
Satellite Television Instructional Experiment (SITE) 210, 214–215, 220–221, 223–224, 226, 229–235, 237–238, 242
Sathi aacharam 192
Savari 19, 133, 143–149
Savarna(s) 138–141, 143, 150–151
folk 157
hegemonic 140
hegemony 147
Scaffolding 158
Scribal practices 107–108
Script(s) 16, 18, 21–22, 104–106, 108, 115, 117–119, 178–179, 181, 187, 196, 235, 289–295, 297, 299–301, 303–304, 306–309, 311, 320–321, 324–333, 347
Bangla 320, 329, 332
change 309
conferences 325
culture 347
debate 324, 333
expert committee 325
foreign 294
invented 326
Meetei 22, 320–321, 325–328, 330–332
modifications of the 307
modified 308
proposed 326
reform 303, 306–309, 311
reform movement 303, 311
representation of the 306
revivalism 326
Roman 325
scholarly and practical aspects of the 292
selection 320, 330
simplification of the 289, 306
standardisation 309
syllabic 306–307
Yelhou 326
Scriptures 12, 114, 344
Sculpture 142
Section 377 156
Seem, Mark 135

Anti-Oedipus 135
Segregation 63, 135
Self
Dalit-Bahujan 140
presentation and orientation of the 138
sense of 149
singularity of the 193
Self-consciousness 61
Self-discipline 191
Self-reflexivity 28
Self-rule movement 185
Senefelder 103–104
Classic 1819 Treatise, The 104
Sense 7, 12–15, 17, 33, 54–55, 60, 64, 68–69, 73, 75–76, 85, 96, 98, 107, 134, 137–138, 141, 146, 149–151, 157, 160, 165, 167, 169, 190, 196, 211, 215, 217, 220–223, 226, 230, 232, 235–236, 257, 259, 308, 321, 324, 343, 357–358
economic 141
indeterminacy of 138
Jungian 169
rational 141
retroactive 215
Sensibility(ies) 36, 137, 149, 292, 351
Victorian 351
Serials 38, 214, 225, 228, 231, 236
sponsored 225, 228
Sex(es) 57, 63, 156–166, 168–170
consensual 163
interaction between the 63
life 164
Sexual
desire 79, 161
minority(ies) 156–157
orientation 164–165
relations 48, 53, 57, 68, 74, 80
Sexuality 48, 61–63, 75, 84, 87, 137, 158–159, 169, 183
female 62, 183
Shafa Labari Shuni 65
Shafi school of law 112
Shettanaufi, Sheik Abdul Hasan Ash 112
Bahjathul Asrar va Maadinul Anwar 112
Shyness 64, 75
Siddha
medicine 179
practitioners 191
Singapore 40
Siras, Shrinivas Ramchandra 163–169
Paaya Khaali Hirwal 167
Sivaraj, N. 183
Skills 16, 103, 140
agonistic 16
technical 103
Slave/Slavery 132, 323
Slum 221, 231, 261
Soap operas 213–214, 225, 228
Social
development 1, 254
history 168, 178, 192
issues 214, 234
media 137, 147, 197
order 59–60, 63, 78–79, 132
problems 63, 68
production 257, 261
relations 52, 59, 86, 238
tensions 62, 64, 79
transformation 61, 211
values 76, 79
Social change 53, 57, 59, 61, 79–80, 84, 223, 226, 240
contemporary 53, 61, 84
direction of 79–80
Socialism 220
Sociality 192, 251
Society for Promoting Christian Knowledge (SPCK) press 349

Society(ies) 1–2, 4, 8, 47, 53, 58–65, 68–69, 71, 78–79, 82, 86–87, 97, 110, 115–116, 118, 120, 143, 159, 181, 183, 186, 188, 197, 216, 220–221, 227, 273, 324, 331, 339, 352
African 47, 59, 86
Hausa 59–62, 64, 68, 71, 79, 82, 87
Islamic 59, 63, 110
Muslim 110, 115–116, 118
Nigerian 58, 61
non-Western 216
postcolonial 78–79
Tamil 273
Socio-religious-economic needs 111
Solidarity 10, 135
Songs 46, 57, 85, 140, 142, 162, 220, 223, 258–259
Sonority 20, 143
South Africa 176, 180
South Asia 2, 6, 9–10, 13, 27–32, 34, 36–37, 40, 156, 176, 323
book history of 13
colonial 27–28, 31–32, 34, 36
history of 10
Southeast Asia 111, 176
South India 5, 95, 176–177, 195, 276
Soyayya authors 48, 64, 65, 67–69, 73, 80, 83
Soyayya books 18, 47–48, 59–62, 64–76, 79, 80–84, 86
complaints against 81
'educative' nature of 83
mass culture of 79
pernicious effect of 84
rise of 65, 86
success of 79–80
Space Applications Centre (SAC) 234–235, 237
Spatiality 14–15, 20–21, 252, 256, 265
relative 14
urban 252
Specificities 11, 55, 86, 252–253
economic 252
geographical 252–253
historical 11, 86, 253
social 252
Spectatorship 214
Sponsorship 225, 230
Srinivasan, Rettaimalai 183, 185
Srinivasan, Rettamalai 194
Śṛṅgārarasa 351
Standard universal type 105
Stark, Ulrike 36, 338
An Empire of Books 36
State 2, 18, 20, 22, 58–59, 63, 80–81, 87, 139, 178, 212–213, 215, 304, 338, 357
modern 139
postcolonial 58–59
TV 20
Straits Times, The 40
Structural Adjustment Programme (SAP) 65
Subaltern 6, 17, 142, 178, 180–182, 184, 192, 194–196
Subhadra, Jupaka 19, 149
Kongu 19, 149–152
Subjectivity 15, 77, 147, 157, 165, 169, 216
Sugnana Grantha Ratnavali 352
Suicide 10, 69, 74, 76, 79, 259, 263
Super-commentaries 111–112, 118
Superstition 216, 241, 354
Suri, Cinnaya 345–349
Nīti-candrika 340–341, 346–347
Suryodhayam 282
Swadesamitran 281
Swadeshi(s) 181, 185–186, 275, 277, 282

reform 185–186
selfish 186
Swadeshism 278
Symbolism 278, 285
folk 278, 285
Syriac New Testament 114

Tafseers 116
Ta'leeq 111
Tamil Buddhism 180, 182–183
Tamil cartooning/cartoons 283, 285
Tamil classics, recovery and publication of 178
Tamil Dalits 143, 180, 193–194, 196
Tamilian, The 180–181, 192
Tamil journalism 273, 282–285
cartoon into 273, 282–283, 285
pre-independence 273
Tamilnadu 110, 282–284, 321
Tamils 179, 185, 255
Tamil Sangam 194
Tamil textbooks, history of 338
Tamizhan 179–184, 187, 189, 192, 194
Teaching and learning 109–110, 113
Techniques 16, 105, 140, 142, 235, 281
metal-engraving 281
Technological
forms 96, 100–101
progress 290, 306
revolution 18, 29
transition 18, 29, 37
Technology(ies) 3–5, 7–17, 19–22, 27–31, 34–35, 37–39, 41, 72, 95–97, 99, 101, 103–104, 107, 113–115, 120, 135, 139–140, 143–144, 148, 181–182, 219, 235, 254–256, 266, 281, 290–291, 293, 295, 304, 310, 347
history of 27, 37
new 3, 12, 28
printing 7, 19, 95, 97, 99, 101, 113–114, 120
role of 30, 35
transfer 29, 291
Telangana 350
Telecommunications 30–31, 37
history of 31, 37
Telegrams 28, 30–31, 36, 38–40
foreign 30, 39
Telegraph 10, 27–30, 35, 37–40
as an imperial 'tool' 29
Telegraphic communication 29–30
Telegraphy 18, 27–31, 35, 37–38, 40
as an instrument of censorship 35
history of 29, 31, 37
use of 28, 30, 35, 37
Television (TV) 16–17, 20, 46–47, 56, 72, 156, 158, 164, 175, 210–234, 236–242, 332
channels 211
commercial 215
commercialisation of 227
consumerist 214
development of Indian 214
domestic 46
ideologies of 211
localise production 232
mismanagement of 213
national 164
satellite 210, 221
shows 233, 237
studio 240
terrestrial network 220
Telugu cultural production 22
Telugu intelligentsia 341, 352–353, 357
Telugu textbooks 22, 338–341, 343, 348, 352, 354, 358

history of the 338, 358
Temple 6–7, 14, 59, 139
Temporality(ies) 8, 15–17, 139
Tension 22, 28, 53, 57, 59–60, 62, 64, 76–79, 137, 152, 190, 217, 264
Textbook committees 339, 341, 343–344, 349
Textbook(s) 17, 22, 32, 100, 275, 301, 331, 337–58
chronological history of 339
Laccadive 100
printed 338, 346
school 331, 340, 348, 350
science 352, 354, 356
vernacular 337–39, 352–353, 355, 358
Text(s) 4–6, 12–13, 51, 56, 73, 86, 95–106, 108, 110–113, 115, 118–120, 137, 139, 143–145, 162, 166, 178, 181–182, 186–188, 194–196, 251, 256, 289–290, 303–304, 306–308, 310, 338–341, 343, 345–348, 351, 355, 357
anti-caste 144
Brahminic 137
Indian 51, 355
literary 181, 196, 338
Malayalam 100
printed 104, 162
reproduction of 103
sacred 13, 108, 120
Sanskrit 346
Sufi 111
Telugu 338, 345, 351
travelling 4, 112
written 112, 120
Texts and traditions 96, 103
Textuality(ies) 19, 152, 189
Textual sources 137, 169
Thass, Pandit Iyothee 20, 143, 175–176, 179, 194
Ilakkiyam 187
Oru Paisa Thamizhan 143
writings 180–181, 183, 193
Theatre 2–3, 238
Thi. Ja. Ranganathan 273
Thiong'o, Ngũgĩ wa 337–338
Third World 48, 228
Tilak, Bal Gangadhar 6, 277
Times of India, The 38–40, 159–160, 163
Times, The 36
Tollywood 251
Tradition and modernity 18, 76, 85
Tradition(s) 2, 4–10, 14, 16, 18, 48, 50, 53, 57–58, 76, 78, 80, 85, 96, 101, 103, 110, 112, 115–116, 118–119, 137, 142, 150, 152, 161, 182, 184, 188, 190, 193, 195, 197, 231, 284–285, 292, 308, 322–325, 351, 355, 358
emergent 7, 9–10
oral 101, 152, 182, 197
performative 2, 4
religious 5
textual 112, 195, 292
vernacular literary 4
Transmission 29, 34, 38–39, 224, 230, 234, 290
Travelogue 109
Tribal/Tribe 83, 144, 227, 325
Typeface(s) 289, 297, 299, 304, 308
design of the 299, 308
making 295
Typesetting 293–295, 297, 306–307, 309
Devanagari 309
machinery 293
mechanical 293–295, 306–307
problems of efficiency in 306
Typographical/Typographic
change 290, 311
design 309

developments 292, 294
engagement 311
font 296
limitations 290
network(s) 290, 295
printing 99, 105, 117–120
printing blocs 105
projects 295
technical constraints 119
type 100
Typography 21, 100, 103–107, 115, 117–119, 289
Arabic 117
failure of 119
impersonalisation in 105
impersonality and regularity in 105
Typography and lithography/ lithography and typography 103, 105, 117, 119

UNESCO 218, 238
United States (US) 40, 146, 157, 160, 210–211, 219, 296
Devanagari development in 298
University Grants Commission (UGC) 2
Untouchability 151, 190–191, 234, 237
Untouchable(s) 138, 179, 182, 185–188, 190–191, 235
Upayukta Grandakarana Sabha 349
Urbanisation 59, 61, 251
Urban planning 251, 260
Utterance 105, 120

Valluva Nayanar 187–188
Kural 187, 188
Vavilla Press, Velcheru 345, 351
Venkatachalapathy, A. R. 3, 9, 21, 178, 274, 279–280, 338
Province of the Book 178
Verghese Committee 221
Verghese Report 223–224
Vernacular past 6, 343, 358
Vernaculars 17, 305–306, 355
Video 47, 48, 51–52, 54, 65, 72–73, 236
Vidya Vilasam Press, Kozhikode 95
Vijnana Chandrika Mandali 348–350, 352, 356
Violence 58, 61, 141, 145, 157, 159, 188–189, 197, 255
Viresalingam, Kandukuri 340, 347, 349, 355
Nīti-candrika 340–341, 346–347
Virtual reality 148
Virtues 16, 75, 77, 85, 97, 224
Visibilisation 159
Visibility 1, 31, 152, 157, 159
Vivekavardhini 340

Wages 237
Water painting 134
Way of life/Ways of life 187, 191, 192, 217, 323
Wa'z (pious exhortation) 116
Wealth 60, 77, 181, 187, 277
Wedding 74, 77
West Africa 53, 86–87
Western culture 51
Westernisation 57, 59, 61, 63, 86
West/Western cultural imperialism 19
Women 8, 47, 57, 62–64, 67, 69–75, 78, 135, 139, 143, 145, 147–150, 152, 160, 182–183, 220, 225, 227, 233, 236, 260, 356
childbearing age 63
Dalit-Bahujan/Dalit-Bahujan-Adivasi 139, 148
education 183, 356
marrying age of 62
outcast 149

status of 62
unmarried 63, 75
Wood's Despatch of 1854 343
World War II 216
Worship 7, 180
Writers' clubs 67–68
Yash Pal 210, 235
Yelhou Mayek 326
Yemen 101, 109
Youth 48, 52–53, 61–62, 64, 68, 75, 77, 80–81, 83–84, 212, 220, 265
contemporary 61, 68, 83